ALSO BY RAFI ZABOR

The Bear Comes Home

I, Wabenzi

RAFI ZABOR

I, Wabenzi

A Souvenir

[VOLUME I • APORIA]

FARRAR, STRAUS AND GIROUX

NEW YORK

Farrar, Straus and Giroux
19 Union Square West, New York 10003

Copyright © 2005 by Rafi Zabor
All rights reserved
Distributed in Canada by Douglas & McIntyre Ltd.
Printed in the United States of America
First edition, 2005

Excerpts from *The Twenty-Nine Pages* © Beshara Publications,
Roberton, Scotland, 1998. Used by permission.

Library of Congress Cataloging-in-Publication Data
Zabor, Rafi.
    I, Wabenzi : a souvenir / by Rafi Zabor.— 1st ed.
        p.   cm.
    ISBN-13: 978-0-86547-583-0 (hardcover : alk. paper)
    ISBN-10: 0-86547-583-0 (hardcover : alk. paper)
    1. Zabor, Rafi. 2. Novelists, American—20th century—Biography.
3. Brooklyn (New York, N.Y.)—Social life and customs. 4. Music
critics—United States—Biography.   I. Title.

PS3576.A157Z466   2005
813'.54—dc22   2005007200

Designed by Cassandra J. Pappas

www.fsgbooks.com

1   3   5   7   9   10   8   6   4   2

IN MEMORIAM:

Harry Zabor
Sadie Zabor

Agrins and Zaborovskys all

Mahmut Rauf
Bülent Rauf
Blair Tremoureux
Lena Zellweger
Layla Shamash Norland
Daniel Furman

Most recently, alas: Hakkı Bey

PART ONE

I see that I shall have to speak about myself. The only possible justification is for me to be honest *about the animal.*

— STENDHAL

It there was one time here an individual known under the name of Jim Smiley; it was in the winter of '49, possibly well at the spring of '50, I no me recollect not exactly. This which makes me to believe that it was the one or the other, it is that I shall remember that the grand flume is not achieved when he arrives at the camp for the first time.

— MARK TWAIN,
"The Frog Jumping of the County of Calaveras"

Surely we created Man with the most beautiful of constitutions; then We brought him down to the lowest of the low.

— ALLAH,
The Quran

1

I CAN'T REMEMBER who first told me about the Wabenzi. For a long time I thought it might have been Yale Evelev, over the phone from the New Music Distribution Service, where he worked press relations for a few years before producing a series of world music albums for Nonesuch. Yale's family came to the States from Russia some decades back. To take on a more American coloration, Yale's father changed the family name from Evelov to Evelev and named his firstborn son after a great American university. (It takes a while to develop an ear in any language. My father for one never made his way completely into English.) In any case it wasn't Yale: when I asked him recently, he said he'd never heard of the Wabenzi. Maybe it was Kip Hanrahan—he'd had the New Music gig just before Yale. But was he the source of the Wabenzi? I'll have to ask him sometime. Let's for the sake of argument say it was Kip.

I forget how the subject came up, but there I was on the phone with ol' Kip, probably trying, in my capacity as jazz critic to the nation, to finagle a few dozen free records out of him, and I suppose he must have mentioned the Wabenzi; or maybe I went into the story of how, in my battered parental grey Chevy Malibu, I had only that week contested a Lower East Side parking place with some space-usurping yuppie kids from Connecticut in a new-looking royal blue two-seater 380SL, and how I won the point—each of our cars partway into the space, mine backed halfway in, theirs nosing in from behind to ace me out of the spot—by revving my engine and shouting at them in a voice so full of a barbarian and pure Brooklyn savagery that it shocked even me, "HOW'D YA LIKE A BIG DENT IN YOUR NICE NEW FUCKING MER-CEDES!" Heavens, where had I found such an unexpected reserve of class consciousness in the generally nondiscriminatory precincts of myself? or was it only because I was late for a meet with a notoriously impatient friend? Those kids backed out of that space in such a hurry I wondered how I must have looked to them, some ragged-ass embodiment of urban yawp and slumland fury thrust out a car window all beard and teeth and garbage cans around me as if I had built and ruined the neighborhood by myself (when in fact for all my boho credentials I'd never once lived in it). Little twerps—there were five or six of them in there, a regulation two in front and at least three more crammed into the semifictional backseat fit only for a suitcase or two—they were probably in the nabe to swallow goldfish, scope the beggars and score some coke: I probly saved them some trouble they were such marks. Anyhow, I parked and went off to see Hakkı Bey.

"In Africa, they have a word for them," Kip, or whoever, told me.

I recradled the phone on my shoulder. "They have a name for who exactly?"

"For the people who drive Mercedes. The way they form tribal names . . . well, take the Watusi for example. The *i* on the end signifies the plural, *wa* means People or the People of, and *tus* the place they're from or the characteristic they'd like to be known by. Watusi therefore means the People of Tus. Africans call the people who drive Mercedes the Wabenzi."

The Wabenzi. I felt illuminated by the concision, the aptness, the im-plied perspective on character and culture, the kind of fools we make of ourselves, given world enough and time. I hoped to be capable of equiv-alent wit some day. I was certain that I would never, ever be a member of that particular tribe.

For one thing, I have never, at least not since junior high, when the exactly right cut of tight black wee-jeans seemed crucial to all I possessed of personhood, been that keen on the symbols of worldly status. I am one of the least worldly individuals you will meet this side of the monastery or Notville, and in general, I have been so out of touch with the iconog-

raphy of loot that when Hakkı Bey told me some years back how he
and Shareen used to pull up to the one-buck movies at St. Mark's Place in
this black Mercedes—I think this was when he was hooked up with those
spoonbenders from outer space up in Ossining and they used to let him
borrow the car—it was such a goof that heads would turn—"Hey man,
imagine me and this skinny little black girl carrying our baby getting out of
this big Mercedes to catch a couple of East Village movies for a dollah!"—
well, I didn't even get the joke, or pick up on the polarities that made it tick.
I thought Mercs were these sober-looking European cars, essentially modest, some kind of better-executed Volvos. Although I remember too, some
years after Hakkı's remark, tooling south down the Thruway between
Woodstock and the City in an old '67 sky-blue Volvo 122S—in my early
thirties, my first car—whose exhaust, toward the end of that vehicle's natural life, poured grey-blue through the firewall and the dashboard, then
over me and out the windows. In winter I'd wear my Turkish white sheepskin coat and hat and crank the windows wide open so as not to croak of as-
phyxia before my time, tearing down the highway something like a literal
house on fire, two plumes of blue jetstreaming out behind me carrying the
souls of dead brain cells and fabulous with poison. I had some king-hell
headaches halfway down and provoked commentary from the tollbooth at-
tendants at Harriman. "You bet," and "Yes I will," I told them, "just as soon
as I can." I remember thinking, amid my monoxides of delirium while
peering through the streaming blue and grey at larger, more majestic chas-
sis steaming south—they gave me plenty of leeway in the process, mind
you—that Mercedes in some unnoticed interim had changed, the older,
more modest ones having been replaced by elongated distortions of themselves whose most wretched excess was their stacked taillights and the
strange, raised and slanted moldings along the interior undersides of their
windows: functionless leatherette swoops which moreover would make it
difficult to rest one's arm upon the sill in summer. Little did I then know
that these "new" Mercs I so disliked were merely the S series then current,
the larger items Daimler-Benz had always put out, the lux models, Hitler-
size, always a tad pompous but much to be desired, top of the line.

Anyhow, years passed and I learned a number of things.

IT WAS AFTER my parents' deaths, and I was worn out.

I had gone back up to Woodstock in the hopes of starting my life up again after two or three years of unrelenting misery, and my friend Danièl—note the accent on the second syllable; I'm going to leave it out of the typography from here on because it looks like a false moustache— Furman was living in my Brooklyn apartment, where the furniture would not creak beneath the weight of memory for him, or the air clot with images of my mother raving while my father struggled for breath, and death looming but taking its time, making sure that every hope of mercy was crushed in its turn before mortality itself broke the door in and collected what was left. Where I had parked myself upstate, the winter's cold seeped through the dark log walls no matter where I sat in the room and the overhead light in its outsize Japanese paper globe swung so wildly in the periodic blow from the forced-air heater that one seemed also to be at sea, on the wrong day, pitching on some bitter North Atlantic of the soul. I practiced drums, visited friends, gazed wistfully at green mountains, paid hapless, too-mournful court to a local saucer-eyed Irish beauty, tried fitfully and without success to write fiction, watched interminable television, clicking discontentedly on the zapper from zilch to shining zilch in the hope of spending a minute or two without pain, and when I woke up in the sleeping balcony and looked out the small casement window beside the bed at the bare branches nodding outside in the grey morning tapping on the walls in an indecipherable but all too obviously minatory code, blindman to blindman and dead to the dead, I found it impossible to imagine how in a month or so they'd be green again, covered in the lushness of leaves and lifted by warmer breezes: the world was a cold barren empty place to which life no longer had the strength to return.

IN EARLY SPRING, my friend Nick Prestigiacomo called to ask a favor.

The spiritual healer he was favoring that year needed a place to work out of on his forthcoming trip to New York. Could I make my parents' place available?

I asked Daniel, and it seemed I could. He wouldn't mind spending five days in another friend's apartment.

So I came down to town, the world in leaf again, straightened the joint up a bit and prepared to receive visitors. Ken Lawton was a large-size genial limping Englishman about sixty with snuff all over the front of his immemorial grey tweed jacket—he kept a stash loose in the right front pocket and carelessly helped himself from it every couple of minutes. His wife, Alice, seemed, despite an elaborate, nearly court-Chinese arrangement of jet black hair piled atop her head, uneccentrically middle-class, the very soul of English teatime. I put them up in what had been my parents' bedroom and I slept, as I had during my parents' calamitous decline, on a thin, stowable foam mattress on the living room floor. Nick and a number of people to whom he had advertised Ken's powers started coming from the City to be healed the next morning, praising the pastoral calm of fair Brooklinium—the people say hello to you on the street! there are so many trees! it's so quiet and friendly and you pay *what* for rent?

"Brooklyn is the Borough of Homes and Churches," I informed them.

Alice had gone off to the City or for a walk in nearby Prospect Park, and I found myself in the living room, trying to read or write but actually answering the doorbell, greeting the pilgrims and making coffee to keep them busy while they waited. Ken kept them in the bedroom about half an hour each, accepted only a modest fee and sent them home ecstatic. "I was suspended above an abyss on a golden cord attached to my navel," one of them told me. "I was lifted. I revolved." Later, Ken gave me a freebie in exchange for the use of the flat, and when he laid his hands on, or rather over me, I had the pleasant but unspectacular sensation, not vision, of invisible barriers gently crumbling, like sandstone walls powdered by the rains of some other, subtler spring. Ken confessed his puzzlement at the wealth of internal cinema people managed to conjure up when he worked on them. He also told me that he felt sure, and he had talked it over with Alice and she did too, that I had quite literally been through hell but that good things were going to happen for me quite quite soon.

I had already pretty much decided to go to Turkey again by way of Europe, and probably on from there to Israel. It was my habitual route of self-renewal, and it might work again.

I found myself saying as much over coffee to Max Rosenblatt while he awaited his turn with Ken, me on the sofa, Max in the armchair and our white china cups of coffee—the *good* dishes, the ones my parents never used—on the large triangular glass Noguchi coffee table that went with nothing else in the room, all false late forties antiques heavy with needless ornamentation and ancestral karma. There were leaves and branches nodding yes outside the window, five storeys up, and a bit of a breeze wafting into the room. I must have gone on to describe the physical problems I was having—the paralyzing pain in my right knee that kept me limping, something like Ken, and unable to walk more than a block without stopping, staggered by the penetration of the ache; and the at least equal agony in my right elbow that stopped me cold every time I tried to pick up anything the weight, say, of a hardcover book—and that consequently I would be unable to travel in the manner to which I had become accustomed, heaving a suitcase on and off trains and buses, through the bare or busy streets of exotic or forbidding cities into cheap hotels and off the edge of civilization into caves in the desert, holy tombs, Anatolian steppes, wilderness, undiscovered country, annihilation, adventure, sometimes even love. "I'm gonna have to buy a car," I told him.

I probably failed to notice Max's face brighten. "Oh yeah?"

"Yeah, and the thing is, since I'm going to Turkey I've got to buy something I can get parts for there, which comes down to a couple of old model Fiats and Renaults the Turks manufacture under license, not great cars, but if you need a part for anything else you could be stuck for months. And, oh yeah, you can get parts for Mercedes, but that's kind of out of my league."

"Not necessarily," Max said, brightening still further, something a trifle manic widening his eyes behind their heavy specs. His large, bullet-shaped head, with its time-heightened brow and close-cropped black hair along its sides, seemed momentarily to expand. "A couple of years ago, when the dollar was really up there, you could pick up a used Mercedes for like three thousand bucks—"

"Whaat?" (Somewhere in there I must have learned what Mercedes meant, and cost.)

"—and now that the dollar's sliding a little you might have to pay four or five."

"No shit?"

"No shit. You could pick one up, drive it around a few months, then sell it for about what you paid."

"Five'd be about my limit," I figured, "and if I could sell it after . . ."

"No problem," he assured me, a broad gesture of arm and hand calming whatever waves of doubt might have risen in the room.

"A Mercedes," I speculated. "It's a good car."

"It's a GREAT car."

"Safe in a crash," I said, letting the siren sing to me in a voice for all the world like that of reason, "no small virtue with all those loonies on the road in Turkey . . ."

"Safer than a Volvo," Max told me.

"Really?"

"Oh yeah. In crash tests . . ."

And Max went on awhile, excited now, a car nut on the loose, and I joined in, about how I'd do best to buy one in Belgium, no import duties and it'd spare me a trip to Germany, I spoke French of a sort and there was no point trotting out, among Germans, a version of their language composed mostly of scraps of the familial Yiddish. And I remembered Belgium, walking the cobbled streets of Ostend one night with a British actress on my arm, stopping for a cold beer here or a brass band playing in a gazebo there, the unevenness of the stones sending the side of her breast against my left arm shoulder high (she was tall, Megan, and wore boots with heels, hence her need, on those treacherous continental stones, of my invincible arm): outward bound eleven years back in 1975 on my first trip to Turkey, where I had my best mystical experiences, lived at Mahmoud's, bless his departed soul, came down with pneumonia and wrote all those terrific unintelligible visionary poems. I wrote the first poem of the journey sitting next to the actress aboard the ferry just before docking beneath chalk cliffs in the dark before dawn, and saw her for the last time on the passport line, except for once in a spy-thing on television. Twenty-nine years old back then! Could those bones still walk at almost forty? A Belgian Mercedes sounded reasonable. I had some money, most of it inherited, it is true, rather than earned, felt more dead than alive and could not for the life of me put together a credible impersonation of a functioning human being. A trip to Turkey seemed in order, a car seemed necessary, and as Max painted the picture a Merc did not appear all that extravagant. I did not remember that Max was a former mental patient who had flipped out while tending the chicken house down at the Gurdjieff plantation in West Virginia and that it had taken the statutory ten strong men to subdue him. Worse, later on he would be damn fool enough to buy a lean and low-slung used red Alfa that put a look of crazed adoration on his face but hardly ever ventured out of the repair shop.

AFTER KEN AND ALICE LEFT, Daniel came back and I took the subject up with him. "As your attorney," he said in his crisp Eastern European accent, fluttering the r of "attorney" like a morsel of lark's wing off the tip of his tongue, "I advise you to steal a bicycle." He settled himself further into the armchair Max had sat in and made his grinding chuckling sound. "Although if you intend to quicken the pace at which you are squandering your patrimony, a Mercedes will almost certainly serve you better than the collection of former girlfriends and impecunious male friends you currently support."

I should probably explain about Daniel. Ah yes, but how? See him anyway, settled into the faux-Victorian armchair with the aqua, cross-hatched-but-less-than-tweed slipcover, a tank of a man about five foot six, a natural heavyweight now considerably heavier, fat on his powerful limbs and a preposterous beachball of girth crammed between chest and plumbing fixtures, nothing drooping about all this weight, though; nearing the age of fifty now, his wiry, kinked, reddish brown hair cropped close and, like his aggressively well-trimmed beard, salted here and there with grey; something military in his bearing still, and in the precision of his speech, and one tooth missing, a small one in the lower deck, right. He might be wearing a suit, or more likely a shirt that would go with one, and perhaps a tie, loosened; cuffs on his trousers, no unemphatic endings on this man anywhere; and as usual an amused expression on his face. His eyes, there is no other word for it, twinkle. Although only recently accredited as a member of the New York bar, he has degrees in Renaissance and medieval history, was one of the principal contributors to the *Encyclopedia Judaica*, is a seemingly unassailable authority on a host of subjects if not initially obscure then quickly made so by his mazy command of dizzying detail, and he is still broke. That is why he is camping in my apartment. One of these days he is supposed to come up with some rent. At the moment, he is supplying me with a few legal services, gratis.

I first ran into him in Paris, summer of '66, when I was a nineteen-year-old stringbean on his first summer abroad and Daniel was someone sitting in an armchair and biting on a meerschaum or a briar at the back of Shakespeare & Company. He was beardless then, and only medium heavy, still only ten years my senior though I took him for a man of forty. His hair was a bit thicker then, though still on the short side. He wore a white shortsleeved shirt with brown and black tattersall squares, khaki slacks, sensible brown shoes, and had no need of glasses. His eyes still twinkled, with perhaps 35 percent fewer ironic complications, he had about the same grin, similarly discounted, and his conversational laugh, a short, wooden bark, was less explosive than it would be twenty years later. He was posing, effectively, as a man of experience.

I forget now the text of his first monologue, whether it was the one on how to take over Europe with twelve well-trained men or Switzerland with five, only in Switzerland life was so boring and regular it would be months before anyone took notice, or the one about how, when he was a sergeant in the French Foreign Legion, he would punish his platoon by waking the men at three in the morning, compel them to stand at attention in the yard while he lectured them on the *dolce stile nuovo* of Guido Cavalcanti and, toward dawn and weakening knees, Dante. He would make them memorize a number of sonnets in the original antique Italian and order them recited in chorus. Or I might have heard the series of talks on his experiences during the Algerian revolution, which demonstrated the falseness of all written history. On the other hand it might have been the discourse that began with the unanswerable question he posed after sufficient minutes of fashionably left-wing talk had passed in his company: "Excuse me, but hev you ever *lived* in a communist country? Personally I count myself very lucky to have escaped one. And I would volunteer to join the American army in Vietnam, were I not unwilling to fight in another losing war." (Daniel's penchant for shocking conversation persisted until the end of his days, but as it turned out, he did make an attempt before leaving Paris to enlist in the American army. This multilingual soldier-scholar, veteran since early childhood of several wars because born half-Jewish in Yugoslavia in 1937, was turned down as a likely spy.) Or it might have been the one that came after I had made a little speech myself and this after all rather formidable figure leaned forward to say, "Ah, I see that you still possess the *visio beatifica*."

"And you think that's funny," I said.

"On the contrary," he told me. "I envy you, because I no longer enjoy the privilege of that vision myself."

I spent some time with him over the six weeks I stayed in Paris, and learned that he visited Shakespeare partly to talk literature, philosophy and war but mostly to pick up tourist girls, that he roomed with a defunct Moldavian prince named Dmitri who looked like a pirate of the civilized-but-cruel typology whom Daniel had worked up into a credible if wholly ignorant international lecturer on metallurgy for a firm that wanted a prince on its payroll even if he had straw in his head: Dmitri memorized a speech Daniel had written for him and referred all questions to an aide de camp. For his own living, Daniel managed the domestic staff of the Paris Hilton on, he said, strict Legionnaire discipline.

I left Paris for Copenhagen, as did Daniel for his own complicated reasons weeks later, and I didn't see him again for eighteen years, and failed to recognize him when I did. He no longer smoked a pipe, although often enough he seemed to. With his short, bulky form and conversational capacity for life-enhancing irony he reminded me of Stendhal, a writer my high regard for whom he found inexplicable.

In Brooklyn, Daniel kept the apartment in scrupulously clean regimental order, although my father's bed had collapsed beneath him so many times he finally left the mattress and box springs on the floor, with the old mahogany posts, sides, and headboard framing them like a palisade around a compound, and he left a pungent natural smell about the place that seemed to me humanly analogous to a bear's.

"Well, D.," I told him, "I wasn't thinking of getting a fast one . . ."

"They are all fast."

"Even something on the order of a 230E? Two point three liters, that's not a very big engine for a car of that weight."

"Less pickup but still able to cruise comfortably at one hundred miles an hour. I drove a number of Mercedes when I was working for the film company in Italy. They are well made, overpriced when new, and when you drive them they seem, how shall I put it, to be of a piece with your body."

"Do you think I can pick one up for less than five?"

"In Belgium? Possibly." He puffed on the invisible, extinct pipe. "A diesel will cost you less to run and maintain."

"I don't know anything about diesels—"

He started to say something more general but thought better of it.

"—and they're such poisoners. That pall of black smoke. Unthinkable." I remembered breathing in pounds of the stuff in Turkey. Inanoz bus lines. That's where I'm gonna punch you. Ina noz. Do unto others. Not to mention the atmosphere. Even if it costs you. Global warming. Here comes the flood. Though anything that puts New York City under water can't be all bad. Argal: no diesel. Preserve, protect, defend.

Daniel shrugged. His chosen weapon was a Mini. He no longer had the one his aged mother had smuggled into the States for him, but he had thought for a while of opening an informal Mini concession in New York; with each tiny car sold he would provide a booklet he proposed to write listing parking places around Manhattan legal for Minis but denied other cars: between crosswalks and the nearest parking meter, say, on such a corner, or an ambiguous spotlet near a hydrant on another— Daniel maintained you could park one virtually anywhere in town.

He had other cause to distrust me on the subject of cars. In its last days I had done him the favor of giving him the sky-blue Volvo, which by then had a virtually smokeless rebuilt engine under its hood. (By then it was known as the Raccoon: I had met a couple of Gypsies in a supermarket parking lot, and they had done some cut-rate fiberglass bodywork for me, much of it around the rusted headlights and grille, then sprayed their handiwork matte black, leaving the car with the likeness of a masked face on its front.) The car which had initially cost me $750 and eventually four or five thousand cost him between two and three grand as a gift, and on the day he finally called the junkman to collect it he was kept waiting overlong and was so late for his flight to Brussels that he boarded, at last, by walking out onto the tarmac suitcase in hand: they wheeled some steps into place for him and instructed him to knock on the locked door of the plane, whose name was Sabena, until a stewardess opened it up to let him in. He had to knock for quite a while. Picture it: in this age of terrorism, a heavyset, trim-bearded man in a trenchcoat, carrying a large leather suitcase, knocking on the gleaming, curvilinear door of a plane. What could they have been thinking in the left-side window seats of first class?

"When do you think you will leave Turkey for Israel?"

"Autumn?" I guessed. "Some time in autumn."

"Good. I should be there by then. I will show you my Jerusalem. I do not recommend travelling overland from Turkey through Syria and Jordan. Not for a person of your physiognomy."

"It's a temptation I will avoid. I will follow my nose."

"Then you will go far. And catch many fish. You will sail from what port on the Mediterranean?"

"Marmaris. Unless I can sail direct to Cyprus from Adana."

"If you sail to Cyprus from Adana it will be to Turkish Cyprus, and you will be unable to cross to Greek Cyprus and thence to Israel. So: you will sail from Marmaris to Rhodes, and from there board a ferry to Haifa."

"*Insh'Allah*," I told him.

"*Deo volente*," he said.

2

NOT LONG BEFORE I left on this proposed *Wunderfahrt*, my friend Elan Sicroff, a concert pianist and piano teacher with a cheerful, gratuitously obscene sense of humor—a Mozart influence? but he was a Beethoven man—came to town from Princeton in order to see his friend the Venerable Bhante Dharmawara, a hundred-year-old Cambodian Buddhist monk who was, as usual, just passing through. In this instance Bhante's passage involved the inauguration of a Buddhist temple in a rambling wooden Brooklyn pile on Rugby Road, not half a block up the street from the high school gym I used to go Friday-night dancing in when in junior high—wearing those pipestem wee-jeans, sneaking smokes outside in the dark, nerving myself up to dance and just barely talk with dark exotic Bobbi Raskin. Later on, when my father bought the local liquor store and I had come of age, I used to deliver liquor to unsteady tenants in dim doorways in the neighborhood.

"Hey, Riff," Sicroff asked me as we looked up at the Buddhist prayer flags depending from the eaves and the bilingual temple sign arched over the entrance, "you think I should pull my fly down and walk in with my schlong hanging out?"

"Uh, probably not, Slip," I said.

Riffraff and Slipslop, to give us our full names, approached the temple across its impressively pillared porch, the old floorboards groaning, who knows, sentiently beneath us with each step we took. Once inside the front door, which had been left ajar, we came face to face with two startled young Cambodian men who stared at us and spoke no English in response to our own. We walked through what had once been the living room, now massed with six-foot-tall candles in monumental sconces, a golden effigy of the Lord Buddha seated at the head of the room and much devotional art arrayed about him along the walls. Incense, flowers, the smell, perhaps, of ceremonial butter. We passed a kitchen doorway through which we glimpsed two or three Cambodian women cooking something smoky and obscure, then, following the pointing fingers of the staring, silent men, we climbed three flights of creaking stairs to usher ourselves into a plain, barely furnished attic bedroom in which Bhante, taking note of our arrival, rose from his daybed nap to say hello, ancient in his faded orange robe, his translucent, lined, hardly still human face breaking into a smile of greeting. He had unusually small and even teeth which might actually have been his own, a shaven head and long-lobed, pointed ears. His skin was the color of blond Virginia tobacco and had a healthy sheen. He moved terribly slowly, as if prone to breakage, but with a definite frail grace, and at so evenly measured a pace as to seem in another region of spacetime, inching along beside us in parallel but with an entirely different relationship to the velocity of light. I had never met him before. Elan had known him well for years, first in England in the company of Gurdjieff's spiritual descendant J. G. Bennett at Sherborne House, then down at the late Mr. Bennett's Gurdjieff plantation in West Virginia, where Elan had often done the wretched cooking of which he was so proud for a number of the master's meditation retreats.

Elan and Bhante had some things to catch up on; a few familiar names percolated through the conversation although I could not follow the plot, and then Bhante, like a very slow, experienced planet, revolved in my direction from the daybed's edge. On the wall behind him were a number of color photographs of Cambodian men and women who had evidently come to the attention of the Khmer Rouge, some with missing limbs, others with enormous burns or slashes on their torsos; some were living and others dead; it was not always possible to tell which. I had never seen a photo of a woman with her breasts hacked off before. After asking me a very few questions and receiving terse, shy, uninformative answers about my parents' deaths and my so far unsteady attempts to find a life in the aftermath, Bhante reignited his grin and his eyes took firmer hold of me. "To take on the suffering of others," he said in his small, quavering, accented, barely audible voice, "is the . . . *noblest* . . . thing a man can do," and here the crawling pace of his speech accelerated to its conclusion: *"but you have taken on too much."* He paused, perhaps not for effect, but the pause was effective all the same, then repeated: "You have taken on too much." He began chuckling and nodding his head yes. Elan and I couldn't help it, we both laughed.

Perhaps that's what I had done, imperfectly and inexpertly at the very least, most often in a disorderly fugue of intertwining, inevitable failures. When I attempted to size the event up in retrospect, the two or three years of the worst of it, one particular incident most often shuddered its way into my mind, not because it represented the bottom of the pit or could serve as adequate summary but because it was the introit to the full scope of the suffering, the taste and the length and the nitpicking thoroughness of the deaths.

BACK THEN, when it happened, I was still dividing my time between Woodstock—actually Mount Tremper, New York, a bend in the winding, creek-following road ten miles from Woodstock, in a small room of a large house full of musicians—and my folks' apartment in Brooklyn, attempting to maintain the fiction of a personal life, although by then my parents' drama had begun to obliterate my own and my time down in Brooklyn to exceed my stays upstate; it would not be long before, arriving one day in the land of trees and hills and brooks and the last green grass of my youth, that it would dawn on me, over the course of a few quiet seconds, that however shellshocked and in need of a retreat I was I no longer belonged there and that my proper business lay back in town. But that was still to come.

In early March of that year, I was awakened one morning, lying on my thin bit of mattress on the living room floor, by the sound of my father choking to death in the kitchen. On second thought, it occurred to me, maybe he was only having a little more difficulty than usual coughing up his gob of phlegm, although I had never heard this particular long, drawn-out strangulation of a sound before. I lay there on my back beneath the blanket, hoping for the best, or perhaps, already wearied by the daily pain deposited like a newspaper at my door, I was too beat to move unless I knew for sure. Worse, maybe I was partly ready, in a dozy, sadistic, barely conscious laziness, to see what the death of a father might be like. I heard a plastic water glass clatter and splash to the kitchen floor and then my father's panicked footsteps coming my way, and I knew that he was having one of those spasms I had heard about but never seen, in which his windpipe shut tight and he began to suffocate. These spasms were caused by one of the medicines he used—each year a few dozen asthmatics are found dead on their floors, a portable inhaler clutched in their hands or lying beside them: one of the risks of the treatment—and he had saved himself, once, after uselessly pouring water into his throat, which sent it back clear and unswallowed over his chin, by falling belly-first over the back of a chair, and once, having tried the chair and failed, by rushing in his underwear out of the apartment into the hallway in what had seemed his last living moment and attempting to shout for help at the closed brown doors of the other apartments on the floor: on the third try his windpipe popped open and out came the sudden sound of his voice. The most recent such attack had come only a little earlier in my mother's accelerating senescence: with his armchair pulled up to the bed-room TV and my mother awake in bed behind him, he had looked at her helplessly over the chairback, gargling in strangulation as she canted her head to one side like a parakeet and looked back at him, saying, "Harry? Harry?" He got out of that one, but there was always the possibility that one of these attacks would finish him off.

As his footsteps came my way I threw off the blanket, flung open the folding fiberboard partition in the archway to the foyer—a gesture toward my privacy, installed years before, when I drifted back home on visits—and went to meet my father. I saw that he was not wearing the length of oxygen hose that usually trailed him around the house; either the spasm had surprised him without it or, more likely, he had torn it off when his windpipe shut. The squat brown oxygen machine wheezed and shuddered at the foyer's other end, its red eye blinking.

We acted, for once, quickly and efficiently: he pointed at his open mouth, I nodded yes, he turned away from me and backed into my arms, arranging them around his deep barrel chest and over his rounded stomach so that I could administer the Heimlich maneuver and unblock his windpipe. I hadn't had the chance to put any clothes on, so I was standing naked behind my father. He was wearing an old beige woolen bathrobe open over faded cotton pajamas. Four or five inches taller than he and feeling awkward, incompletely awake, and well aware that my father could die in my arms, with me standing there naked holding on if this didn't work, I held my breath and gave a hard pull and squeeze across his belly. I heard a number of cracking sounds and thought, *good*, as he shook his head no, did not begin breathing and repositioned my arms lower, *well, at least I've adjusted his spine for him.* The second pull worked—I could feel his stomach give way and his breathing suddenly break open— but the sound that came out of him on the first breath was a groan of pain in extremis. When he tried to straighten up, he groaned again. When he raised his arms, the pain was audibly unbearable. When he tried to turn sideways to face me, it was the same. I saw the look of shock in his eyes.

On the first pull, my arms too high around him, where he and I together had placed them, I had dislocated six of his ribs, as I found out later that day when my friend, the curly, blond, hale and irrepressibly hearty ("How ya doin', Ria?" "GREAT!") Ria Eagan, recently licensed as a chiropractor but as yet without an office, came by with a folding table and put a struck tuning fork to each of his ribs in turn to check for fracture—had one been broken, she told me afterward, the pain of the fork's vibration on the contiguous edges of bone would have sent him screaming through the living room ceiling: a nice test. As it was, my father would be in serious pain, she told me, this on top of his already terrible struggle for sequential breath, for at least the next couple of weeks.

I felt defined; accused, judged, and condemned: I was trying to help my parents; but in the real picture I was increasing their suffering. My mother had tormented me throughout my childhood with a torrent of neurotic accusations. Now she was similarly although not identically tormenting my father, and I was trying to get between them and heal, I suppose, the pain that was tearing all of us to pieces.

"Please, Sadie," my father would beg her, "let me read for a little while, a little peace, a little quiet. I'm a sick man." And she would return with, "Sick? *Sick?* You're making *me* sick. You're making me *cra-zy.*"

In any event, thanks to my most recent aid, my father could now not only hardly breathe, he could barely move. My mother hovered darkly about the apartment, her eyes uncertain, ready to pounce if she could make out, through the fog of her disintegrating perception, any sign of weakness in him. She would not attack me. You could see the look in her eyes, wanting to, but then pulling back when she saw that I was too well armed against her. But my father refused to protect himself. "She's as innocent as a little bird," he would tell me—in his rumbling, heavily accented voice, that of a warmer, kinder Boris Badenov, or a more organ-toned Akim Tamiroff, whom he resembled physically. "How can I say a word against her? A little bird." He would not even distance himself from her emotionally, as I told him he should, if only for his own protection. Any step backward felt cruel to him. You can see how the situation worked. Perfected torment, better, in general, than your garden-variety steel trap, more balanced and conclusive than algebra. It was a psychodrama to which I was only very occasionally equal. After twenty minutes or less, sometimes a good deal less, of rational peacemaking, I would wake to find myself screaming, usually at my mother, who could not grasp the point of what I was trying, however loudly and ineffectively, to say.

THAT NIGHT MY FATHER came briefly out of bed to see if he could read for a while in the kitchen. Reading had been one of the first, and was now the last of his pleasures, although he only read junk now, the autobiographies of actresses and the like. "I can't take any more sadnesses," he would tell me when I came at him with some new novel, by Josef Skvorecky, say, that had appealed to me, or recommended that he have another go at his beloved Tolstoy. "If you want to do me a favor, go to the library and find me another one like Joan Fontaine," he said, referring to an admittedly superior example of the genre. The steroids that helped keep him breathing had destabilized his emotions even beyond what my mother's onslaughts had accomplished; all he wanted from a book now was a little distraction from his pain; to read something even parenthetically authentic about suffering or even unhappiness was intolerable to him.

There was a line in *War and Peace*—the book that dominated the bookshelves of my childhood, thick and red, its title gilt on a contrasting black band, and for frontispiece a multicolored map that compared Napoleon's advance into Russia with Hitler's; an edition that had been printed in the darkest days of the war that early on consumed my father's family—which like so many others had struck me, in my most recent reading of the book, as a definitive pronouncement of an all-seeing, God's-eye genius. It comes late in the book, after Pierre's capture by the French, when he is trudging west as their prisoner through the lethal snows of their retreat. He has been imprisoned, marched up to a firing squad, seen other men executed and expected himself to be shot next, then marched hungry and freezing through the white death of the Russian winter: "He had learned that there is a limit to suffering and a limit to freedom, and that these limits are not far away . . . that in the old days when he had put on his tight dancing shoes he had been just as uncomfortable as he was now, walking on bare feet that were covered with sores." It is an audacious statement in the middle of a stretch of narrative that may be the most fully realized portrait of the activity of Enlightened Mind in the whole of Western fiction, but it is untrue.

Even without recourse to the concentration camps my father had escaped by getting to America just in time, or to the increasingly quotidian incidents around the world to which the mutilated bodies on Bhante's bedroom wall bore prosaic witness, it was possible, even within the relative comfort of a three-room petit-bourgeois Brooklyn apartment, to set sail for another country in which pain was infinite, exquisitely well aimed by a mysterious knowledge of your most occult and tender workings, and utterly without recourse. Sitting in that kitchen, and still able to acknowledge that his suffering represented a small drop in the world's oceanic supply of the stuff, I could see, over the shoulders of the border guards as they poked at me with their pocketknives or laughed at the inadequacy of my papers, I could see my father lost in the depths of that country, stunned and without a passport, progressively stripped of his human attributes, his memories, his ability to think and feel, his identity, his name. I could see the look of shocked recognition in his eyes, and hear the echo of the blows as they came up from the depths.

His eyes were beginning to fail him too, and he read with a lamp drawn down close to the pages of his book through a large round magnifier in a brown, imitation tortoise-shell plastic frame. He had the pleasantly simian features that had earned him the mockery of his brothers in the old country. "Such a flat nose! With no hook to it!" they had teased him, cruelly laughing. Recently I found his features in a black-and-white photo of a particularly soulful gorilla from the Geneva zoo: it appeared to be crooning and dreaming in its cage. Most of my father's hair was gone and the skin on his head was blotched cancerously with brown, and in addition to the fairly new black-and-grey bristle on his upper lip he wore a second moustache of clear plastic with two prongs that went a small way up his nostrils: oxygen. The fat brown machine huffed behind him, visible in profile through the open doorway to the foyer.

It was painful for him to sit at the table, but more painful to lie in bed, with some of his weight invariably pressuring his dislocated ribs. I sat in my chair at the oval table's opposite end. To my left and his right the wallpaper depicted, approximately and in three colors only, the Seine flowing past the Île St.-Louis in Paris—on a white ground, the basic line was black, the shadings medium-pale blue and green. The electrical outlet that powered both his reading lamp and the clock that told us the irrelevant hour was situated in the middle of this depicted river: hydroelectric energy, as we used to say in happier times.

"I'm so sorry about the ribs." I must have said this a number of times that day and night.

If he had tried to shrug, it would have hurt him.

"I'm so sorry."

"It's terrible the pain." Not once did he admit to complicity in the placement of my hands on the first try. This omission amazed me: for all the accusations I had hurled at him over the years, with the unspeakable cruelty that only a loving, beloved, too symbiotic son can manage—sharper than that Shakespearean serpent's tooth by a long shot—this was the closest he had ever come to accusing me, of anything.

We heard my mother's smallish footsteps shuffling up the corridor from the bedroom, the slap of a slipper when now and then she raised one of her feet from the floorboards. She paused at the dining room door, stooped, uncertain, a diminutive woman with short, thinning white hair, and features, despite the alternately absent or accusative look in her eyes, that were beginning to acquire, it seemed to me, an extraordinary intellectual distinction (later I would realize that what I saw emerging through her thinning hair and simplifying facial expressions was the shape, vanity being endless, of my own skull, with its high forehead a proscenium between prominent ridges of bone). Having been born in America, barely, she spoke without a European accent; just the trace of a first-generation Brooklyn broadening of the occasional vowel.

"Sadie," said my father.

"Sadie," she replied, not in confirmation but in the identical tones, an echo.

"Do you want it maybe a glass of hot milk with water?"

"Water with milk?" she inquired, her voice faltering upward.

"Or water with milk," my father allowed. "Pull up a chair. Sit down with us awhile."

I got up to heat a pot of water on the stove.

"Where are you?" my mother might have asked him.

"Sadie," he would have answered, "I'm here, in the kitchen, with you."

"I saw a cockaroach in the bathroom," she said.

"Sadie, it's not a cockaroach. It's a crack in the tile. Do you remember? We put your finger on it? It didn't move. It didn't run away."

"A cockaroach. Look," she said, pointing, then paused as she realized she was not in the bathroom anymore.

"Sadie."

The trained ear could hear the beginnings of a modulation toward fury as she insisted: "A *cockaroach*."

And I would have gone to the stove to tend to the water. I would have selected two clean highball glasses, poured an inch or two of milk into them, then filled the remainder with the heated water: an insipid drink my parents had taken to in recent years.

I would have sat down at the table with them, and hoped for something milder than catastrophe.

And, if no special horror intervened, later that night I would have put them to bed, and still later my mother would have insisted on lying atop the blankets instead of beneath them despite the cold of the night—"I *always* lie on top of the blankets!" she would start to insist, shaking with increasingly cold rage, or, shocked, ask my father how *dared* he, dirty man, *to come into my bed*, and then my father would begin to weep like a child because if she stayed like that she would be stiff with ache by morning and because he could do nothing with her, and I would come in from my momentary refuge (ice cream, television) in the living room and get inside my mother's timing, ask her to excuse me a minute but would she get up—hah?—and, yes, okay, you can lie back down now, there, I'll tuck you in, have a good night's sleep, good night, Mom.

And looking at the small mound of her under the blanket my father would ask me, how did you *do* that?

And I would say, you just have to distance yourself a little from your emotions and see what will work in a purely practical sense.

And he would say, I can't.

And I would say, because you think it would be cruel?

And he'd say, helplessly, yes.

And I'd say, but by doing it you can actually help the situation a little, reduce the suffering all around.

Yes, he'd painfully admit.

And I: do you have to take every arrow directly in the heart?

And he wouldn't know what to say, because taking every arrow directly in the heart was the best he could come up with (taking on the suffering of others is the . . . *noblest* . . . thing a man can do).

And I would say, good night, dad.

BUT THE DISLOCATION of my father's ribs was not the crucial event.

The very next morning I woke to the unexpected sound of water, an unaccustomed torrent of it, like the sound of the bathtub being filled only louder and impossibly more cataractine, and my father's unbelieving voice coming from a distance from behind a door: "No. Oh *noooo* . . ."

This time I had the leisure to pull on the pair of jeans that lay folded on the armchair beside the mattress, but the water sound was getting louder and now my father was groaning in pain, so I hurried past the kitchen doorway and along the parquet flooring of the hall. When I turned right at the corner I was not prepared for what I saw. Around the edges of the tightly closed bathroom door, water was gushing as it does in submarine films, when a depth charge has hit and the crew tries, inadequately, to shut the watertight doors against the flood. It rilled up over the bathroom doorsill—pressure behind it giving the water a bit of loft—and from around the sides of the door to an elevation of say three feet. I tried to imagine the bathroom, with my parents inside it, filled from floor to ceiling with water—a Marx Brothers riff, my parents paddling in the blue, exhaling bubbles, I'd open the door and *whoosh*—an impossibility, but apparently the news of the day. I was standing in an inch of ice cold water that rushed over my bare feet, but the visual image had greater impact: *this is too much*, I thought, meaning the words literally, and although I had as yet no notion what the actual state of affairs in the bathroom might be, I understood instantaneously that all my ideas of life and what could happen to you in it were as of now insufficient, that all my attempts to stem the tide of suffering, to protect either myself or my parents from it, or to place limits upon it, were overmastered and in vain. That everything I had most feared all my life, the shapeless, final, unknown pain that would find my unprotected core and destroy me at last, was upon me and there would be no protection. I walked through the deepening water in the hall and pushed the door open against the pressure, with no idea what I'd find on the other side apart from life changed forever.

Nearest me, my father, his face soaped but only halfway shaven, had fallen sideways across the bathroom basin, clutching the ribs I had dislocated the previous morning. At the other end of the room, my mother was standing bent over beside the toilet with her pink-and-white housedress hitched up her thighs and her plain cotton panties pushed down around her ankles. She was looking behind her puzzled at the spout of water about four inches in diameter roaring out of the wall where the toilet fixture had been attached; it came with such force that it travelled the ten-foot length of the narrow bathroom with only a slight curvature downward before it hit the flat of the bathroom door it had slammed shut behind me. An immense volume of water was pouring into the room. The water felt freezing cold; it was early March. "Pliers," said my father. "Get a pair of pliers."

"You first." He was drenched in cold water. I pulled him upright, he groaned, and I hustled him into the bedroom, pulling his soaked pajamas off and getting him under his quilt, then returned to the bathroom where my mother, a diminutive woman, you will remember, with thinning white hair, was still comparatively dry because she was standing to one side of the gusher, still bent over, looking alternately at the water jetting from behind her and at the wad of toilet paper gathered in her hand. I stooped in front of the toilet to pull my mother's panties up and was amazed at the violence of the bonechilling water as it hit me, as if from a fire hydrant wrenched open. I worked the panties up her legs, then led her into the bedroom, stripped her and got her under the blankets on her side of the beds. "Pliers," my father pleaded again, but I tossed another winter blanket over him and still another over my mother. "A pair of *pliers*."

I ran to get them from the kitchen—the entire apartment was flooding now, a tide of water running along the hallway, taking a left into the kitchen, reaching the living room now and pausing contemplatively as it encountered the edge of the light brown living room carpet—ran back to the toilet and with the water hitting me in my bare stomach, began tearing at a bolt on the toilet fixture for about ten seconds until I realized that the water was coming directly out of the wall, unattached to any fixture, and there was no bolt I could turn, no helm to lash myself to in the storm: sorry, sailor, wrong movie.

"I've got to find the super!" I called to my father, and ran splashing through the deepening water through the apartment into the hallway and then down the polished stone of the first flight of stairs. Actually, because I was still wearing only jeans and my feet were slick with water, I lost my footing, fell, and slid down to the fourth floor mostly on my backside, my right leg folding under me. I could tell that I had broken a toe, and this surprised me: this would have been the time to break a leg, or my back, or land inverted in a heap at the bottom of the steps on my head, concussed. On the fourth floor, doors were opening and neighbors were rushing out of their apartments, only to find me, wearing only blue jeans, sprawled and sodden at the base of the stairs—*Enter Mariners, wet*. Phil and Mary, the old couple who lived directly beneath us, looked the most thoroughly stunned. "What the hell's going on?" said Phil, over eighty, full head of white hair, in a voice that boomed like a trained bass-baritone's even in normal conversation. "Water's running down our walls, down the wires, the lightbulb in the kitchen fixture just blew up—"

"Flood," I said while running. "Gotta find the super."

I slid down the better part of the next three flights wondering where the hell I was going to find him. Miguel was a notoriously difficult man to locate when you needed him, probably could sense the prospect of work coming toward him across a sizable radius of time and space, chant some spell and mysteriously evanesce.

My luck was unbelievable: the short knotty Dominican was just coming out of the incinerator room at the bottom with a metal bucket in his hands. "Miguel! Flood in the apartment, turn off the water *fast*—"

"What line?" he asked.

"My parents' place!"

"What *line*?" He had forgotten.

"Five U, the bathroom, hurry up, the place is—"

He hightailed it to the basement and its rank of valves. By the time I got upstairs there was no new flooding at the source, the waters were abating on the plain, the dove coming back with its bit of olive branch as I pulled back the blankets, bent over my naked parents, one male, one female, and dried them with towels, giving my father back his oxygen hose, wincing when he moaned moving his arms to receive it; telling my uncomprehending mother everything was all right, and all that uncertainty in her eyes. Miguel, famed for his lack of industry but a man who had seen my family's troubles over the preceding months, came up with a large yellow bucket on wheels, a big mop, and uncomplainingly swabbed the place out even though most of the water was seeping down to Mary and Phil's through the floorboards, and the living room carpet was sopping up some of it too . . .

"BUT, DAD, HOW DID IT HAPPEN?" I wanted to know that night, thinking of how my mother would stand at the front door of the apartment, fiddling uncertainly with the locks for a quarter of an hour, trying to get all three of them open at the same time, usually in vain. "Did she unscrew the pipe from the wall?"

"How could she unscrew it the pipe from the wall?" he asked me, a plaintive *Yiddische* downturn wringing his voice, avoiding the outright lie, worried that I would be angry enough to yell at her, scream, carry on, make the whole thing worse than it already was. Only months after my mother's death did my father tell me, in passing, that she had indeed fiddled with the flushometer—they had to call it *something*—as if it were a doorlock or a dial instead of simply pushing the lever down, and, impossibly, the damned thing had popped off the wall and initiated the flood. "Do you know how little strength Mother has it in her hands?"

"Not much," I agreed. "So it just popped off when she flushed?"

"Ye-es," he said, "when she flushed."

Later, my mother, standing in the kitchen and comparing her height with the chair rail around the room, would insist that the entire apartment had been flooded, "up to *here*," indicating the chair rail waist-high, the level at which the waterspout had in fact come past her.

"No, Sadie," my father would laugh weeks later at this recital, his ribs sufficiently healed by now to allow some laughter, "it wasn't like that, my sweetheart," but found himself unable to explain how it really was.

It was still possible to laugh, if emptily, but we had all three of us fetched up, after the flood, on a bare and unimplorable shore on which all human gesture failed. We would be there for a while.

* * *

ONE OF THE LAST THINGS I did before leaving New York was to meet Daniel in a Greek luncheonette on a hot July day, sit across a formica table from him with my little black plastic battery-powered typewriter in front of me, tell him how I wanted it, and then at his dictation tap out the preposterously detailed clauses and subclauses of my will.

We ordered glass after tall glass of seltzer. I divided my realm, like that wise king, Lear, between three women—Sara, Saaque and Siddiqa.

"Never tell anyone," Daniel instructed me, "that we drew up the will in this manner. I will be disbarred."

"Trust me." After all the clauses had been nailed into place—nine pages of single-spaced text that attempted to take into account every exhaustive eventuality that might befall a mere mortal and his more immortal money—all the seltzer had been poured down our throats and back out of our pores into our light cotton clothing and the waiting air, and we had dog-paddled out into the smog and such daylight as could penetrate it—New York had all the charm of an overloaded ashtray that summer—"you know," I said, "after all that typing, all those goddamn clauses and exceptions, like what if one of them dies the week before I do and another one sneezes in the wrong county, it seems a terrible waste of labor, not to mention a failure of taste, to go on living." I started laughing, and almost immediately the laugh got out of control. "I mean really—hold on a second while I catch my breath—I'm not talking about how, how, how *wasted* I feel in general, just about all that, just about all that *fucking typing*." It was too funny for me. I grabbed hold of a passing lamppost for support and panted myself upright until new laughs convulsed me. "Really, man, I should die right here. Jesus. That truck . . . ah, Christ . . . that truck coming up the street should do just fine." The laughter subsided for a moment.

Daniel chuckled but cast me a serious sidelong glance. "Go to Europe," he advised me, "buy a car, go for a drive in the world and enjoy yourself."

"Enjoy myself." I rolled the concept around in what I could assemble of my mind, in an attempt to locate its foreign unfamiliar savor.

"Try."

"Try." I rolled that one too.

"Make an effort. Go for a drive."

"Oh all right already I will."

3

I DROVE MY UNCLE AVRAM EAST through Long Island to the cemetery in the grey Chevy Malibu Classic with the bench seats you slid all over the place on when cornering even when you had the seatbelt on, and the main gasket that drooled oil out the sides of the cylinder block every time you pushed the thing past sixty on the interstate. This sluggard, contumelious car featured a three-speed automatic transmission that habitually left you in the wrong gear when you accelerated to pass, phlumph, or slowed to make a turn. Bought from a Brooklyn Hasid's used-car lot for $3,500, it needed periodic work and upon subsequent closer examination turned out to have been cobbled together from two other like-minded Chevys. I don't know what was Classic about the machine or, for that matter, in what way it might have savored of Malibu. It was a squarish, widish, blockish sort of car. Its leaky air-conditioning system poked irregular holes in the planetary ozone, its black vinyl upholstery was cold in winter and an abomination in summer—that *rrrrripp* when you rose from it having even lightly sweated—and, although a genuine enough four-door sedan, it had been designed with rear windows which could not be rolled down. A rear butterfly window would admit a small trapezoid of breeze if you were observant enough to notice it and applied yourself sufficiently to the ambiguous and recalcitrant hasp. The immovable rear windows seemed the car's churliest feature but not, all things considered, its worst. Its slewy handling took the biscuit. This Malibu Classic handled like a top-heavy rubber duck in a tempest-torn and gong-tormented bath. Zabors (we were the only ones in the phonebook) have never had particularly good luck with their cars. When buying them we tend to turn greenhorn. The Zabor *qua emptor* approaches with calflike facial expression and an upturned hand that asks for fairness if not mercy in this world and knows in its bones and by frequent rehearsal that it will receive neither. Implicitly, when it comes to buying cars at least, we beg to be wounded, short-changed, to be taken, in short, for a ride. Our kingdom is not of this world.

"Even though I tink when you ee dead you ee nothing," Avram told me as I drove, "it feel important I don't know why to see your father grave."

"Sure," I said, although I thought that when you ee dead you ee still pretty present and for that reason, or perhaps because I saw enough of them in dreams, I had no interest in visiting my father's grave, or my mother's beside it. Let's say at least that there was an iceberg of ambivalence, most of it duly concealed underwater, floating in the sea of my mind, in this regard.

Avram, who retained the suffix "-ovsky" that my parents had had removed from the family name when I entered grade school, was another, altogether more primitive kind of Jew. Viewed across that black vinyl banquette he seemed normal enough, a taller version of my father with a larger, hookier but unlaughed-at-in-childhood and perhaps therefore more assertive nose, and a face whose putty had been roughed up with a bit of hasty thumbwork on the part of its ministering angel. Tufty whitening hair plumed out around his ears but was shaved short and high on the back of his neck. That neck might have provided a shrewd observer with his first clue to Avram's real strangeness: a tapering pillar that rose from shoulders that did not appear unusually large—there was no bulk as such on the man anywhere—lifting that beaked head in an eaglish bareness into its heights, it was braided, this pillar, with muscle you didn't ordinarily see on human necks, much less on those belonging to men in their eighties. From this neck, if you noticed it, you might pass to a consideration of Avram's wrists, which seemed thicker than wrists had any right to be; they looked like heavy rope each tributary strand of which was of at least maritime tensile strength. Having taken these in, one might notice the animal grace with which the old man sat even in that insufficiency of a Chevy, no hint of either a youthful or an aged slouch to him but a certain self-lofting quality, a feral wakefulness, the echo of a panther body instinctly alert: not a bad effect for a man of eighty-some. Underneath the distant uptown Manhattan bed in which Avram slept beside his necessarily docile wife Pearl—pronounced "Peril," with a lightly gargled, nearly French uvular *r* in the middle—lay a 1930s axle from a Ford truck. Avram had brought it up (along with the *ee* that peppered his speech but which had lost much of its functional resemblance to the Spanish *y* from which it derived) from South America with him in '48; it was the perfect weight for his exercises, he said. I had never seen anyone else able to lift it by one of its ends and with wrist power alone or rigidly extended arm raise it to the vertical and slowly let it down again, or anyone beside him, let alone anyone his age, who could squeeze a bathroom scale in his hands and without strain run the dial past its 250-pound limit bang into its endpoint; but the most quintessentially Avramic demonstration of strength I could recall came at a family party in a Bronx apartment about a decade back when some vague cousin or other entered with one of his children, a boy about twelve years old and of normal size for that age, and Uncle Avram—a couple or six straight double vodkas to the better—who had not seen the child in question for a few years, put his wide right hand under the kid's bottom and lifted him at arm's length for the assembled company to see, saying, "Oh look what a beautiful child," while standing unaffected by the child's weight at the end of his arm with roughly the immortal poise of the bronze Poseidon in the Athens Archaeological Museum: Avram had seemed supported by some force familiar with the stresses of gravity but which had chosen not to have much to do with them for the moment.

His voice was not the thundering instrument you might have expected from such a figure; slightly throat-strained and not at all deep, it tended to quest slightly upward during the course of a sentence.

Examined casually the man offered nothing special to the eye. Avram's peasant face was usually pale and looked somehow dusted lightly with fine flour, like a bialy. Looking into his face straight on you noticed that although his small eyes were keenly watchful they were not particularly expressive, as if the light of personality had penetrated into them once or twice but had not thought to linger. Wolves' eyes look warmer and more cognitive.

WE HAD FLED MY PARENTS' GRAVES, Avram and I, quickly enough across the bare ground on the freezing late January morning we put my father's body in the earth: a wind cut us through our clothing and we ran from it like cowards from a knife in the hand of an unknown quantity. The haste with which we beat it shocked me: my devotion to my father collapsed by a gust of windchill, and Avram, fleeing the graveside after barely managing a Kaddish . . . well, it was hard to believe. The family wildman lived in an apartment, as I remembered, incorrectly, from childhood, with the windows flung wide open in all seasons; back in the old country he'd kept himself in a cabin apart from the rest of the family and lived by his own fierce and eccentric rules. Sometimes he'd take some of the farm animals in to live with him, conceivably for warmth. When the successive waves of armies—German, Russian, White Russian, Red Russian, German, Polish, etc.—came through the unpronounceable town during the First World War and the Russian Civil War that arrived festively in its wake, Avram took the family's animals, the cows and the chickens and the horses and the geese, into the forest and lived with them there, no doubt eating one or two to help pass the time, until the ravening armies had come and gone for good. He had returned, my father told me when I was a child, carrying a staff, flanked biblically by animals and wearing a beard down to there. My father had filled my childhood with Avram stories, mostly of his supernatural strength: shouldering startled plowhorses athwart him into the air for exercise; putting my father behind him and tossing a gang of attacking Polacks, as my father called them, over a wall hup one-two-three-four like a circus act; picking up a man (who had given my father a ride on a windmill blade, woodblocked the mill to a stop and left him hanging at the apex), holding him for a moment in his large hands while saying something on the order of Don't ever do anything like that to my kid brother again, then putting him down unconscious, nearly dead, a doctor said later, and all Avram had done was pick him up by the shoulders and hold him in those big hands awhile.

More recently, on a visit to his younger son Victor in California, when Avram was in his early seventies, Vic took him to meet a friend of his, an immense young man who appeared to be all rippling bicep, who was, in fact, the official arm-wrestling champion of California. After chatting for a while about this and that, Victor mentioned that his dad was pretty strong. Would the champ like to arm-wrestle with him? Said champion looked dubious, and let on that he was afraid of hurting the old guy. "No," Avram told him, "I not worried." So they sat down across a table from each other and got into position. The champ gave Avram's arm a little push at perhaps 10 percent of his power. "It's okay," Avram told him, "you can do more." The champ gave it a little more, and then at Avram's suggestion pushed it up another notch, and then another, until by increments he began exerting himself to the utmost, muscles straining and veins apop while the funny-looking old guy with the accent looked calmly back at him across the table. "Is that it?" Avram finally asked him, and the champ, popping blood vessels, puffing and pouring with sweat, nodded yes. "You *are* strong," Avram told him without irony. "O-kay," he concluded in a two-note singsong, and took a couple of seconds at most to smoothly press the champion's hand to the boards. The only uncharacteristic touch in this story is the hint of Avram's deliberate humiliation of the younger man, but I'm sure that my uncle's interest in their relative strength was purely academic and that he meant to inflict neither physical nor psychic harm. It probably never entered his mind that he might.

In the petit-bourgeois tidiness of my mother's household, and of her sister Rose's more sophisticated shrine to the gods of domestic order in the apartment just next door, the alien Zaborovskys periodically burst through like a travelling circus troupe, a medley of uncivilized and parti-accented eccentrics, all talking at the same time, all loud, all disagreeing about everything, all clashing like cymbals to a tune of indecipherable trivialities, their features irregular, their color sense grotesque or non-existent—orange slacks, green suits, crisscrossed yellows, blues, browns, unassimilable stripes, indigestible plaids—endlessly competing for the floor, *yes yes yes* beaten back by waves of *no no no*, unanimous only in their certainty that the kepitalist economy would start collapsing any day now Herry and the longed-for revolution come. Although *Sam* (emphasis added), the oldest of the brothers and the self-declared patriarch of the bunch, conducted himself like the King of the Visible Universe, wearing well into his late eighties a full head of coarse wavy hair still more black than grey; a year-round tan; blindingly bright blue shirts; pleated, impeccable, white trousers; gold lamé loafers without socks and a shiny armature of unassailable judgments that were blazoned forth, from this tower of might, in a definitive, basso-profundo voice that could level small buildings at forty paces and shake, when he required it to, the foundations of modern physics—in my child's mind Avram had always led this impossible and lunatic pack of cards, this band of piebald, contradictory, *Lobachevskian* humanity, and it was with a part-bewildered still partly childish love that I continued to love him.

"Ee I tink you don't care to see your father grave."

"It doesn't matter that much to me. I'm happy to take you."

"I don't have car. How else I go? Whew. Is hot."

"You want me to turn on the air conditioner?"

"Air conditioner? Why for? You sick?"

Some vacationer in a red Plymouth Fury cut me off while changing lanes. I braked and swerved to avoid him, cursed the Chevy's slew and thought wistfully of the lightfooted Raccoon, then draining Daniel's wallet instead of mine. I didn't like American cars. I sneered at them in general and at the reckless Fury in particular before returning to conversation with my favorite, hold on, make that only living uncle. The Zaborovskian ranks were thinning out, all that vitality and excess no proof against the tide of time, and the initial footprint that particular peasant culture made, not to be repeated ever in the stomp and tread of history, tipped by whitemaned coursers onto the American shore, was being washed away even as we rode to the cemetery, and would soon be illegible on the sand. "No, I'm all right," I said. "I thought you might want it." I stepped on the gas and the car responded like one of the seven sleepers of Ephesus; I tromped the pedal into scat gear and repossessed the center lane.

"Me? What I care for air conditioner?"

In this extrovert and farraginous family my father was the youngest, quietest, most modest and intellectual member. In his modesty he had a model in the strong, deliberately gentle blacksmith who was the clan's father. (I have his picture with me: a broad, bearded face with large, dark, impossibly soulful eyes; in another photo, taken shortly before the Nazis let the Poles have a party and club the town's Jews to death in the square or slaughter them like cattle hung from hooks at the kosher butcher's, he sits with other elders of the community, his hair and beard gone mostly grey, his large hands placed calmly on his thighs and a bright, unmistakable halo ringing his head with light: there are no similar distortions elsewhere in the picture.) My calm, iron-wielding grandfather had remarried after being widowed; my father had a different mother than the older crop of Ovskys. He was born underweight and was a sickly child. His lungs were the problem from the beginning: asthma, with a classic psychological etiology, and successive bouts of pleurisy, in war-torn times and peaceful intermissions, sent him into the wavery borderland between life and death a number of times before his bar mitzvah—once he woke from a fever to find that his parents had taken him out of bed and placed him on the floor so that he would die without so much painful struggle, the family standing vigil in a rough circle around him and waiting unhappily for him to go. (For him, one of the conclusive signs of Tolstoy's genius was the exact and unmelodramatic series of hallucinations Prince Andrei suffers on the way to his reconciliation with Natasha and his death: a voice whispering nonsense syllables, a shirt that resembles a sphinx, and a network of needles building itself on his face, more terrifying, my father insisted, than the grotesquer inventions of lesser writers, because true. My father knew these night visions well, in his case a haunted shirt hanging on the back of a chair that rose and fell with his labored breath and a blanket that grew uncontrollably large as it lay on him, filling the room to the ceiling and then receding, only to swell again.) At the age of thirteen, he was a thin, pale intellectual youth who did not breathe well and was not expected to live very long.

It was this too mortal wraith whom Avram took conclusively in hand. After the armies had gone, Avram had something like the following conversation with him while walking along a road.

—Herschel, do you want to live?

—Of course I want to live.

—You'll die before twenty unless you let me help you.

—What do I have to do?

—Come live with me next winter. Do what I do, eat what I eat. Stay with me for one winter and you will live to be an old man.

They would wake early and exercise at Avram's direction. Avram and my father would then fetch in buckets of snow. Avram would rub my father's naked body down with snow and they would exercise some more. My father could only eat food that Avram himself had prepared. My father never approached his older brother's inexplicable strength—who could?—but he became a thick-bodied powerful man who lived to the age of seventy-eight and would probably have made it to ninety-plus, like Sam, if he hadn't taken up smoking cigarettes when young.

"Ay, your father save whole family," Avram told me as we rode.

"I know."

"If not for him I dead, oh, years ago, in Uruguay."

"He loved you very much."

"Of course. We was brothers."

"No. He *loved* you."

"Of *course* he love me. We was brothers."

Avram: in physical culture a prodigy, in conversation, a wall.

Uruguay: Avram stumbling into a village after being lost in the forest for a few weeks, the villagers offering food, Avram eating an entire roast sheep, drinking five or ten gallons of milk, then lying down to sleep for three days while the assembled villagers waited for the giant to die. From my father's stories, all of them true, you could construct a mythic creature named Avram; it was only later, in conversations with the actual Avram, that I learned that in Uruguay he had been a shopkeeper and occasionally went off peddling in the sticks somewhere.

"Your father save all of us. What we do without him?"

"Avram, what would he have done without you?"

"What I do?"

Well, when the Poles were about to jail my father the second time for his revolutionary activities, Avram had come to him and said, "Herschel, this time you won't survive it when they torture you," and, altering a document or two, he had gone to prison in my father's place—that counted for something, I guessed. My father never ran down the full list of Polish entertainments, but he did mention once in passing when I was seven or eight years old that the pain of having hot needles pushed in beneath your toenails was "unimaginable."

My father save whole family by means of Paradise Drinks. This was a sliver of luncheonette attached to the side of the Loews Paradise, a movie palace two doors down from the Apollo Theatre on 125th Street; so narrow that I can remember, when I was of an age that left me shorter than the lunch counter, barely squeezing past between the stoolbacks and the wall. I also remember: never having seen so many Negroes in the street; "The Great Pretender" in heavy rotation on the jukebox; being let in free next door in the middle of *Lust for Life* and wondering what Kirk Douglas was all worked up about; the fascinating hamburgers you sliced off a kind of hamburger-salami and stacked in the cooler, separated by squares of wax paper; the clean, wet-wood smell of the back room and the darkly lumbered walk-in fridge, its door heavy as a vault's; and that the couple of colored guys who worked for my dad seemed incredibly glad to meet me. The boss's little son! Everybody likes me!

My father had bought into Paradise on credit after arriving in New York with thirty-five cents and a small bag of marijuana in his pocket—it was good for his asthma, he said—hauling cement sacks in Rockaway for eleven dollars a week (six of which he sent back to his parents until Stalin acquired them through the nonaggression pact in '39 and there was no longer any prospect of buying their way out), then getting his cook's training flipping burgers in someone else's Harlem joint, the only place an over-thirty immigrant stumbling through English could get work—when asked, once, to cancel the coffee, he continued putting milk in it, saying, Here's your cancelled coffee, ser, until the man threw the cup at him and left my father a small scar above his left eye for life—where black people danced to the jazz he would never be able to unhate (except for Coltrane in his hymning mood) and enormous, long-toothed white Norwegian rats gobbled the fat drippings beneath the grill, brushing with chilling territorial arrogance against his feet. Somehow he persuaded Loews to front him two months' rent, Coca-Cola to advance him syrup and Trunz the necessary meats; he then pulled the brothers and sisters who had mocked his nose in childhood and done nothing to rescue him from impending Hitler (Sam, who had his own business already, had gotten him out, but that's another story), from their various shit-jobs around town and informed them that they were his partners. After the war, when Paradise Drinks was going like a bomb, with each of the partners pulling in the equivalent of a doctor's income, he brought Avram, his wife, two already gigantic sons and a truck axle up from Uruguay; knowing that this lone wolf could cooperate with no one, my father bought him his own dive elsewhere in the neighborhood. My father's devotion to the family had never asked for anything in return; he had, however, wanted to get them all out of Harlem even before the convulsions of the sixties, but the others chose to sit tight with a sure thing, wary of his several plans, at least one of which—picking up the Nedicks chain for a song during a momentary lapse in that firm's prosperity—would have made the fortunes of them all.

In my parents' last years, Avram had visited regularly, a two-hour-plus subway ride from his hilltop eyrie in Washington Heights, near Manhattan's northern end. He would massage my mother's neck, then simply lay his outsized unmoving hands on her to give her some of his energy and would press the flesh only when she wondered why his hands weren't moving—this back in the days when she could still frame such a question—sit for hours across the table from my dad, talking with him in the Yiddish I had never learned to speak or understand very well.

Once, Avram was just finishing up one of these visits as I was about to take the Chevy into the City to hear some Shostakovich. "Avram," I proposed, "I'm going to Carnegie Hall. Come with me in the car. I can drop you at the A train station on 59th Street and you can go on from there without changing trains."

"No. What for?"

"It'll be faster than the subway, it's a nice evening, we can talk on the way . . ."

"No, I take train."

"He likes to take the train," my father pitched in.

"We going somewhere?" asked my mother, looking around for her purse.

In the end, I prevailed over Avram's protests, and my uncle permitted himself to be led to the Malibu.

A short distance from the house, he asked me to stop the car. He got out and picked up a cracked table lamp from a trash heap. How he had spotted it, at speed and in the gathering dark, I will never know. "Nice lamp," he said, "ee lying around. I fix up, maybe keep, maybe give to neighbor."

Soon we had left the streets behind and entered the Prospect Expressway, City-bound. The sun had gone down but smog had turned the twilight several spectacular shades of purple, a blush of red at the base, then levels of magenta ascending darkly into indigo and eventual night. Below us, as we rode the rising hump of the Belt over the Gowanus Canal, lights were on in the oblong windows of a line of Edward Hopper tenements ascending an incline, their redbrick faces turned to the street, clotheslines and ailanthus commingling at the rear. Once my father got himself more than slightly established in New York, he saw that the people lived like ants, hordes of them disappearing into holes in the ground, working, working, finding niches to live in, reproducing, working, soldiering on: like ants. Yes, *exactly*, I'd told him with some heat, and disregarding me he'd continued: And I was happy to be one of the ants. Oh I was a happy ant in those days, he said, his voice retrospective and fond.

All I had ever really loved about Brooklyn per se—I mean apart from its skies or the sound of wind passing through the highest leaves of its trees on Lenox Road—was that Jackie Robinson played baseball in it, and that was a while ago.

"Tell me," asked Avram.

"Yes?"

"You going Carnegie Hall."

"Ye-es."

"What is Carnegie Hall?"

"You've never heard of Carnegie Hall?"

"No. What is?"

"Avram, you've lived in New York for forty years and you've never heard of Carnegie Hall?"

"No, is first time I hear. Is some kind theatre?"

"It's a famous concert hall. You've really never heard of it?"

"No."

"They have concerts there, symphony orchestras, sometimes other kinds of music."

"So is kind theatre."

"Okay, sure."

At length we rounded the horn of Brooklyn beneath the Heights and came alongside the black water, and there was your insular city of the Mannahatoes, black obelisks of the Battery pocked with light against the purple grades of air. Much as I hated New York—and I hate New York with a ferocity I believe its lack of heart deserves, even though I know that my very vehemence is a signpost pointing elsewhere—I still found Manhattan a beautiful prospect from this distance. We swung beneath the Promenade and could see the lit ladder of the City ranged uptown, the Brooklyn Bridge a noble stone-and-cable necklace strung with lights across the river as its gate. To our left and slightly behind us, pale green, the Statue of Liberty had turned its back on Manhattan and was gazing off to sea, its torch upraised. Save the lady and the bridge and *sink* the rest of it.

"Tell me," Avram said, gesturing at the Brooklyn Bridge as we got nearer to it. "What bridge that?"

"Avram," I said, "you don't know what bridge that is?"

"No. What is?"

"That's the Brooklyn Bridge, Avram."

"Oh, *that* the Brooklyn Bridge," he said.

"Yes," I said, and shook my head. "You've never seen it before?"

"No. How I see? I don't have car."

"You've never seen a picture of it?"

"I don't tinkso."

"But you must have come this way by car with us at least a couple of times. Avram: that's the Brooklyn Bridge for Chrissakes."

"So *that* the Brooklyn Bridge," he said.

When we were halfway across it, Avram pointed out the right-hand window at the Manhattan Bridge, its blued girders uglying their way across the East River to our immediate north. "Ee tell me. What bridge that one?"

"You don't know that one either?"

"No. How I know?"

"That's the Manhattan Bridge."

"Oh, *that* the Manhattan Bridge."

I dropped him outside the Colosseum at the 59th Street A train stop—he raised his cracked lamp in the air as parting salutation—left the car nearly in front of Carnegie on 57th just as parking turned legal at 7 p.m., picked up my ticket at the box office and went to the Carnegie Deli for dinner, where the world's largest matzoh ball confronted me from a bowl.

Wonders, it seemed, would never cease.

NOW WATCH: in the time it takes me to eat my way through this matzoh ball, I'll tell you how my father managed to con his way to America. The year was 1938, my father was the last of his brothers and sisters still alive in Europe, and the Poles, inspired by the example of Hitler next door but still a tad more cautious, had begun by means of discriminatory tax laws to legislate away the property of their resident Jews. My grandfather's never very large spread had been stripped of its farmland, barns and animals and been reduced to the family home and the blacksmith shop. Others, more mercantile, more thoroughly embedded in the economy of the towns and cities, had been stripped of their commercial holdings and reduced to peddling their wares on the roads, where the Poles were free to kill them for sport.

It was not hard for my father to feel the comprehensive waves of doom that were rolling in. He wrote abroad pleading for help to get himself and his parents out, but did not get much in the way of response, even though, as good leftists, most of his brothers and sisters had sound doctrinal reasons for taking Hitler seriously: now that the workers' revolution had come and day was about to break over the darkened earth, the forces of reaction would do their worst to smudge the nascent light and Hitler was the avatar the oligarchy had been praying for—so, at least, went the legend. But even if they'd been willing to help this runt of the litter, could his brothers and sisters, rootless noncosmopolitans making less than their fortunes in the *goldeneh medineh*, have done anything for him? And my father was in at least a double bind: as a godless Jewish commie organizer who'd done time twice, on record, for subversion, there was no way the Poles would let him slip the noose and bugger off to Ameriky.

But, if my father was such a revolutionary, I can hear a voice in the cheap seats asking, why didn't he trot off to suck the waiting paps of Mother Russia? To which I can only reply that my father was not a fool. You did not have to swear by the prophet Trotsky or know about the famines or the Gulag to understand that the revolution had been betrayed: if nothing else, the show trials of the thirties—in which all the planners of the Bolshevik revolution save Stalin and the late Mr. Lenin confessed to having been no-good spying wreckers in the pay of the German or British secret services all along and then demanded to be shot—made it plain as day to anyone with a working set of eyes what manner of darkness was breeding in the shadow of the Big Moustache. With my own splendid, painlessly acquired hindsight I can make out a sufficiently bloody gloom germinating behind the Dynamic Brow and beetling from beneath the Small Goatee, but my father wouldn't have run to the Soviet Union even if Lenin had still been running the show. He could gauge the size of the coming war by the immensity of the cloudfront preceding it. Besides, if you wanted to raise a family you went where a decent life was possible, and dialectical materialists were *sposed* to think smart: America was the obvious, the necessary place. Bejesus, it was in indisputable fact a paradise. So with Hitler to the west of him, Stalin to the east, and no ready prospect of escape, my father was inspired, his mind concentrated wonderfully by the prospect of being hanged in the morning, to do some creative thinking.

He began by initiating a friendly correspondence with his oldest brother *Sam*, who was living in New York and had become, at least since his service in the American army during the First World War, an American superpatriot who wholly rejected the leftist politics of his lesser siblings. In the Great War, Sam had served his nation on Staten Island, a beleaguered outpost off the coast of lower Manhattan, and had joined the American Legion upon being demobbed. All I know about his army life is one family legend: that he was caught sneaking back one night into the post after going AWOL for a while—already married then, he had scarpered off only to enjoy the fruits of a divine command operative since the tactical retreat from Eden. To the "Who goes there" of the watchful guard-at-arms, Sam bellowed back "GENERAL SHMAI!" and urged his horse through the gates unmolested—nay: the guard snapped to and saluted him smartly—seated as mightily as any bronze hero on a statue horse.

My father, who in his own time would serve his country heroically during the Second World War heaving the diminutive cutlasses of a barber in the state of Oregon before being court-martialled, acquitted, then honorably discharged for largely bogus medical reasons, began his correspondence with Sam innocently enough, giving him news of the old country and the old folks at home, etc., etc. But he had taken the measure of Sam's pride decades before: once their correspondence was established my father began slipping other bits of information into the mix, finally letting word fall that the Finkels, the mere Finkels, were laughing up their sleeves at Sam, because even though Sam was such a bigshot in America they, the Finkels, had been able to get Harry Finkel out last year, whereas Sam, whereas Sam . . .

In my father's possibly suspect telling of this story, Sam's response was an immediate and explosive WHAT! and the sudden demolition of the door to the office of the biggest general the New York City branch of the American Legion had to offer by the volcanic rearrival of General Shmai laying down the law to whatever lesser officers might since have sprouted in the land. In relatively short order my father received a summons to the American Embassy in Warsaw to pick up his papers. In order to get there he had had to load the goods truck that took him there and in consequence arrived in time to see the gates closing and the handful of the Saved walking away, papers in hand. It was the last day on which his papers would be available—this detail seems unconvincing, but Avram guarantees it—and in some panic he called out to the diplomatic compound, his hands clutching the wrought-iron bars that separated him from a future, any future.

"Go away," someone shouted back, but my father called again. "What's your name?" the someone asked him this time.

My father told the man.

"Zaborovsky? Why didn't you say so? Wait a moment, I'll get the key."

Once inside he was given the papers that would enable him to live awhile longer, but before he was able to leave with them, an American official drew him aside to ask a question. "You know," this official told him, "the gates to America are closed now. The quotas are full, it's impossible to get in." Here he tapped at my father's immigration papers, and my father flinched. "I've never seen papers like this in my life. You're stamped all the way through, no normal procedure, no questions asked. So what I want to know is: who is this Sam Rogers who is sponsoring you?"

"My brother," my father said.

"But what is he, a general? I tell you, I've never seen papers like this in my life."

Sh'ma. Shazam. Shmai.

My father debarked from Hamburg and ate heartily all the way across while others puked their immigrant guts up.

When he arrived in New York, he was stripped of whatever valuables he had brought—including a silver sugar bowl, with bicephalous eagles for ears, that my father would later insist came from the Winter Palace, given to the family by a grateful Red Army boarder when that army withdrew—and saw them distributed to people in the family who had done nothing to save him and who had no thought of saving his parents now.

But he fell in love with America when he saw that soldiers neither inspired the familiar, pavement-shaking European terror nor were even accorded any special respect when they walked down the street, and that you could buy a suit of clothes without having to wheedle away at the price. The large signs in shopfronts everywhere that read TO LET confused him because he could imagine no reason for so garishly pointing out the location of a toilet, but he did better than his brother Julius had upon his arrival: when offered a banana he said thanks, downed the thing peel and all, said it was good and asked for another. My father was sent to work immediately, with no English, no instructions and for almost no pay, in a hot dog grill tucked into the curved, blue-tile flank of S. Klein's department store on Union Square. They didn't even tell him how to turn on the gas; my father had to pull in a passing old Jewish man to show him where the valve was and how to work it, but remained at a loss when people asked him for Apackaluckies or Apackacamels while pointing at the cigarette rack, where all he could make out by his own lights were Lootskiy Streekyeh and Tsyamel.

My father toughed it out and stayed on the job, and took an interest in the ruling family despite their cavalier treatment of him in the hot dog trade. In particular, he pleaded with them to get their nephew Avezzah out of Europe before the war came. You have the money, he told them. Get him out. They objected that Avezzah was not like you, Herschel; he's too primitive to make the transition. But my father persisted, told them that the war was really coming, the alternative was certain death, and at length Avezzah was fetched to America.

One morning my father arrived at work to find this Avezzah already *in situ* behind the grill. "Avezzah," my father asked him, "what are you doing here? This is my job."

"Get out of here," Avezzah snarled at him.

"But Avezzah—"

"Out!" Avezzah bared his teeth and brandished a large knife above his head and chopped the air with it. "OUT!" (I remember this Avezzah in his old age, a rude, white-bearded image of a peasant patriarch, red-faced, with wild eyes.)

My father never really forgave him, until the end, for this humiliation and several others. After a few more confrontations with this savage figure, and some equally fruitless pleading with the chieftains of Avezzah's family—the Finkels, as it happened—my father took off for the Rockaways and his appointed burden of cement.

SPEAKING OF WHICH and strangely believe it: that matzoh ball is gone.

4

"HOW YOUR FRIEND JAKE?" Avram asked me back in narrative time present.

Jake and Avram had gotten to know each other in the limo on the way back from my mother's burial on the Island. "Living in Israel. We write to each other. I'll see him there if I go."

"What he doing there, Jake?"

"Some translating . . ."

"Hebrew?"

"Mostly Yiddish into English. Adventure books for religious kids. Doing some writing for a rabbi."

"The rabbi *paying* him something?"

"He'd have to. Jake can't afford to work for nothing."

"He living where, Jerusalem?"

"Near his wife's family in Tel Aviv, but he wants to move to Jerusalem."

"Sure he want to live in Jerusalem, believer like him. Where else he want to live? A believer," Avram said incredulously, astonished that the species could still exist amid the century's fine progress in the destruction of belief. And believers.

"That's Jake all right," I said.

JACOB LAMPART HAD COME LATE to my mother's funeral because of some subway tangle in the Hadean tunnels between the Upper
West Side and Brooklyn; I had missed him during the service and only
spotted him—poking by alongside the funeral home in his old black suit
with the uncertain body language of an immigrant or the even greater
hesitations that afflict the living when they approach the territory of the
dead—as I sat in the lead limo waiting for the cortege to take off for Nassau County and the family plot. Naturally I invited him in.

On the ride back from that burial, about five miles distant from Beth
Moses, I noticed with surprised recognition the emotions doing their instantaneous New Orleans turnaround from somberness to sudden happy
sociability. Jake got into an animated three-way with Avram and my father,
asking them about the old days in the old country and Avram unwinding a
story or two, my father checking the gauge on his portable liquid oxygen
unit before launching into one of his own; before very long they were flying
inscrutably by me in Yiddish, and I sat there on the foldout seat, my hands
composed upon my knees, feeling exactly like a tourist. Finally, "Do you
think you can do this in English?" I asked them, and "Hah?" said Jake or my
father or Avram, like sleepers awakened, before condescending into English
for me for a minute or two until Yiddish resumed.

Like most of my friends, Jake had thought highly of my father. He had
visited him in the hospital a number of times and even came to the Intensive
Care Unit where my father spent the last ten weeks of his life—a pilgrimage
not many had cared to make, and in the end, my father died only a couple
of days before Jake and his wife moved back to Israel for good: they took off
for the Holy Land, and he departed severally for a patch of earth and the
immensity of the skies. What skies? Oh, I'll tell you later.

Even though he wore the black gabardine jacket and knitted skullcap of
a yeshiva *bukher*, Jake and I had looked essentially alike back in college: two
long thin dark-haired mordant Jews writing nihilistic short stories, waiting
to turn twenty-one and get on with the rest of the catastrophe. Jake's dark
good looks and thick long black hair had earned him the nickname Angel in
his yeshiva days. Angel's stories were both better and more nihilistic than

mine. His prize-winning "Aszy's Worshippers," published anonymously in fear of his Orthodox father's wrath, concluded with an aged, paretic couple enabled to fuck by the woman reciting the oration for the man's future funeral. "It's over. Off of me," Aszy said, with all the Lampartian tenderness of that period, when the lovemaking was over and the oration complete. ("In life he was a simple man. He asked for little," etc.) Jake's influences at the time? Beckett, Malamud, and a real-life father and mother who had emerged alive from between the grinding stones of Hitler and Stalin. Jake was born in Poland just after the war and had lived briefly with his parents in Paris before coming to New York. Yiddish was his first language, and although he spoke American English without an accent, his writing sometimes had the complex aura of translation.

I remembered picking Jake up in the family car near his family home in the late sixties on Friday nights after dark; he'd wait for me hidden in some still darker doorway, wearing a jacket with the collar pulled up to conceal his face, and a pair of heavy black Italian shades that only made him more conspicuous in the dark. Only when the car had come to a full stop would he emerge from the doorway, scuttle across the pavement and climb in, hunching his shoulders. "Let's go," he'd say, sweeping his yarmulke off but keeping his shoulders hunched until we'd left the neighborhood. Usually we'd end up at Garfield's gigantic cafeteria at Church and Flatbush, with its glittering two-storey-high mosaic walls depicting dismantled Venetian motifs in burgundy, black and gold, and we'd talk about writing over French toast, coffee and cigarettes for hours.

Jake had written some strange stories in those years. "The Ball-Licking Belle of Atlantic City," in which the decrepit, near-dead agonists shoot a paretic porno movie without film in the camera. "Hungry," in which there is nothing left to eat in the nameless abstract-European village but chicken-eye soup, and the woman who gets the eyes has to be begged for them, usually with sexual favors of which hunger has made the beggar incapable. This story finally had scared Jake a little, had seemed a definite lapse across the border into the wilds of outright madness, and, living in a Boerum Hill apartment with an unobstructed view of the brown massif of the Ex Lax Building—then the *fons et origo* of the chocolate laxative, later a block of luxury apartments—he began to consider the wisdom of a tactical retreat from the abyss.

We'd stayed in touch through the wanderings of the intervening decades, with California and Israel for him and me all over the map. We'd even been neighbors once for a six-month stretch in 1976, stacked in two apartments above a small synagogue in a narrow, green-tinged brownstone on the Upper West Side. My apartment had trapdoors cut in its floors; in the High Holy Days the synagogue's women would use the apartment as a kind of balcony—I'd be confined to the living room and kitchen then—so that they could peer down through the opened traps at the services below. One morning on my own I'd innocently opened the parquet square cut in the living room floor and looked directly down on a circumcision, the child cut and crying, the drop of sweet wine wiped across his lips that silenced him, the penis quickly swaddled in cotton. Jake, who had once lived in that apartment, which had seemed to me a mirror of his personality, had moved up to the larger flat on the top floor, made his living as a substitute teacher but kept banging out variants of what had begun to seem one long story of sex and Jews and death. In one, the narrator suggests that after the Holocaust there weren't enough Jewish bodies to go around and so sometimes two souls, both full of recent anguish, were crammed together into one—I've had a number of friends whose parents survived the concentration camps that Jake's had managed, miraculously and by a whisker, to escape, and some of these friends eventually killed themselves, but none of them seemed as deeply marked by the burnings of that war as Jake did, or so indelibly dyed with its colors. "Under the Hasid's Knife" was only one of several fictions in which the dead hand of the past materializes to snuff out any possibility of already corrupted new life—the Hasid coming through the door knife in hand just as the protagonist, a man with a museum of faked Holocaust pornography in his apartment, is about to go to bed with the old woman next door who has survived Auschwitz—but Jake had managed to publish two more normal stories in *Commentary*, and like the good shoemaker he

stuck to his last. The sustained rumble of his Selectric on my ceiling encouraged me; I'd listen to it for a while and think, Why not? In the six
months I spent sandwiched between Jake and the synagogue I wrassled
into shape the hundreds of pages of poetry I'd written in Turkey—most
of it at Mahmoud's house—and Israel the year before, and wrote a modest short novel based on the time I'd spent recovering from Turkish
pneumonia while living alone in a cave in the Sinai Desert. In our stacked
firetraps, Jake and I read each other's manuscripts, talked a lot about writing, less about religion and mysticism, and kept the intimate things
slightly generalized. Since the synagogue had no interest in profit and
only wanted the building occupied for security reasons, I paid $110 a
month rent, the winter passed from 1976 to '77, and I learned a thing or
two about how to get it onto the page.

BY THE TIME HE MET AVRAM in the anteroom to the Intensive
Care Unit in which my father lay dying, Jake was a different, gentler but
still quite odd sort of writer—he'd always been a gentle person, soft of
voice, the soul of solicitude and consideration—and had returned to the
Jewish Orthodoxy against which he had been in so painful yet so covert a
rebellion back then. He had acquired a potbelly and blander features.

As for lean, trim, eighty-something Avram, he still managed the one-
handed axle lift but looked a little uneasy in the corridor. He had to watch
his step in Lenox Hill. Murray might have shown up at any moment.

Murray Rogers was the huge, dark, dignified son of *Sam* and a power at
the hospital, the head of the department of respiratory medicine. Sam had
found even an extractive Ovskyectomy insufficient, changed his last name to
Rogers during a stopover in Sweden on his way to the States and had remained marginally furious that only one other of his brothers, Julius, had
followed his footsteps into the soundness of this American name. Although
a fully fledged Dr. Rogers, Murray looked like a golden-skinned throwback
to the steppes of Asia and had made a hobbyhorse of thinking that the name
Zaborovsky derived from the Zaporozhian Cossacks famous for having pro-

vided Gogol with Taras Bulba and for telling the Ottoman sultan to go fuck himself six picturesque ways from sundown.

Murray was also my father's doctor, and he could not abide Avram, first because of Avram's crackpot notions of medicine, prime among which was that anything, up to and including cancer, could be cured with applications or ingestions of cold water; second because Avram had told the whole family that if *he* had been in charge of Sam's old age instead of Murray, the old man, gangrene schmangrene, leg schmeg, would still be alive and probably live to a hundred; and, last, because after the patriarch's funeral, during the family gathering at Sam's daughter Edie's house in Canarsie, Avram and his wife Pearl went missing and were discovered in the basement—so went Edie's story, anyway—emptying the contents of Sam's closets and dressers into a pair of large cheap suitcases: when Edie, in her booming voice, asked just what the *hell* they thought they were doing with her father's clothes, Avram replied, logically and in utter surprise at Edie's vehemence, "What he need clothes for? He *dead*."

Murray had more or less sworn to kill him on sight.

So it was with the occasional sidelong glance at the entranceway that Avram said to Jake, "For young man you have big belly."

Jake blushed and acknowledged that he had. "You know how I can get rid of it?"

"Of *course*," Avram said expansively. "I write whole book on exercise."

"Is it published?"

"What published? In my *house* I have."

"Well," Jake asked him, "could you tell me what I could do to lose this?"

"Hold in," Avram advised him. "Like thees." He sucked his own flatness concave.

"Hold it in?" Jake had heard some Avram stories over the years and had expected better. "Is that all?"

"Sure. Make muscles stronger. Also hold in stomach, make big steps." Avram demonstrated, raising his knees high one at a time, very nearly introducing them to his nose. "Like thees. One, two. One, two. One, two. One, two. One, two. One, two. One, two. One, two. One, two. One, two. One, two. One, two. One, two. One, two. One, two. One, two. One, two."

"How many times?" Jake, the student of Talmudic exactitudes in him responding to the call, had taken out a small notepad and a pen, ready to record the number.

"Two three hundred maybe, ee five minutes."

"Five minutes?" asked Jake. "Do you think I could do that many? Wouldn't it be better for me to start off slower?"

"Sure," Avram said. "What you like."

Jake repoised his pen. "How many times, then."

"Fifty."

"Fifty," said Jake, writing.

"Sixty."

"Sixty," Jake repeated.

"Forty."

"Should I do fifty or sixty or forty?" Jake wanted to know.

"Fifty, sixty, forty. Forty, fifty, sixty," Avram said.

Jake pencilled in an adjustment to his notes and looked up. "And then what?"

"Excuse me," I told them both, "I'm going to look in on my dad."

I hightailed it into the ward, where my father was lying on his back in the uptilted bed, the corrugated translucent plastic hose of a respirator jammed into his mouth and down his throat, the machine breathing him in and out through its cylinder to the accompaniment of beeps, wheezes and small red and green blinking lights. "Dad," I told him, "Avram's got a convert. Jake's taking notes on exercise, but cold water can't be far behind."

My father started laughing around the respirator hose; I could tell he was laughing because his face had turned red and his breath convulsed laughwise, but of course there was nothing to hear except the respirator, having neither a sense of fun nor any particular liking for Zaborovskian family humor getting its own motor into gear, trying to enforce its regular tread whether my father felt like laughing or not. They had tried taking him off the machine a couple of days before, and he had not been able to make it. The first thing he had said, when they pulled the hose from his mouth and he was able to speak, in a hoarse whisper to the nurse and in my presence, was, *"I want you to take a needle and pierce my heaart."*

Sometimes they got him out of bed and sat him up awhile in a chair beside it, the network of hoses and tubes looming over and into him, the machine like an alien robot rising dominant behind: he had lost a lot of weight by then, and looked like a small child being tormented by unnameable agencies for unspecifiable sins. They had not yet cut the hole in his throat for better ventilation, and jammed the hose into that.

"Should I go back and bring you reports?"

Still laughing around the thickness of hose, with a little saliva foaming at its edges, he nodded yes, yes.

I went out past the rows of beds. At the rear of the ward, Mrs. Cruz in her coma presided over the other beds like an Inca corn goddess, surrounded by her sad-eyed family, a husband and two daughters, who had brought her in the week before for a routine procedure, a series of barium X-rays; something had gone unaccountably wrong, and she lay there, dark-skinned, radiant and unreachable upon her bed, a smile of extraordinary calm and beauty on her wide, Indian features, and her arms extended beside her, hands open, palms up. Her family had dressed her in an oversized T-shirt with a rudimentary golden sun on its front. She looked, in her radiance, as if she were conveying life and warmth to the whole world, which would shrivel to a cinder without her attention, which was constant and absorbed her completely. The only people, it seemed, her solar warmth could not suffuse were her own family, whose eyes were abysses and to whom it might never occur to sue the fucking hospital for zillions after the machines were shut off and she split for good. The other patients, with their grey complexions and hospital whites, looked like bits of paper strewn along the wayside. I had gotten to know a few of them and a number of their relatives. I was there every day, and my father lasted a long time. For all I know he set a record for duration in the ward.

"Well," Jake was saying as I rearrived, "I see *you're* in great shape. Why don't you tell me what *you* do?"

"I lift axle," said Avram, as if that should have been obvious.

"No. I mean, let's say, how do you start your day?" Jake still had pen and pad at the ready.

"I wake up."

"Early?" Jake prompted.

"Sure early."

"And you get right out of bed."

"No. I stay ee bed another hour."

Jake noted this down. "Why?"

"Who like to wake up so quick?"

Jake crossed something out. "Then what."

"I drink two qvarts cold water."

"Two . . . quarts. Then breakfast."

"What breakfast? I no eat breakfast. *Exercise*."

"And after you exercise, breakfast."

"What breakfast? I told you: *I no eat breakfast*. After exercise two more qvarts water."

"But isn't breakfast good for you?"

"I eat one big meal ee afternoon," Avram said absolutely.

Jake wrote this down. "Is that really better than eating three?"

"Better I don't know. Less trouble."

Jake was still writing things down, although he had to do a lot of crossing out.

"Ee before lunch I drink two more qvarts cold water."

"*Another* two quarts?" Avram's capacity for water was remarkable. I tried to imagine what would happen to anyone else who tried to match it. Probably not the abruptness of an explosion; more, after the initial enlargement, a slow deflation, a leaking away, leaving God knows what pudding of flesh as residue. "And *before* lunch, not during."

"Yes, before," confirmed Avram.

"Ah, that's interesting: you're in agreement with the *Rambam*: Maimonides said that you should drink before meals, not during."

"Yes? Maimonides say that?" asked Avram, impressed. "Me too."

"Before."

"Yes, before." Avram paused to consider how he and Maimonides, on this subject, had thought alike. "Also I drink during," he added for good measure.

Jake crossed out another note but maintained the pad earnestly at the ready. "And the water is cold," he persisted. "Always cold."

"Yes, cold water," Avram confirmed. "Always cold. Cold water good for every ting. Cold water best ting in whole world. Cure everyting. I cure cancer two three times with cold water."

"So the water is always cold, then."

"Yes. Of course, always cold. Only for lunchtime I warm it up a little."

"Excuse me," I said, and ran back to report to my father. He laughed silently around the hose, turned bright red with the pressure, shut his eyes, and nodded emphatically yes when I asked if I should go back for more.

When I came back, the conversation had begun its shift from the physical to the metaphysical plane. "Tell me," Avram asked Jake, "you believer? I tink you believer."

Jake smiled and adjusted the yarmulke he had resumed after an intermission of about a decade. "Yes."

"I wonder, how you can be believer? You modern man, intelligent, smart, college. How you can be believer?"

Jake exchanged a smile with me and told Avram simply, "I am."

"Your mother father they religious?"

Jake nodded.

"When I young man—*young*—I was believer too. Herschel," he nodded toward the ward where my father lay awaiting the next installment, "Herschel was believer too, but me, I was fanatic."

"You?"

"I was *very* fanatic," Avram assured us. "But, then I live more, I have experience, ee I tink, ee I know better."

Jake exchanged another gentle smile with me; I was hoping my own beliefs were not going to be asked to join the conversation.

"There no God," Avram said.

"No?"

"Look," Avram said firmly. "You intelligent man. We have here," he made an oddly clumsy hooping gesture about his hips, "what we have. We have sun ee earth, we have plant, ee animal, ee men, yes?"

Jake admitted this.

"We have wind, mountain ee season ee field, tings grow ee we eat. Yes? Tell me," he said importantly, giving us the look, "if all of a sudden sun go out, what happen?"

"Everything's over," said Jake. "Everything dies."

"You see?" Avram made the open-palmed gesture of the self-evident conclusion: "What God? Where God?"

Jake smiled again, and even I was about to tell Avram that he hadn't really thought this one all the way through, but Avram turned to me first.

"A long time ago, we have Renaissance, yes?"

"Renaissance?" I asked, amazed.

"Yes, Renaissance," he said firmly, and I thought, holy shit, Avram, my uncle Avram who'd never heard of Carnegie Hall and couldn't recognize the Brooklyn Bridge, was about to tell me about the Renaissance and the birth of the secular humanist tradition, the libertarian perspective. "Big animals," he added.

"Big animals, Avram?" I asked, thinking of unicorn tapestries perhaps.

"Big animals," he said again.

I peered into this fog for a moment, trying to get my brain to conform to the convolutions of Avramian dialectic, and at length saw the possible answer emerging from prehistoric mist. "Avram, do you mean *dinosaurs*?"

"Oh yes," he laughed delightedly, getting his trisyllables right. "Not Renaissance. *Dinosaurs!*"

"I'll be right back," I said, holding it in with great difficulty.

My father's laughter nearly put the respirator out of commission, and a nurse came running to check the dials and meters.

A LINE OF TREES ALONG THE ROADSIDE to our right tugged uneasily at my memory. The landscape had just become disquietingly familiar. I had driven this way to visit my mother thrice weekly in the place we had buried her for the last few months of her life—as surely as I've buried her in this narrative.

When it seemed, not for the first time, that unless I separated my parents, my father would certainly die of the strain within a week or two, we found a little private house just over the Suffolk County line where a patient, enterprising woman and her son, who was a day-shift nurse at a local hospital, looked after five or six women during their last disintegration, and ladies and gentlemen of the jury we put Sadie Zabor née Novack there. I can remember trying to push a bit of brown, fecal-looking blender exudate on a teaspoon past her resistant lips and gums as she sat in an armchair in front of a television on which an old Japanese monster movie was showing, Godzilla clumping up out of the sea and stomping Tokyo again, or saving it from some monster even worse than he—the shrieking tricephalous Ghidorah perhaps—and my mother, barring the spoon's way again, said, "We had Japanese food last night." It was the longest sentence I had heard her complete in months. She was smiling vacantly and nodding—it was odd how docile she had become since leaving home.

"Did you?" I asked.

"Yeah. Japanese food," she said, her eyes on the screen as I knelt beside her and held the spoon at the ready. Her lips were stained with brown purée that had not gone in, and some had run down her chin. In my other hand I held a bit of damp paper towel with which I wiped her off. My mother had wonderfully unwrinkled skin, so that she had retained her own younger face into age. (Would it be still more grotesque than usual for me to add that her breasts were still in remarkably good shape at seventy-eight? For years afterward, the most vividly remembered naked female body I carried in my memory would be hers. After all, I had bathed her, wiped her bottom, fed her, much as she had done for me thirty-nine years before, when the tables were turned the other way; but had the sight of my infant body made sex—made all human generation—seem as grotesque and delusive to her as the reverse view made it seem to me? It was, for a while, difficult to find a basis for desire. What could there possibly be, in another dying body, so reminiscent of hers, to desire?) Her face growing serious as Godzilla splashed around in Tokyo Bay, heading for those electric towers again, she continued, "and then there was a flood, the water was up to *here*, and her sons—*two big men!*—came in and they took me and they put me!"

"They put you where."

"There," she said furiously and indicated the back yard, "in the, in the, in the."

She meant the green dumpster up against the side of the garage. It had claimed her attention before and begun to figure in her increasingly fragmentary stories of persecution.

Sitting in chairs elsewhere around the room, while the television presented its tottering rubber monsters and fleeing hordes of Orientals, were other old women, each of them dithering, as Tolstoy might have put it, in her own way.

From these colloquies with Mom I would return through impenetrable depths of depression along this same highway autumn evenings in this same grey Chevy—muttering to myself *Look what we've done to her Look what we've done to her* and hoping I'd miss the bottleneck at Kennedy to get home in time to cook my dad a sufficiently early dinner. Out there on the Island, Howard Stern's was the only show I could pull in on the car's not very good AM radio to help keep me awake as I drove—"Do you have *really* big breasts? C'mon, take your bra off right now and rub 'em on the telephone, while everyone out there's listening. Ooh, I can feel it. Mmm. This is great. This is great radio"—knowing without a shadow of a doubt that in this stunned and leaden state of mind, and my subconscious raging in its abyss beneath, I would die in a car crash by midwinter and that would be the end of the story: what a waste of time and effort, no human being produced at the end of my labors, only a man consumed unconscious by his own beginnings, a forty-year-old dragged backward into adolescence, swept into the wave from which he had issued and, unable to rise to the effort implicit in the confrontation with diurnal light and shade, returned by a powerful undertow to the undifferentiated green of his prenatal sea.

My attention would slip for the crucial instant, the Chevy's miserable handling would have done the rest, and in a few seconds' worth of crumpling metal and sharding glass, this consciousness, which I had labored to maintain intact and tried to fill with some kind of significant content for as long as I've been stumbling to and fro on earth, would have snuffed it on this side of the Great Divide. I would wake in the peaceful wood of Eden after my eyeblink's length of life, restored to wholeness but feeling what? about the venture.

"WHAT?" I asked Avram, heading east in sunlight, dolphin-torn, gong-tormented, alive.

"Hakkabi. Hakkabi."

"What about Hakkı Bey?"

"How he is? You see him?"

"He's fine. We go to the movies."

"You go to movies? Where you go? How much you pay? Is expensive. Television not good enough?" Avram had a television which, if you warmed it up for an hour, then hit it just right on the side of its head, would surrender two-thirds of a swaying, snowing image in black and white whose signs could almost be decoded and soundtrack made out through an abrasive sixty-cycle buzz. Avram seemed to enjoy watching it now and then. No man else could.

"I watch plenty of television, Avram. I watch too much. These days I can hardly turn the damn thing off. It's gotten to be a real habit," ever since it had begun providing shelter from the unvarying realism of my parents and me being ground to bits.

But I was probably the only person in America not to have seen the big news on TV the morning of my father's funeral. By the time friends, neighbors and family began filing into the funeral home, it was all anyone was talking about. "Murray," I asked the first person I had reason to think would be coherent, "what the hell is everyone talking about?"

Murray loomed over me, massive, handsome, his throwback complexion midway between olive and tobacco, full-faced, around sixty, waves of hair still full and black, and a deep voice so harmonious coming out of him it should have been enough to heal anyone on its own. "Do you mean you didn't see it?" he asked me. "The space shuttle *Challenger* went up and exploded in midair."

"*No.* On television?"

He nodded. "A ball of fire. They were all killed instantly, of course."

"Ah, I see . . . Murray, listen, thank you for coming, no, listen to me, and thank you for everything you've done."

"Your father was a wonderful man," he said, and placed a hand on my shoulder. Since we were already in the middle of a handshake, this move locked us in place for a long sequence in which he said loving things about my father, I said grateful things about Murray, Murray said complimentary things about my behavior and I denied them, pleading multiple moral and spiritual failures.

"You mean you couldn't save their lives. No one could have saved their lives," Murray said.

"No, it's not that," I protested, worried how I was ever getting out of this lifelock of handshake, shoulderhold, heartfelt words.

"I hope you'll understand that I can't come to the burial—"

"Of course, your duties at the hospital—"

I still wasn't getting out of this embrace, we'd be standing there forever, but then I saw Hakkı Bey swimming into view through the crowd toward us—hey, he'd found a suit somewhere, and it fit—and I was able to say, "Murray, I've got a friend to tend to. We can talk later. *Hakkı*," I said, stepping back from Murray and forward to field my friend—he looked excited—just in case.

"You see the space shuttle go up on TV?" Hakkı asked me as Murray receded at last.

"No, I'm probably the only—"

"Rafi, *wasn't that fantastic?*" Hakkı small and dark and well formed, his almond eyes flicking left and right, his deep voice curled expressively around the words. "They thought they were going on a trip and they *really went on a trip.* The first thing I thought, Rafi, was that I would have *loved to be on that rocket.*" The enthused curve of Hakkı's voice continued the shuttle's trajectory through its skyburst into a greater brilliance in which the colors were more true and the souls of the travellers, already crouched in the expectation of adventure, were projected into a new world for real, their bodies remade, finer and more pleasant to live in, their eyes filling with inconceivable light, the great thing at last, all constrictions exploding, categories of thought tumbling to their extinction and Hakkı Bey's eyes bright with the longing for it, God's own hipster on the shadowland of earth with no fear of fire and in love with the light behind the puppets, the world outside the cave, and the rhythm of the whole show as it moved from light to dark and again to light. Whoops: Hakkı clocked the room, a funeral, people in suits, and composed himself, tucked his aura in, compressed himself back into a space where death might still have dominion. "How you doing, man?" he asked me.

"I'm okay," I said. "Thanks for coming. I'm probably the only person here who didn't see the thing on TV."

Hakkı shook his head. "Man, you should've seen it. It was beautiful. Oh man, that's my idea of travel. Rafi: I would have *loved* to be on that rocket." Hakkı had a way of repeating himself, modulating his way through a series of key signatures until he found the cadence that completed the statement: "Man, I would have *loved* to be on that rocket."

I had first met him when I was nineteen and he seventeen years old and I was going out with his sister, Sharon, a dancer who tended to pop spontaneously out of her costumes onstage in the middle of some leap or thrust. She could also take an innocent walk down Broadway and find her panties down around her ankles. ("I don't know how it happens, honest.")

I met her oddly. I was in the spring of my third year at Brooklyn College and at the ripest point, perhaps, of my adolescent visionary phase. I got a call from a high school friend I still hung with sometimes, a budding satyr named Gene Teper who had taken to haunting City College and auditing a course or two so he could look for women. He was excited on the phone: "I met this girl at City, I've been talking to her in the cafeteria and man, let me tell you, she's got the most incredible pair of tits I've ever seen and I got her to say she'd come meet me at a party Friday night. Wanna come along?"

The party, as I remember it, took place in a vast East Village apartment with ochre walls, no furniture unless the blasting stereo counted and no curtains on the big windows. The joint was literally jumpin': packed wall to wall with at least 150 people jumping up and down to the beat of who was it, the Stones, Aretha, James Brown, Stevie, all of the above, and it seemed wholly characteristic of the crowd that across that ocean sea of bobbing heads and through the pot smoke my eye found Chuck Mittman, the only guy at my high school aside from me who had refused to pledge allegiance to the flag; I played at the protest once or twice, but Chuck persisted through the thick and thicker of procedural appeal. And here we were in 1966, man, had never known each other well, but waved and grinned wildly atop the pack when our eyes caught, recognized and held.

I was over by the beer stash, not much of a drinker in those days but it was too hot to dance, so I'd anchored myself near the tub of ice and bottles. Gene was out there circulating through the pack, searching with some anxiety or eagerness for Sharon; he passed in and out of view, lost himself in the mix and then emerged, looking my way for a high sign and nodding when I shook my head *No, not yet*, or shrugged. His description of Sharon hadn't been very precise—I think he got off the tits once or twice to say short brown hair—but must have been vivid enough to get across, because when Sharon came through the doorway of the party room I spotted her right off by her dramatic profile as she wandered inside looking around for Gene.

And here was the odd part. I had never been a cutter-in. It was not in my nature and I'd never done it, but as Sharon's gaze raked the room and reached me at the beer tub I thrust my right arm in the air and hailed her, waved her over, and may have mouthed a large-scale *Geeeene* and pointed vaguely into the crowd so she'd know.

I watched her weave and do-si-do her way through the crowd, her face serious, almond eyes lowered beneath a prominent, shapely forehead, her full lips compressed but not severely, and when she reached me I had a cold beer open for her in its sweating bottle.

"Gene's out there looking for you," I told her, and introduced myself, and then to my considerable surprise launched the longest sleekest jag of sweet talk I'd ever sent out on the chancy social seas in my young life. Sharon's beauty hadn't shot the blind bow-boy's arrow into my heart, and aside from a certain natural curiosity about what went on under those clothes I wasn't even particularly attracted to her, but I remember going on about sincerity and the soul, and in fact came out with an unusual narrative under the circumstances: of a girl named Abby I'd met in high school and fallen so profoundly in love with I could hardly speak to her, even when in lab techniques she came to my table almost daily, inclined her graceful neck and asked if she could share my microscope. Fawnlike, delicate of feature, elegant of form and duskily complected: I followed her up the hall after class and admired her ideal curve of calf, and the little golden anklet that graced the slender ankle beneath it. The love I felt for her was so profound and as if sacred that not once in those pimpled anguished years did I use the thought of her to fuel a bout of masturbation—I was seventeen, and that is not chopped liver. Neither did I—idiot—invite her to join me some weekend evening at Birdland or the Five Spot, as she clearly would have liked me to do.

Until we got to Brooklyn College I was too stupid to be sure she felt anything for me, but sometimes we'd see each other at opposite ends of a long walkway on campus and the very instant my heart thudded and fell and began to beat me up from inside out, I'd see her mouth fall open and her pace falter, nearly fall, as her eye found me. God knows what she saw in me, but there it was. Unfortunately it was the love, on both sides, that dared not speak its name, and to this day I could kick myself for being such a dunce—really, for all my life's many fuckups, I have only three actual regrets, and that's the first of them. I remain convinced that however our conjunction might have turned out it would have changed my life, sweetened it while young, and kept me out of the serious trouble that eventually shattered everything. Four years of Brooklyn College; perhaps by the third I'd already heard that she was having an affair with a radical young psychology professor.

In any case it was an odd story to tell a girl it seemed I was trying to pick up with every bit of sociosexual heft I possessed. I used the Abby story, primarily, to demonstrate the high-grade quality of my soul, but what I remember best is the velocity and insistence of the telling, the thrum and thrust of energy, the coils of talk as I spun them out, draped them around Sharon and reeled them in, all the while amazed that I was stepping so far out of character as to do this to Eugene.

What is more remarkable is that it worked, and when Gene found us maybe ten minutes later the fait was so obviously accompli that he gave up the prize without a protest, and to his credit never laid the least legal brief of reprimand on my head and shoulders in the aftermath or ever.

When I started dating Sharon she told me she couldn't go to bed with me right away because she was recovering from an abortion, so we made out a lot in her mother's East Village apartment sixteen storeys up—strange place: her estranged father, a tall distinguished Levantine-looking man, had moved out but had begun dating his wife again, and came to call the same night I did once or twice. He was quiet and dignified, Sharon's mother attractive, flamboyant and loud. There was also a wise-ass younger brother, and a brilliant fucked-up older brother, then in juvey jail: they called him Jack. The family name was Shema, but they pronounced it "Sheema," and when I said How could they, and effused about being named for the *She'ma*—Hear O Israel, the Lord is God, the Lord is One—Sharon said Oh who cares.

I didn't meet Jack Shema the future Hakkı Bey right away, only on the fourth or fifth date, when he was out on a weekend pass, where they'd finally sent him, I think, after a blown second-storey job on a doctor's office, or a drug bust, I forget, and by then Sharon had told me a lot about her brother Jack, how brilliant an artist and amazing a guy he was, how although just sixteen he'd been on the streets for years, how rough he was with her—say it straight, he'd hit her a couple times—and I'd seen a brilliant but cruel line drawing he'd caricatured her in for a custom birthday card: a dazed, raggedy-feathered newborn chick with a helmet of shell lopsided on its nod and its chest burst outward through the feathers into flesh by a perfect rendering of Sharon's breasts. Her brother existed symbolically in the picture as a jet plane flying overhead trailing a banner reading HAPPY BIRTHDAY SHARON! The Sharon-bird was looking up at the airplane in stupefied awe. "That's how he is," Sharon told me, "flying by up there somewhere, while I'm stuck down here." It was a fiendish, jabbing piece of work I couldn't like, but the pen-and-ink work and the quality of line were distinctive.

I wasn't exactly prepared to like this guy, but a strange thing happened when I saw him for the first time. Sharon met me at the door, My brother's here she said, then let the door slowly open, and as I entered, the apartment dimmer than usual, I saw a small dark guy sitting cross-legged on the floor, holding a Spanish guitar across his lap and listening to some music or other playing quietly on the stereo. I was already in the thick of my second set of visionary experiences—the first had been all ve-hemence and breakthrough but the second had expanded and softened: without the aid of any drugs, my heart chakra had hatched from its own bit of eggshell and I had discovered that battered back by sufficient an-guish or longing the insufficient mummery of phenomena could scroll away and more real vistas emerge in which the most overwhelming and all-redeeming fact, shining over the hills and valleys of existence like a sun, was that God was omnipresent and His nature Love—well anyway I caught a piece of it. Although fatuously proud of having had a peep of such scenery and especially vain at having managed the trick without the psychedelics that had begun to produce a billow of instant visionaries among the lesser humans of my generation, I had begun to affect a mys-tical gentleness of manner and had replaced Ivan with Alyosha Karama-zov as my role model for a soul model.

What happened when I first saw Hakkı Bey, which was not his name at the time any more than mine was Rafi, was that without warning something fast and massive plowed through my heart as packed with freight as any mile-long midnight train, and I saw in fugitive flashes—huh?—images of deserts, palm trees in moonlight, men in white playing music on ouds and drums or perhaps chanting names of God; other pic-tures went by too quickly for me to catch, and then, before I could cen-sor the sentence with the normal machinery of my self-consciousness, the surprising words spoke themselves aloud inside me: *This is a real holy man.* Instantly I felt ashamed of my half-hearted spiritual playacting, how vain and bourgeois I was, my real timidity of vision and the thinness of my stance before experience, my gaping insufficiency of being.

It was a wallop, with pictures and a voice, and I'd never experienced anything like it. It had happened so *fast*. Any slower and I would have throttled it before it could walk.

When he and I got to talking, about simpler things of course, it turned out that we liked each other. He was intense, radiant, funny, inspired, street-brilliant at nearly seventeen, but, in the grip of the glamor of crime and chatting avidly about the variety of drugs he took, he was obviously self-destructive to an extent I had never imagined in my sheltered life; the image came to me of someone setting a match to his own nerve endings one at a time just to see the way they burned, digging the light he came up with, smiling at it, thinking, yeah, let's light up another one. I figured he had about three years left to live, and although twenty years later he was still skating close to the edge, he hadn't gone over it yet. Or rather, he'd gone over it more than a few times and against all one's sense of human possibility had as many times come back.

You know, Sharon told me in some amazement, you're the first boyfriend of mine he's ever liked or wanted to know at all.

Midway through my inconclusive time with Sharon, Jack and his girlfriend Gina invited Sharon and me up to their place on West 10th one Friday night—he was out of jail by then. It was the spring of '66, I had booked my summer flight to Europe and was looking forward to the great adventure, had smoked pot a few times but hadn't gotten high on it. Jack's secret well-laid plan was to get me stoned and ask me for a loan, but before the first joint was rolled Jack mentioned that Gina needed an abortion, illegal in the States those days, of course. I asked how much money he needed and then, wondering why I found myself saying this— in fact, telling myself in a surprised, distinct, internal voice *You don't know why you're doing this*—in fact too, experiencing a strange sensation of something happening in the air above and behind my head, on my left, as if a phantasmal hand were stirring the air with its fingers: whut?— mentioned that I was all set for my summer trip and could lend them the necessary $150 easy. Then I got ripped out of my mind for the first time in my life on some very good grass rolled in wheatstraw paper, and drove with Sharon through billowing multicolored tents that spanned the highway hanging in the air all the way to Brooklyn, where Gene let us use the bedroom of his apartment on Ocean Avenue, and where I proved myself, at that stage of my development and despite the inspiration with which Sharon's stupendous body should have supplied me, a remarkably inept lover. When I came back from Europe a changed man that autumn, I dutifully tried to look Jack up for the money but Sharon said he was somewhere in New Jersey doing anatomical sculpture for medical schools, but—the strangest thing—he actually wanted to pay me back, and she'd never heard him say he wanted to pay anyone back before. And the following spring, when on the deadly trudges of my own abortion inquiry I dropped in on Gina at their old apartment, she told me Jack was out of town somewhere, vanished, she didn't see him anymore, he was gone.

I wouldn't see Jack Shema again for another six years. Yeah, he'd tell me then, she was great, Gina, look how she covered for me, man.

Since that second meeting we'd always stayed in touch, with intermissions for voyages between continents, distinct from each other but in some ways like brothers: I had other friends, some of them closer, but without Hakkı I was an only child, and it was through him that I met Mahmoud, without whom I would have had an only father.

There were other links as well. A year after that loan of a hundred and a half I would visit the same abortionist Hakkı (and Sharon before him) had used, with a by then more than borderline psychotic girlfriend vomiting out the car window all along Bergenline Avenue in a stretch of suburban New Jersey that looked all the more alien for resembling disconnected patches of my native Brooklyn. On arrival at the doctor's, the scene had grown unexpectedly sinister since Sharon's last report, with two characters sitting on the porch in suits and shades demanding that I wait for Barbara not in the office as arranged but in my car parked at least two blocks off and don't come looking, she'll come out to you when it's over. Had the Mob moved in on the operation? Even though by that time Barbara had attempted suicide twice, not very convincingly, murder once—with a kitchen knife I dodged pretty easily—and had threatened to run away, have the baby, raise it on a leash, and teach it to bark instead of talk, I couldn't put her through the abortion in Jersey. In the end it would take all the money I had saved up—to move to Paris and be the next big thing after Samuel Beckett on: I figured it would take a year's work, maybe two—to fund a nightmare trip to Japan in the second trimester of the pregnancy, achieve the desired result on or about my twenty-first birthday, and to change my life beyond recognition in the aftermath.

NOT SURPRISINGLY, Hakkı and Avram hit it off in the limo on the way back from the burial. As after my mother's funeral, the mood was doing a turnaround, the talk getting animated, stories coming out of hiding to tell themselves and establish a livable sense of time after the ceremonies of death. I liked watching Hakkı and Avram talk.

A story from Avram's Harlem days: "Ee I walk down subway ee someone take me for the neck. I tink, is someone I know making joke, but, no, I see *he really take me for the neck.* So: I move my head, he fly over land in front of me ee I ask him 'Why you take me for the neck?' but he run away."

I found it touching that Hakkı told Avram how highly he had thought of my Dad.

"We more close than brothers me and Herschel. Oh, it surprise me how I cry. How I cry. It surprise me." Avram's body jackknifing at the graveside, sudden tears squeezed out of his eyes in the cold. "I usually not crying man."

"He was your closest brother," Hakkı told him.

"Oh yes."

"When *I* cry, Avram," Hakkı told him consolingly, "I'm worse than a woman." I had seen Hakkı extending the same courtesy to other people, admitting to a weakness not his own, before.

"Ee oh yes now I remember. One time five men they come in to counter ee they show me knives, I tink why they show me knives? Then I see another one, he put his hand in cash register. So now I *see* what they doing. I move my hands, the five fall down, then I take other one from the wrist and squeeze him till he fall down. Then they pick him up, ee go."

"You're a terror, Avram," Hakkı Bey said. "You're a real terror."

"I what? Terrible? Why for? What kind of man you are then?"

"Worse," Hakkı Bey said. "And not as bad."

"How you know? You don't know mine character."

"I'm *sure* I don't, Avram," crooned Hakkı Bey.

"How many pounds bread you tink I bring home on mine bicycle yesterday?"

Hakkı Bey looked my way and I mimed quantity by widening my eyes.

"Twenty pounds," Hakkı Bey guessed.

Avram looked pleased as he said, "*One hundred* twenty pound."

"That's a lot of bread, Avram. How long will it last?"

"Four, maybe five day."

"A hundred and twenty pounds of bread in five days? You're a dangerous man, Avram."

"What dangerous? When I walk out door of mine building hundreds ee thousands of every kind bird come flying down from rooftops—they *know* me. You know, in Europe we have only four kind bird. We have black like crow, we have sperrow, and we have small kind bird make mud nest always under the roof sticking out nest—"

"Swallow," I put in, thinking of my father's love of swallows, and my own.

"Svallow," Avram pronounced. "But here in Ameriky you have every kind bird: *every kind bird!*"

"You had storks in Europe," I remembered.

"I don't mean stork. I mean small bird."

"Wait a minute," Hakkı Bey said. "If you don't mind my asking, how do you get a hundred and twenty pounds of bread on a bicycle?"

"I have *lady* bicycle," Avram explained, "so I have plenty plenty room. Bakery give me old bread, I tie on bags of bread with cord and push bicycle careful careful back up hill to mine home. Sometimes the goals see me coming and they scream so. So hungry the goals."

"The what?"

"Goals. White kind sea bird."

"Ah," Hakkı said. "Gulls."

"Yes, what I say: goals. And so many! They see me come they fly, they scream, they go in circles all around me—they very hungry birds, goals— and I sometimes embarrassed maybe some person see me and what they think, maybe they frightened if I say hello to them, and maybe I am able to help some person but I don't say hello to him because of all the goals, all the hundreds and thousands hungry goals, Hakkabi, and then I feel bad because maybe I not help some person who need my help. Last week I pass by man in wheelchair just like this with all the screaming goals and later I feel bad I don't say hello, and every night I have dream about this man and feel terrible I don't speak to him and maybe help him . . . Ay," Avram sighed. "Here in Ameriky you have every kind bird, Hakkabi. Every kind bird."

By the time we got back to the apartment, my friends Maryam and Susan had swooped in from upstate and cleaned the place up, my cousin Frank had swept in with enormous platters of everything from his delicatessen, and, to my surprise, Jake was overseeing the array of goodies in the living room like a headwaiter and serving glasses of seltzer to a klatsch of old folks from the neighboring apartments.

"Jake," I said. "I'm surprised to see you. I thought you were already . . ."

"No," he said and shook my hand. "Ora and I don't fly to Israel till tomorrow." He smiled and shook his head. "It's just that this time . . ."

"You got stuck in the subway even worse than last time?"

"I think I missed you at the funeral home by five minutes. I'm sorry. How are you feeling?"

"Fine," I said with surprising energy, and Jake looked at me strangely because he had not been party, this time, to the ride in the limo and might have forgotten how grief had flipped to affability after my mother's burial. "I mean, I was walled up with my parents for three years, I haven't even begun to deal with the change and my father's death . . . my father's death . . . I mean, nothing could be more . . . more . . . but Jake," and here I drew him by his elbow into an unpopulated corner of the living room, cased the joint for snoopers and dropped confidentially down to sotto voce, "but right after my shower this morning, I was standing on the bathmat bending over to dry my right leg and I saw my father—"

Jake looked at me with compassionate alarm. "Where?"

"In my mind's eye, Horatio," I reassured him, but actually there had been a certain extra-ocular objective-visionary component to the sight. "He was up there, swimming in an ocean of light—it looked like a stage set, a scrim, yellow and gold, layered, with blue behind it—and Jake, he was free of all the suffering he'd been through, he was remade, his body was young and unpained and he was so happy in it, so refreshed, and I could see for the first time what an *ardent* spirit he was. Jake, you should've seen him. He loved to swim, used to get out there past the waves and float for hours in a kind of bliss, but this morning Jake he was stretching those new muscles, pulling those long strokes. After all the horrible shit he'd been through he was finally free . . ."

But Jake had put his hand out and touched my arm as if to steady me, his eyes quizzical and tainted with worry.

"No, really, Jake, I promise, I'm okay . . ."

But then again maybe I was in fact a little strained and manic. When I turned aside from Jake to tend to my guests, in the words of Bobby Darin there was a party goin' on. I was splishin' and a-splashin' and the dancing-on-the-grave bayou backstep was in full swing everywhere in the apartment: sure the note was forced, but the cold cuts and Danish were good, there was plenty of beer and coffee, and for the moment it seemed to be some kind of big festive event in which life and death were no big deal and we all knew—not just wayward comet friends but old declining neighbors of my parents' generation—that light comedy for all was the order of this and every day on both sides of the Great Divide and meanwhile let's be affectionate and merry. Before long the apartment was wall to wall with people, I was swigging down good cognac and pouring some out for others, telling stories, eating open-faced pastrami sandwiches and insisting that I brew up the necessary pots of coffee myself. It had to be just right! Brewed with bottled spring water! The perfect strength! Maryam! Susan! You have to leave? Jeez, thanks for doing such a great job! Try the pastrami or at least the corned beef! Take some with you! Of *course* I'll come up and visit.

I saw that Hakkı Bey had backed a panicked-looking cousin into a corner saying, "So I said, 'That guy's got a really *anal* personality,' and they asked me 'You mean he's uptight?' and I said, 'No, I mean he's an *asshole.*' Hey, that's pretty good on the spur of the moment, huh? 'No, I mean he's an *asshole.*' Pretty good on the spur of the moment." I decided not to rescue the cousin: let him sink or swim. I circulated like what I took to be a pretty virtuoso host but must have seemed, to the outside eye, at least a little jagged, and somewhere in there found myself at the kitchen table, where my father had done all his reading. I was sipping another snifter of VSOP and starting to tell Avram The World's Greatest Joke—I always gave it that preface, the surest way to kill a laugh, later to say, You see? Isn't it? and generally the audience would have to agree. "You mean I never told you this one?" I asked my uncle.

"Joke? I don't tink so. You know, I not one for joke really. I like joke, but not special."

"You'll like this one."

"Yes?" He made a noncommittal shrug and followed it with a two-note cadence: "O-kay."

I took a swig of cognac to light the way. "It starts out in an old synagogue somewhere in Eastern Europe, a *shtiebel* really—"

"Yes, is what we call small synagogue in Europe, *shtiebel.* Means *room,* no how you say balcony, silver, fancy tings. You know this word?"

"Yep: *shtiebel.* This one's really run down, there's a lot of dust in the wood, a broken window's patched with brown paper, the first light of dawn's just beginning to sift into the room . . ."

"*You don't need all that shit,*" Hakkı Bey rumbled from the doorway, leaning in the frame with his own glass of cognac in hand, a large one I noticed, a tumbler, half full. I thought uh-oh, knowing what Hakkı could be like when he'd had a few. "In fact, Rah-fee," he said heavily, "it's *my* joke."

"I know it's your joke."

"*I* got it in England," he continued. "*I* told it to *you,* and *you're* telling it *wrong.*"

"Oh hello Hakkabi," said Avram, turning in his chair. "How you are?"

"I'm fine, Avram, fine, but he's telling you the joke wrong."

"So: you tell."

Hakkı Bey slugged down the remainder of his firewater and helped himself to a refill from the bottle of Rémy on the table, then pulled a chair backward and straddled it. "The rabbi," he said, and paused.

"Comes in for dawn prayers," I prompted.

"Watch it," he said.

"I can't tell my uncle a joke in my own house?"

"*Not today.*" Hakkı turned to Avram. "The rabbi comes in for dawn prayers. He's the first one there, and he goes up to the front of the synagogue."

"By the ark of the Torah," I said. "To wait for the rest of the minyan."

Hakkı shot me a look but said nothing. "And suddenly he looks up and says," Hakkı dramatizing it, spreading his arms, raising his almond eyes to heaven, "'O God: I am nothing . . . I am nothing . . . I am nothing . . .' And each time he says it, he sees his nothingness in a new aspect, as if, as if, Avram, his nothingness is a multifaceted gemstone being turned in the light. So he begins to repeat it, faster and faster. 'I am nothing I am nothing I am nothing I am nothing. I am nothing I am nothing I am nothing.'"

"Yes," Avram said, nodding in acknowledgement. "I am notting."

At this point Jake, probably having heard this familiar chant from the living room, appeared in the doorway to lean on the frame with a glass of seltzer in his hand and an almost dreamy smile on his face.

"A second man, the teacher, comes into the synagogue," Hakkı Bey continued.

"The *melamed*," Jake inserted.

"This . . . *melamed*," Hakkı Bey continued, "sees the rabbi up there, strikes himself in the chest and says, '*I* am nothing,' and before you know it he's up there next to the rabbi, saying 'I am nothing I am nothing I am nothing I am nothing.'"

"Ye-es," Avram said.

"Actually," Jake said from his post, "if that had happened in a real synagogue . . ."

"*What?*" said Hakkı Bey, turning to Jake with dangerous velocity.

"Oh, hello Jake," said Avram, half turning in his seat. "How you are?"

Jake nodded fine but said nothing.

"A third guy comes in," Hakkı pressed on, "the little old man with a broom who keeps the place clean—"

"*Shammes,*" Avram said. "He called *shammes,* Hakkabi."

"He's sweeping the dust up, Avram, and while he's doing it he looks up and sees the other two, the big shots, up there," and here Hakkı Bey stood up, bent in an old man's body, sweeping the floor with a short invisible broom, "and after a while he starts to sing along in this cracked little voice, 'Ehh . . . I am notting . . . I am notting . . . I am notting . . .'" Here Hakkı Bey touched Avram lightly on the shoulder to indicate that the punchline was up. "And the second guy nudges the rabbi, nods across the floor at the little guy in rags and says to the rabbi, 'Hey, *look who thinks he's nothing.*'"

"Ye-es," Avram said.

"That was it, Avram," I said.

"Yes. I see. The rabbi think he notting. Denk you, Hakkabi. Good joke. Not exactly my style, but is okay."

"Actually," Jake said from his post, "I think I remember," he said, "that the source of the joke is an eighteenth-century story about Israel Salanter, the founder of the Mussar movement. His followers were sometimes called the Mussarniks."

"The *what?*" said Hakkı Bey.

"Was only joke, Hakkabi," Avram said, leaning forward to pat Hakkı on the forearm. "The rabbi tink he notting."

"The misser*what?*" Hakkı Bey asked Jake.

"Wait a minute. Hold on," I said, raising gyroscopic fingertips to my brow, not so much in fear of a Hakkıan cannonade but because my father had died, too many of my disparate worlds were colliding before me in my kitchen, I'd spent three years compressed in this same apartment with my extravagantly disintegrating parents, I was coming off my favorite joke and a bout of postfuneral mania and at any moment expected a house call, claw and talon and righteous unanswerable accusation, from the Eumenides . . . but at this point a fog of cognac covered everything, and as Gogol might have put it, nothing further is known about the incident.

"I LIKE THIS HAKKABI," Avram told me, on the road.

"He liked you too. You two are a lot alike," I said.

"No. How?"

"Well . . ." I began, but we had reached our exit. I had to consult the little map they'd given me back at the funeral home in Brooklyn. Within half a minute of our leaving the highway we were passing one field after another in which New York had buried its dead. I did in fact know that death had undone so many, but what surprised me was that there was still room for more of them on the Island, Manhattan turning out dead bodies faster than Nassau and Suffolk counties could produce living ones, a real estate race between the quick and the quicker dead. God, and presumably also the Mafia, knew how much longer there would be room for any of them.

It was a hot day, and as we passed along the grey stone walls of the enclosures I was more aware of the green expanses within them than of the stones laid out in lethal, ordered rows upon the grass. Beth Moses was the third or fourth cemetery in an unbroken sequence of same, although the religions kept changing. We entered between the granite pillars of its gate. I drove up the straight approach road and pulled into the parking lot in front of the cemetery offices, a grey brick building whose suggestion of white dome atop and pillars at the front recalled Jefferson's Monticello and therefore the ultimate democracy of the dead, in which neither the Jews in Beth Moses nor the Catholics next door automatically had a better view of the prospects of eternity. I insinuated the Malibu Classic into a spot between a Dodge Masada and a Chevy Caporetto and switched off the engine.

"I'll go in and talk to them, Avram."

"I wait outside." I left him in the parking lot, sniffing down lungfuls of greenscented suburban air. An obedient dove mourned nearby with a dying fall and a broken ritardando between the beginning of its one known tune and its subsequent decline.

At a counter inside the building, I handed over a maintenance check—part of my payment toward the perpetual care of my father's grave, my mother's having already been paid for in full—to a woman who searched through the files and then marked out in pencil on a printed map the location of my parents' last abode.

They weren't hard to find, up an avenue on the right, then slightly inland from the road. "Is there," Avram said, then took a yarmulke from his pocket and readied himself to say Kaddish. He appeared not to see anything wrong, but I was appalled. The large headstone spelled out unequivocally ZABOR—*my* name, not anyone else's, not my mother's nor my father's but mine—and at my parents' buried feet there were parallel six-foot slots of property for me and the wife I hadn't found yet. The evergreen shrubbery that had been planted atop my mother's grave was thickening into a trimmed, rectangular mat about two feet high, but my father's grave was the site of some terrible subterranean collapse, a sundering, an open pit, dry soil fallen inward with the suggestion of collapsed beams at the sides, and I was the culprit. The check I'd just written out had been for two scheduled installments: I had lost my way in the blizzard of paper that had pursued me since my father's death and missed a quarterly bill. My father's grave was a disaster area, a deconstruction site, a gaping wound in the earth.

"Yis gadal v'yis gadash sh'meh rabboh," Avram began the only prayer I had ever found beautiful in the synagogues I had disliked from childhood, Aramaic rather than Hebrew: the sounds had appealed to me before I knew what they were for, but as I listened to them now a second guilt-excavated abyss had opened in the pit of my stomach: Oh my God Dad what have I done to you now? The footstone I'd ordered hadn't been put in place yet but so what? It was the grave or what was left of it that slew me: it wasn't as if, looking down into the dry soil of the almost sandy pit at my feet, as Avram prayed to a God whose existence he considered to have been disproven by Renaissance dinosaurs, that I expected to see a corner of the casket revealed at the bottom, a nightmare rat gnawing a hole in it or appearing face first out of the burgled coffin with a mouthful of Dad on show—though Christ the collapse seemed deep enough for that. It was more that, in the gnawing that was working its way up from the pit of my stomach to my already swiss-cheesed heart, I

almost expected to see my father's hand emerge from the earth—no, too melodramatic, too cold-mad-feary-fatherish for that warm, almost infinitely forbearing man—or to hear the pained, disembodied equivalent of his voice, its infra-Jewish twistings so familiar through the years of his torment, exclaiming, "What have you done to me please don't I even have some peace even finally in my graaave?" But of course this didn't happen, and Avram, Kaddish done, turned to me as if nothing were amiss (although years later he would tell me he suspected the cemetery keepers of having stolen my father's body) and asked, "You say Rose ask me to make Kaddish also for Joe?"

"Yes," I must have gasped, and Avram moved next door to the stone marked AGRIN, my parents' nearest neighbors in death as they had been in the years of my childhood, Zaborovskys in apartment 5C, the Agrins in 5D, the alphabet of my earliest experience strung between them backward from Z to A. My mother's sister Rose couldn't stand Avram—she had barely tolerated my father—but had asked, when I told her we were going out for a visit, if he could say a prayer for her husband there, my gone beloved Uncle Joe.

Avram finished the Kaddish faster than I could have done, then asked me, no fuss, "We go?"

"Wait for me a minute," I said, never more grateful for the impersonality of his eyes and his apparent lack of conventional perception—or was it, I wondered, a generosity that he extended to me then, invisibly and without trace, looking past the world of guilt and blame at another, more impersonal reality, who knows? As he retired to the roadway, inhaling again lungfuls of air that smelled of cut grass and summer trees, I did my own prayers, in English, Aramaic, in the heart's unworded language, and then in a fragmentary Arabic in which I invoked the aspect of God the Forgiver, hoping somewhat desperately at the moment for the best; and when I was done I beat a path to the office, asked them how much I owed on the balance of the account, paid it in one check now instead of three over the rest of the year and asked them for God's sake to fill in the hole and yes I'll write another check for yew trees but for sweet Jesus' sake and mine please fill in that gaping hole in the earth now.

5

IT WAS TAKING ME FOREVER (you may have noticed) to get out of New York. Summer was upon me, and my travel plans were vaporizing in the heat. The idea had always been, sailing to Byzantium in the car I proposed to buy in Belgium or possibly France, to arrive in Istanbul around the beginning of September, when the north wind sweeps down the Bosphorus out of the Black Sea to blow off the oven heat of summer and clear the sky of hanging soot. I'd make my usual rounds in town, wander down the Aegean coast at least as far as Ephesus, hook eastward into Anatolia, do some hang time in Konya, the home of the whirling dervishes, among whom I had friends, and then finally get that tour of easternmost Turkey done, giving the bloody, terrorized Kurdish southeast a miss—I'd been through there once and it had been a little scary: village idiots chased and stoned in the nighttime street, too-solicitous army officers asking about my travels in such dangerous and untouristed country and my cover slipping, checkpoint submachine guns thrust through cab windows into my face: not what I had in mind this year—and getting up northeast to Erzurum, Kars, and if possible the Armenian ruins of the Temple of Ani hard by what was then the Soviet border. I particularly wanted to see the dramatic view of Mount Ararat from Doğubayazit, the stark ancient walls and towers of Ishak Pasha in the foreground, bare dun mountains grading upward behind them into snow and the immense blue flank of Ararat—an enormous whale surfacing beside the tiny boat of your outlook—commanding the horizon, the perpetual snows of its endless lateral summit shimmering indivisibly into cloud. I hoped, with a fatuity that was partly apparent even to me, that this vista, one of the most romantic in a country already overstocked with spectacular views, would deliver me some final essence of wild, untappable Asia, where my spirit had run free in the past and might learn to do so again.

Fata Morgana.

It wasn't only, or even mostly, that I was ditzing interminably around, my way lit by guilt's fitful lantern, in the psychological labyrinth beneath the House of Zaborovsky, where a momentary minotaur in traffic-cop blues had seized my arm with a fateful "Hold it, bub," and asked for a look at my ID and any particularly painful secrets I might be transporting across state lines—although I'll admit it was a complicated departure that year. But even at the best of times it takes me a while to work up the velocity to break free of Gotham. What slowed me that year, as the months passed almost before I'd had time to notice their arrival and the prospect of good weather in eastern Turkey by the time I got there iced over in the distance, was mostly straight material-world legal business concerning my parents' Last Will and Testament, although these things never rumble into town without a freight of symbol in their cars.

By this time I had closed up shop in Woodstock and moved back to Brooklyn preparatory to finding someone to sublet the apartment for the six or nine months I proposed to be away—however long it took to get some imagery into my mind's glazed eye other than my dying parents tottering through the stages of their dismemberment, then their fall. Daniel had moved to a spare room in a lawyer friend's large apartment across Prospect Park from me and was spending about half his time down in Georgia, where a wealthy Swiss friend of his had bought a farm and was being robbed nearsighted if not blind by the management company that ran the place for him in his absence; he hired Daniel to go down there, count the cows, assess the amount of acreage actually given over to the cultivation of rice, ride a rent-a-car up and down the dirt roads and paper trails and otherwise mess with the locals. Daniel had already turned up the first hard evidence of thievery, had been unprovably threatened with violence and offered a bribe to, uh, get off the case. A couple of million dollars were tied up in the property, there were obstacles to proving the theft in a court of law and, it seemed, a deal of some sort would have to be engineered.

Daniel had also begun to think of carrying a gun.

"It is either that or hire some Pinkertons for my protection, which considering my military background would dent my *amour propre*— humiliating, but preferable to a bulllet hole between the shoulder blades. I think I must buy a weapon. A magnum is an effective deterrent, although of course it is no more accurate than any other handgun, and it will spoil the line of your jacket on less formal occasions, such as buying a cheeseburger at the local diner. One does not want to assume the position over a lunch counter, after flirting with the cute blond waitress, for a pair of state troopers who may also be your enemies' friends."

"You sound remarkably sensible for a probable psychopath."

"Vee aims to please. There are some very nice nine-millimeter automatics out there, but they are expensive and I am not sure that my client will recognize a pair of them as a legitimate business expense."

"You know, I've halfway thought of picking something up in Istanbul and stashing it under the car seat if I do get out to eastern Turkey."

"The well-known Anatolian Exploding Model. You are worried about Kurds? Pardon me," he said, loosening his tie and switching to the Turkish government locution: "Mountain Turks."

"I was thinking of bandits. I've heard too many stories about shotgun blasts and quick throat-cuttings at crossroads on the steppe."

"Traditional Turkish entertainments. Delights."

"Best people in the world," I said. "But since I don't know how to use a gun maybe a Bogart effect will be enough and all I need's a trenchcoat. Got any you outgrew a couple of hundred pounds ago?"

Furman raised an eyebrow, then lowered it, like a churlish drawbridge. "By the way, my impertinent friend, should you ever actually need to shoot someone with a handgun, it is best to place the feet so," he rose to demonstrate, "then pivot the torso to the left, extending the right arm transversely across the chest and holding the pistol firmly in your right hand while grasping the wrist with your left. Let me move this chair out of the way and show you . . ."

"You're slipping, Furman. You already did this sketch. Also how to kill with one blow of the hand."

"Yes, but have you *tested it in the field*?"

"I only kill parents," I told him, "and I do it slow."

Between southern trips, Daniel went to work for me in Brooklyn, refusing my repeated offers of payment. There should have been no complications with the will: I was my folks' only issue, the document named me such, wished me all applicable riches, and no strange voice had risen from the gallery to contest my rights. But the attorney who had drawn the thing up for my parents years back had, in his innocence, underestimated the majesty of the Law.

In a medium-shabby room on the second floor of Surrogate's Court in sylvan downtown Brookliana, over a countertop across which the possibility of direct human contact had been eliminated by a plexiglass partition, Daniel encountered the first of the wearying clerks who stand guard before the Law. Roused for the moment from his newspaper and unwrapping a fresh Rolaid, this individual told Furman, no doubt with a spiteful twist of pleasure, that my parents' will was invalid and would not be honored by the court.

"What's wrong with the thing?" I asked Daniel the next day, sitting in the living room with him, sensing a chill mist beginning to emerge from the dark wood into which my parents had gone. "Explain it to me as simply as possible."

"The will itself is all right," Daniel began, "although almost any will can be contested and broken if there is sufficient motivation for doing so—you may remember the number of clauses we had to insert into your own will to eliminate the possibility of error. The difficulty with your parents' will lies not in how it was written but in the way in which it was witnessed."

"Yes," I said again, but felt less than positive. The fog had dismalled its way to my feet and lay there resting; my antennae picked up the first anticipatory perturbations of heavy mental weather.

"Look." Daniel flipped open the document's grey cover and ticked through the thrice-creased sheets of bond to the fourth and last page, poking a thick index finger on the signatures at the bottom. I recognized my father's craggy, effortful scratching and my mother's gracefully flowing line. Below these, in the document's coda, two witnesses had signed their names.

"Daniel, it's witnessed. What's the problem?"

"Yes, these people witnessed the will, but it was also necessary for them to sign a second time to bear witness to the fact that they had witnessed the will and signed it above."

"They had to witness their own witnessing?"

"Precisely."

"That's nonsense." The mist had thickened about my ankles and now licked interrogatively upward toward my knees. "That's complete and obvious nonsense."

"Of course it is, but they will not accept this will in Surrogate's Court as currently witnessed."

"Usufruct," I swore.

"These laws," Daniel patiently explained, "with all their minute particularities, hev been designed solely to protect the legatee, viz. yourself. These good intentions pave the road to a small legal hell in which your parents' will has not the power to walk upon its hind legs and leave," and here Daniel raised an eyebrow, "if I may be permitted so extravagant an expression. Hev you put a controlled substance in my seltzer?"

"Nah, I'm just fucking with your dialogue a little. You don't sound like yourself on the page unless I push the language some. What if I were to go down there with you, brandishing ID and wearing a plaintive expression?"

"I have met these people. They will not accept the will." Daniel permitted himself a thoughtful look down toward the gathering unclarity at my feet. "Unless possibly . . ."

"Yes?" I said hopefully but without real conviction.

"Unless you can get these two witnesses to sign again, bearing witness in a separate document that they witnessed the will in the first place. Do you know these people? Mae Rogers?"

"My aunt Mae, Julius' widow. No problem. She lives in this building, on the second floor. In fact, it's because she and my uncle Julius lived here when the neighborhood I grew up in was turning into Murderer's Row that my parents . . . never mind."

"And Dinah Daitsman?"

"Dinah is Mae's, let me see . . ." The mist reached up to circle my head, and advanced a finger brainward to show me that it had the power to cloud men's minds, like the Shadow do. "Mae's . . . daughter's husband's mother. Mae's . . . does that make them sisters-in-law? Anyhow she's Mae's virtually inseparable friend." The mist's larger body waited, content at having demonstrated its strength. "Heh," I added.

"Heh?" Daniel asked. "Might I inquire why you say: Heh?"

"Dinah Daitsman has an apartment just down the hall." Not having much of a choice, I let the mist cover me completely. "She's a sweet little old lady about ninety-five years old, her hair still mostly black and never sick a day in her life till last Tuesday when they carted her off to the hospital after she suffered a major stroke. I think she's in a coma."

Daniel compressed his lips and gave off a businesslike vibration before setting his sentences marching, in their usual manner, like an Israeli armored division advancing on Egypt. "We will go down to your Aunt Mae's apartment on the second floor and secure an affidavit from her. I will return with it to Surrogate's Court tomorrow, where perhaps her signature will suffice. But there is a lesson in this: may all your wills be witnessed by young, healthy and if possible immortal beings. All the same, as you say: Heh."

"The very word," said a voice which must have been mine. But the speaker could not be seen.

THE ONE-SIGNATURE GAMBIT didn't play downtown either, and Daniel instructed me to visit Dinah Daitsman in the hospital—this is what I'd been dreading—get her to make a mark on a piece of paper, and if that proved impossible, to secure an affidavit from her son, certifying the authenticity of her original signature at the bottom of my parents' will.

"Do I have to?" I asked him.

"If you wish to retain the will there is no alternative. Otherwise we will hev to declare your parents to hev died intestate, and further complications may ensue. In short, yes: you have to do this."

"Son of a bitch," I said. "Which is what I'll feel like if I pursue Dinah Daitsman on her deathbed with a piece of paper."

But that night, when I telephoned her son Frank—the one who'd shown up bearing trays of delicatessen goodies the day of my father's funeral, zooming out of the apartment before I could stuff money in his pockets—he said No problem, he understood the situation, and when I went looking for him in the corridors of Brookhaven Hospital the next afternoon, what I felt like was a ghoul. There was a long-established confusion in my mind—rooted in a view of Brookhaven from a car window in childhood and a childish need to render my birthplace tangible—between Brookhaven Hospital on the eastern reaches of Linden Boulevard and the Beth Israel somewhere else in which my mother had had such difficulty bringing me to birth in August 1946; so that I also felt, on that hot day in search of Dinah Daitsman's room, as if I were on some inverse uterine journey with a dying old woman in a hospital bed at its end. A queasy sweat poured from me as I took another sip of ice water from the fountain next to the elevator or ducked into the men's room before turning the corner around which I was supposed to find Frank waiting for his mother to die and for me to show up with Daniel's affidavit.

MY OWN MOTHER, not only short of stature but narrow of hip and turning forty-one while I was dreaming myself up inside her, did not have an easy time delivering me to daylight. In fact she miscarried early on. Her obstetrician, a Dr. Adnopoz (rhymes with Inanoz), had an office in a brownstone well west of Brookhaven but likewise on Linden Boulevard, and a young son, Elliott, who was fixated on cowboys to a degree unusual even in the Brooklyn of that era. Elliott, my mother told me, although I never caught his act, used to stroll down to his father's waiting room from the living quarters upstairs wearing shiny two-tone cowboy shirts, jeans, hand-tooled boots, spurs, leather chaps and the latest thing in capguns. He would draw, give his guns a twirl on his fingers, shoot his father's patients where they sat, then mosey back upstairs. Later, the world would know him not as Killer Elliott Adnopoz but as Ramblin' Jack Elliott, the cowboy singer from Brooklyn from whom Bob Dylan lifted much of his vocal style.

As I'd always understood it, a couple of months into her pregnancy my mother bled herself of a messy discharge. In panic or the beginning of grief or conceivably something else, she rushed the two blocks to the doctor's office. Adnopoz told her she had lost the baby, and he performed whatever tasks were necessary to clean her up. I can only guess at the emotions that seized my mother, who had probably despaired of marriage and childbearing as her twenties passed unwed into her thirties, and these passed too, leaving her irretrievably alone, only to be taken up, when she was possibly past the fruitful age, by the passionate and unlikely suitor Harry Zaborovsky.

My father had returned from the Army and the narrow squeak of his court-martial to his sister Fanny's Bronx apartment early one morning while the war was still on. Fanny, a she-wolf of a woman about four and a half feet tall who usually spoke in a throaty shriek that she heightened still further for especially histrionic occasions, like watching her son Irwin eat dinner, was burning breakfast at the stove when my father, still in uniform, let himself in with his old key. Without missing a beat Fanny turned her head toward the bedroom and called out to her husband Martin (a smiling, docile man whom few had ever heard speak but who played cool-headed, killer chess and retailed a line of wicked humor when Fanny was not around), "MOTTN! You don't go to work today Herschel's back he can open the store!" My father about-faced without dropping his duffel bag and took a bus upstate to a left-wing resort in the Catskills, where he encountered my mother and at once set about confusing her with his intentions.

"This . . . funny guy kept following me around," my mother told me once, shrugging and allowing herself one of her few little laughs. "We all went out on a nature walk, and this . . . funny guy kept falling behind. I thought he was about to drift off and get lost, and whenever I looked at him he was . . . I didn't know why, but he was looking at me, puffing on a cigarette and sort of . . . following me around. And that night . . ."

"Oh yes that night," my father said, laughing quietly.

"That night he wanted to come visit me. He got all dressed up . . ."

"I put on cologne even, too much cologne, I spilled it the bottle . . ."

"He put on all this cologne," my mother agreed, "a brown jacket and blue pants . . ."

"The pants were green."

"Blue, and then your father decided to take a shortcut through the woods to the women's bungalows instead of taking the path like everyone else—you know he always has to be different, your father has to do everything his way—and he took the shortcut and fell into this hole . . ."

"A peet," my father said.

"A pit," my mother agreed. "And he let out such a yell . . ."

"I let out such a *gevalt* they had to come all of them with ropes and ladders to get me out of that peet."

"Your father," my mother said, as if presenting him to me for the first time. He had run with the free love crowd in the old country and had even assisted the surgeon in an abortion of his own begetting—in America he had run through a string or two of showgirls before meeting Mom—but this absentminded and unlikely Lothario, as soon as he set eyes on the pretty if unglamorous Sadie Novack, recognized in her the stable, faithful mother of his future sons and daughters. Actually, considering both their ages, maybe one child would be the most they should hope for. They were married about a year later, but even before that, using money abstracted from Paradise, he set her up with an apartment in far-off romantic Brookyelaine—"I was a kept woman," she told me before I knew what the phrase meant—and bought her the nose job she seemed to think she required.

A couple of weeks after the miscarriage, my mother went to the doctor for a follow-up examination, was shot to death again by Elliott in her chair, and informed by the frankly surprised Dr. Adnopoz that she was still pregnant: my mother and father had conceived twins, and there was still one in there, clinging to the uterine wall, alive and possibly undamaged. There were no further mishaps during the pregnancy, but my mother's labor about seven months later at Beth Israel was painful and protracted, and the doctors were readying the patient for a Cesarean when unexpectedly, about an hour after midnight, I made my move.

I SQUEEZED BETWEEN HER SLENDER HIPS in a room along *these same green corridors*, I told myself, erroneously, almost forty years later, as I nerved myself up to secure legal witness from the dying Dinah Daitsman or her son Frank in the halls of Brookhaven.

Frank was a tall thin number about a decade my senior, with thinning sandy hair, a long friendly face and a protuberant Adam's apple that seemed to have wandered onto the front of his neck from the throat of a Midwestern farmer in a genre painting. He greeted me with an easy affability surprising in someone waiting in a hallway for his mother to die, but then I was used to the anomalies of the process.

I began by expressing my concern for his mother, then apologized for being there. A phantasmal dagger appeared before me in the air, and I stabbed myself in the belly with it.

"It's okay," he said. "But my mother isn't going to be able to sign anything for you. Not today. Probably not ever."

"I'm sorry, Frank."

"It's how it is," he said.

"Then, if you don't mind, if it's not too much to ask, I've got something for you to sign. My lawyer says you'll never have to appear in court to back it up."

"Anything to help," Frank said. "Got a pen? I don't think I have one on me."

I escaped from Brookhaven with Frank's signature, convulsed with guilt in the traditional manner, and conveyed the document to lawyer Furman, who in turned carried it to Surrogate's Court in downtown Brooklyn, where they read him fresh clauses of legal phantasmagoria and sent him packing.

ONE MORE ODDITY AT ABOUT THIS TIME: I was sitting up
late in bed one night, reading I think, or maybe watching *chazzerai* on
TV, when I heard a cry from the street, a woman's voice sounding lost,
and when I went to the window and looked five floors down to the concrete walkway between the two fenced-in gardens that filled the building's forecourt, I saw a smallish white-haired woman in a floral-print
summer dress, at that distance for all the world like my dead mother, lying on her side where the walkway gave onto the sidewalk by means of
two little steps. She moved her legs—her feet, like my mother's, were
clad in short white socks—as if she were upright and hesitantly walking,
and her repeated cries—a soft, wandering Ohhhh, not quite a sob but
as involuntary—were the unintended ineffectual cry of dementia, a plea
with no sufficient answer in this world.

So: there was a woman remarkably like my mother lying on the pavement outside my window at three in the morning. When God lays it on
with a trowel, I thought, God lays it on with a trowel. It was not so much
that I took things on the order of dead mothers doubled on the ground
outside my window in stride as that such festivities no longer came upon
me entirely unexpected. The laws of probability were not what they used
to be: anything could happen to anyone at any time. In their new config-
uration the laws were above all no respecters of persons.

I threw on some clothes and a pair of sneakers and ran down five
flights of stairs to the street.

When I pushed through the main door into the soft summer night
she was still there on her side, fitfully moving her legs. I had hoped to be
the first to reach her, and I had gotten my wish. I approached her slowly,
let her see me—her eyes took me in, held for a moment, forgot me and
passed on—then hunkered down in front of her and when I was sure that
she had seen me again, said, "Hi," my voice soothing I hoped, and the
rest of me making no sudden moves.

"Hello?" she said. I tried to gauge by the tone of her voice and the look in her eyes the stage of her mind's undoing, but she was not my mother, and no two dementiae sing the same tune. Neither was her face my mom's, I was relieved to observe: it was a wider, squarer construction more coarsely and conventionally given over to the latticework of age. Marked strength of jaw there. What had she been like once? What was she like now? And by what declining music of self had she been played from there to here?

"Did you fall down? Would you like to get up?"

"Maury?" The mere trowel had been set down and a large shovel taken up. I didn't know the woman; she might have come from anywhere, might live anywhere, could have come out for her walk from this building or wandered over from somewhere up the street or farther off—the night was young, and full of possibilities—but of one thing I was sure: this Maury for whom she had tentatively mistaken me was her son.

"Your son, Maury?" I ventured.

"Maury?" she asked me.

"Is that your son's name? Maury?"

She searched my face and found that it was not the one she was looking for. "Where is he, here?"

"Well, let's see. Do you think you can sit up?"

"Sit up?" she echoed. She looked me in the eyes before her glance slid off again, lacking sufficient cognitive grip. By the unobstructed movement of her neck as she looked around at her several gathered nights I determined that she had not injured her back and might safely be sat upright. In all probability she had fallen softly, more a confusion of limbs and motion than a deadfall or a faint, had lost track of her body in a moment's forgetfulness and then found herself lying down, wondering why and where and possibly, give or take a few decades, when.

"Here. Sit up against the fence and we'll see if we can find Maury for you." You know how to do this, I told myself. You really know how to do this. I tilted her up against the cyclone fence that held the chest-high hedges in. "Ohhh . . . ," her involuntary voice said as I moved her, all of Brooklyn righting itself, her internal compass slipping untellably out of kilter—and taking her by an ankle I straightened up for her the haphazard tangle of her legs. She had one bedroom slipper on; its fellow lay upside down on the lower of the two concrete steps, next to scraps of paper trash and a flattened beer can. Slippers were a hopeful sign, I thought, and improved the odds that she'd come from this building and not some God-knows-where farther off.

"Okay. What do you say to just sitting here awhile?" I asked. "Maybe a little later we'll get you all the way up."

"Hm," she said, and for a moment a more routinely thoughtful expression crossed her face.

I heard a window open above and behind me, and looked back over my shoulder to see a trembling of the veil in a window three storeys up the dark of the wall. "Could someone call 911?" I called loud enough to be heard, I hoped, without waking anyone else. "We might need an ambulance here."

"She hurt?"

"Don't think so," I said. "Confused. But we need some help. Do you, does anyone up there know who she is?" No answer came. "Will you call 911?"

"You got it," the voice said, and the gauzy white curtain drifted shut.

I had it? The situation well in hand? The Alzheimer's gene myself?

In the words of Fats Waller: one never knows, do one.

6

"IT'S UNBELIEVABLE," said my aunt Rose when I told her the story in her large, modern Greenwich Village apartment a few days later. "That such a thing should happen to you, of all people."

"It was mostly happening to her. Besides, I'm getting used to it."

"So tell me: what finally happened?"

We were sitting in Rose's long, pleasantly daylit living room. I was at one end of her sofa and Rose, a woman even smaller than my mother had been, and now mostly sightless after a couple of botched cataract operations, her figure bent and her hands gnarled with arthritis, sat on the other. Her white hair, very fine and nearly straight, was cut like a cap on her small head, and from this thinning cap her face descended through the marks and harrowings of eighty-five years—Rose did not have my mother's ageless skin—to a small chin still delicate despite the loose flesh wattled beneath it. Her eyes seemed contemplative in their sightlessness, but also were dulled to a not quite leaden grey sitting there day after day in a life of almost no incident or interest, her husband Joe dead some fifteen years now. Between eyes and bones she did not get around much anymore, and only made it outdoors holding on to the arm of one of the Caribbean or Philippine "girls" she found so much to complain about; if the weather was nice, maybe up the street to Washington Square Park, sit on a bench, see if she could make out the arch in the gloaming.

Today she wore a well-tailored, tufty mauve suit with navy piping, its style derived from 1950s Chanel or just possibly an original. In any case Rose had a well-defined sense of taste in clothing and décor. The furniture in the room, much of it familiar to me since childhood, when I had treated the Agrins' next-door apartment as a handy extension of my own, imitated the same period as the things my mother had bought, probably with Rose's guidance, but were more augustly and tastefully designed—fewer gew-gaws, finer wood and fabric—and by now were much better tended. In the daylight behind my aunt, seen through a bank of three windows and slatted by uniformly canted venetian blinds, successive planes of brick in shades from rust to ochre presented themselves, intersected and fell away, greenery upflung between them here and there in a materialized prayer to light whose intensity and limits had been accounted for by the architect. A couple of 8th Street shop fronts were visible through a slot at the bottom of the view: cubist Manahatta with a slice of Hopper at the base.

It's odd to report this but nonetheless true: as I sat there, a dark blur in Rose's vision and Rose a small human tumulus silhouetted against the daylight in mine, I had the subliminal but powerful impression of the two of us sitting in a sea-cut cave: we were in the dry part, but around the bend behind her, irregular corrugations of rock tunnelled away and led to the lapping salt and interminable sea. In retrospect it seems the control-ling image of my visit. I gazed leisurely around at the paintings of mixed quality on the walls—two of them portraits of her daughters, Gloria the brilliant one (first in her class back at Columbia Law) and Ruth the beauty (when young, frequently mistaken for Elizabeth Taylor, but I'd always thought Ruth leaner, better-looking and about a third of the way from Liz to Audrey Hepburn gracewise); both middle-aged now, both di-vorced, but only one with brain cancer: Gloria lived in an apartment up-stairs and did not want visitors. My eye took in the gadrooned silver-alloy lamps, the blackstone scrimshaw six-inch Eskimo whose spear Joe had replaced years back with a small wooden paddle so that the smooth fat greystone seal at his feet seemed safe now from all but Ping-Pong; the pale green onyx ashtray with a tarnished bronze ibis overlooking the oval concavity; and the one small photo of Joseph Agrin, her departed husband and my likewise uncle, in which that urbane man was posed with uncharacteristic stiffness in a business suit before a vague grey curtain; but if I allowed my essential impression of the scene to come through that other curtain, the mostly omnipresent veil of phenomenal being, there we were in a column of air the surf had cut through living rock, seated on stones, the sound of the sea distantly in our ears, its salt breath registering in our nostrils and grey-green sealight cooling the space between our dreaming forms.

This admittedly strange impression—I've checked it with my lawyer, who had visited Rose once, and he told me it was based on something real—may have been intensified by the fluid, amniotic question I wanted to ask my aunt. In all my life, and despite the sad, revealing conversations I'd had with my father in his last year, which uncloaked so many mysterious forms that had hovered, flapping their sheets and making dim and unintelligible noises at the back of my life for so long, I had never succeeded in learning if the miscarriage that had eliminated my twin and nearly taken me out of the picture was an innocent accident or something my mother had consciously or semiconsciously done on her own. The evidence I had in hand was suggestive but inconclusive, and Rose, I thought, might just have the crucial piece of information. But could I ask her for it? I was frightened not just by the delicacy of the question and her potential response, but by the whole damned subject.

THE FIRST I'D HEARD OF MY LATE TWIN I was probably five or at most seven years old—it's a guess, but the memory has the cognitive temperature of that age. "You know," my father told me one day out of the blue, sitting at the rectangular maple dining room table of our old apartment—in place of the Seine a matching rusticated brown maple sideboard stood along this first kitchen's wall to my left and his right: "You know, originally you had a twin brother or sister, but it died when it was still inside Mother."

It probably took me some time and a handful of questions to assimilate the technical side of the question, to the extent that my father was willing to confide it—my concept of sexual plumbing was primitive; these things are simpler if you grew up, as my father had, on a farm—but what occupied my attention more powerfully than any tenuous grasping at the specifics was the unfamiliar emotion that had walked up behind me and laid its large hand on my shoulder. In response, a dark space opened inside me, the first shock of which was that something so fundamental to my existence as a missing twin could have existed for so long without my knowing about it: it was a numbing blow to my illusion of autonomy, a sense of having been robbed, not yet of a nebulous twin but of my integrity, of the clarity of my outline in the world. Farther in, I didn't know what to feel. It was my innocent impression at the time that being an only child was the common state of nature and that brothers and sisters were exceptions to the rule. I could not in an instant reconceive my life to include retrospectively a male or female Other standing there beside me for the duration, his or her hand in mine, and . . . wait a minute: what if it'd been an *identical* twin? another Myself looking back at me in a mirrorworld—a possibility too weird to compass without some long and heavy thinking . . . although a *girl,* think of it, might've been even stranger. Then some glimmering of pride, which likely hid a selfish glee at still being solo, attached itself to the absence of this unborn Whoozis: this hadn't happened to anyone else I knew: it marked me out, made me different, *special*: my hidden gestation, unlike others', had been an adventure, with dangers and near-death escapes, like something in the movies. But behind this facile semiglow pounded an impenetrable absence, and inside that, something fundamental in me reached out for the missing Other, although I barely let myself feel this at the time. "Why did it die, Daddy?" I finally must have asked.

And here my father—to the end of his life he had a horribly covert way of communicating an emotional subtext—planted the still hidden but audibly ticking bomb. "You know Mother what a hard worker she is. She, ah," and here his glance slid precipitously aside, and my soul tumbled after it off the margin of daylight into a darkened world of illegible text, "she, ah, worked . . . a little too *hard* one day and it made her kind sick and the other one it died." This last word had two syllables: di-èd: al-most Elizabethan: and as I tried to visualize the dissolution of my womb-mate inside a visualization of my mother, some secrecy inside myself closed over the subject like a cloud in which a storm was being born. I knew, without being coached, not to ask my mother about it, and I never did.

I did, however, pursue the subject with my father a second time, when—I think—I was just short of pubescence and the warfare between my mother and me, although already in progress, was not quite as open or as furious as it would shortly become. "What did you mean," I asked him one day, "that she worked too hard? What was she *doing* when it happened?" The only work I had seen her do was the ceaseless, repetitive cleaning of the apartment, but on hearing about this unformed "work" of which she had done too much, I'd eventually imagined my mother in a department store composed in roughly equal parts of the ground floors of Macy's and A&S, where in the midst of exercising some mid-managerial function, my mother put a tremulous hand to her stomach, or alternatively to her brow, then went pale and fainted beside a counter on which a fanshape of colorful silk scarves was spread. Despite my close questioning—I was on the hunt this time; I had a motive, and cued by Dad's well-remembered sidesliding glance, my widened nostrils sniffed prey—he husbanded his information carefully, only letting a corner of it show. Then, when he had sidestepped all my lancing questions, all on his own he dropped the crucial card, his tone of voice speculative and ad-dressed apparently to himself: "What I don't understand it is that Dr. Adnopoz had just told her, now you are this much pregnant, don't give yourself any more enemas, it's dangerous for the baby—Mother used sometimes to give herself an enema—and just the next day," and here his glance slid terribly off to his left again, and I tumbled out of my seated, out-of-its-element body after it, "and just the next day she gave it herself an enema, and that's what happened, the other one it di-èd. I don't un-derstand it," he said, shaking his head. "She must have forgotten what the doctor said."

This was not quite the instantaneous bombshell it might have been—

it was a slow jump to the obvious conclusion for a child who had not yet worked out a concept of the subconscious in action—but it lay there inside me and in my adolescence gradually revealed itself, blossoming like a black rose, as something very like a charge of murder: in the half-sleep of the mind, my half-dreaming mother had tried to get rid of us, of *me*, and she had cheated me of a brother, a sister, a twin, a lifelong companion, a friend. Or maybe the crime had been my mother's cleareyed, completely conscious attempt to rid herself of the nasty dirty life that had begun to infest her. It fit exactly with the insane, accusative way she had treated me from the beginning! I could see her doing it! etc., etc . . . It must redound somewhere to my credit that during my teenage years some sense of honor, of my mother's honor if not my own, prevented me from charging her in the middle of one of our screaming, hysterical arguments—in which on occasion I'd had to physically propel her out of my room and across the apartment to keep myself from pummeling her full-strength with my fists—with the murder of my double and the attempted murder of myself. It's not that I made a conscious choice: it simply never occurred to me to fling this cruellest of daggers. Had it appeared before me at a sufficiently dramatic moment—reflex Freudians are gonna love the imagery—I might well have stabbed her with it and twisted it with all my strength in the wound. Some unconscious discretion must have kept it unseen. So all I did was bellow out my usual mantra: LEAVE ME ALONE! WHY CAN'T YOU LEAVE ME ALONE!

I asked my father about it a third time in the shellshocked calm we shared in his last year of life, after my mother's passing—the two of us sitting alone now, blown out, exhausted, few illusions left—wanting to know the facts of the matter insofar as they were knowable; he told me then about Adnopoz's surprise at my mother still being pregnant after the miscarriage, but nothing more. I remembered the red rubber douchebag—"enema" had been a euphemism of course—hanging from the bathtub faucet all my childhood long, its unintelligible serpent hoses with their metal clips, at the end of one of them a long black upcurving longitudinally ridged plastic thingamajig gradually swelling toward its end. Is this the messy, tubular stuff of which a life is made or unmade, all the rest an airy fabrication and the ultimate reality this pink-red rubber *thing*, luke-warm water, a moment of unconscious action and slippery loss, a spill of thickened blood in the bath? In retrospect and on a background of neatly grouted small square white tiles, this reddish rubber bag rattled auton-omously on its faucet and annihilated everything across the years be-tween myself and it. The remembered smell of its rubber entered my pores and took some fundamental possession of me. It comes down to this. Rattle rattle. There you are. Hubble bubble. You're gone. Hotcha gotcha. You never were.

Some delicacy or terror or politesse kept me from pressing my father any further on the subject this last time.

NOW, SITTING IN THE LIVING ROOM with my aunt Rose, or on rocks in a sea cave with an aged and blinded crone whom I hoped might prove an oracle, but washed fairly clean of vengeance, I only wanted to know where to set this crucial stone in the uncertain pillar at the foundation of my life. Just to get the facts straight. Just to know. Just, perhaps, to be a less subjunctive person in the world.

"*Nu?*" Rose asked me. "Are you going to tell me what happened or not?"

"What?" I gathered myself back from other shores and regrouped. "I was thinking of something else."

"*Tell me what happened with the woman.*"

"The paramedics showed up in five or ten minutes. I talked to her un-til they came, and while we were all trying to figure out where she lived and if they should take her to the hospital, a woman I knew, a neighbor—d'you remember Lillian? Did you meet her?"

"Whatsisname's—Phil's wife?"

"No. Someone else. Long face, square jaw, a little leathery, nice lady."

"I can't remember all the A.K.'s in your building."

I nodded. "Anyhow this Lillian came out of the building in her housecoat and she knew the woman. They were next-door neighbors. Funny I'd never seen this woman before, I thought I knew them all—"

"All the *Alte Kakkers*," Rose said, perhaps thinking I needed a translation.

"Right," I acknowledged. "All the A.K.'s. Anyway, Lillian talked to her and the woman seemed to respond a little, so we got her on her feet. She was a little wobbly and we helped her walk. The paramedics came upstairs with us, carrying emergency gear. The woman was still a little shaken. It was an open question, with no one present who could claim legal responsibility, whether or not they'd take her to the hospital. We sat her down at her kitchen table, made her a nice cup of tea, and Lillian gave me her son's phone number—"

"Maury."

"Maury. *'A real son of a bitch,'* Lillian mouthed in a big stage whisper to me as I was dialling. *'He won't take her in, the bastard.'* It was about four in the morning. I got him out of bed and he didn't much feel like driving over."

"So he *was* a . . . no-goodnik," Rose politely equivocated.

"Not necessarily."

"Not everyone is like you."

"Look," I recited. "When it got really serious with Mom and Dad, I was living upstate, I wasn't married, I wasn't even writing that much for the magazine anymore . . . I was able to give it my time because I had the time to give. Not everyone has the luxury . . . "

"Some luxury."

"You know what I mean. Anyhow this Maury had a regular job he had to get up for in a couple of hours, and an apartment down in Sheepshead Bay."

He asked me to sit up with his mother until she could sleep and maybe he'd come see her tomorrow. I recognized the unwillingness, the resistance in his voice and could remember its equivalent in mine.

"Look," I'd told him, "Lillian and I are both with your mother but she's disoriented and upset, she's been asking for you. I understand it's four in the morning and you need your sleep . . . but if you don't come the paramedics won't leave without her. Right, they have to have a legal next of kin. They'll take her to the hospital and you'll have to come down there tomorrow after work and get her out and it'll cost you and there'll be paperwork." *Shit*, he'd said finally, wanting to tell me off but answering instead that it would take him maybe forty-five minutes to get there. I told him that Lillian and I would wait.

In the event, Lillian lit a cigarette, made herself a cup of Nescafé and told me to take off; I went back to my place on the other side of the building, and Lillian—who wrote the woman's rent checks for her and often cooked an extra dinner so that her neighbor would have something to eat—did the waiting-up and received Maury when he came.

"SO: YOU SEE WHAT HAPPENS TO PEOPLE," said Rose, and looked across the living room away from my story. Her jaw quivered. "I always thought," she said, her voice tremulous now, "I always thought, after Joe died, that whatever else happened, Sadie would be there, that I'd have Sadie . . ." A tear began its way down her small lined face but before it could get very far she wiped it away with a peremptory hand. "And look what happened to her. Who could have imagined it? Who could have imagined what happened to her?"

"Not me," I admitted.

"When she stayed here with me that week—do you remember?"

"Yes."

"She swore, she was *convinced*, that I had beaten her up all night. 'You came into my bed! You beat me up!' And there was no way I could convince her otherwise. 'You beat me up! Look at the bruises I have all over me!' 'Sadie,' I told her, 'there are no bruises.' 'Look at these bruises on my arms!' 'There *are* no bruises on your arms.' 'Look at them, they're bruised all over.' *Then* I saw what you'd been coping with in Brooklyn. I didn't know. Until then I just didn't know."

"Yes."

"I blamed your father for exaggerating. You know what a histrionic personality he had. I blamed him."

"Yes."

"But I didn't know. Not until I saw it with my own eyes."

"Yes."

"And why am *I* kept alive?" she asked now, leaning insistently toward me as if it might just be my fault. "I've seen enough. I've seen too much. If it weren't for what it would do to my grandchildren I'd put an end to it tomorrow. I have enough pills, and if not, then I wouldn't be afraid to turn on the gas or put myself out the window. Who *needs* it? Who needs to live so long, in this condition?" She turned her eyes toward me and squinted, straining to see the darkish blur I was a bit more clearly. Her voice narrowed, her diction grew still more exact, driving in the nails one by one with perhaps a certain grim satisfaction. "I ask you: what is the point? Is there any point to prolonging my life when it's just—you see what it is: would *you* call this a life? This is not a life."

"Two. Forty. Five. Pee. Em," said a precise but disjunct computer-generated male voice from a black plastic cube on Rose's end table; her mottled, vein-congested hand rested on the clock after relinquishing the button.

Call me cautious, but this didn't seem like the right moment to pop the question about my mother's possible role in my near-abortion.

"Can I offer you some more coffee?" Rose asked. "I'll make you another cup, but if you want seltzer or ginger ale, if you'll pardon me," she waved an arm in a backhand sweep of welcome, "you know the way to the refrigerator, please get it for yourself."

"I'm fine."

"I'm sorry I have nothing else to give you," she said a bit testily. "If you had given me a little notice I might have had something to offer you for lunch, but as it is, the way you come, when you want, if you want, with one day's warning . . ."

"It's okay, Rose. I'm not here for lunch. I came to see you."

"There's not much left to see. To speak frankly, I'd be better off dead."

I examined the dregs of my coffee and considered munching on another tight curl of rugelach. It couldn't be her own, I thought, although it tasted confusingly like the things she'd made once. But she couldn't be baking anymore. How would she manage? In simpler days I'd never fail to cut loose from my mother's apron strings Friday mornings and run next door squealing "Fry-day is Bake-day!" (an early pun), Rose's kitchen brilliant with sun, and the heady smell of baking already in full possession of the air, Rose turning out loaves of coffee cake, smaller twists of pastry nuggeted with nuts and raisins, big gleaming brown braids of challah, their egg-glazed tops lightly speckled with poppyseed—man, did that place smell good! I'd buddy up to her on a stool, climbing up the black rungs of its base, wiggling my butt to get settled, watch fascinated while she worked, kneading the dough, knotting it into interbraided ropes of future food, and would accept, when at length it was offered, a small munch of uncooked dough from her finger's end. I would do my best to ignore my mother's uneasy summonses homeward, and vibrate impatiently until Rose told me that my favorites, the *tsibbeleh kichlach*—hard crisp rumply nearly rhombic onion biscuits: if you haven't had them you just don't know—were cool enough to eat. I can recognize now how characteristic of Rose her baked goods were: relatively small, less yeasty and sugared than the norm, well structured, a bit hard and tight, and of the first excellence, and generously offered, in a warmth of welcome that must have characterized all our time together in those years.

On the other six less exultant days of the week I would also champ at the bit for a release into the world of 5D, in which the living room, narrower, darker and infinitely more plush than our own 5C's, left me free to pursue the textured light and shade into the welcoming embrace of cloudy fantasy: the ranked cumuliform carvings of the dove-grey carpet, the dark purple velvet on the plumebacked chair seats against the push of my fingers, and my mouth pronouncing silently the vees and ells of velvet to taste the hidden place the word had come from, vee the push of my fingertips against the plush, elve the yieldingness that caressed my hand in a fore-image of sexual love and the tee at the end a soft landing for all that lushness: *velvet*, a perfect word. I also loved the dark-blossoming clouds, black with soft brown edges, that bulged out of nullity into form when I pressed my fingers onto my tight-closed eyes just right. Nor were these adventures always solitary. I would run happily into the arms of

Gloria, a short-haired proto-beatnik whose eyes had always seen something in me they especially liked—a recognition daunting to me even now. Usually she'd be sitting on the floor in old soft flannel shirt, jeans and sandals, or I'd watch her painting at her easel—Goya, I used to call her, before I could articulate the syllables—fascinated by the wholesale transfer of a couple of fraybacked books and a wooden sleeping-Mexican bookend from the three-dimensional apartment to the flat of her canvas, the background dark maroon and the folds of the mestizo's cotton but really carved clothing caught just right, his sombrero covering his head just the way it did in, um, life: an amazing thing, just amazing, a talent I'd never begin to possess even though Gloria tried to get me started. Elsewhere in the apartment the younger, graceful Ruth might also have started painting by then, since eventually she developed a finer gift in that art than Gloria, more impatient and intellectual, ever would, or might have begun working her way through the beginnings of some music on her Spanish guitar. Ruth would welcome me too, although in a more generalized way; and although I was drawn to Ruth's slender graceful Italianate beauty, it is Gloria to whom I remember being particularly close, and whose regard for the wide-eyed little twerp I was harbored some particular perception of who might actually live there behind my clear grey eyes. She was the most accommodating female presence in my infant world, and easily the most intelligent person. Sometimes when I'm looking past my fading denimed legs on a summer day, as now in Paris, where I'm freeloading in a friend's apartment—Gloria lived here awhile, spoke fine French and had a friend named Anne-Marie who was shot down in a plane she flew for the Maquis during the war: I looked up at her in some awe—or watch my hands buckling on a pair of sandals, I wonder how deep a mark Gloria left on me, the relaxed but graceful manners of her youth, the warmth of her welcoming body through the flannel, those brushes moving over the surface of a small stretched canvas leaving form and colors behind . . . A few years ago, before Gloria's cancer reached her brain, when I told her I still had the picture she'd made of books and bookends—I didn't tell her time had torn one corner of it—she laughed and hoped I'd chuck it down the incinerator please and I told her sorry, no dice, absolutely not.

And there was still more music in 5D, its source a tall Victorianesque obelisk in dark wood, the four mock-pillars at its corners vertically grooved and fluted, with technological innards that played 78s under a heavy hinged lid, and when you opened the door on the front a mysterious green eye that dilated and winked in unison with the mysteriously sourceless music of the radio—all we had in 5C was a small brown-and-gold Bakelite Victrola that played "Mule Train," "Rudolph the Red-Nosed Reindeer" and some very funny Danny Kaye. When I reached a certain age, Rose and Joe let me put the records on for myself. I remember the music coming out of the magical thing and how I used to climb up on a chair to watch the records turn, or, standing back on the grey clouds of the carpet, would stretch my arms wide to embrace the sacred object, pressing my body close, wishing my arms were long enough to go all the way around it, when at best I could manage only a side, grasping the edges, stretching, hanging on as best I could. My tastes? Khachaturian and Tchaikovsky. Forty years down the line, hey lookit, I've made it all the way to Shostakovich.

But why, at the base of some of Rose's dark, faceted mahogany furniture, should a harpy's claw seize a brass ball with savage fixity right there on the tame domestic carpet? It seemed to me that the clawfoot tables and chairs and chests must either obscurely contain or symbolize the whole animal to which the totem foot belonged. Had the furniture once been alive? Was that why they called it a living room? Had that wide breakfront been extruded outward from the wood-dark, white-bone geometry of an animal body? doors its flesh, shelving the ribs, all trace of blood refined down to dovetail joinery, polished curve of wood and ornamental filigree? Was each *chest* with doors also the other kind of *chest* of a slain animal, rendered into this shape through a transubstantiation of its flesh or an appropriation of its spirit? One way or another, had the furniture been killed into what it was? If so, what had been done with the organs? Were they the *bone*-china tchotchkes on the shelves? Did the tables call back to the forest dark of their origin? Fur. Bodies. Night. Was that the secret of the tamed world of Rose's living room? A chair sat up and demonstrated its trees. I heard a bearlike breathing, heavier than my father's and smelling more of tree bark than tobacco.

What was the secret that was hidden here?

I was fascinated but not frightened, because above all, Rose's apartment provided a world in which I would not be pursued by the sudden sharp accusation of "What are you doing? What are you hiding from me? *What are you thinking?* You're up to something! . . . *You're trying to drive me* crazy!" I only had to be alone in the bedroom of 5C and the shrill voice would come, repeatedly, out of absolute nowhere, and I would look up from my marbles—long since lost I'll admit—or away from the patterning dust motes in the sunbeam slanting down from the wooden venetian blinds in the window, and there my mother would be, an inexplicably violent presence, her lips compressed and eyes narrowed at nobody in the whole wide breathing world but me. *"Wait till I tell your father when he gets home!"*

The plot would thicken during the course of the day, its elements assembling mysteriously and in my absence, taking form from a small seed of what exactly? a too-long examination, out the window, of some incinerator smoke disappearing into the larger air while I tried to deduce from this the relative volume of the atmosphere? or my marbles, among which, it is true, a large white one with brown veins which I had named Egypt had, in my wars between good and bad marbles, a certain moral ambiguity? some parent-testing or merely too-spontaneous gesture?—who knows?—but once started the procedure would proceed, my mother gathering the strands, adducing fresh evidence of my constant plot against her from any stray thing I might do or say, reading the meanings in, her eye on the deep structure of the text, and by the time my father came back from Paradise Drinks there it would be, the whole narrative fully achieved, my mother screaming and in tears about every rotten thing I'd done or more often had only planned to do specifically to drive her mad, my small hysterical arms raised shaking in the air behind her, my voice raised to a scream: "She's lying! Can't you see she's LYING!" and even when my father had hugged my convulsively weeping mother to quiescence and gathered me up in his warm arms I still felt walled away from the world by the incomprehensible behavior of this woman who loved me, who hated me, who loved me, who loved me not—impossible to tell—and whom I had not myself quite ceased to love, whom I would

108 • RAFI ZABOR

have given anything, I think, to love freely and without mortal pain. My father sided with neither of us, only poured a soothing oil upon the waters so that the facts of the matter, whatever they might have been, were never ascertained, and I was left feeling as if I lived in a crystalline and invisible jail whose walls rose almost daily on a foundation of unforeseeable pretexts to shut me in and shut a world I wanted to live in out. I never understood a thing about it, never even got a whiff of why the intricate workings of this operation should have been turned upon me.

My father's return from Paradise, my voice rising in a wail, then my father's smoothaway response and my mother weeping in his arms.

The particulars are swept from memory, though I do remember one day, once only, for some reason, I was able to prove her wrong and my father had to accept the facts as I gave them. My followup was pure spite: case proven I announced that I was going into my room and have a good cry. I wanted them both to feel as miserable as possible.

And once too I came up with an intricate dagger of a wish, a really twisted blade forged in bitterness and perversity. At the end of another screaming episode my father had smoothed away I told him: "I hope you die before she does, because I don't want her to die and for you to cry about it believing she was good! Because she's not!"

Okay, so let's fess up: I could not only have been a smiley dreamy child trailing regulation clouds of glory and gazing at bits of Brooklyn smoke vanishing into the innocent air. On present evidence I am prepared to believe that I was from birth headstrong, willful, purblind, stubborn, wrongheaded and as difficult to lead as any fractious horse. No doubt I had my childish-spiteful moments. It's not incredible that I could have driven my mother to hysterical speculation. Neither is it hard, after all, for a sufficiently uneasy personality to perceive in the normal activities of even a predominantly contemplative child the instrument and the work of the devil. If you fear your own human nature or have been bludgeoned early into keeping it under wraps, a child's spontaneous selfishness can terrify you with a vision of evil, an aura that will wrap it from head to toe so completely that finally the child itself can no longer be seen. Even though the child is only trying to grow its way into the world according to the branching of its blood and the lawful grasping of its nature, it may seem, to some troubled other, the work of God to suppress its burgeoning individuality, to smother its nascent criminal sense of self as one's own nascent criminal sense of self has been smothered; to do so appears to be an expression of an objective order of being, a part of the way things are, ever have been and shall be. The only remedy for this perceptual set, I think, is love consciously chosen, although, and there's the rub, the ability to make the appropriate discriminations in situ presupposes either great resources of character which if present are often cancelled out by the spot you're in, or sufficient background in meditation or some other mental discipline conducive to the right kind of detachment from the autonomic passions of the instant, and even then it is the reverse of easy: we all know what it's like to try to deal with the powerful forces we find already gassed up and throbbing within us.

The terrible thing, of course, is not that my mother was next door to a nutcase—after all, my abuse, to call it that, was small potatoes compared to what goes on in the world and now is reported widely—no, the terrible thing is human nature as currently understood in this part of the forest: a jerry-rigged and slapdash thing in which, for example, a series of strange and unnecessary dramas was the only medium my mother could find through which to articulate the anguished nature of her love; a humorless Rube Goldberg contraption in which the omnivorous maw of my unconscious could take all that gratuitous melodrama in and from its miscellaneously reflected shards construct a buried mirror-world that would in some measure shape my inner sight and workings for the rest of my life no matter what consciousness I achieved or what physically and metaphysically transcontinental adventures I managed later on. Before the industrial revolution's multiplication and democratization of wealth, the creation of a middle class and the rights that went with it, Zaborovskys and Novacks, their kin and kind and first-begotten, could seldom afford to purchase the immaterial luxury of an individuated self in the modern sense of the term; and if therefore the ungainly intermixture of consciousness and its obverse that we experience at present is no more than a sticky interstice in the evolution, assuming there is such, of the human race, even so: at the end of the second millennium did it add up to no more than this? Was consciousness provided only to be crammed, like cable television with its couple hundred channels, almost exclusively with complicated but profitless *chazzerai*? Did ordinary people stop living like slaves and being killed like cattle only for their consciousness to amount to *this*? Maybe bad for a first run, an early attempt, but even so . . . When there wasn't some blind war to die in, couldn't we do any better? Can a man be tripped up by such flimsy lianas as these? In a word or two, *you betcha*.

It would sometimes be my conviction, if I were still capable of having one, that the third-rate stage sets of our subjective selves have not so much to be understood as to be *harrowed*, and what light enters with the harrowing, that's the light you get to see by.

You know, no one told me it was going to be this hard to write a book about a car. The next time I pass a copy of *Motor Trend* on a magazine rack, I shall tremble with incredulous respect.

"PEOPLE LIVE TOO LONG THESE DAYS," Rose was telling me. "Medical science keeps us alive long past the point—"

"But Rose," I objected, "medical science hasn't had anything to do with keeping you alive. You just happen to be free of any lethal condition . . ."

This assertion received the muffled snort it deserved.

"Now Joe on the other hand—"

Rose spoke quickly: "Joe would never have had a single heart attack if it hadn't been for the blood pressure medication that doctor gave him."

"Was that sometime around 1950?" I asked, for my records, but Rose was in midstride and would not stop for me.

"Joe took the pills he'd been prescribed, lay down in the bedroom for a nap and when I looked in on him half an hour later he had turned *blue*—blue from head to toe except for his lips. His lips were bright purple."

"I know, Rose. The doctor who prescribed the stuff came over and sat up with him all night—"

"That doctor," Rose said acidly.

"—expecting him to die, but Joe made it. He had a heart like a locomotive."

"He had a heart like his *mother,*" Rose corrected me. "She lived to
ninety-seven God bless her without being sick a day in her life and passed
away in her sleep and if it hadn't been for that *fahrshtinkener* doctor Joe
would never have had a single heart attack in his life, let alone all the
heart attacks he did have, and he would still be alive today."

"Yes," I said. I had always adored the man, although in childhood I'd
been a bit unclear as to his status, never sure who was related to whom by
which marriage or what precisely an uncle was, and although I am told
that in my crib I used to look back and forth between Rose and my
mother in confusion as to which was which, I have no memory of quar-
rying that quandary but can recall quite clearly having to enumerate at
say the age of four the differences between my father and Joe: my uncle
the one with the pencil-line moustache, the squared-off, jowlier face, and
his thinning hair combed straight back from his widow-peaked forehead
with a bigtoothed comb so that the regular lines showed through to his
skin; Joe smoked a pipe instead of my father's periodic cigarettes, and often wore a certain navy blue polo shirt with three thin horizontal bands
of red, green, and yellow stripes mid-chest high, but confused the issue
later on by giving this shirt to my dad so that I had to work their identi-
ties out all over again. Before going to bed on Bakeday evenings, I would
be summoned to 5D's dinner table for the Friday night *khmalyeh*: this was
a punch Joe ordered me to deliver with all my might and no cheating to
his upper arm as he sat over his second cup of coffee and his first pipe of
the night. I would stand beside his chair and take aim; it was his left arm
I had to hit, just below the deltoids. In the beginning, since I had no wish
to hurt my uncle Joe, this ritual *khmalyeh*, although I loved the thunder-
ous sound of the word, confused me—it occurs to me only now that the
Friday night shot in the arm may have been in some obscure and most
likely unconscious sense Joe's atonement for no longer observing the
Sabbath of his ancestors—but after a while, once I saw that I was not
hurting him, I looked forward to the plosiveness of the *khmalyeh* through

the doldrums of the week, enjoyed it tremendously when it came, revelling in its license and giving the punch everything I had. I was upset when it was cancelled after his first major coronary. My heart palpably sank, but "You're too strong for me now," he told me, characteristically displacing the abrogation of the ceremony from his new vulnerability to my growing strength.

Joe's first major, *khmalyeh*-stopping coronary caught him during a business trip to Providence, Rhode Island, shortly after Hurricane Carol had flooded that city: I remember going up there with my folks in our first car, the black '53 Dodge Coronet, to visit him and paging through a photobook of the flood, my gift from Joe, while dawdling in the hospital, vague about the seriousness of his condition—Joe had nearly bought the farm—but impressed with the grainy black-and-white shots of flooded city streets and high-water marks brassed in memoriam more than one storey high onto the facades of downtown office buildings. It was more from these dramatic photos than from Joe hanging out for some reason in a foreign hospital that it got through to me that something, anyway, had happened. Even smart kids are dumb as shit sometimes.

About two decades and a dozen or so heart attacks further on, when Joe had finally begun to acquire a pale and beaten look, I visited him in Intensive Care at St. Vincent's on 7th Avenue after a rough one. "They wanted me this time," he said, with a vestige of his old smile, "but I was still a little too tough for them." His eyes, tired but still managing a glint of humor, told me implicitly that if he made it through this one, the next would be his last; but a few years later he looked a lot more chipper when I came to see him in a Catholic hospital on the Upper East Side after a big one had knocked him unconscious near Gracie Mansion alongside the East River. He'd been visiting a client when it hit. "I think you'll like this," he said. "The first thing I saw when I woke up was *that*," and he pointed past his feet under the sheets at a dark bronze foot-high Christ agonied on the Florentine-brown wall beyond the foot of his bed, "and a nurse leaning over me, adjusting the IV drip. The nameplate on her blouse was practically in my eye, and it read: JEWHATE." He spelled it out for me. "The first words out of my mouth on coming to were, 'Excuse me miss, but how do you pronounce your family name?' Until she said 'Hewett' I wasn't sure I hadn't died and ended up in the Other Place."

Joe Agrin, I think, was my earliest model of what it meant to be a civilized, intelligent human being; all subsequent, usually European modifications of the image have settled on his shoulders without much strain and no untoward jostling of continents.

Joe had sailed with his family to America from Odessa, fleeing the intensifying pogroms that celebrated our century's opening with what, in view of what was to come, turned out to be a fairly delicate touch. He was twelve years old on arrival and had already read the complete works of Tolstoy and Shakespeare in Russian. Arriving in the refuge of America at that age, he was able to assimilate his way into the culture, as later my father would be unable to do at thirty, acquiring more than a homemade shtetl intellectual education and speaking cultured and unaccented English. Like my father, Joe would have preferred a scholarly or literary career—Shakespeare turned out to be even better in English—but he had to support his aged immigrant parents and so went into accountancy. "It turned out that I liked it," he told me. "In fact I loved it. I've been fortunate. I've been very, very lucky."

He prospered, building a distinguished firm without ever getting exactly rich, but he and Rose took the cruises and the trips to Europe that my parents never did. Finally, the Agrins climbed out of the trough of Brooklyn to the Village—old tenements going down, apartment blocks shouldering skyward in their place—in 1955 or '56, shortly after replacing their old blue Pontiac with the two-pane windshield and the sloping trunk with an impressively large squared-off grey one, a '54 Star Chief: old Chief Pontiac's dark orange glass face, with its prominent nose, lit up on the hood ornament when you turned on the headlights. The consequent change in my life as that face steered the Agrins over the bridge to Manhattan, the loss of my second home, was a geological shift. As these things go, seismic. Small kid, world still inscrutably large, and no refuge from my accuser.

7

HOW WAS YOUR TIME on earth?
What did you do there?
How did it feel to you at the time?

Isn't it amazing that such a little eyeblink could have occupied you so?

Is it possible I have so much less to say about the women in both my families only because none of them are storytellers and the men are almost, um, to a man? For a notion of my mother's childhood and a picture of life among the Novacks all I have to draw upon are some shadowy, generalized images of a Depression childhood with a few particulars emerging nacreous and pearlescent through yellowing layers of old lacquer: a series of one-room living quarters behind a series of small failing shops, dominated by the shrill presence of a mother who was always sick and usually bedridden. In these images, it seems, bed linens were perpetually boiling in a big pot on the stove, releasing acrid blasts of steam into the room, and my little mother stood on a chair to stir the pot with a wooden paddle while the voice came at her from behind in Yiddish—pour in more bleach, more bluing, stir the pot more, make sure everything is clean, *oy I'm so sick!*

At the age of twelve, my mother was ordered to leave school to stay home and play her repetitive role in these scenes. When not stirring the bitter pot of her young life, she worked at outside jobs while Rose was permitted to go on into the larger world of education, even unto graduation from Erasmus High. At home the rancid steam rose to fill the room, my mother stirring with her paddle, her face pale and sweaty in the heat as *vey iz mir, gevalt,* and the weight of duty drove her steadily into in-expression, her father coming home from the constricting horizon on which yet another business limped toward death—although the schemes he worked up for other people always seemed to take off like rockets—or the job at the trunk-and-suitcase factory that provided his customary shelter after a fresh collapse of enterprise. At the back of my childhood closets his busted unstrung fiddle lay unplayed, like his unplayed soul, in its case: I don't know when we parted ways with it and wish I still had it. "He was . . . such a *kind* man," my mother would say in the tenderest mo-ments she allowed herself in my presence—it was the deepest note I would hear her sound until the end of her life; until, in fact, the very last time I saw her alive—the tears gathering in her eyes and voice with a thickness from which you could infer the scarcity of kindness from other quarters of her world in general back then.

But surely this bequest from my mother presents a melodramatized picture, an ascription to external circumstance of an internal condition of the soul. I have a few old black-and-white photos, however, that may prove more objective.

I can't find the one of the luggage workshop, an industrial loft blasted white from the room-long bank of windows on the left with a daylight in which the men, having taken one step back from their work and turned their heads calmly to the camera, stand in their black aprons solid as the very building blocks of capitalism; so the first significant photo I have in hand is a family grouping, formally posed in a studio on Victorian-looking furniture and a Persian carpet amid similar bric-a-brac, framed by drap-ery left and right and a leaded window at the right rear. The faintly smiling grandfather who died before I could meet him hardly looks Jewish here—it's mostly that near-handlebar moustache, a likely stab at assimilation—but he displays, seated in a chair at the left of the picture, the baldness he passed on to me, the maternal grandfather, I'm told, being the crucial party. My grandmother is standing right of center wearing a very proper, high-collared black shirtwaist dress and has lifted her head for the camera, looks straight at it with ironic or perhaps only defensive hauteur and a fine intellectual light in her eyes. She betrays no evidence of her signature illness, and the artfully pinned-up mass of black hair atop her head does not square with the thin grey straggling strands of the ill old woman with salty fingers and not much English who lived with us during my infancy. The three children, with the two girls slightly fore-grounded, are arrayed right to left in descending order of age. Seated rightmost, Rose seems to assert her pride of place with the level gaze and near-smirk she directs at the camera. Sitting beside her in a lower chair, my mother seems vague, her I-don't-get-it look aimed nowhere in par-ticular, and her body seated as if she weren't very conscious of it, the arms awkward, hands distressingly limp; one elbow is almost leaning on Rose's thigh, as if seeking support or shelter. Their infant younger brother—a promising young man who died in his late twenties and of whom I have apparently always reminded everyone—whose mother holds him sitting splaylegged and upright on a pedestal table in the picture's center in frilly unisex baby whites, looks plainly stunned by the inexplicable occasion and the gesticulating cameraman, not to mention the explosion of the flash, and his dark hair stands almost ideally on end, his eyes staring help-me wide.

Poor Sadie my mother, as I seem to be saying in one of my father's lo-cutions, you see how easy it is to constrict and bury someone's heart in the soil of this world: it is the commonplace work of a few years, accom-plished with only slight attention and too inextricably a part of the back-ground to be much noticed at the time, still less changed later on. In lurid sum, driven by a sick, frequently hysterical mother and dominated by her older sister, my mother never got to articulate the self she came into the world with, never fully bloomed after her early blights. It's odd, although she didn't look visibly unhappy as a mature woman, how few times in her life I saw her smile, and then with an embarrassed facial cringe of self-defense; she laughed still less often, and it was usually at something on television rather than in life—but at the right things: it was Sid Caesar and Ernie Kovacs, not the odious Berle, that brought her out, and some-times Gracie Allen, whom she resembled a bit in the face and the way she did her hair—and a hand rose to cover her mouth, reflexively ashamed at the pleasure or perhaps only the spontaneity of laughter. In general she was a reasonably attractive woman who communicated neither uncertainty nor shame but an assured and stable presence: she looked like she belonged. But, Sadie, it was a cover, and even a man with all my father's solar warmth could not bring you back to your destinate fruitfulness, and it would be your infant son's spontaneity that drove you to distraction. With this old photo in hand—one you carried clutched stiffly to your breast from room to room of a strange house in your last weeks of life, your eyes like those in the picture, only much, much worse—I think I can follow the trail from your shuttered childhood through the years of office jobs, your girlfriends who also never married, the lesbian who approached you once and shocked you cold, your gratefulness at Joe's generosity after he married Rose, taking you out with them on road trips in that eventful old Buick of his. It's easy for me to find you, or to imagine that I find you, because some portion of my apparently contractual solitude is an echo of your own. You were valuable in those office jobs—the best of them that upper administrative position with *PM*, a left-liberal evening paper long gone now but highly regarded in its day—with your practical capacity for self-abnegation and the organizational talent in which you found refuge from the demands that were made upon you by all sorts of voices, sick voices, dear voices, your own voices . . . By the time you met my father at the end of your thirties you were not expected to marry, and when you did make your married home with him you moved into an apartment next door to your long-married sister, whose expectation of dominating you was scarcely subject to alteration by then.

This Zaborovsky person? A sentimental peasant bumpkin with a good heart but no manners and less taste. She was lucky to have caught anyone at all, doubly lucky this one had a thriving business even if it was only hot dogs in Harlem . . . So, at any rate, Rose may have thought.

In later years, when I visited her in the Village with my folks, Rose used to turn to me in the middle of some semi-suppressed disagreement with her brother-in-law and say, "You know your father and I always argue. We fight about everything because we just don't see things in the same way, and because he's so . . . *Anyway:* he knows that I love him. And I know that he loves me." To this declaration my father would seem faintly to nod his assent, but in my earliest years his battles with Rose for the control of my mother and then of me were fought in earnest.

THE READER may already have recognized the dishonest compensatory note sounding amid the heartfelt, reverent music that plays whenever I write about my father. The fact is that as an infant arriving in the big world already peopled with its giants, I picked up on the clues everyone around me let fall as casually as cigarette ash: the general disapproval of my father's accent, emotionalism, absentmindedness, peasant manners and utter lack of interest or taste in clothes or home furnishings (although this can at least partly be attributed to the general Zaborovskian blue-green color blindness that he stubbornly insisted he did not have): so that along with the yeasty Bakeday air of 5D I breathed in a universal condescension bordering on contempt for this man to whom even Joe Agrin would sometimes refer in desperation after a political discussion— although both were, or still thought they were, fairly orthodox lefties— as The Polack. At least in the army they'd had the courtesy to call him The Russian. So, casually I learned to despise this bumbling, ill-dressed man who could not distinguish sheets from shits or find or even name his hat or glasses—"Sadie, where is, where is, where is my watchoucull?"— when usually he was wearing them. Even though well into my middle childhood he could wake me at three in the morning after subwaying home from the night shift in Paradise and I would rise with spontaneous delight to embrace this fundamental source of human warmth in my life, in the logical world of daylight I divided my heart against him and joined the opposite party even though it included my tormentor. Years later, in my teens and early twenties, with all the regulation stupidity of such psychological civil war, I would exhaust myself trying to battle back to what seemed the other side of my only available nature. There were Mom's characteristics and Dad's; Dad's were now the good ones, Mom's the bad, etc., etc. The conditioned self inhabits a plane, metaphysically inferior to others I could mention, on which it is almost impossible to get anything done without producing stupid backfires in at least two or three unsought directions.

"Yes, what can you expect," I can imagine hearing Rose say to Joe in their kitchen. "Sadie was lucky to get anyone at all." *But what did they make of the daylong hysterical screaming crescendos they could not have avoided hearing from next door, my mother's voice raised against mine, mine struggling back?*

"Oh, Harry's all right," I hope Joe would have said.

"But the rest of them," Rose shuddered. "*Sam.* And that preposterous Tarzan . . ."

Gloria, as I recall, had a fundamental regard for my father, saw the more that did not immediately meet the eye.

Even so, even so . . . the tone, the implication was that there was something distasteful or at least embarrassing about the man . . .

But it is difficult even for me to realize how cool and clear an eye my father had. He could be the most level and sometimes most merciless evaluator of people, and this from long habit. Used to being belittled, one of his strategies was not to seem to see. *Ecce*, therefore, a realist with his sun in Scorpio perhaps giving him a tendency toward the hidden stinger. Certainly my father never turned the basilisk eye of his judgment upon me unveiled, and qualified himself with every kindness, although in the quiet behind his eyes, unsparing accounts were kept and worldly odds knowledgeably tallied; he saw me, and how the world wagged its people's tails, all too well, and it was the nature of his intelligence to seek a practical result.

In any case, his very sensitive seismic apparatus had no trouble discerning every tremor of insult that shuddered his way from the Agrins and little difficulty locating their epicenter in Rose, and although he could not, as he learned, win my mother's subtlest workings back from her, he'd be damned if the woman was going to run me too. He could see the marks being etched onto my open face by my mother's hysteria and the usual social acids, and knew himself at a disadvantage in the struggle, lamed by his accent, manner and local reputation.

I HAD NO IDEA of it at the time, in fact no idea until my father's last year, my mother already gone and both of us exhausted, sitting across from each other in the kitchen making up for conversations we had never had.

"Dad, those fights I had with Mom when I was a very young kid, how often did they happen? Once a week, once every two weeks?"

"Almost every day. Sometimes every day."

"No."

"Almost every day I came home from work to a screaming. You had done this terrible thing or that terrible thing. I saw that Mother couldn't express her emotion without . . . she had to bring it to a climax, a kind spasm, otherwise she wasn't able to express it."

"And when I told you she was lying, that she was making it all up . . . you *knew* what was going on?"

"Of course. I knew all what was going on."

"Christ, Dad, *why didn't you tell me?* You always smoothed things over. I felt walled off, I felt completely isolated, and no one knew. If only you'd told me . . . I was so completely cut off, alone."

The music in my father's voice modulated into a key I hadn't heard before, a spare, last-things realism sounding unexpected chords: "You poor guy. You haven't had much of a life, have you?"

I was startled by this: "Me? Are you kidding? Look, aside from Mom I had a pretty happy childhood."

"You deed?"

"Yeah, and after that, sure, there were some terrible times but I've had a few fantastic years."

"You have?" he asked me, an odd, surprised look dawning in his face.

"Absolutely. Some fantastic stretches."

"Really?" he said. "Good *years?*"

"Sometimes a few in a row. Count on it."

"Joel," he said. "In my whole life I haven't had two good weeks together."

Incredulity stopped my breath. "You're serious."

"Quiet serious. Not two good weeks together, in all my life."

I stared at him and he looked levelly back at me and nodded. It wasn't possible: how had he kept a heart like his alive if that's how it had been? It wasn't possible, but we were among last things, final honesties, the wraps off. We sat silent, face to face, the information ticking through, then his voice entered quietly: "I knew, between the time Mother and I became engaged and the time we got married, I knew there was something wrong with Mother. Something not right with her, in her mind."

"You did?"

"I deed. And I thought of not going through, not marrying her even, and I saw it that if I left her it would destroy her, it would destroy Mother completely, and I couldn't do it."

"You knew going in?"

He nodded. "And when it started these yelling and accusings I saw all what it was doing to you. I saw all what it was doing and I thought I had to leave her and take you with me."

I sat there listening as if my hair, all of it, were standing on end.

"And I saw it, Joel, that I couldn't leave. They would take you away from me, Rose and Joe. Gloria was a lawyer. And they knew all kinds other lawyers, people with influence, professional people, and what was I, a poor man, with the worst English in the world and my frankfurter stand on 125th Street."

"Dad, I had no idea."

"I thought it over for a long long time, of leaving, and I couldn't go."

"You stayed because of me."

"I saw it that if I left you would have no chance of becoming all what I saw you had in you to become . . . They would take you and they would have you, *Puppeleh*."

He hadn't called me that in decades. I sat staring at him across the table at which we took our meals, and he looked back at me, the shape of his life changing massively behind him: he was becoming gigantic again in my eyes.

"What an appalling picture," I said. "It's unbelievable. God. How did you *do* it? How . . ."

And I saw, too, why he had been unable to tell me that he knew what my mother was doing to me: I would have used the information against her—"He knows! Daddy knows you're lying!"—she would have run in tears to Rose, and the false, frail structure of our life together, roof, windows, walls, would have fallen in on us. He had already lost one family to the war. In his forties it would have been an intolerable defeat to lose another. In his seventies, in what we both knew was his last year, not because he had planned to but from sheer exhaustion, he was telling me about it.

"Ye-es, they would have taken you away from me, *Puppeleh*, and me, they would have broken me into pieces, if I tried to take you with me."

IT WAS TRUE. The Agrins would have taken him to court and had Paradise in escrow and his son in their hands if he pushed things too far; and even short of that breach, he could not for the most part fight openly with Rose without provoking unhealable rifts between people living in close quarters, but he had to do something. He would have to work, as we used to say in the sixties, within the system.

What may have irked Rose most was my father's clear refusal to be condescended to or insulted in any fundamental way: he would surrender trivial ground, but none in which his heart's blood was invested: this probably got Rose's particular goat by the nostrils and yanked hard. He could be a stubborn, infuriating enemy once he set his mind to the task, in this case partly because the precision of his calculations demonstrated a degree of intelligence Rose was determined to deny him. If only, she must have thought, the uneducated savage would crumple beneath the hieratic power of our glare. But he had the gall and obstinacy to stand there coolly looking back.

We rented the back half of a vaguely mission-style white stucco house in Belle Harbor, near Far Rockaway, for a couple of summers—rounded archways, tiled steps, terracotta roof tiles, bright sun and breezes, three houses from the beach, the bracing whiff of ocean salt, grains of sand getting into everything, and the owners downstairs an Orthodox Jewish couple named the Appels who lit mysterious candles and chanted foreign words at their table in the early dark of Friday evenings: my atheist-quietist parents let me attend as an observer: I was fascinated but found it a little weird, candleshadows wavering on the walls, the bread raised up in both hands during the chanting, and the cloth napkin I was asked to put on my head.

It was from this summer rental that I made my first attempt to run away from home: with a troublemaking kid named Barry one year my senior I escaped eastward along the beach below the boardwalk at dusk until the sky began fading to bruised dark orange and massing indigo while up on the boards the milling people's faces began to seem alien and strange—just the kind of thing I go in for now that I'm grown, but it scared me to a stop back then. A police car was spinning its red domelight in front of the house when Barry and I came back under our own steam. I was not quite five years old.

The scene I have in mind took place in the back garden with my father, on the grass beside the moist dug-up earth of the Appels' bright flowerbeds. I can hear my voice exclaiming in received fastidious disgust, "But it's *dirty*," and my father laughing, telling me, *Puppeleh*, dirt is earth and earth is good. Look where flowers grow from and all what we eat, *Puppeleh*. Ten minutes later when my mother appeared, frozen in horror on the back steps, my father and I were laughing, happily covered in dark brown loamy soil—it was in our hands, in my hair, all over both of us—and releasing ourselves into the equivocal largesse of humanity and its earth. Scary, anarchic stuff to Mom, to whom cleanliness, if not next to godliness exactly, was a buffer against incursions of terror from chaos and void.

"Ha-*rry*!" shrilled her voice from the missionary steps. "What are you *doing*?"

"Playing," said my father in his most musical voice, a basso laugh at the bottom of it. "Having a good time. Come join us!"

"*Ha*-rry."

Though the Rockaway dirtfest took place away from the command post in 5D and not, memory tells me, during one of Rose's visits to our sandy little Arcadia, it does by inference indicate the general disposition of the troops.

In war it is essential, Daniel tells me, to understand the strengths and weaknesses of your enemy with impersonal objectivity and in the greatest possible detail. In her automatic assumption of tactical superiority Rose probably failed to appreciate that like the God of Israel my father was long-suffering, slow to anger, but could roast her to a crisp on the spot if he chose to. When the time came for him to confront Rose directly, he blocked her way like a burning bush or, let's tone it down a little, a Russian tank in a country lane. There must have been a few such occasions, but the one my father mentioned most fondly and most often and which Rose herself acknowledged in conversation had to do, of all things, with how to tell a story and what to put in it.

When I was a little *pisher* there were a number of books I loved—*The Train from Timbuktoo to Kalamazoo* loomed large for a while, but gave way before *The Jungle Book* and never survived the upgrade—but my father, when night gathered its folds around me and the world settled down and softened, preferred to tell me stories of his own devising. The one I remember best was a nearly monthlong serial about the Little Pony—orphaned, loved by a boy, lost, gone picaro to survive many adventures before being gathered back into the safeties of love and home—but it was another long story that brought my father's and Rose's opposing armies into the field, flags aloft, their excited horses snorting and flaring their nostrils and, perhaps as in Tolstoy, in the still pristine grassy field between them before the bloodshed a small brown-and-white dog, barely out of puppyhood, ecstatically rubbing its back on the ground and frisking its legs in the air. This dog, of course, was me.

The story in question was about a man, his wife and his children. They lived, as did the people in all my father's stories, in a "Europe" that seemed to have lost its Western half. I don't know in what sort of detail my father described this Europe, but in memory its composite is a hilly place of small rough cottages and deeply rutted roads. In some of these stories my father himself walked these roads, usually followed by his cow, Lola, who loved him, taught him communism and whom he loved in return—*honi soit qui mal y pense*, y'all: keep it clean out there. On the way to town in the first of three episodes, Lola cruised through a fencegap into a passing field to munch some farmer's fallen apples and while salivating happily over the next sweet bruised item in her path was attacked by the angry farmer who proclaimed the field and everything in it to be his own. In leading Lola back to the safety of the public road, my father realized that the cow was smarter than the farmer, and he suddenly understood what Faulkner said King Ikemotubbe knew, that land could not be owned and that all such ownership was a presumptuous and ineluctably evil fiction. In a second story it was my father sneaking into a field after unfallen plums, property having already been defined as theft. He was attacked, not by any farmer but by the resident bull with blood in his eyes and a pair of horns ready for unequal battle, when Lola appeared out of nowhere, interposed herself between the bull and my future father, and made cow eyes and batted her lashes at the beast until my father could escape to safety. It may have been the third story that textured those European roads: finally reaching town, my father proceeded along the rough wooden sidewalk only to find that Lola had followed him onto the boards; shocked townies and angry merchants raised the cry, and unable to shoo Lola back into the gutter on her own, my father was obliged to walk with her in the ankle-deep mud of the street: Huckleberry Ovsky strides again.

Naturally enough Rose had nothing to say against Lola—if she had, my father might have vaporized her. But in the crucial, all-offending story my father told, the man, wife and children lived in this rough-hewn Europe through which terrible armies passed and where the sky looked more dramatically roiled with trouble than the skies of home. The story-family began well enough but life was hard, work was hard, the alfalfa crop failed and the man began to drink. He quarreled with his wife, started smacking the kids around—one son, one daughter, in my mind mysteriously both the same age—backhanding them at the dinner table and sending them to bed hungry when the twisted fault was all his own. Soon he was beating his wife, and not long after that he took to the roads, leaving his family defenseless behind him and his heart churning with bitter rage and self-deception. He stole, he drank, he didn't shave, he woke up in the cold dew of open fields, took a job at a sawmill and got into fights with his co-workers, beat up the boss and ran, eventually was impressed, as people were in my father's time and place, into the passing Russian army, got horsewhipped by Cossacks and was trudged twice into the storm of battle, the war between metal and men. Finally he escaped when the army began the slog back to Mother Russia. Meanwhile back at the ranch, life was going hard for the wife and kids: it rained, it snowed, the roof leaked, the stove smoked, and as in a silent movie the landlord showed up full of wily insinuation and diabolical menace.

Rose flipped. How could he tell me such cruel, such bestial stories? What did he want me to think of people? Of the world? Of life? What kind of horrible ideas was he putting into my head?

My father must have seen that this was an issue over which Rose might be openly and solidly opposed. I want him to know, my father told her, possibly reverting to the Yiddish of which he had so eloquent and literary a command, I want Joel to know everything about how people are. Rose, do you think this world is a fairy tale? It is not a fairy tale. I want my son to see it all, and to know how life really is. Moreover Joel is *my* son, not yours, and I will raise him as I choose to raise him, not as you would have me do. You have your children, Ruth and Gloria, and I would never presume to say a word about how you should raise or teach them. And neither will you raise my son. I do not agree with you about how to raise him, I will not agree with you about it, and I will not let you decide how I will raise him in my own home. I am glad that he is welcome in your home, and there of course you have the freedom to do with him as you like, and I approve. I see that you love him and that he loves you and I am grateful for it, but here, in my home, in what I do, you do not have the right . . .

Und so weiter. It would have been difficult to recognize behind this measured and implacable emanation of will the softhearted bumpkin of popular legend.

So after this confrontation—hardly an epic clash of armies I'll admit, but to my mind's nose the sharpest whiff of cannon smoke from a war whose subtler, usually undetectable scents were worked into the weave, day in day out and year after year, of the book of my childhood's binding—my father continued his story. The unshaven man woke in a ditch one morning all at once overwhelmed by remorse. He would never drink again. It had ruined him, made him into a monster, destroyed his life— my father wouldn't buy the liquor store for another eight years—and the lives of those he loved. Yes, loved. Gathering his ragged jacket around him and shivering with inner and outer winters he made his way across the hilly, rutted landscape back to his former home and begged his wife and children to take him in, swore never to take another drink and that he would sooner cut off his right hand than ever again raise it against them. And he wept and fell to his knees and begged. And finally believing him, they took him back. And because this time he had really learned his lesson, he worked hard, he repaired the house, improved the land, and they lived . . .

Happily ever after, Daddy?

Yes, *Puppeleh*, I think so, said my father, knowing that he himself was stuck behind enemy lines for the duration. Maybe that's why he also told me so many First World War stories, his mother tramping across the fields with pancakes bundled in her apron to where her children hid in a ditch behind a line of trees; the Cossacks dragging my grandfather between two horses out of the stableyard and into the field where they were going to chop him to pieces, my father and his brother Julius wailing after them and a Cossack captain riding up at the last minute on a steaming, snorting horse to say, "Let him go. Don't you see the man has children?" My father had one now, having made it to the safety of America and into the regulation entertainments of the middle class of the epoch.

Yes, *Puppeleh*, happy ever after.

Like you and me, Daddy?

Like you and me.

The drunkard story may have taken a month to tell in its entirety—I didn't get an installment every night; for starters my dad did two night-shifts a week in Paradise—and its length helped compose a Europe in my mind more real to me than America would ever be. Beneath those skies with clouds gnarled and complicated as human thought, the corrugated land was invested with deeper meaning than the Great Forty-eight or Shifty Fifty would ever afford me, and years later when I came back happy from the rough illuminations of Anatolia my father asked me incredulously what it was I'd found there and I was blank-minded with surprise at the question, not because he had to ask it but because I myself had lost track of at least one obvious answer: rough roads, dramatic skies, rough earth, unvarnished experience, the fullness of life and the richness of the world. He had been a good storyteller, my father.

"BUT DAD, really, not two good weeks together?"

Still there in the mortal exhaustion of the kitchen as if conducting an autopsy on the body of our lives, the inaccurate Parisian Seineside scene wallpapered beside us providing foreign imagery in reduction and taunting me: the beauty of the world, from which it seemed I'd been barred again. And maybe nothing now would revive its magic for me, ever.

My father sighed, then readjusted the clear plastic moustache that rode his real moustache in black and grey, got the oxygen prongs less uncomfortably settled in his nostrils. "Not two good weeks together. And our . . . sex life, with Mother, it was terrible."

"Jesus, Dad."

"In Europe as a young one I was with advanced people, modern. The women . . ." he said, pausing in uncharacteristic embarrassment. "We were an advanced group, politically, and also . . . the women . . ." he looked down in something approaching shame, not at the action but for the difficulty of speaking about it to me, "the women . . . used their mouths."

And I felt like reaching across the table and slapping some congratulations on his shoulder. All right, Herschel!

"Oh yeah?" was the most I could manage, but I must have smiled.

He nodded, then managed to look up.

It was such a violation of the decency of his speech, but what was left we couldn't say to each other now?

"But with Mother . . . There was no watchoucull. Spontaneity. No laughter, no what is it."

"Joy?"

He shrugged. "Everything was on schedule, prepared. Mother got things ready, put a pillow on the bed, as if to say Put it there, mister. I felt, it was like it being in a brothel. There was no watchoucull, and after, in the bathroom, the . . . hot water bottle, already was full and ready. It was a miserable thing."

"Oh Dad," I mourned, wanting to say I'm sorry it was such a chore getting me. That there was so little in it for you, except me, and what kind of reward for a life of effort did I look like, across the table? I wanted to tell him I won't fail you, I'll get on with it somehow, but I didn't have the energy to convince him or me, just then.

So we sat there, breathing in and out, but it felt like only breathing out.

In an infinite universe, even when you've finessed your way around Hitler, starvation, Stalin, the most that could be managed of a life, it turned out, was this.

"You know," my father said, "maybe I'd like to have a cup of coffee, if you don't mine."

"I'll make us some," I told him. "But if you think I'm gonna use one of those fff . . . one of those paper towels forget it."

Something my parents had done: folding a length of paper towel, putting it in the cone and filling it with Martinson's, even rinsing it out for a second and third use after I'd shown them the awful chemical flavor it imparted to the coffee—chlorine and who knew what other bitter poisons. Even after tasting and admitting the difference they left the Pyrex paper in the cupboard and used the paper roll, inured to the taste of it, saving the phantasm of a penny. When I wasn't there my father persisted in the habit.

"It's so expensive, that paper," my father said.

I gave him a levelling look.

"Use what paper you like," he said. "But if you don't mine, is there, I know you drink it black but do we have it any milk in the house?"

TWO MORNINGS AGO, freeloading in my friends Peter and Nicole's big Paris apartment this summer while they're down in Bordeaux with the kids, I woke up, my heart pounding fresh from a dream in which I'd been walking with my father. He was on my left as we went, and when the dream faded in we had already spoken of a number of things, now indistinct. Then, all at once filling with fear—perhaps the old dread of not knowing what to do about money but also a terror creeping in from the margins to the effect that I had gotten life fundamentally wrong and that from the position into which I had worked myself it might be too complicated for me to ever get it right: yes, I was getting it wrong and would be judged for it in the harsh court of justice that is this world. I asked my father to help me, to advise me please, to tell me the thing I so much needed to know, which I had all my life long kept relentlessly excluding from acknowledgement and view; and against all precedent my father compressed his lips shut, turned his face a harsh quarter-turn away and quickened his pace so that without taking me by the arm he led me firmly until there was a wall, and around the corner of this wall, there on a bench alone in a faded floral-print cotton dress— and, in a fearful symmetry I didn't plan two chapters back, white cotton socks and bedroom slippers—looking thin and bare and vulnerable, her eyes on me and body bent away as if to avoid a blow I might deliver at any moment, sat my mother. The image held for a moment and then I woke from it into a consciousness so lucid that I never doubted—and once you start messing with dreams it is of the utmost importance to distinguish carefully between the subjective ones and the rare ones that have some purchase on objective truth—that the dream was a veridical record of a real encounter.

I am doing my best to be accurate and honest, but, to say nothing of my poor dead and now defenseless mother, I am also irretrievably aware that Rose, for one, is being painted more luridly than she can possibly deserve. I've tested the residues left by acid truthfulness with the *solvae universalis* of compassion, then the result against the obsidian of fact, and I still don't know if I'm doing something worthwhile or if, fundamentally blinded by the greed of writing or by simple stupid vengeance, I am walking into a world of further crime and consequence, or—what's that other game show?—Truth and Punishment; my hands bloody, axe adangle.

Whatever the verdict, I'll remember the way my mother looked on that bench, her shoulders rounded, her hurt face bent away.

Poor Sadie my mother, I seem to be saying again: after forty years of solitude life fitted you out with an incomprehensible creature who emerged alive from your own body, whom you nourished with your blood and covered in skin you yourself had made, who as he grew larger and stranger and stronger screamed at you to keep away from him when all you wanted was closeness and love given and accepted. For a finish, life reduced your brain to smithereens, unstrung your music until it lay there without design in your hands, and then set me over you, put you in my care, and let me live to write about it after.

What a scheme of things. How exactly measured a divine economy, and what strange exchanges within it when the only uncounterfeited coin in play, as I still believe, with all the shit I've been through and you've been through and we've all been through, is the unalloyed and solar gold of mercy, knock it on the counter and you'll hear it ring and ring, for all the poverty of our experience.

IN MY EARLY CHILDHOOD, the accusative storms of terror apart, she seemed to be everywhere at once putting up protective fences around me, but the warmth of intimacy was usually conspicuous by its absence. The atmosphere was close, but she loomed over me without actually touching, or seldom. Once in a while she hit me, but more than that she was everywhere, a nice-looking woman with her black hair going grey in streaks and waves, perpetually bustling about the apartment seeming to clean the same things two or three times a day; her palpable anxiety for my well-being filled the space around us with an invisible geometry which, inherently unstable, was perpetually threatened with disruption from the teeming world outside: her protection had a crystalline, rectilinear feel to it, and I experienced its form rather than its essence, which of course was an immense unreasoning love, and its only secondary obverse a nearly equal fear. My mother could not, as I begged her with increasing volume and hysteria, leave me alone, because if she did, something terrible might happen at any time. She could imagine these terrible things happening, and before too long, without noticing the transition, since that is how things happen down here, she herself was doing them.

There must have been something of a respite in my middle childhood, when I was distinguishing myself as the smartest, best-behaved nurk in my grade school and was no longer so defenseless an individual at home. I can recall being happy with her, particularly when listening to the radio. At the time it was my impression, despite the evidence of my Victrola and their records, that Frank Sinatra, Patti Page, Eddie Fisher and Doris Day used to spend their days taking taxis from one radio station to another, where orchestras awaited them and after brushing the city soot from their coats they walked up to the microphone and sang their current hits. My mother and I used to listen to them on the oblong maroon plastic General Electric clock radio that sat upon the maple sideboard in the kitchen, the clock set behind a square of clear plastic between two symmetrical wings only one of which held a speaker, in those days before stereo. We would sing along with the music. I had a good voice in childhood, could sing in tune over two and a half octaves, and my mother's wasn't bad either. On long afternoons the music composed itself into an intermediary between us by means of which deeper dissonances could be resolved—how much is that doggie in the window?—and I must have prayed that by means of this magic the intervals of nightmare could be banished completely and for good.

With due respect to Norman Rockwell, I must add that for a while we had a green-and-yellow parakeet name of Pepper who used to join us in these singalongs, perched alongside the radio on the rim of a rocks glass full of ginger ale, dipping her blunted beak down for a sip of the bubbly between happy chirps. This Pepper—hail to thee, blithe spirit!—also liked to lie on her back in the middle of the dining room table and toss a swizzlestick up and down in her feet. Mornings, she would wake me for school first thing out of the cage at 7 a.m. by flying from the kitchen to my bedroom, landing on my head and chirping away until I budged and groaned. Then she'd hop down to the pillow and rub the downy top of her head gently in my still-closed eye until I'd sit up to play with her and say a friendly word, although she never learned to talk back. Her best stunt was reserved for my father. When he sat at the head of the kitchen table to count the money he had brought home from Harlem by subway in a rumpled brown paper bag, Pepper would waddle up and close her beak on the corner of a bill from the top of one of the stacks (singles, fives, tens, the occasional twenty), waddle to the far end of the table with it, let it go and follow its oscillating descent to the floor with a left-right-left of the head. As in a Buster Keaton sketch, my father would creak himself out of his chair, bend wheezing over the belly he had begun to develop, and stoop to pick up the bill while Pepper ran back to the stacks. By the time my father got back down in his chair, Pepper had grabbed a fiver and begun waddling away across the table with a corner of it in her beak to let it go, left-right-left, so that my father would have to get up again, exclaiming with a half-laugh, *"Pep-per,"* and . . . you get the drift of the routine. This bird-and-papa two-step would last until the whole family was laughing and my comically frustrated dad, having already tried to push Pepper away with the back of his hand and gotten angry uncomprehending chirps of protest in return, would finally have to jam the bills back into the bag and quit. Pepper eventually found her way out the kitchen window when the screen was loose and no one knew it till too late, but before this and then despite this, oh, we were happy, happy: happy as a bunch of bozos on a Grecian urn, pursued by the suspect intentions of an ode.

I used to wake early and crawl into their bed Sunday mornings—they slept on a convertible daybed in the foyer, having ceded me the bedroom with its two giant mahogany-frame beds and matching furniture once my grandmother was shunted off to the Home. (Of course they doted on me! Of course I was spoiled! Rotten! This should have been obvious from page one!) Once in their bed I'd feel their warmth, listening to my mother's regular breathing and my father's congested purr, which was occasionally broken by long scary pauses, five seconds, ten, then a soft growl of exhalation, yup, he's still alive. I'd smell my mother's familiar scent and my father's bear-smell—I liked her better—and raise my hands part translucent to the daylight streaming from the kitchen window and through the doorway into the foyer, and look at their backs wondering if my hands were really red inside, if the light was coming through them or just around them, then bending. I wondered if that light had anything to do with the pretty spheres of light that used to come into my bedroom at night and play with me when I was very young, wondered where the consciousness that called itself Me came from and what was its relation to my body, which came from those man-and-woman pictures in my copy of *How Things Work*. I remembered the summer road trips we took to Washington and New England in our first car, the 1953 black Dodge Coronet with a semi-automatic transmission and a charging ram for a hood ornament, and how my mother was a clearminded, decisive driver, and my father hopelessly muddled as to which way to go, often leaving us stranded on a median between choices A and B or twenty miles down the wrong road—I liked her better. By then the size and awkwardness of my father's emotions embarrassed me too, and the way he walked into the Shoreham Hotel in D.C. wearing shorts and carrying a bucket, thinking they would give him a room looking like that, my mother scolding him, correctly I thought, when he got back to the car and Dad saying, incorrectly I thought, that they said they were full up because we were *Jews*— I liked her better. On the other hand, when we visited a dairy farm in Virginia once, he knew how to croon to the cows and stroke their throats so that they turned their big emotive eyes to him and loved him wholly— God knows it may have been the only time in those years I thought him really worthy of my respect. But, oh Lord, he would try singing sometimes too, not along with the radio *like a normal human being* (my mother's phrase) but on his own and without words—ty-rye rye *ree*, went his usual text—standing in front of the bedroom mirror in his undershirt, inflating his barrel chest and unleashing a voice he said was beautiful and cantorial and had been envied in all the synagogues of Europe but which sounded to me like a cross between an animal growl and a seven-storey building falling down. Everything he did was the wrong size, but really, everything was fine, everything was perfect and okay and we could live inside the music when my mother and I blended our voices and sang along with the radio: Love and marriage, love and marriage, go together like a horse and carriage. Oh my Papa, to me he was so wonderful, to me he was so good. Take a ring, and it is round round round as it runs along the ground till it leads you to the one you love. "Mother loves you," my father used to tell me when I seethed with hatred of her later on, in adolescence, when it seemed to me that fighting my way free of her influence, her dominance, her *sexual repressiveness* (I was learning new words) was a fight for my very life. "Mother loves you with an animal love. She is so attached to you . . . Do you know what I mean it by an animal love? the incredible devotion of an animal mother?"

And I would think, in my teens, in my twenties when I visited, even in my thirties ditto, of her automatic face at the fifth-storey window awaiting my return home dreading what might have happened to me in the anonymous night—in which, as it happened, I'd begun to find my name—and I would ask my father, "What good is it?" And I'd use a metaphor peculiarly loaded for him: "She won't let me *breathe*."

But once started, my father would go on dipping the gourd into his own well of memory: "You see, in Europe we always used to say it that the child is either a colt or a calf. The colt," which he pronounced cult, "stays by the side of the mother, it stands against the mother's legs, it leans on the mother's body and looks out from behind her with such big eyes at the world, and it never leaves the side of the mother and goes wherever the mother goes. But the calf it goes away on its own always and the mother full of insecurity has always to run after it . . . The cult or the calf. And you were always the calf, we had to run after you where you went . . ."

And if I was the right cruel and stupid age, in my teens especially, I would have asked him why he was telling me this *shit*, using the word specifically to wound him, or if saying nothing then shooting him a look that amounted to as much. At the root of my anger toward my father you would have found buried a stone rage that he had not protected me from her earlier, when I had no defenses: the impossible task of being a parent, who must be more perfect than God and still more omnipresent or stand accused, no matter what unknown sacrifices have been made.

But with the self-sustaining insularity I have inherited from him too in my fashion, my willful or oblivious father would go on, in the warmth that was his own protection and mine: "You were always the calf. How you made me run after you! Oh, how you made me run. I remember the first time you got up on all fours on your hands and knees and looked around at the world with such a pleasure, look what I have done, like you were a god, looking around at all you could see . . . I'll never forget the look you had on your face, the light you had it in your eyes. And I thought, I would do anything for you. Give up my blood, my life, anything what you want."

"Yeah, right."

"Do you know what I mean it by an animal love? Once in Europe I was out in the field and all of a sudden I couldn't breathe, I fell down, and my mother saw it and she came running and picked me up in her arms and began to run like the wind to the house with me, and I looked up at her eyes above me and I saw this love, this animal devotion, this fierceness that would do anything for me for this love, and—pop!—I could all of a sudden breathe, I was fine. This is the love of a mother. A father can't know a love like this. This is the animal love of a mother that Mother has for you. Some day you will see it."

"Dad, it's the reverse. She won't let me breathe." All I could remember was her, huge and screaming at me for no reason with murder in her eyes.

"No, you don't understand," and, remembering his own mother, able to see past the heartlessness of his son, his eyes would moisten and the warmth would pour from him in waves.

My mother's incapacity for effusive self-invention, for the effortless fabulizing that Zaborovsky men took in with their mothers' milk and breathed out along with carbon dioxide and the smell of onions, leaves her without testimony in this courtroom. But I remember sweet times too, especially once school had freed me from her all-day supervision: she took me to music school on Saturdays, where I played recorder and sang in Earl Robinson's chorus, and she ate burgers and shakes with me at a big midtown Walgreens afterward. She took me to see Maria Tall-chief dance *The Firebird* at City Center. I was fascinated by her name and that she really was an Indian, was pleased to see that she was in fact tall, and especially remembered her at the end of the ballet leaping over paper scrims of gold and orange fire at the rear of the stage into the free blue beyond . . . Memory flails, memory fails, the images drain of their colors, and I can't go back there with better wisdom, turn it all into love naturally expressed and heal us all.

So there we are: my father, my mother, and me, seated together on the comfy sofa of middle-class life, where foreign armies seldom intrude, and most of the wounds are imaginary. Specimen lives, otherwise what possible reason for telling them?

Recently I had a dream that may be relevant.

It lacked the telltale veridical clarity of the Mom & Pop apparition of a couple of weeks back, although in the end it pierced me with a parallel shaft. The imagery began in a subjective muddle in which several times and places were confused, but as it snapped into legibility in the middle of a memorable gathering of family and friends, I said aloud, "I've got to run upstairs and get the camera to take some pictures of this," and in the dream I ran up the several flights to my in fact current waking-world Paris crib, past the layers of scaffolding and plaster dust by means of which the building, an elite *lycée* consecrated to the arts, is being shambled to bits and reconstructed while I ramble solo in an apartment at the top—Peter and Nicole are still down in Bordeaux with the kids. Looking through my dream camera bag I could only find an absurdly long tele-photo lens of at least one thousand millimeters and a still more unwieldy monopod on which to prop the camera—in the world of fact I own neither of these items—and impeded by them I stumbled back downstairs to what was now a fairly blurry family gathering. When I got the camera upright and the lens focused, I could not, because of its awkward focal length, take a picture of anyone in the room—all of them too close to frame—so I pointed the thing at an unrecognizable child five or six years old in a polo shirt and shorts idling in a doorway farther off. Behind him blurry impressionist trees blazed almost uniformly golden in the sun. I got the kid into focus and began to snap away as he rearranged his splayed feet or looked wistfully off left: these pictures, I thought, were going to be good. Joe Agrin materialized at my side out of the indistinctness to say in an irritated voice, the first such he had directed at me, ever, "What are you doing? What good is that fancy lens of yours? All you're doing is taking pictures of my nephew," and I woke from this muddle thinking, nephew? What nephew?

Once I got my mind unstrung from sleep I could appreciate the ingenuity of the construction, and the familiar hammer hit me: Oh. *That* nephew.

DEEP, as Thomas Mann so memorably put it, is the well of the past. To which I would add: deep, making it Deep is the well of the past, deep; or Deep, deep is the well of the past. Another deep would kill it, brevity—I always say—brevity being the soul of wit. Deep, deep, deep is the well of the past sounds like fifties doowop, and you'd also need well, well, well, and past, past, past, for the purposes of parallelism, and a little triplet beat, making it Deep, deep, deep is the well, well, well of the past, past, past, with some background singers going Deep-deep-deep; whereas Deep, deep is the well of the past, deep, sounds like there might be frogs in the well, and I've fallen into it even without the repetitions. So, fine, scramble back to the present tense, don't think just do it, sitting with neither a seacave crone nor an amphibian oracle but a real, nearly blinded, arthritic and unhappy old woman to whom I was inextricably related. Perhaps it was not the living room but I who had turned to stone.

"Sometimes," she was saying, "if I put the chair sideways next to the television and look at the screen out of the corner of my eye, I just manage to see a little bit of a picture. I only watch the news on MacNeil-Lehrer. There's not that much to see, MacNeil or Lehrer, Lehrer or MacNeil, but sometimes it's a relief in the evening just to see the face of another human being."

"Yes."

"But after a while, the strain hurts my eyes. Ahh really: what's the use? At this point, what, is, the, use?"

Rose had made me another cup of coffee by insisting that she wanted one herself and that I might as well join her, so I was sipping Martinson's blue-label without milk or sugar while her own milky cup sat untasted on the ivory-veined black marble of her coffee table.

"What your mother went through," Rose said, "was the worst of all."

I paused for a moment before replying, checking to see that I wasn't being partisan, only exact, and said, "Actually, what my father went through was worse."

There was rage in Rose's return snap: "What Sadie went through was *horrible.*"

"Absolutely. You'll get no argument from me. But she suffered less than he did because, except for rare moments, she didn't know what was happening. It was no picnic for her. Everything she did was going wrong and she experienced terrible confusion and dismay, but she was spared the consciousness of it." There was something pedantic in my tone of voice, but as far as I could tell I was still, strictly speaking, correct. "On the other hand my father, while struggling for his next breath of air, was conscious, minute by minute, as if his eyelids had been sewn open, of the destruction of my mother's individuality and his own."

"Sadie *knew*," Rose insisted, her voice beginning to shake with a rage that had some kinship with my mother's, and sometimes even I come to a stop.

"Maybe so," I said. "After all, I only know so much."

"That's right," she underlined, *"you only know so much,"* and watching the shape of that small woman's fury I knew that I would not be able to ask her the question about my aborted twin, the undermotive of my visit.

She would see it only as some ultimate, defining treason, and it would tick over in her brain that *blood will out,* and I had signed the tribal contract of the Zaborovskys.

I found myself staring thoughtlessly at a familiar lamp that stood beside a loveseat in front of Rose's triple windows, a three-legged freestanding mahogany lamp about five feet tall. Around its waist it wore a hexagonal table with a dadoed ornamental rail. On loan to us until the Agrins took flight from Brooklyn, it had once stood beside a squarish magisterial tasselled green armchair in our living room, my father's chair, the one in which he used to read the papers in the evening—books were read at the kitchen table—by the light of that lamp. One evening in early childhood I had come to him there and asked him despite his reading—I might have been feeling more than usually illegal and excluded—if I could climb up into his arms. He had said Of course, *Puppeleh,* anytime, *Puppeleh,* and I climbed up into the warmth and tobacco smell of his embrace as if I were finally being told that there was a place for me in flesh and on earth. The memory of this trivial incident had come back to me several times during the years of my parents' destruction, and had explicitly rematerialized on my father's deathbed in hugely altered form.

"I might be able to finish that novel about the Bear," I told Rose, who had asked me, by then, to change the subject, what, really, I would be up to in Turkey. The Bear was a literal bear who, in an otherwise realistic novel, talked and played alto saxophone on the New York jazz scene. It had been serialized in the jazz magazine I wrote for and signed up by a publisher, but I had lost track of the character's warmth and humor halfway through. I missed the Bear. He'd been a comforting presence in my life until the cold got to him. I hoped he was only hibernating. It wasn't much of a hope.

"That thing? How long has it been?" Rose asked me.

"Too long. I should have written it quickly. You know, I should have told the magazine to find another editor and written it straight through. I could have finished it in six months but instead I decided to act responsible and adult for a change, and work at the magazine and publish a chapter every six weeks. I should've stayed a kid. I'd have a book out. It would help."

Rose shrugged, as it seemed to me, skeptically.

"It's a little late but I'll give it a try," I said. "When I get to central Turkey—Konya—I'll plonk my typewriter down and give it a shot. It's all plotted out. I just haven't been able to find the right note. The lost chord," I said, doing a small Durante. "Ah cha-cha-chaa." The project sounded doomed even to me.

Rose was not amused. "I hope you'll have a good vacation, if that's what it is, and get yourself back together. Only one thing."

"What's that."

"Don't drift."

Good Lord, I thought. She knows me.

My big question was still unanswered, but it was time to make my escape.

"Is there any chance," I asked Rose, even though I knew the answer, "that I can go upstairs and say hello to Gloria?"

"Gloria doesn't want to see *anyone*."

Her cancer-bald head wrapped in a white turban, the last time I'd seen her.

"And when I go up there," Rose was telling me, "she blames me for *everything*. For what, I don't know. She treats me horribly."

"It's the tumor talking." Chemotherapy had not conquered it, and it was swelling inside her skull. "She loves you."

"She's angry about everything, about dying too—and she has a right to be. She's angry about everything, but she takes it all out on me. Do you know why she should take it out on me?"

"No."

"Have I given her any reason?"

"None. Is there any chance I could go up there? Maybe I could help."

Rose frowned at me for this vanity. "She told me: she wants to see *no one*. No exceptions."

In her turban, face pale and doughy, amid all those packed book-shelves and fine art, my childhood buddy, my brilliant friend later on, my Gloria.

When I had shouldered my bookbag and as we loitered by her door,

Rose started telling me about the recent visits of her grandchildren. "And the other week, Andy"—Ruth's older son—"even sent a car for me and I went up to Westchester to visit them and Nicholas was just wonderful, what a beautiful child, and the twins, well, the twins . . . They're such beautiful little girls."

"That reminds me," I said surprised and supercasually, but my spy's heart was beating hard. "I always wondered how far along my mother was in her pregnancy when she lost my twin."

"What?" Rose asked me, and a strange smile, the first I had seen on her during this visit, played about her features.

I repeated the question.

"What are you talking about?" she said, her face still lent unexpected innocence by the gentle spontaneity of her smile. It was the smile of a young girl. "What do you mean?"

I recited the well-known facts in their least accusative version: "You know, some time into her pregnancy she had a miscarriage, as Adnopoz told her, but when she went back for a checkup a week or so later it turned out that she was still pregnant, and that was me. Originally, there had been twins."

The tiny woman, still smiling, took a half-step back. "I've never heard of this in my life," she said.

"What?"

"Ne-ver. Where did you hear this?"

"From my father. Several times. In childhood and again last year."

"It's not possible," Rose said.

"My father couldn't have made it up."

"*I would have known.* Your mother and I lived, not just in the next apartment, but the same life. She would have told me."

"My father couldn't possibly have made it up."

Rose laughed quietly and shrugged. "Strange."

So we stood there at the door of her apartment, as I began to leave then didn't leave, and parsed the event awhile, coming to no conclusion; but what was strange, apart from Rose's ignorance of the now only alleged event, was the curious lightness, the day's first, that had enveloped us, a spell of innocence in which all partisan feeling had dissolved. My pre-birth adventure had begun to float in a pleasant lack of gravity, in a sort of roseate glow, an amniotic aura I did not penetrate beyond deciding for myself that since my father could not have made the story up and Rose hadn't known about the miscarriage, the miscarriage would have to be dated earlier in my mother's pregnancy than I had thought. Before they had told anyone about the pregnancy at all. When perhaps they weren't sure, until Adnopoz told them it was over, that my mother was pregnant at all.

I saw all of it in a flash and thought it out later.

My father and mother, he thirty-nine and she forty years old at the end of 1945, the Jew-annihilating war barely behind them, guarding this flame that flickered between them, are hooped around the pregnant silence of a maybe child. They tell no one, not even the symbiotic sister on the other side of the wall. They are weaving an invisible nest. They are the geometers of a matrix of a possible soul. When the miscarriage comes they tell no one, because their sense of possibility is not yet exhausted, and to tell the story to anyone would expose their still-living hope to alien air it had no lungs to breathe. This argues my mother's innocence: the contract of hope between my mother and father had not been broken. Neither treachery nor murder has intervened—my father would have left her if he'd thought they had. At the very least there would have been a tremor of conversation betraying veiled rage and it would have sent my mother weeping next door to Rose. There would have been wall-piercing volume to the indictment and the defense. There would have been open warfare, and no secret left.

They hardly knew that she was pregnant. At that point a so-called "enema" would not have signified anything about her will, and all it would have done was eliminate a twin whom my mother, who barely managed to get me born, never could have brought to term. In fact, in the unaided normal course of events she probably would have lost us both. The "enema" may have saved the only life she could have borne.

In other words, my mother was off the hook and free to leave the court.

It was over.

Wasn't it?

And I'd long since forgiven her everything anyway.

Hadn't I?

I enveloped Rose one last time before leaving—she had grown so tiny that a mere hug was no longer possible. Now she barely made it to my breastbone. She seemed as frail as if her bones were hollow, like a bird's. I bent to kiss the thin hair atop her head. This disproportionate hug got the little laugh from her it usually did.

"So: go already. Get yourself together and come back."

As the elevator lowered me to earth I still felt half-dazed, and as I tripped east along 9th Street, the visit to Rose, despite its oddly pleasant conclusion, still felt like one of those glorious occasions, and there were so many of them that year, on which life sticks a pin through your thorax and fixes you to the mounting board when all along you had hoped to get by on your colors, on the useless beautiful outstretched incandescence of your wings.

8

EAST BENEATH THE GREEN HANDS of the trees, the hallucination of personality gradually gave way to the hallucination of New York. Civilization prevailed for about a block, but at the first major intersection the masquerade was over: Broadway was a grey trench choked with poisonous smokes, its walls implacable but glittery about the base with rectangles of commercial lure, its dominant voice the grinding of engines. When the first beggar stumbled at me out of the gears through the smog of the city and the fog of himself I emptied my pocket of change for him. They had stopped hitting me with the mystical double entendres of yesteryear—Elijah or Khidr references generally—but out of a crowd of a thousand they could still pick me out even unseen, eyes down, with only the mercy beam for rangefinder.

As I walked farther east more beggars appeared in the slipstream, the sidewalk a busy weave of bodies from whose colors they emerged, ashen signposts marking the stations of another pilgrimage, another way. In the crowd those not mortally wounded were armored to the teeth, hard eyes going past atop impenetrable fashion statements, haircuts of offput, emanations of Don't Bother Me. I might have been among them if I'd still been capable of the insularity, but I walked through them leaking money from my pockets and the subtler blood of hope from wounds that seemed to be just everywhere on my body. The occasional apparition of a beautiful woman stunned me—improbable in this place, under obvious attack from all sides: loved, hated, coveted, resented, exploited, feared: some of them going by postered on the sides of buses, showing the holy curve of cleavage: what the place had left of Deity. A sentence from a lost chapter of the Bear ticked through my mind: men take refuge from their own ugliness of spirit in the beauty of women.

A block east of Broadway through stone gloom and oven heat, space opened out for Cooper Square and the matte black cube standing on end in the middle a chunk of public art that gave no light back to the day. Life had been better around here once. What had happened to the place? It looked more like a medium-heavy Buddhist hell populated by overcoated tenancies in which obscure and tyrannous obsessions ruled, manshaped cosmological hulks in which the learning process, immured in ever denser materialities, had grown very very slow. The poverty bazaar spread multiform on the sidewalks: whole suits of clothes going cheap, flights of grounded wingtips, the big busted radio of the world. A young girl all in black going by, ostentatiously kissing the shaggy pet rat she held up in front of her like a hood ornament, her eyes bright with self-display and the peculiar shape of love her experience of the world had left her.

WHEN I GOT TO East 10th Street, a third of the way along a southside row of tenements catching the afternoon sun, Hakkı Bey was shooting the breeze on the stoop in a mix of English and Spanish with a couple of Colombian smoke dealers.

"Heyy," he looked up smiling when I got there, "the Lone Ranger."

"How you doing, Hakk."

He spread his arms to indicate the basking block and beyond it the world. "As you see. *Qué pasa?*"

"*Bupkes,*" I replied.

I nodded hello to the Colombians, a dealer-and-lookout pair, and they nodded edgily back. They had their stash taped to the underside of one of the local trashcan lids, and when a Yupmobile eased to the curb or someone in white shirt, dark tie, black briefcase and new haircut walked by nodding a covert yes, the big soft-looking guy with the faint moustache would amble out to talk terms while the smaller cat with the skinny neck loitered near the cans waiting for the nod okay and how many fingers up.

"*Hola*," I said, nodding as amiably as I could.

"*Hola*," and a very equivocal nod were all I got back. I was wearing sandals, faded jeans and an old red Hawaiian shirt made in Romania, but it didn't name that tune. I looked a suspicious outsider to them, and in effect I was one. Fact is, my aura didn't swing too much that year.

Hakkı Bey's block was about evenly divided between art galleries and dope dealers just then. Hakkı was cool, more or less, with the whole population, though he didn't think much of the local art scene and let the gallery owners know it. They didn't know quite what to make of him, this quick little darkish guy—what was he, Persian? Armenian? Arab? Italian? some strange kind of Jew?—in a muscle shirt and street manners saying something fast and deprecatory about the local daubs and letting slip the occasional reference to the refractive properties of oil and acrylic.

"Aaa-*ah*," said my buddy, stretching his arms, I thought, a little ostentatiously. When he'd started drinking again a few months back his liver pains had returned and he went to the gym most days to work the toxins out. He used to have the body of one of the slimmer Greek statues but now that he'd reached his late thirties he'd begun to bulk up, and muscles popped impressively as he stretched. "You're a little late for a Friday movie. It's what, almost four o'clock, and I'm due at Edith's at seven."

"I told you I'd be late. This visit was never about a movie. It's about goodbye." It was also about telling him what I planned to do once I got to Turkey. The prospect of getting Hakkı's blessing for work on Mahmoud's grave worried me, as if with my private sack of griefs I might look like a poacher coming across the fields.

"So you're really going," Hakkı Bey said.

"Thursday."

"Damn, Rafi, you've been talking about leaving for so long I figured . . . you know . . ."

"Ticket paid for. Stuff halfway packed. The apartment full of other people's cartons. Sublet City. Action Comics."

The Colombians began to take their leave with a series of elaborate salutations to Hakkı Bey—they called him *Condorito*, the Little Condor, after a Latino comic-book character, something about the way he'd put on his hooded sweatshirt and roar off on his motorcycle to work—and another set of equivocal nods and gestures for me.

When I looked back at Hakkı Bey he was lighting up an unfiltered Camel. My brand had been Camels too but it had been thirteen years since I'd given up the habit.

"So," he said around an exhalation and a squint across the street, where one of the young Tibetan monks, in mufti, had come to the door of his little shop and waved hello on seeing Hakkı, "you're going off to Turkey and leaving me alone in this fucking wilderness."

"That's the idea."

Hakkı gave the monk a wave back. "Thanks a lot, man." He picked a tobacco shred from his lower lip and blew out a grey-blue spume of carbon precipitate. His deep voice coiled about the syllables. "You know, every day I wake up and it's not too bad until eventually I have to go outside, and then I walk out the door into the . . . unbelievable coarseness of this culture and the delusional state everyone moves through like fish through water, like fish through water, man, and after a minute or two I lose my meditation and I get sucked right in, the brutality, the violence of so-called normal thought . . ." Hakkı looked toward the corner where the Second Avenue Deli sign hung from a shaft. "The whole *schmeer.* New York's bad for me. I've got heavy roots here, a bad past . . . And now you're going off to Turkey. Thanks a lot, old pal."

"Any old time."

Hakkı squared his shoulders for a more general pronouncement and turned to look at me full on with his dark almond eyes. "I look at this as a very dull incarnation on one of the universe's least interesting planets. The only thing I really like to do here, if you'll pardon my coarseness, is fuck. But that's *it.* If I ever had anything to contribute, it's either too late or it's over. I'm ready to leave, any time at all."

"You'd do all right in Turkey."

"Yeah, thanks again for leaving."

"Look Hakkı, I've got to do something. I've lost the ability to hold my life lightly. That's called being stuck. So I'm going back out there. It's what I know to do."

"Let *me* loose over there I'd be just fine, man." He got up from his seat on the stoop to demonstrate his essential uncontainment, then gestured at East 10th Street. "I can't believe I'm sitting still for this shit. I can't believe I'm not in the Middle East or the Caribbean just because I don't have the cojones to quit my job. Thirty-eight years old, the first straight job I've ever had and I can't believe it's turned me into such a fucking coward. I'm afraid of losing my *health insurance.* You believe it?" He ran a hand through his thick black short-cut hair. "I've even started thinking about my *retirement.* I never expected to live long enough to retire from *anything.*"

"Welcome to earth," I told him.

"It's a dull planet but I'd do all right in Turkey or the Caribbean. The Dominican Republic, man, the sun, the sea, miles of beach, all those gorgeous honey-brown girls. Bottle of rum. I'd do fine. Afghanistan."

"They've got a war on there."

"So? There was a war in Pakistan when I was there with Sufi Barkat Ali. We used to sleep outside on the ground and they put tarpaulins over the dome of the mosque so the beautiful turquoise tiles wouldn't reflect the moon and give the bombers a target. Those were the days, man. I had some vision back then. I used to be a contender. Not just another schmuck from Manhattan. All I really want to do is meditate. I'd like to put on a loincloth, walk off down the street and leave it all behind."

"Do it without the loincloth," I told him, "they'll give you a nice little cell to meditate in and three square meals a day."

Hakkı seethed at me for a moment. He didn't like it when other people got the punchlines.

"Look," I said, "I ain't setting my sights all that high this year. I'm just looking to get by."

As I said this I was struck by the contrast with my first departure for

Turkey eleven years earlier, summer of 1975. I'd talked modestly then too, but I hadn't believed a word of it. Aimed like an arrow of longing at the Absolute, I'd been half-wild with the prescience of a pilgrimage to appointed places, a succession of established stations along the capital *P* for path. I talked a line of modesty, even to myself, but that was a hedge against my egoism, pure self-defense. Hakkı had come back from Turkey just that spring—for the last long stretch he'd been living with Mahmoud Rauf, a man then known to me only through a handful of colorful stories and one color photo I'd seen in England in January 1973: a thin, elegant old man with a large curved Ottoman nose, European rather than Asiatic coloring, a thinning backswept mane of white hair and a straggly white moustache. The photo, shot from above, found him sitting on an old wooden chair in worn-out clothes, lacquerless floorboards beneath him and a black potbelly stove out of focus behind him: the three-by-five glossy had been passed in front of me and I'd said *Who is that beautiful old man?* and had practically fallen into the room in the picture, felt the temperature of the air and the dryness of the old stove's heat, the dust trodden into the floorboards, the particular time of day. Touching base with Hakkı Bey before my departure in '75 had felt like a necessary ceremony, then as now.

When Hakkı came back from Turkey then, I'd been living up in Boston in a rundown townhouse, playing jazz in the clubs at night, working in a record store days, writing what little I could in my spare time, and one night late in March I saw Hakkı in a dream: he was playing on a beautiful little Gretsch drumset and Turkish cymbals in a style somewhere between my own and Tony Williams', and then, abruptly, we were sitting in the bleachers facing my high school athletic field slicing the palms of our right hands open with a hunting knife and doing the blood brother handshake. A skinny little brownskin girl—whom neither of us had met yet but who would turn out to be Shareen, the future mother of Hakkı's daughter Rabia—leaned forward and said, "That's *heavy*. That means whatever happens to *him* is gonna to happen to *you* and whatever happens to *you* is gonna to happen to *him*." The next morning my Boston phone rang and it was Hakkı calling from Queens to say he was back in the States. His oldest friend Gregory Volkhonsky's parents had died on vacation in Mexico when their plane crashed into the ruins of an ancient Mayan city, and he'd come back from Turkey to take care of his friend in the aftershock. Three days later I drove down from Boston—for a few weeks my folks had lent me the then current family chariot, a dark-blue Dodge Dart whose punctured body my father had patched here and there with tin-can lids he painted navy—drove down through an ice storm, the slate sky streaming sleet, past galleries of bare black trees, each distinct branch and twig encased in a crystal integument, and the roads lethal with a smooth unseeable variant of that enchantment all the way to the Volkhonskys' death-shuttered, storm-beaten house in Forest Hills. Hakkı and Greg, Greg's kid brother Peter, and Peter's girlfriend Holly, who looked like Nefertiti, and I mean *exactly* like Nefertiti—despite the swelling proportions of her second-generation Jewish-American vowels and the lack of Egyptian headgear, Holly was the unimpeachable image of the famous bust of Akhnaten's queen—were living in Greg's suddenly gone parents' brick-and-timber house, the bathtub full of unwashed dishes, Gregory snorting a little smack, and Hakkı Bey, although joining in for a comradely line now and then, starting to whip the joint into shape and tend to its grieved and spaced-out residents. Hakkı and I shook hands hello, definite twinning mirror effect in the thinning scrim of house, furniture, rambling human forms. Later we went calling on a friend of Greg's a block away: as it happened there was a neat little Gretsch drumset in the basement and Hakkı and I took turns on it. Hakkı hadn't played anything heavier than hand drums in fifteen years but had retained a surprising amount of touch on the traps, and three months later, lofted by a sudden wealth of unemployment insurance money the agency had inexplicably let accumulate unpaid for months, twenty-nine years old and at the peak of my vital energies, I was on an airplane heading east into the radiance of what is still probably my favorite year, while Hakkı was pairing up with Shareen to beget their daughter. Whatever happens to *him* is gonna happen to *you*, and whatever happens to *you* . . . My first Turkish year—Hakkı had so recently left Mahmoud's that our ice storm meeting seemed a handoff in a relay race—had been filled with an order of visionary experience in the midst of which, if you had told me that in ten years' time I'd be stuffed back into the darkling basement beneath the Mom & Pop store of subjective psychology—a place like Blake's chinked cavern of the Senses Five, only very, very Jewish—well, I would have laughed in your face and told you I was beyond that stuff forever. But sitting there in the warm declining light of 10th Street eleven years after the ice, I felt unrevivably weak and empty, with no energy or will to offer up in sacrifice or trade for radiance or vision. "Really, Hakk," I said, "it's a cold world this year. Someone offers me a warm corner to lie down I'll probably take it."

He regarded me from beneath a cocked eyebrow. "If that's the way you're thinking, you haven't got a chance," he said.

"Thanks."

"You gonna see Tash in London?" Hakkı asked, sounding a chime of our worldflung unofficial family. "And Siddiqa?"

"I'm staying at Tash's when I get to London," I said, and rolled my eyes. "Sid later, I imagine."

"You know, Rafi, what I always remember about Tash is that no matter how awful his personality gets, I'm always aware of a higher level of reality acting through him."

"Yeah, and what's worse is he knows it."

"But even when he ruins it," Hakkı said in an instructional tone, "it's still there, Rafi. Try to remember that."

"When'd you last see him, ten years ago? The way he's drinking now . . ."

"We're all drinking now, Rafi. He calls me at four in the morning sometimes, drunk out of his mind, a real pain in the ass, ordering me to come to England and yammering at me in baby-talk Arabic, and even then . . ."

"But you're right," I told him officially, so he'd drop the subject. "Even when he's at his worst, that higher thing is always working."

"Anyway, tell him Hakkı Bey says hello. Sid too."

He examined his cigarette and rolled the edge of its cinder carefully round on an edge of concrete step. "Think you'll see Bulent?" Bulent was Mahmoud's immense, surviving brother.

"He's usually in Turkey in the summer. I'll probly miss him."

"I'd really like to see Bulent, man."

"I only have two real regrets in my life, and not spending enough time with Bulent's one of them. The other one's about a girl," I laughed, "I wish I'd taken out in high school."

"How old is Bulent now?" Hakkı Bey asked.

"Seventy-something. And there's been another cancer operation."

"Well, *I'll* never see him again in this world. Have a nice trip, and if you see Bulent tell him Hakkı Bey says hello. Maybe I'll get lucky and die quick of natural causes."

"Keep drinking your way into liver pain and you might make out. And AIDS ain't just for homosexuals anymore. You use condoms with your girls from Eileen's?"

"I use 'em but they break."

"You break latex condoms? What the hell you doing in there?"

Hakkı Bey shrugged, it seemed to me, rather modestly under the circumstances. "They break." He stretched his arms in front of him, interlocked his fingers and cracked them backward. "You want to come in for a couple of minutes? I've got a few things to do before I go to Edith's."

"Whatever's right."

He dragged himself standing and looked down the street both ways. I remembered a conversation we'd had, somewhere in the neighborhood, just before I left for Turkey in '75. "Well Rafi, they say that a pilgrimage," he'd told me importantly, and drawn a large circle in the air with his index finger, then spiralled the circle smaller to end on my heart, "they say a pilgrimage really only takes place *here*." And fingertipped my breastbone for emphasis. I'd said something in answer about how sometimes you have to go through the motions of the lesser pilgrimage in order to accomplish the essential involutions of the greater. How, if you do it right maybe they're the same. Hakkı had nodded his approval at the time.

9

I N T H E S E L A T T E R D A Y S he lived in a slot at the back of a slot, a narrow three-room railroad flat at the back of the straitened circumstance of the tenement's ground floor, his doorway stuck in a corner behind the cramped ascent of stairs. "Rafi," he asked me once he had worked his keys through the gnashing metal challenge of the locks and we had entered his lair, "isn't this place terrific? I mean everybody and his brother wants to live in this neighborhood and I found this *unbelievable apartment.*"

"Uh-huh," I said without real commitment, but allowed for the fact that it was a fairly recent acquisition. Hakkı acquired so few things.

"I mean *really*," he said, filling a small aluminum kettle from the tap at the little sink in the corner and pivoting across the tightish entrance-kitchen to put the kettle on the stove and light the burner, "who'd believe it?"

He did have a point. Hakkı Bey was paying the kind of rent that no longer really existed in New York. Until recently he'd been living, not far off, in a room in his mother's flat sixteen flights above First Avenue; his mother was away most of the time in the Merchant Marine, working on military ships in the Mediterranean, and the other rooms were given over, so Hakkı told me, to mental patients just out of hospitals and psychiatric halfway houses trying to reaccustom themselves to the world. What they got was Hakkı Bey: there had been some comedy, though nothing, really, you could sell to the TV networks by the half hour. Just that winter, his mother had come back from the Med and stayed awhile, padding around the apartment and letting the former mental patients have a piece of her mind. It dawned on Hakkı that he had to get out of there. Following the beam of his perking psychic radar, he walked a couple of blocks in the rain and looked up at a heavyset Dominican man leaning in a tenement doorway sipping from a pint of rum in a brown paper bag. Without thinking twice Hakkı pulled two C-notes from his pocket for the key, the fixtures and the goodwill, and moved in a couple of days later. The rent was $140 at the time and had gone up in increments since but had yet to reach $200 a month. When you considered that Hakkı Bey was making enough money to live almost anywhere in town, the flat was an easy landing for someone who didn't much care about his place in the material world. "It's all right," I allowed.

"It's a *great* place," Hakkı told me, "an absolute steal."

Five nights a week at around half past six, Condorito flipped the hood of a sweatshirt over his head, carried a black helmet in his hand and made his way past the terracotta frieze of smoke dealers on the stoop to his motorbike—a 500cc one-cylinder Suzuki thumper, a scaled-down chopper slung low enough to be the only bike Hakkı had ever owned astride which he could put both feet on the pavement—then blared his way midtown to the mostly dark offices of one of the major TV networks, where, installed in his glassine booth in a row of other such cubicles, all untenanted, he would switch the computer on—one of the most advanced and expensive in the nation—and turn out elegantly nuanced backdrops for the network's national breakfast yammer show. Hakkı had also designed the show's nationwide logo, a red sun rising from steely letters that spelled out the program's name, the design sense sound and Hakkı's old touch evident in the varied luster of the steel. The once-visionary artist of mindscapes, spacecraft, dervishes and *djinn* had adapted his skills to fit the demands of the working day, and a certain otherworldly finesse still glimmered from his productions.

That he had gotten the job at all and held onto it was remarkable in itself: having surreptitiously read the file upside down on the desk of the state employment officer who'd told him, I can't send you there, until you get your portfolio reshot—at the time his life was a choice between subway fare and a hot dog—he'd been hired as a walk-in, a temp for two weeks one winter. Occasionally parading behavior that scared most normal humans half to death and helping himself regularly to slugs from a pint of Smirnoff hidden in his satchel, Hakkı did work with the airbrush that was so fast and fine that the network kept him on past his original term, renewed him, then renewed him again, and when the first generation of powerful art computers evolved, they bought two out of the extant three and put him in training. The computer skills were electronic extensions of everything Hakkı had learned about pen and ink, ink and air, and when he learned to work the virtual equivalents faster than anyone else in the program they'd told him, Young man, you've got a niche. His first year on the box he'd stat his work onto slides and keep them in a portfolio out of pride or just in case, but a while later he just let them hit the air and go. Hakkı Bey accepted his slot as given and devoted no thought to hustling himself an independent career with book jackets or record covers or a studio of his own. Although he was making good money, he didn't get a commission for particular coups, like the logo the nation's eye saw daily on air and go past on the sides of buses. He said he was working for scale and was paid on schedule, like everyone there. He'd been on the job a couple of years and had bitched about it from the outset, but he worked unsupervised at night, he was making rent, putting money in the bank, and although he hadn't given up the one-night girls he met around the corner at Eileen's Broadway Bar, he'd recently begun a steadier weekend liaison with a Chinese woman, Edith, a couple of years his senior, in which actual sentiment seemed to be involved. Regular employment may have cramped his style here and there and kept him from leaving the corrosive city in a loincloth or the known surface of Earth dressed only in his body of light, but it had also, it seemed to me, stabilized him a little.

I pulled the fridge open. "Glad to see success hasn't spoiled you. You still have the traditional contents: lightbulb and a pack of Luckies."

"Look in the door."

"Hey. Half a quart of flat Pepsi. Way to go."

"And in the next couple of minutes I'll mix you up the best rum and Coke you ever tasted."

"You actually got a lime?"

"Rafi," Hakkı Bey said, "go into the other room and sit down for a couple of minutes while I shave. Then, if I don't punch you out first, I'll make you an absolutely fantastic Cuba libre."

"Deal," I said, and went one room farther in.

Hakkı's middle room had, on the left, a red lacquered door that opened into a small closet with a toilet inside. Farther along that wall a shower-bath was concealed in tall darkstained plywood boxwork. Across the room from this, an old white metal kitchen cabinet with glassed-in shelves in its top stood beside an aluminum card table with a grey mother-of-pearl top: exemplary items of New York Nondescript. I loitered beside the card table to look at the photos on display: Hakkı Bey wearing ceremonial whites, shaven head wrapped in a turban, among darkskinned dervishes in Pakistan, '70 or '71, Hakkı for once the tallest person in the picture, his eyes intensely alight, his arms around his buddies' shoulders; a recent snapshot of his honey-brown daughter Rabia smiling prettily from Portland, Oregon, at the age of ten; a fading poster of a rampant bull elephant that had come with the apartment; a slickly photographed motorcycle calendar, heavy on sculptured chrome curvature gleaming out of darkness; intensely green postcard palm trees from his natal Caribbean; and a smiley shot of the Dalai Lama.

"The other morning," Hakkı said, appearing in the kitchen doorway, shaving brush in hand, his face partly lathered, "pardon me while I scrape the hair off my vehicle."

"Sure. The other morning what."

He withdrew. "The other morning," came his voice, altering its timbre as he stretched his face to lather his neck, "I woke up and the first thing I came back to myself as—no tricks, just how I woke up—was an arc of beautiful blue light. An arc of blue light, Rafi. After that, the other colors of the spectrum precipitated themselves one by one, and I lay there thinking, Isn't this wonderful? isn't this a wonderful experience? aren't I lucky to be having this wonderful experience? After all the colors settled, I recognized myself as a subtle body and only after that as material form, as a body made of flesh. Isn't that something?"

"You've been meditating again," I told him. Over the years I had gotten used to the idea that every time Hakkı Bey went out on a new vision-quest or only up for air, he would come back funny for a while. On occasion he'd do time in Bonkersville, and take a few turns around the town square ringing the bell of the famous Bonkersville trolley, but eventually, better refitted for the uses of this world, he'd resume the familiar form of the man I knew: my wilder, braver brother, sometimes getting a mindburn for having flown too near the sun: my brother whom the shores of madness daunted not. No, sometimes he dove for them grinning and inspired, or just as often plummeted like a dumbbell. Nobody's perfect, but I'd always thought him a better man than I, for all the din of his act. Of all my friendships that were based upon an implicit twinship, my link with Hakkı Bey was the twinniest. He was the only person of my generation I really trusted on the difficult, essential things. When he wasn't wholly nuts at least.

"You know that dream?" he asked me, stretching across the kitchen doorway to dip his shaving brush into the boiling water in the kettle on the stove, then applying it roughly to his face. He reddened with the heat, but did not wince or flinch. "Let me show you how a *man* shaves," he growled, laughing.

"I'm so impressed. Which dream."

"The one . . . wait a minute." He gestured with the brush and withdrew. "You know the dream," came his voice, "where you're flying alongside a star?"

"Not really."

"Well, the other night," Hakkı said, briefly back in view again, this time with a stripe of cheek shaved clear, "instead of just flying past the star, I thought, wait a minute. I turned around and, Rafi," he made a swan-dive motion with his arms, the razor in his right hand scattering droplets of water, *"I flew right into it."*

"How'd you make out?"

"Fantastic."

The star-dream seemed wholly characteristic of a man who in a certain circle could be referred to without need of further identification as the Human Torch—but it also seemed to me that outer space had not always brought Hakkı Bey his best luck. He had done fine among the dervishes, I felt, both in the Middle East and the Declining West, but when he hooked up with the spoonbenders from outer space, it was not long before he disappeared over the rim. It was never clear to me just how he ran into Uri Geller and Andrija Puharich, but when I came back from Turkey in '76 he, Shareen and the newborn smiling butterball of Rabia—born, of course, with a perfect five-pointed star inscribed by nature on the sole of each foot—were living in Puharich's house in Ossining, New York, a big white colonial job called Lab Nine that was chocked with psychics and mediums busy tuning into extraterrestrials who regularly beamed them, Hakkı told me excitedly, the larger physics, including the immaterial orders, of the Unified Field Theory: the whole bandwidth of being, the entire sine-wave curve of which humans with their limited sensory and intellectual apparatus had so far only deduced a stretch of middle segment. I'd visited Lab Nine once on a drive down from Woodstock with my friend Sara and I'd thought Hakkı was overawed by the psychics. Behaving with elaborate humility, he described himself as no more than Lab Nine's houseboy, helping to keep the place running, washing the dishes, sweeping the floors and keeping out of the big people's way. Lab Nine was popping, Hakkı told Sara and me at the vacated dinner table in a half-whisper as he sponged it clear of crumbs while the big folks—in their neat clothes and regulation haircuts they seemed like junior execs, or mid-range academics drawing a bead on tenure—had gone into the other room to watch something on the big TV. Silverware, Rafi, was spontaneously bending all over the place, a full-grown oak tree had appeared overnight in the middle of someone's backyard, Uri Geller had dematerialized from midtown Manhattan one afternoon and rematerialized twelve feet in the air above Lab Nine's porch: when he fell through the porch roof, scattering shingles and landing ass-backward on the loveseat, everyone in the house thought the boiler had exploded and we all ran outside: Oh, hi Uri. What are you doing *there?*

While Hakkı told me the story, Shareen sat with burbling Rabia in her arms and, like Sara, kept her own counsel.

Hakkı Bey's big trouble probably began with the government surveillance of Lab Nine. At Puharich's urging Uri Geller had gone public, bending spoons and popping IUDs on commercial television, speaking only slightly more privately about flying saucer people; and there was a lot of speculation at the time, often in connection with Geller, about psychic warfare with the Russians. Some of Uncle Sam's darker minions had come calling on Geller to work for them early on but had been turned down flat, or so went the legend. Puharich himself had begun his psychic researches as a doctor in the American military, and had quit because he didn't like the uses to which his research was being put; so the Powers, one understood, were onto him from the beginning. Hakkı Bey's particular problem was that his mother happened at just that time to be working on one of the U.S. Navy's more sophisticated electronic spy ships in the Mediterranean, and even though her particular work was nonsecret, this conjunction was too significant for the Surveilling Powers to overlook. One morning at his mother's flat in Manhattan, as Hakkı tells it, my buddy surprised two athletically built men in dark suits and steel-frame shades going through the morning paper that had been left at his door. An attractive young woman who was not a matriculating mental patient moved into one of the spare rooms and began playing up to Hakkı Bey and asking him a lot of pointy questions; when she asked him to do a healing on her, and he laid hands on and inevitably embraced her, she convulsed and vomited out an enormous volume of thick black bile; the next day an athletically built young man with thin lips and neatly cut hair was seated immovably in a chair at the door of her room, admitting no callers and answering no questions. That night a second similar piece of gristle took his place, so Hakkı said. But as is famously well known, even paranoids have enemies: one fine day in Ossining, Lab Nine blew up and burned to the ground, fortunately when no one corporeal was at home. Something hasty and official was said about the boiler, but no credible cause of the explosion was ever ascertained. One day soon after, Hakkı went driving to Washington in a car with the sexy black-bilious government agent, and the car crashed, rolled, glass fragments flying everywhere—the whole rending experience in slow explicit experiential detail—and then, one radically discontinuous moment later, he found himself sitting alongside the girl on the roadside next to the uncrashed car, its engine peacefully idling—for material discontinuity, it was his version of Geller's porch dive. Employees of the Agency later approached Hakkı Bey—how much of this actually happened it is now impossible for me to know—offering sums of money, and in the presence of his visiting mother—he had insisted on her presence—laid out a contract for a book deal: a number of books "authored" by him would appear in print and generate such-and-such an income the first year, so-and-so the second. For this the Agency would enjoy the pleasure of an occasional chat with him. Hakkı declined the offer, but his mother, Hakkı told me, sitting at the kitchen table over the cups of instant coffee she had made for everyone—sugar?—revised her conception, as he had intended, of her firstborn son's wandering sanity.

But of course, as Chico told Groucho, everyone knows there ain't no sanity clause: somewhere in Hakkı Bey the chaos of the inner world met the chaos of the outer and blurred, the doors of perception got painted funny colors, borders were crossed by funny-looking troops in irregular fashion and some unfortunate chemicals were thrown into the cocktail shaker of events and the contents got splashed around. Before long Hakkı Bey—though it pained me to see it, since paranoia is such a low order of imaginative invention—was uncovering federal agents everywhere, in that rug-cleaning van parked over there or, bam, grabbing hold of some startled passerby on the street—"Rafi, I'm too fast for them, I'm blowing their agents off the *map!*" This was in Colorado: a bunch of his friends were there and we all tried to help him—"I know ya woikin' fo' the C-I-A," he sang to me when I chanced one more intervention—but he left for New York, where one night, at about 3 a.m., he was typing a letter in his mother's kitchen and one of the former mental patients came out to ask him to please stop, I'm trying to sleep, and Hakkı was inspired to understand that the sound of his typing had triggered trace memories of this federal agent's machine-gun training, which was why he was so upset. So Hakkı dragged him out onto the balcony, sixteen storeys above concrete walkways, small fenced-in geometric gardens and an empty flagpole with its fastener banging in the nightwind, and held the guy off the edge awhile, probably snarling something memorable in his face for the duration.

At about this time, I proposed to some friends that we get Hakkı Bey out of the country before he killed somebody or got killed himself, and we raised the money, shipped him to England, thinking madness would not be noticed in him there. Besides, we hoped Bulent might agree to help him. But Bulent, for all his years, experience and generous disposition—although he had also long urged us not to confuse the spiritual life with psychotherapy: if you have a problem, see a doctor—surprised us by not particularly wanting to see our orbiting friend; through intermediaries, he suggested that Hakkı wear twenty-four peas around his neck on a string and eat one pea a day: when the peas were finished Hakkı Bey would be well. What could we say? Give peas a chance? Bulent's usually impeccable input had seemed, in a difficult psychic season, only one more suggestion from Nutville that year, and besides, draping a string of peas around Hakkı's neck was more than a little akin to the mouse plan to hang a bell on the housecat; so Hakkı landed without a medicinal festoon of *Pisum sativum* at Siddiqa's little Cotswold stone house in a small Gloucestershire village. He chased her around the furniture awhile, repeating *mascara, mascara*—Sid had always favored silver jewelry and a fair amount of makeup. Her son Aaron, who ordinarily didn't see things, kept noticing some kind of flame-beings out of the corner of his eye around the rooms and when he came back from school in Cheltenham every evening fully expected to find his home burned to the ground. Clearly, Hakkı would have to move on. After a number of stops with other friends who found themselves likewise unable to house the Torch, he transferred his presence to the abandoned Cambodian Embassy in London—the Khmer Rouge were in genocidal sway back home, and outlying bits of the old official apparatus were appropriated by the random forces of international crashpadism: Hakkı slept on the cold littered floor in the secretariat and wrote visionary doggerel on Embassy stationery. "Put your aces where your face is, and the places be the same," one verset advised us: something to do with the effect of enemas on one's chakras. There were many poems about "the old warhorse that was reshod in the field." After some months, Bulent cannily sent two attractive women as emissaries to fetch him to safety up in Scotland, but it was too late: by then Hakkı wanted only warmth, and even Bulent's was not enough. His search for the sun led him to the French Riviera, where the green sea calmed him and he made a small living setting up umbrellas and deck chairs for the rich folks on the beach. From there he graduated to the crew of somebody's fabulous yacht, sailed the Mediterranean awhile— he might have crossed wakes with his mother or turned up on one of her ship's omnipercipient screens—sometimes playing flamenco guitar for the nighttime cocktail get-togethers and collecting the occasional C-note in tribute to his art. Eventually the yacht careered across the Atlantic to cruise the Caribbean, and all in all it was a couple of years before Hakkı Bey trickled back perfectly sane onto American soil.

ALL OF A SUDDEN my brain registered what my eyes had been seeing for some time. There was an old blue tie hanging over the back of the flimsy wooden chair pulled up to Hakkı Bey's table. Hakkı Bey didn't wear ties but I'd seen it there in times past. I couldn't take my eyes off it, and when Hakkı asked me some question from the kitchen and I didn't answer, my nonresponse produced his inquisitively leaning upper body in the kitchen doorway. He clocked me staring at the tie, then me staring at him.

"Aw man, say it ain't so," I told him.

"Rafi, I'm all right," Hakkı said.

"Famous last words."

"Leave it alone, Rafi."

My heart turned leaden and hit bottom. It must have shown in my face.

"Okay Rafi, I'm gonna tell you about it and then we'll drop the subject. Last weekend I was getting ready to go over to Edith's, and I knew we were gonna do a lot of drinking and my liver already hurt, so I figured I'd give my liver a rest and I went out to cop, and Rafi, it was the funniest thing."

"I'm in stitches."

"I came up on these two guys on Avenue D and asked to buy a few bags and they looked me up and down, and you know, I look healthy, I've got muscles, a tan, my eyes are clear, and this guy said, 'Maan, I wouldn't sell you a pack of *Marlboros.*'"

"They made you as a cop."

"They made me as a cop and so did everyone else on the block. I had to ask Pablo out front to cop for me and he did."

"How was it."

"It was fine, Rafi."

I pointed my jaw at the tie slung over the chairback.

"Not today," Hakkı said. "And I'm not getting a habit. I know what I'm doing with the stuff. I know my limits."

"Famous last words," I said again.

"I'm not getting a habit, and that's all we're gonna say about it or you're leaving."

I thought about it and the answer was no, both out of fear of a farewell dissonance and because there were still things he and I had to say. "Hakk, I hope you do know what you're doing with this shit."

"I do. That's it, Rafi. Finished? Stay or go."

"Finished," and I did my best to let the subject and its attendant weight fall free.

I wandered into the last of Hakkı Bey's three in-line rooms, and my eye was drawn to his remaining guitar, hanging from a nail in the shade of the loft bed, left. He had beautifully embellished its lady-shaped curves with an intricate woodburn of winding vines and precisely articulated leaves, but acoustically it was not much of an instrument. I could hear him saying, in a variety of discontented voices down the years, that there wasn't *time* to be an artist in this life, that there were more important— more unalloyedly spiritual—things to do. It had never seemed that way to me: I had never seen the separation and in fact for me the two categories of experience were essentially the same.

Once upon a time Hakkı had been wonderful playing the guitar: his flamenco technique never flamboyant, its necessary fires cultivated but contained, so that their heat was realized in the listener, not as pyrotechnic display. Hakkı Bey's approach came out of the classical rigor of Sabicas and especially Niño de Ricardo rather than the flash of Manitas de Plata or the pure virtuoso command of Carlos Montoya. He was not an incredibly fast player in any case, but he sounded his notes with a fine precision of feeling, and nailed them savvily into place in the serious impassioned structure of *cante jondo*. Hakkı's hands were not large, and there was a fading black jailbird tattoo heart at the base of his right thumb. His pose with the instrument had been a good one too, the guitar resting on his raised, triangulated knee, his body bent over the wood and strings, his head inclined, dark features now explicitly Gitano, eyes compressed almost shut and the stub of a cigarette burning down in a corner of his mouth, lips tight and a blue thread of smoke ascending: it made a great picture. Women swooned, some of them, and guys, some of them, thought, Damn, *that's* how I meant to be. His old guitar, the Spanish one bought from a small skillful maker somewhere in the dry heat of Al-Andaluz, the one he'd played in restaurants and road-show companies of *Man of La Mancha*, had gone missing in his saucer-people period, lifted from him one night by thieves and junkies in Union Square. "All I had left in this world was my guitar, Rafi," he told me on the phone at the time, as I sat there in Colorado with mutual friends listening on an extension downstairs. "They took my guitar, so *I took the park*. You hear me? All my uncle left me was his moustache," a complex reference to the deceased Mahmoud, "so I walked in there, man, and I *took the fucking park*."

Happily, it was at about this time that we succeeded in raising enough money to ship him to England.

The loft bed was pushed nearly to the ceiling by heavy darkstained beams and a rudimentary ladder fixed to its foot. He kept a TV and a telephone up there. Bookshelves were distributed here and there about the room: paperback thrillers, eclectic bits of history, the odd literary novel. The rear wall was veiled left to right by a bright blue synthetic curtain he'd found there when he moved in, one edge pulled aside to reveal a narrow window with heavy vertical iron bars inset: you could see a brick wall about ten feet off and what seemed a perpetual sifting down of city ash. In front of the curtain sat a white ceramic giraffe three or four feet high; Hakkı had found it on the street, glued its broken neck together and tied a red bandanna around the join. The ceiling of Hakkı Bey's backmost cell was high, the walls lacquered, on this face or that, white or light blue. The overall effect was that of oddments fetched up in a hermit's cave.

I sat down beneath the gallows of the loft bed in the square foam armchair Hakkı had also pulled in off the street, and looked across the room at the two high wall-mounted bookshelves he had consecrated to esoteric lore: a run of Sufi volumes, some Vedanta, then a uniform blue march of Alice Bailey occultism with its proliferating emanations, bodies and rays; but commanding the center of the upper shelf was the posed black-and-white photo portrait of Bülent Rauf, our late friend Mahmoud's surviving brother. Bulent and Mahmoud, two Turkish brothers born near our century's beginning, had been so unalike—Bulent the fat rich epicurean mystic, Mahmoud the thin impoverished devotee of Freud and Jung—resembling each other only, it sometimes seemed, in their high Ottoman ancestry, the subtlety of their culture and the expressiveness of their eyes. They had never got along, and the Mutt and Jeff stories of their opposition had, in some circles, been played upon and raised into the blurry, too-revised realm of fable to dramatize an opposition of principles, a clash of light and dark or yes and no. In the photograph, Bulent smiled a mite uncomfortably for the camera, not particularly liking to be shot but acceding to the general demand for a portrait. He looked at the viewer with bagging, Rembrandt eyes. In fact, Bulent looked more than a little like a late Rembrandt self-portrait, and if his eyes were as full of time as any the artist had ever painted, the echoes of loss in Bulent's were not fundamental, a secondary shade that lent poignancy and depth to an at least equal measure of, what to call it, twinkle. But what exactly twinkled there? It was quite a face.

"You know," I called to Hakkı two rooms off, "one time I was sitting with Bulent—"

"What?"

"Wait a minute." I creaked myself up from the too-low foam chair, rucked my jeans down off my knees, walked to the entry-kitchen and leaned my shoulder in the doorframe. Hakkı seemed to have finished shaving but was examining his face critically in the glass, stretching its leather here and there. "I was sitting with Bulent after lunch one day up in Scotland with this English upper-class guy named Aziz, actually the future Lord Locke, hereditary seat in the House of Lords, the whole she-bang—and Aziz had Bulent sort of buttonholed—"

"How do you do that?" Hakkı asked me, roughly reshaving the face that was by now swept almost completely clean of lather. "How do you buttonhole *Bulent*?"

"He's not as fierce as he was when you knew him. Anyhow Aziz said in his plummy upper-class accent, 'You know, Bulent, I had the oddest dream the other night,' and Bulent blinked those eyes at him and said, '*Cheese.*'"

"CHEESE," Hakkı Bey said. He threw his head back and laughed. "*Ah* ha ha *haaah.*"

"That wasn't the punchline," I told Hakkı, but he didn't seem to hear me and I waited for him to subside. "So Aziz asked him, all polite and very English, '*Cheese*, Bulent?' And Bulent said," and I did Bulent's fat, ripe, fluttering voice, "'They say that if you eat cheese before going to bed that you will have strange dreams.'"

Hakkı Bey chuckled appreciatively.

"Anything to avoid hearing about Aziz's dream, right? but Aziz was oblivious. 'I don't *think* I ate any cheese, Bulent, but in this *particular* dream—' Bulent took a sip of coffee from the dregs of his demitasse and asked him, 'Shall I tell you the *worst* dream I ever had?' Well, what could the guy say?"

Hakkı Bey rinsed his face clean of remaining lather and leaned down into the basin laughing to himself.

"'Yes, Bulent, please,' Aziz said. 'Well,' said Bulent," I told Hakkı Bey, still doing the old man's voice: Turkish with an aristocratic English overlay, voluptuous, plummier than anything Aziz could summon up, "'it was a *long* dream, it was a *very* long dream. It was the longest dream I've

ever had, and it always seemed that I was about to meet someone significant in it: something important was always about to happen. But all that
ever happened was that I met *another* group of people, who were always
about to take me to *another* place and this *other* person with whom the
significant something would take place. But when we got there, that
person had just left, and we had to go on to still some *other* place, and *another* group of people among whom the significant something again
was promised . . . You see how it was, my *dyah*,'" Bulent's pronunciation
of "my dear" ample and unsentimental, the English substitute for the
unimportable Turkish informality *janım*: my soul. "'I kept going from
one place to the next and from one group of people to the next, and
the important thing was always deferred, until finally,' and Bulent paused
here for another sip from the bottom of his coffee, 'until finally I had
no choice.' 'Yes, Bulent?' Aziz and I said more or less in unison. Bulent resumed: 'Finally I had no choice: I woke up.'" I finished the story
laughing.

"That's very heavy, Rafi," said Hakkı Bey in his most signifying voice,
patting his rinsed and shaven cheeks hard enough to raise their color again.

"Huh?"

"He was talking about his *life*."

"Oh. Jeez. Right," I said. "I missed it completely. It was his *life*. Of
course." Bulent had slid the parable right past me. Duhh.

I went into the middle room, sat down at the table and waited while
Hakkı poured Pepsi into two heavy glass beer mugs, cut two sections of
lime and came my way for the bottle of rum, which he kept on a shelf
above the table. It was dark Dominican stuff and he poured a lot of it into
the Pepsi, then stirred the drinks lightly with a long spoon which he then
placed carefully in an unused ashtray. "Try that," he said.

"Strong," I said.

"A *man's* drink," he laughed. "No, seriously. Isn't that the best Cuba
libre you ever tasted?"

"Yes," I said, since I'd never had one. The Pepsi was kind of flat.

Hakkı settled into the other chair and drank deeply from his beaker of the full south and I sipped again from mine. I felt the alcohol start to ease me, and realized that I'd been tense.

"You know," I said, starting my little between-worlds inquiry off slowly, "I was wondering . . ."

"You were wondering what."

"I was sitting in the apartment the other day, the place was stacked with heaps of cartons, things the people subletting from me shipped over, and I was knocking out a fast set of liner notes. I was sitting on the sofa, the record was on, I had my little plastic typewriter balanced on my knees, and out of the corner of my eye, I saw the hem of my mother's housedress go by the corner of the coffee table."

"She was upset about the disorder in her apartment," Hakkı said.

"That's what I figured. I stopped typing and talked to the air, told her it was only a sublet and I was leaving but I'd be back. I also asked her if there wasn't some other place she'd rather be."

"Rafi," said Hakkı Bey, "it's probably more that she left so much of herself behind there as, you know . . ."

"As her mind came apart," I finished for him.

"Hasn't it occurred to you that maybe you saw her because she was worried about *you*?" Hakkı asked.

The suggestion landed with a thump. "Huh," was all I managed, and took a long sip of my drink. Hakkı gave me the moment. "I was wondering," I asked him, "if you've seen any more of those scenes with my mother and me in the kitchen . . ."

While my father was busy dying that winter in the Intensive Care Unit of Lenox Hill Hospital, I'd wandered through Chinatown late one night with Hakkı Bey looking for dinner, my feet cold and damp in my boots and Hakkı going on in practically sacerdotal tones about the bowl of crabs he'd been served in a restaurant right here, no, maybe on the next block—let me tell you, man, it was *some* bowl of crabs, and for only *two dollars*. I'd said, Hakkı I believe you it was some bowl of crabs but it's getting late, I need my sleep, and I have to get back to the hospital early tomorrow; and after intricate and time-consuming searches up this street and down that alley, exasperated—I knew Hakkı Bey could be compul-sive, but this ultra-nudnik mode was new to me—I pulled him into a noo-dle joint on Pell Street before the dawn found us. Once we were settled at our Formica table beneath harsh fluorescent light and surrounded by mirrors, warming ourselves on tea, I mentioned that in the year since my mother's death, my father had dreamed repeatedly of her calling to him from a cold bare place saying, Harry, come to me, I'm cold, I'm alone, come to me, come to me here. For my father it was just another dream, but for me it was more than a little spooky.

She hasn't landed well, I told Hakkı over steaming Chinese vegeta-bles, and Hakkı paused for reflection. Then he said that he had seen me and my mother in what he called a clear-light dream—his distinction between the subjective mechanical stuff and the rare veridical ones—seated in a room very like our Brooklyn kitchen: I was explaining things to her, calmly and clearly and, Hakkı said, he had had the impression that this was a regular get-together and that the encounter was going well. Dreams were equivocal instruments, but amid the fears and wor-ries attending my father's deathwatch, Hakkı's dream had calmed me. He was probably the only person with whom I'd let myself have such a con-versation. Especially when he wasn't in a Bonkersville period, I trusted him on those levels. "Have you, um, seen anything new along those lines?"

"No. But I think she's all right. I think she's moved on. Want another one?"

"Huh?" I looked down to see that my mug was as empty as his. "You know," I said while he was in the kitchen slicing lime on a cutting board propped across the stove's burners, "I think I had a clear one about my fa-ther last week." What the hell, I thought, my tongue loosened by demon rum. Let 'er rip.

"Wait till I come back," he said.

"Of course. Right." Hakkı Bey's sense of decorum in these matters was, as usual, exacting.

The second drink, still mixed strong, tasted better than the first.

"When I became aware of the dream, my father and I were finishing a long talk. We'd run through a number of things: life, death, my future probably, but I didn't remember the specifics. There was a good understanding between us. It was calm and normal and we were as we were, but without the tensions of being father and son. I was facing him, and I could see a river flowing behind him from left to right. It looked like the East River seen from midtown, but inside the dream I understood it to be the river of life, or being, or time . . ."

"Right." Hakkı plucked his lime slice from his mug and squeezed it into the remainder of his drink, then rubbed the rind roughly across his foreteeth. "The river."

"And there was a visual pun: I could see the big SILVERCUP sign over his shoulder. The one you see from midtown there. The bread factory across the river in Queens. My father looked relaxed, his arms were stretched along the back of the bench he was sitting on. I wish I could remember everything we said."

"You weren't supposed to."

"I guess not."

Hakkı and I sat over our mugs, which were either half empty or half full, as we reached what was for me the leading tone of the music we were to play today. Fact was, in an attempt to find my way into Hakkı's key signature, I'd been playing a prelude to bringing up the grave of Mahmoud Rauf and what I planned to do in Turkey.

"Do you remember the dream I had," I told Hakkı Bey this side of the veil, in present time, "after Mahmoud died? The one about the house."

Hakkı lowered his eyelids and said, "Tell me," as if wanting to hear a familiar tune again.

The first word of Mahmoud's death came on a postcard from a French-Canadian woman I knew—Lise had just come back to Scotland from Istanbul and sent me the news. I was living sandwiched between Jake and the synagogue on West 103rd Street at the time, early spring of '77. Perched on my cheap sofa as if on the lip of an abyss instead of just above a synagogue, I read and reread the card, a color photo of Jelaluddin Rumi's beautifully ornate tomb in Konya on the obverse, and knew without hope of error that I'd abandoned Mahmoud the year before by leaving. Although we hadn't exchanged a word on the subject we'd both known he would die the following year and that he had wanted me to stay; and I thought of the long winter and how painful it must have been for him in that old house on the hill, his thin body, the cheap tobacco he smoked, those insubstantial walls, the damp rolling uphill from the chilly Sea of Marmara, his long congested coughs gathering critical strength until finally—Mahmoud I'm so sorry: I left knowing you'd die because I'd also had a premonition of my father's death, and while it's impossible to choose between one's fathers I felt that I should be here, in New York, if he went. For myself, I would rather have stayed on with you. In the event, Dad only had walking pneumonia and you, you're gone. I tried to get Nick to go to Turkey and stay with you but he wasn't up to making the trip.

But that blank night on which it had also been my bitter duty to phone Hakkı Bey in California and tell him that our friend was gone, that wasn't when I had the dream. A couple of months later, when I heard how Mahmoud had actually died, and that not only hadn't he suffered a lingering illness but had gone out beautifully, just beautifully: then the dream came to me.

"I was led into Mahmoud's house by a deputation of Turkish men in old blue double-breasted suits," I told Hakkı over our Cuba libres, "all very businesslike, serious, dignified, grave," and as I began to tell the dream I could see the house again, perched alone on the slope overlooking the Sea of Marmara south a mile or two downhill, the Princes' Islands mounded hazily in the water, at my left hand Asia rolling off in hills to the east, downslope to my right past half a mile of dry sage and scrub the thickening terracotta roof tiles, dark plumes of cypress, first severally then bunched together miles away at the old cemetery; beyond that the town of Kadiköy and the harbor and across the Bosphorus the domes and minarets of Istanbul deliquescing in the haze: city of my dreams. Christ I had loved that old house, the nights I couldn't sleep because the poems kept coming in like airplane squadrons and I had to light the kerosene lantern again to get them landed, write them down, Mahmoud's company the next morning over small glasses of strong tea. The water had come uphill on panniers laid across the backs of donkeys, and we had poured the tins into the barrel alongside the house. "The men held the front door open for me," I told Hakkı. "We went in, they led me down the hall and then to the right into my old bedroom—"

"It was my old bedroom too."

"It was your bedroom too," I agreed, "before it was mine. In the dream the place had been fixed up, the walls were freshly painted white, there were none of those spreading dampstains all over. The French doors to the little balcony were open and I could see the Sea of Marmara down there shining in the sun—it was a brilliant sunny day and the sea was all golden. A wooden table had been set in the center of the room and a big scrolled-up paper was lying on the table and alongside it there may have been a quill pen and a bottle of ink. The men in their suits—six of them, maybe eight—lined up in two formal rows from the table to the balcony, there was some serious throat-clearing and then one of the men took me by the arm and walked me up to the table. 'Now that Mahmoud has gone on his ocean voyage,' the man told me, 'this house has been given to you.' He unrolled the scroll, which was at the same time the deed to the house and a detailed blueprint of it: you could see the layout of the rooms, the placement of the furniture. I was flattered that the house should have been given to me—I thought, Hakk, why not you?— and said, 'I want to thank you for giving me this wonderful house, and I'm deeply touched by the gift, but what I really want is to be with Mahmoud on his voyage,' and as I said it I spread my arms wide and started walking to the balcony and then I was flying off the balcony up into the sunlight over the ocean, not the Sea of Marmara but the wonderful blue of the deep sea and I said, with my voice expanding, *'I want to be with him on that ship,'* and as I said it I could see this beautiful white ocean liner below me, cutting through the water, the water parting white around its bows. It was something to see, that ship, and when I saw it I folded my arms back and dove, I headed right for it, my heart was beating hard and I was getting close to the ship when the dream ended. I woke up clear as a bell, wishing I'd reached the ship and seen Mahmoud and I was trembling with the intensity of the dream. Oh man, the ship was so beautiful and I was going to see Mahmoud. It was so daylit and clear."

"That's a beautiful dream, Rafi," Hakkı Bey said.

"I know. I'd still like to see him on that ship."

"So would I."

"I still miss him."

"Of course," dipping his dark eyes again.

We gave the moment its beat, its breath, but we both knew what one of us would say next.

"Bravo," Hakkı Bey said quietly, the accent on the second syllable, Mahmoud's last recorded word on earth.

"Bravo," I repeated.

We sat awhile.

"You remember," I started out, "that for a while I took the dream literally?"

"Not really, Rafi."

"I thought it'd be a good idea to rebuild the house, put a Turkish family in downstairs to look after it, fix up the upstairs for general use, for you, for me, Tash, Sid, whoever might want to spend time there. It wouldn't have cost much, a few grand, tops, and I thought a few of us could get the bread together and do the physical work. That was before they knocked the walls down . . ."

"Why did they have to knock it down? It's such a waste."

"Tramps were living in the shell of it."

"A tramp," Hakkı Bey said. "A shell. That's all I was."

"You know," I said, "this year I was thinking of doing something stupid. I was thinking of buying a stone for Mahmoud's grave. It's unmarked, you know."

I'd been uneasy about broaching the subject, but the volume of Hakkı Bey's rejoinder and the heat behind it shocked me: *"Well if you want to do something stupid, Rafi . . ."*

"Wha?"

"Because, if you'll excuse me for saying so," Hakkı Bey said, accommodatingly, but still at volume, "I think you want to do this for *yourself.*"

I hadn't expected to find the most blameless of all my affections, that for Mahmoud, to be challenged on moral grounds—but there at my feet was the famously vertiginous drop most people dread and quail at. Was there really no place to run to, this or any other day? Were all my projects blind and rotten? Was it really true I had no right to live? Was everything I felt finally illegitimate? Would nothing even provisionally justify my existing at all? "Why are you yelling at me?" I asked Hakkı Bey, whose name translated as Mister Truth, or Sir Reality.

He turned the volume down. "Because I think you might be doing this not for Mahmoud but for you."

"It's possible," I said, trying to keep my ship steady on its keel, "though that's not how it feels. It's for Mahmoud, even though I know he couldn't care less. I wanted to buy a headstone for him on my last few visits, but now that I have the money for it . . ."

Hakkı had simmered down somewhat but his voice still bulged with judgment: "Whatever you want to do, Rafi . . . Just be careful of your motivations."

"I'll think it over," I promised. "But if it still feels right, it's something I want to do. Of course I'll have to put the proposal to his family."

"To Bulent?"

"To all of them, I expect."

"Where's Mahmoud buried?" Hakkı asked me, down a notch.

"Kanlıca, about a third of the way up the Bosphorus on the Asian side. The cemetery's on a hill."

"Kanlıca. I don't know it."

I remembered going to the graveyard, the *mezarlık*, the first time in 1979, walking uphill from the ferry landing in the rain, asking for directions in my limited Turkish and then telling the large overcoated man, who wondered why I was looking for it, that my uncle—in Turkish parlance, an older friend is your uncle, *amcha*—was in there. The man nodded to acknowledge what it was like to have one's uncle in there, then pointed out the uphill path past the houses into the trees. "Kanlıca's very scenic," I told Hakkı Bey. "It's got a beautiful view."

Hakkı Bey snorted, "That's nice."

"The town is famous for its yoghurt," I added absurdly.

Hakkı snorted again.

"It's something I thought I'd do."

Hakkı Bey still said nothing, but you could see spectral steam rising. "Okay, Rafi," he came out with finally. "Whatever you want to do. You know, when I go, I don't give a shit what happens to the remains. You can put my ashes in a coffee can and leave it at the bus stop on the corner. And I don't think Mahmoud cared any more than I do."

"I'm sure. It's a gesture."

Hakkı Bey seized me by the shoulders. *"Coràggio,"* he said. "Or, what else did Mahmoud say? . . . that line in French."

"L'audace!" I announced, trying to get Mahmoud's voice into it and thrusting a hand into the air in an echo of our old friend's last Bravo. *"Toujours l'audace!"*

"Toujours l'audace, Rafi," Hakkı Bey advised me.

"Nice work if you can get it."

"Adiós, baby."

"Adieu," I agreed.

PART TWO

*Of all the marvelous Acts there is the Act of Mounts, and
thus is the variety of their ways: there are those who abide
in Truth and there are those who cut distances into deserts
of wilderness . . . and upon all of them God reveals His
unknowableness from every side.*

— IBN ʿARABI

*Blues jumped a rabbit, he run for a solid mile
Blues jumped a rabbit, he run for a solid mile
Rabbit laid down and cried like a baby child.*

— TRADITIONAL BLUES

1

I TOOK SOME AIRLINE'S REDEYE out of Newark.

And the blur of travel propelled me through the slow, Judas-goat nuisance of the gate onto the plane: stumble up the aisle, peer outside, bookbag, overhead, underseat, pillow, blanket, buckle, find a place for your legs and finally a prayer for safety as we shuddered into motion, with a doubt dangling from its nether end: was I really sure I wanted a smooth ride and another few decades of the heavy trudge through life? Wouldn't I have half-preferred an easeful planecrash and an after-impact choice of transcendent lights, if such were still on offer?

I asked myself seriously which I wanted and the answer came out even.

Where was my usual boost from the prospect of travel? From the first it had been an escape from my family's sadness and the inevitable degree to which the Depression and my father's immigrant experience colored the atmosphere and stifled hope and motion. I remembered seeing Gloria off to France by plane, Rose and Joe on the *Independence* or the *Constitution* for a European tour—I discovered shrimp at their stateroom party and ate the whole row of them off the rim of the long dishful of cocktail sauce. The good, the free, adventurous life was outside the grasp of the Zabors, who sat indoors, sold hot dogs or liquor and sometimes opened a book in which that famous object The World might appear and at least be read about—though my father had seen the place and was happy to be out of it, in America.

But I wasn't feeling the thrill of liftoff this year, at least not yet.

WHAT HAD FINALLY NUDGED ME off the continental shelf and into chronological narrative was the realization that if I waited for all the technicalities attending my parents' estate to be completed I would go nowhere that year; so I reconciled myself to leaving accusative caws and flutters of legal chaos behind me, transferred cash out of the estate's available bank accounts into mine, made out some powers of attorney so that Daniel could operate on my behalf, and winged it out of there later in the year than I'd hoped—too late for Doğubayazit and its view of Ararat?—on the last empurpled evening of that July.

My friend Peter Giron drove me to the airport. Peter was in momentary exile from France, where he had but lightly established himself before a riot of illness was let loose amid his family back in New Jersey: his kid brother needed a succession of brain operations, his mother a biopsy, and his father's diabetes had taken another lurch forward and put the irascible old man on crutches when he could make it out of bed at all. "I don't know if I'm gonna make it back to France," Peter told me en route to the airport, hauling left on the wheel of his rusting white Datsun bassmobile to avoid a flight of newspaper rearing up out of the windblown soot of the turnpike dusk, "and I'm not sure Nicole's willing to come live here if I can't leave."

Thanks to the weak kidneys that had kept him in hospitals for much of his childhood, Peter sported a habitual greenish pallor beneath the three-day growth of beard on his tough-looking, pockmarked face. He looked embattled at the best of times, and this was not the best of times. I'd spent at least one evening walking up and down the misted road outside his parents' suburban Jersey home, trying to give him the dubious benefit of my experience of illness and death. I enumerated alternative therapies, counselled patience, suggested that failure was the order of the day and that when playing a tune in the key of catastrophe one shouldn't expect to come up with a terrific solo on the changes; and when, finally, in a still, small voice I suggested that there might just be some use to prayer, he growled at me and ended our conversation with an emphatic, fortissimo and all-including *NO*. Peter was an old music friend—and a better musician than I would ever be—a bassist I'd met and started playing with in Boston in the early seventies. Our band was called the Che Giron Revolución—Peter looked like Che Guevara if you squinted right—and enjoyed a spot of local success before we got an agent and everything went kaflooey. A few months after the band's confused demise I headed down to New York and then off for the first time to Turkey.

Years later, when Peter sallied forth from Joisey in search of the larger world, he had lucked out, and even found The Girl. I'd hoped to spend some time with him and Nicole this year in France, maybe even get some playing done, but it wasn't going to work out. That year's version of Peter Giron came on like one nerving himself up to climb into the ring and duke it out with the Godzilla of mortality. Otherwise he wasn't going anywhere.

"You sure Nicole won't move here if you can't go back?"

"I don't know." Peter's mouth curved down another notch and his jaw locked its door. "She doesn't like it here much."

I said nothing, which seemed the best thing to say.

"You know, she's been looking around for those old Renaults for you," Peter said after a sullen mile had passed. Friends of Nicole's were hunting old Renaults—models discontinued in France but still churned out in Turkey—in case I got cold feet about buying the Mercedes.

"I might not even need a car," I told him, even though I knew I was probably hooked. "My knee and elbow seem to have healed up amazingly well. That chiropractor-naturopath I told you about did great work on me, and I'll say it again, he might be able to do some good for your br—"

"Yep, she's been looking around for those cars," Peter rumbled, as if his mood had trodden the clutch and shifted the machinery of himself into lower gear. "She's been sending out the troops down there in Bordeaux."

"Okay, Peter."

"Lot of people you've never met looking around so you can have a car."

"Okay, Peter. Peter, gotcha."

"Domi, Domie, Jean-Pierre and Marie-Jô, they're all . . ."

"Pete. Okay. Relax."

I'd met Nicole when she'd come over to visit Peter early on. She was obviously the best thing that had happened to him since he'd developed perfect pitch in childhood. He'd met her while playing bass in a love-boat band cruising the Mediterranean—she'd been the ship's suave social director; he tended to fight with the bandleader, laugh out loud at the vocalist's intonation, set fire to awnings, throw deckchairs overboard and get into motorcycle accidents in Egypt, emerging from the clinic bandaged like a mummy but still able to make the gig—and in fact he can be seen in his winding-sheets doing a Ray Charles impression in the rear of a scene of the actual *Love Boat* series shot on the boat in question: if you catch a rerun of the episode featuring Eva Marie Saint, Polly Bergen and Kiel Martin, the guy in the shades and bandages rocking side to side at the piano, that's my pal. After a brief return to the States, where he had a fabulous life one flight up from Dumont New Jersey's Pioneer Lounge in a dark apartment strewn with old pizza cartons and gutted bluetick mattresses bleeding their cotton batting onto the bottles on the dustball floor, Peter set out to join her in Bordeaux. Since then they'd shifted north near Paris in Étampes, and Peter commuted to play blues gigs on electric bass in the City of Light until things Stateside had intervened to drag him back by his anchor chain to a sinking household in which everyone seemed to be struggling to pretend that their feet were dry. With Peter back, the decibel level was climbing, the radio room was crackling and the ammunition magazine seemed ready to blow; aside from that Peter hadn't been able to accomplish much.

When we got back to the house through the mist, Peter's father was sitting on a beach chair inside the front door with a glass of iced tea in one hand, naked except for a pair of boxer shorts, his hairless head and body looking as if they had been made of damp pale green clay. "If you live long enough, you get to see everything," he said.

JUST BEFORE THE FEEDER ROAD decanted us into the airport roundelay we skirted a recent accident: a Nissan Accedia had plowed into the side of a blue Chrysler Monad. The drivers seemed unharmed, but steam rose from the Accedia's nose and one of the Monad's windows was broken. What kind of an omen was that?

After a few minutes on the baggage line in the terminal, I was surprised to see Daniel, bulking against the evening light in the airport windows and looking even more like an armored vehicle than usual, his large square head pivoting like a turret in search of me. I sent Peter to collect him.

"Ah Peterrr," Daniel trilled. "How are your family?"

"Phphrrrphr," Peter said.

"And where is . . ."

Peter indicated.

"Ah, Joël," as he preferred to call me. "The Raccoon stalled only three times en route and I was able to drive all the way to the airport without the aid of a tow truck. A minor miracle. Grace attends your going forth. I hev some papers for you to sign."

"*More* papers?" I nudged my bags another notch along the check-in line.

"There are always more papers."

"How come? How can there possibly be more papers?"

"Once the dying starts, everything is possible," he said. As Daniel fluttered the sheets in my face, flocks of unbelief assailed me and a cavern opened in my core. A whir of wings clapped black applause at the enchained consequences of death in the family.

Once, when I was eighteen years old and struggling to be an adequate civil rights worker in Mississippi—"You want to be a good civil rights worker?" Holmes County's SNCC supervisor, in civilian life a Pittsburgh undertaker, asked me. "Go out and get your ass killed 'cause no one gave a shit about what was goin' down here till those two white boys bought it in Leflore"—I was driving a borrowed lowslung white two-seat ragtop Triumph Spitfire down a red dirt road in hill country—the road surface rough, about a car-and-a-half wide flanked by deep ditches to catch that big-dropped Mississippi rain, the encircling trees tall dark humped shapes halfway gone in kudzu—when wheeling around a bend I came upon a dead dog in the middle of the road, although the dog was not what I saw first off: around its body in a doctorish knot a convocation of blackheaded crookneck vultures hooked at the dogsbody with their beaks, occasionally raising a corner to let it fall back in a puff of red dirt. It was about 110° Fahrenheit, as usual. The vultures' wings were dull black, with a suggestion of near-purple sheen, wingshoulders raised and wings partly spread to cover their prey, taloned legs carefully astep and three or four heads raised, in each a round eye that held me in flat tactical regard. I stomped the car to a halt, sliding sideways on the stony clay and then, because I could all too easily imagine myself identically dead on a stretch of Mississippi road—there had been so many casual attempts on our lives that summer it's a miracle that any of us scampered back to our Northern colleges alive—or perhaps only because in the naïveté of my city reflexes I could only register a pack of vultures as evil incarnate, I gunned the engine, punched the shifter into first and with the wheels breaking loose on the road surface then grappling ahead I plowed the car into the vultures: they rose around me flapping themselves and whorls of red road dust into the air: I didn't hit nary a one, but for a moment it was as if their beating six-foot nightmare wings had surrounded me and closed in, clapping me about the eyes and ears.

A week or two before Peter drove me to the airport, prompted by the money man to whom I'd confided most of my inherited funds in my absence, I'd driven the Malibu to a recommended law office in New Jersey—Sliver & Disbranch, let's call them—where in a conference room whose windows overlooked stacked overpasses and chicanes awhizz with freeway interchange, a half dozen tall men in dark suits descended upon me to pick clean the bones of my parents' estate; the Mississippi memory had been irresistible. There wasn't much meat to pick: I owed the Feds no inheritance tax at all and New York State less than five thousand dollars; but the disorder of my papers and the need for multiple verifications promised an extended wrangle and longdrawn remunerative feasts for the firm. In the end I let them get their beaks into me for a couple of grand in fees, then cut the suits loose and returned my bleeding legal corpus to the ministrations of Daniel, against whose unreliability and inexperience that convocation of beak and claw had duly warned me—Sliver's second cousin Sy was a habitué of Brooklyn Probate Court and the clerks wouldn't give him the runaround they were entertaining this buddy of yours with, whats-isname, Furman. Flap flap flap. I couldn't have hit them with a car either.

"Sign this sheet as indicated," Daniel told me.

"Where?" My eyes glazing. Edged my bags ahead.

"At the bottom, there," said Daniel, pointing at the space as marked and taking no apparent note of my disarray amid the wings of paper. "This one twice, once at the top and a second time, let me show you, use my briefcase as a desk . . ."

"Necks," a voice called from behind a terminal ahead.

"With these papers I may be able to prevent the courts from nullify-ing the will, after which, if we fail, we would hev to declare your parents to hev died intestate—"

"What? I thought—"

A voice grew more insistent: *"Necks."*

"It is not as bad as it sounds and in the end it may be the best we can hope for, since no one will contest the natural succession of the estate to you—"

"Necks," a new voice called, meaning me.

"Wait a minute," I told Daniel, "I have to heft my—"

"—and perhaps it would hev been easier, although of course it was impossible to know this with adequate foresight, to ignore the existence of the will at the outset and declare both of them to hev died intestate so that—"

"Daniel, I really have to heft my—"

"Sir," an admonitory voice said from behind a desk, "you're necks."

"Heft my . . ." and while pivoting my two bags of clothes onto the airline scales, heavy with the skins of four seasons—I expected winter to find me on the eastern steppes of Turkey and had packed sweaters and a sturdy leather jacket—I almost audibly ripped out all the wonderful chiropractic work that had been done on my knee and elbow in the weeks before departure: the familiar ailments did their tear-and-crunch routine and the pain took its customary seat inside me. I'd have to sit immobilized all through the flight. Tomorrow morning I might have to take a taxi once I staggered into London. The cost! hysterical-ancestral voices warned me, taxis being against the family religion; but family having died, family habits were dying fast.

I did my ticket-passport-luggage business at the desk.

"Peter," I announced, clapping hands on his shoulders in farewell and trying to suppress any sign of physical pain. "See you in France next month I hope."

"Pph. I ain't gettin' outa here."

"Daniel. Next year, you know . . ."

"I should be in Jerusalem by January. Drive safely."

"Oh listen," I remembered. "There's one last thing I wanted to ask you."

"*Effendim.*"

"I know the word alcohol comes from the Arabic but what's the Arabic word?" I was thinking ahead to Tash in London.

"*Al kahal.* The blue."

"Because of the flame with which it burns?"

"Or because of the blues it alternately gives you or takes away," Daniel said.

THE FLUOROLIT tubiform corridor I sat in hissed and hummed and took an occasional dip that convinced me I was actually flying through the air along with the occasional squalling baby and rows of men and women straining not to fart after dinner. In the row immediately behind me a last American conversation graced the processed air: "Let me one thing . . . there are a lot of very armchair critics who . . . yes no, I'm fully recognizable of the information that he said, and it's about accurate, excetera, but . . . "

"Look, he's a viral young man and quite an athalete . . . but what it is is, is everyone wanted to get rid of him because he was so confrontive . . . and his mind is very highly compartmented . . ."

My own highly compartmented, not to say fragmentalized, mind wasn't working very acutely either. It kept revolving a piece of a French actor's name in its sleepless eye—Michel . . . Michel . . . Lom*bard*?—and my familiar failure to remember this name encapsulated, in a ticky, minor, but almost infinitely irritating way, all my lapses of brain that year.

A pretty stewardess, seeing no sign of trouble in me—why not?—kept slipping by, once I had asked her for the first, with free miniatures of cognac that eased the evening but didn't do much for the pain in my pinioned knee. I should have taken an aisle seat that permitted the prisoner to stretch his legs instead of the window seat that made easier the sleep I knew I wouldn't get anyway.

At least I could ignore my elbow most of the time.

In general I was hurt, I was wounded, and I needed a little comfort and mercy. And where was I going? To England. To Tash. What a sense of direction, what aim.

Michel . . . Lam*part*? I asked myself again, and the same mistaken synaptic shunt repeated itself in the chambers of my brain each time I neared the right, true, proper, utterly insignificant and unapproachable target: Michel Lom*bard*? . . . Why couldn't I remember it? Michel . . . mrff . . . fzzt.

My distress had limits: I knew I wasn't getting a taste of the Alzheimer's disease I might have inherited from my mother. My general inability to think was the obvious result of weariness and shock, but my collapses of memory did worry me in one particular way: I knew how central a part memory played in my ability not just to think but to let fly the one arrow I still might have in my quiver, i.e., the one I could write with: not just the only decent means I had of making a living, but something, oddly enough in the face of my exhaustion, I still wanted to do. Of course I would never stoop to autobiography, which, *pace* Dr. Johnson, is the true scoundrel's last refuge, but I had to be in palpable contact with every word in a work-ing text, whatever its length, sensing the strength and position of each as a spider must every constituent thread in the composition of its web, and that year I could barely put two sentences together and remember what the first one felt like.

Michel . . .

I remembered without difficulty the actor in a number of his roles: in François Truffaut's *Stolen Kisses* he had played Monsieur Tabard, who hired junior-grade private detective Antoine Doinel (played by Jean-Pierre Léaud), employed by the Blady Detective Agency, to find out why nobody liked him, and when Doinel was on the brink of an affair with Tabard's wife Fabienne (played by the unforgettable Delphine Seyrig) he chanted into his bedroom mirror *AntoineDoinelAntoineDoinelAntoine DoinelAntoineDoinelAntoineDoinelAntoineDoinelAntoineDoinelAntoineDoinel AntoineDoinelAntoineDoinelAntoineDoinelAntoineDoinelAntoineDoinel* then *FabienneTabardFabienneTabardFabienneTabardFabienneTabardFabienneTabard FabienneTabardFabienneTabardFabienneTabardFabienneTabardFabienneTabard FabienneTabardFabienneTabardFabienneTabard.*

Wonderful scene. In matters of art I always admire economy of means.

Tall, podgy Michel . . . Lom*bard*? had also performed well in his lightly accented English as the diffident, brilliant investigator summoned out of pigeonshit obscurity to catch the assassin in the John Forsyth/Fred Zinnemann thriller *The Day of the Jackal* (which also featured Seyrig as the haute-bourgeoise Colette Montellier; she had a good scene in it with Lam-part? and showed her breasts, though not to him, and was later murdered in her bed). Spywise, he did a near-genius turn with Alec Guinness toward the end of *Smiley's People* as a spectacularly disoriented Soviet diplomat. When quite young—it might have been his earliest English-language role—he'd played the priest in the cathedral scene in Orson Welles' ver-sion of *The Trial*, though I think Welles himself may have dubbed his lines. As Drax, he was the villain in one of the lesser James Bond films. The only time I'd seen him fail was when, miscast opposite an also miscast Guinness or was it Anthony Hopkins as the Führer—it's an impossible role, period—he played Martin Bormann in one of those things about the last days of Hitler in the bunker. *Why couldn't I remember his name?* And why, once I did remember it—as I might in the course of this flight between unsustainably overpopulated continents, every single one of whose human inhabitants was thinking his and her own thoughts and walking where necessity or the whim of the moment suggested, in what in one of my anxious moments seemed a scarily random swarming pullulation of life going on about its business, just as the gazillion firing and misfiring neurons of my brain flashed through their microscopic tasks instinct with purpose without "my" oversight, though whoever "I" might be was hard to tell, since, let's not forget, throughout the inextricably plural organism I haunted, my highly motivated white blood cells, immune system T-cells each invested with apparent consciousness and intent, my teeming, super-motivated, perpetually regenerating supply of spermatozoa every one of them wild to lash its tail a path to glory, nor yet the hordes of actual alien microorganisms, some of them friendly and working in my casual employ, others that might be inimical held in check by my own autonomic defenses, the whole of life endlessly particulate beyond accounting north south east west and the whole teeming seeming dreaming multifarious shebang, as is well known by now, a less than speck adrift in starpocked infinities of incalculable space—how could you keep track of *anything* in all this? especially if you'd lost your own essential thread.

Why, whenever I had that actor's name free and clear, despite all my disproportionate rage over this lost, quite immaterial penny, why would I almost immediately *forget* his name again? and more to the point, why did it never occur to me to write his name down, once I had it, on a slip of paper and put it in my wallet? In the words of the famous French rabbit I'd seen on TV in that great nation, *Qu'est-que c'est que ça que se passe, monsieur le professeur?*

As far as I could tell I didn't identify with Lom*bard* and had never obsessed about his talent or his personality—although a fine character actor with a personal tone he was no Akim Tamiroff: I looked nothing like him and neither had my dad; he was miscellaneous, a stray—and although I knew it mattered less than the weight of a gnat's wing whether I had his name in hand or not, there I was in an airplane, looking out at a small red light blinking on the end of the nightbound wing, my mind stuck on the windowpane blind and abuzz with twitches of insect incomprehension.

The only connection I could think of, his characters usually seem mildly preoccupied, distracted.

Michel . . . Lam*bard*?

All my fretting over the fate of my busted intellectual organ summed itself up in an inability to dislodge the eyeblinding mote of a French actor's forgotten name.

Of course Daniel's unrelenting intellect and encyclopedic recall had sometimes nettled me too.

For all the pleasure of his company, of which I'd had more, in the months before departure, than any other person's, Daniel was a particular goad to my injured intellectual vanity and a critique, paragraph by ordered paragraph of his speech, of my inability to frame a coherent thought that year. Even at the best of times I would have lacked his brainpower. Daniel's company and conversation were an invitation to a dance of which I was no longer capable, and my weakness of intellectual limb felt like a lethal wound.

One too-hot afternoon not long before my departure, he resolved for all time in my humble Brooklyn apartment what had lately become a central question in the history of the European Jews. Raiding the main branch of the Brooklyn Public Library to the tune of five books a day while freeloading a room at a fellow lawyer's apartment at 135 Eastern Parkway, he finally collided with Arthur Koestler, whose *The Thirteenth Tribe* he read in an hour or two, and didn't buy its thesis—who did? but it was a tricky thing to disprove—that all or most of Europe's Jews descended from the Khazars, a Turkic-speaking North Caucasian tribe that had chosen Judaism in the eighth century as a dodge to keep them out of the Islamic-Christian wars then convulsing the region. This ploy kept the Khazars out of trouble with the Arabs and the Byzantines for two hundred years; it was Koestler's idea that the Jews of Europe were not Semitic at all but descendants of the Judaized Khazars who, he said, migrated west when their empire finally fell to the advancing Pechenegs and Russians in the tenth century. Koestler decided that the Khazars, perhaps lost in the monotheistic dazzle they'd assumed as protective aura, literally forgot who they were and where they came from and so, eventually, did everyone else, and hey presto, Europe had acquired its full kit of Jews.

Koestler's book was published in 1976. I read it, or most of it, a year or so later, on returning from my first trip to Turkey, so that with my own interest, homemade and prone to suggestion, in some sort of Turko-Judaic *tsimmes* stimulated, I might have been working, with no great seriousness and therefore only mild fatuity, on some new version of the family romance: *Zebur* meant the Book of Psalms in Turkish, so might not Zabor indicate . . . and might I not combine in myself two strands of history that historical memory had nodded over in its sleep and unwoven? and had I not, in my heterodox or anyway extremely casual fashion begun to reweave them on the loom of my adventures?

It was fun to think so for a minute but it was no big deal to me.

I'd discussed the book once or twice with my father and might even, for the sake of a discussion or just to piss him off, have tried to sell him the idea. After all, Turkey had restored to me the rough-hewn Europe of my father's bedtime tales—an essentialist landscape deprived of bourgeois varnish—and at the time I would have been mildly happy, such is the shape of human folly, to yoke these couple of continents together for the space of an afternoon.

"Oh, we always knew about the Khazars," my father told me. "We knew some Jews came from there. But all? No. We had all kinds of Jews in our town. Even Kara'im like your crazy musician friend from Boston, whatyoucall."

"Avraham."

"Avraham. Always a few of every kind. But all of us from Khazaria? Not possible."

"Why not?"

"Im-possible, believe you me." My father had pursed his lips, then sent Koestler packing with a small assertive nod. His complacency, and the fact that he had come to most of his conclusions decades back and had not seriously rethought any of them, may have ticked me off. His complacency often did.

A decade later—the battle over and my parents buried—Daniel, looking pleased with himself, was equally definitive about the Khazars. "Do you know why Koestler is wrong? Once you see it, it is completely obvious."

I tried to see it. "Sorry," I said.

A jacket over the back of a chair and a loosened tie indicated relaxation from the constraints of his profession. "There is one constant in the whole of Jewish history," Daniel told me. It was a history Daniel did not invariably admire.

"Guilt?" I ventured.

"A recent import."

"Herring."

"Only in the northern provinces. As I read Koestler's book I saw that he developed his case logically enough and had a fair command of the history, but something was missing. Do you know what it was?"

"No."

"You of all people should know. *Storytelling.* Stories. No matter what has happened to the Jews, wherever and whenever it happened to them, they told stories about it, they generated legends and peopled them with heroic or pathetic characters—whatever the continent or the epoch, the production of narrative was constant, and since they were the People of the Book this lore eventually was written down. But of a migration of several hundred thousand people from well east of the Caucasus to central Europe through territory populated by Turks and Kurds and similar Cro-Magnons—you still don't see it? Of so epic a migration *there is not a single tale.* No legend, no stories of the hero who led God's chosen people through the narrow gap, no epic battles or sly elisions to cover bad events, no near-catastrophes or great escapes—not one word. Therefore nothing remotely like it ever can have happened. And the European Jews whom Koestler says resulted from this migration? They memorialized everything about their history and themselves. Tell me: did they acquire this habit only after arriving in Europe?"

"Holmes, you've cracked the case."

"Thank you, Vatson. *Kefalo* works!" Daniel announced, thumping himself on the cranium.

"I'll tell you something else. In England I know a couple of people who are close to Arthur Koestler. A woman I know named Ruth West—"

"Is she nubile?"

"Shut up. She administers the Arthur Koestler Foundation. There's this guy, Avi, a *landsmann* of yours, another Israeli brainbox. A few years ago he got a job painting Koestler's apartment, probably got the gig through Ruth, anyhow he got into a conversation with Koestler, and Koestler told him about a series of experiments he was doing at the time, his last attempt to establish scientific proof for the existence of the supernatural. Koestler told Avi that if these experiments failed it would leave him in a state of philosophical despair. Avi thought this was a rudimentary error, since to require a proof of the Transcendence by a means that is not Itself, to demand of the Transcendence that It show Itself in a medium not itself Transcendent . . . I'm muddling it. Avi gets complicated with this stuff. Anyhow I guess the experiments didn't work, because Koestler wouldn't have killed himself if they had."

But "Yes!" Daniel said in a sudden outburst, fully animated in the armchair, which creaked and trembled under the onslaught. "That's it! It's completely clear!"

"Huh? What is," I said dully.

"Koestler was unable to enjoy the living presence of the *Shekhina*"— the Kabbalistic term for the immanent, indwelling, implicit presence of God in all things—"and since he was for personal reasons unable to deny the existence of God, *he denied the existence of the Jews.*"

"Wow," I said, or something like it.

This was a shining, self-evident conclusion,* but in the midst of the pleasure I took in it I wondered what had happened to me. I used to come

---

*It should be noted that the Furman Proof of Jewish Continuity was achieved years before geneticists detected the Cohen Modal Hapletite in the DNA of a majority of hereditary Cohens—*Kohanim*, the priestly class—of both European and Oriental descent, proving the persistence of the descendants of a single male progenitor—the converging lines of temporal perspective suggest someone of equivalent antiquity to the first priest, Moses' brother Aaron—throughout the world's Jewish population, even, apparently, the black Lemba tribe in southern Africa, who emigrated to the east coast of the continent via Yemen after the end of the Babylonian captivity, built a great stone city there, but broke the laws of *Kashruth* by eating mice in hard times and were then "scattered among the nations." This information also courtesy of Daniel, but later.

up with a bright idea now and then. I used to enjoy the occasional light-ningflash of an inspired idea. What had become of my mind? What, if anything, could bring it back? Driving around Asia Minor in a car? What bozo thought that one up?

Michel . . . Lom . . . forget it.

OTHERWISE I was in perfect shape.

My elbow actually hurt worse than my knee, but since I didn't walk on my hands and it only hurt me when I picked something up I could forget about it much of the time. Before the stresses of motherfatherdoom, the pain in my elbow was an insignificant twinge I'd acquired while playing cricket with friends up in Scotland. As a kid baseball player who had hit well but fielded badly, I could hardly believe my luck in finding a game in which, if you hit, they let you keep hitting and, here's the kicker to one's sense of the credible, they give you a big wide half-flattened bat to do it with, so I stood there on the Scottish grass hunkered in my ass-wagging Jackie Robinson crouch, duly laughed at by stiff ofay Scots and an assort-ment of even stiffer English twits and poff! poff! poff! kept socking those balls outa there until they hadda stop me 'cause I threatened to put one through the winders of the big house. Take *that*, I muttered in my mind as I retreated obedient but unchastened to a field position, but then, whoa, what's this curious strumming in the tendons of my elbow? Noth-ing much, I hastened to assure myself; and it remained nothing much un-til life and death started tearing me up the following year.

Nowadays I could pick up my plastic glass of cognac without trouble unless I got the angle wrong, but the weight of a glass of beer could stop me cold.

My purgatorial knee had a longer, deeper history. When in my fourth year it appeared that I was mildly pigeontoed—my feet were turned almost imperceptibly inward as I stood, I was told, though I'd never noticed it my-self—my doting greenhorn parents took it as a bird of ill omen—and took me straight to the offices of a Dr. Forest—I was puzzled by the urban set-ting of his downtown Brooklyn office when his name had led me to expect depths of green and birdsong—who fitted me out with a prescription for a pair of outward-turned high-laced brown leather boots that were supposed turn my stance straight as woodsman's arrow. Instead, they twisted my legs out of shape, shunting the lower segment of each knee-joint outward and causing my shanks to curve correspondingly inward as they descended—not that I or, I think, my anxious, cosseting parents noticed it at the time, even though a slight deformity of my knees is visible in some snapshots from Belle Harbor: their primary concern was that my friends would mock me for my funny footwear, but I told everyone, with odd reflexive pride, that I was wearing custom-made *baseball* boots, and in fact I did think they brought me a heroic measure nearer my idol Jackie R. I didn't know I was bowlegged until friends, their eyelight sharpened by the competitive surges of pubescence, began making fun of my legs when I was about thirteen.

After a couple of years of this I evolved a walk I hoped would disguise the facts of the matter, which I had finally verified with the aid of the bedroom mirror: it was true: when I stood with my feet together there was a gap of about four inches between my knees—in fact I'd known my knees didn't meet; what I didn't understand until mocked was that other people's did. Since my problem consisted in my knees' separation from each other I began pulling them together on the step-through as I walked, guided less by touch than by the sound of my trouserlegs brushing together. This serpentine leg motion lent my walk a certain unwonted effeminacy, I think, and also imparted an op-art, bending-pencil, Charleston aspect to my forward progress that occasionally amazed and confused the unimaginative, so that in addition to the walk per se I contrived to approach someone directly as seldom as possible, and would pretend to be interested or distracted by this or that innocent object— building, cloud, tree, bird—alternately to right and left, so that I would arrive at the person who had hailed me, or whom I had hailed, by a series of tacks assisted by a secondary sequence of facial expressions intended to explain the indirection of my advance. I was an imaginative adolescent, and this maneuver should have proved simple enough for me to execute in good grace, but unhappily my new walk had to be added to other gestures of social defense already well established in my repertoire. As early as my tenth year I had noticed two unfortunate things about my head: the height of my forehead exceeded that of my contemporaries, and a photo showed me that my head stuck out like a watermelon in back, not like the ideal head—Rock Hudson's in the Korean War movie *Battle Hymn*, in the scene in which, anguished at having dropped a bomb on an orphanage, he crushed a waterglass in his hand, resigned his commission in the Air Force and joined the ministry. His head was flat in back and his hair looked good on it.

Rock Hudson's head was a shocker. I come to some things slowly: until I was six or so I assumed that human beings lived to be a hundred, the numerical system having been designed around this fixed infallible span. One day while paging through a coloring book I read a caption informing me that the elephant I was supposed to color with grey Crayola lived as long as people did: on average, sixty-eight years. The blow of this intimate subtraction not just of years but still more of surety nearly dropped me where I stood.

My high forehead fell to a simple solution: it took little effort to keep my eyebrows raised in company, and a wrinkled brow at ten was a teensy price to pay for normalizing the anomalous plaza between my eyebrows and my hairline; but it was harder never to be seen in profile and thus conceal my melonhead from unkind eyes—which later would become a point of intellectual vanity, but that faded when I learned that Proust's brain had been unusually small—and it was necessary, by a lightninglike construction of an ever-shifting series of perceptual-behavioral hierarchies built of the brick and mortar of sheer anxiety, to determine who, in a crowd, might see the thing and who, elsewhere in the crowd, must not.

This much I could handle, and in fact had handled until the discovery of my bowleggedness and the invention of my walking system introduced a third variable that sometimes led to exotic combinations, for example walking indirectly toward someone while pulling my knees together on the step-through, trying not to be seen in profile by someone else and keeping my eyebrows raised while looking serially interested in this or that happenstance object as might seem appropriate to the zig or zag of current tack.

Then came the pimples.

I'm not even getting into the genito-urinary bloodclot that delayed the material expression of my sexual maturity until I was nearly seventeen and unleashed in me an unfortunate capacity for secrecy, melodrama and elaborately false autobiographical fictions. (At least these had the ancillary effect of developing my memory, which, since I had to maintain coherent files on a whole series of not quite parallel lies told to different sets of friends, evolved into a truly prodigious instrument—God's dartboard! is there no other way to make a writer?—at least until a circulation problem started knocking off my brain cells by the million when I was twenty-one. Until then I was the kind of person who remembered every conversation he'd ever had and could resume or revise them at any paragraph.) Jeezis how I suffered the secret shame of my failure to pubesce until one day, while taking an innocent pee in my family apartment's immaculate white tile bathroom, I was dropped gasping to my knees by an astounding bonfire of excruciation that blazed its way through the narrow channel of my surprised penis and emerged as a liverish brown blob about half an inch across with an aureole of bloody tendrils, as if it were a little sun. Since I was a nice clean Jewish boy, when the pain dropped me I managed to land positioned over the toilet so that the bloodclot hit the porcelain and slid to the water to float there, the very lozenge of my destiny, the better for me to contemplate it now that it had gone. A few days later I woke up in the lush and ease of milky sheets and thought my life had changed, and only later began to see that the serried battlements and redoubts of the intricately false personality I had constructed around my guilty secret could not be pissed as simply and conclusively away as the liverish clot that had issued without flourish or fanfare and dropped, its lines all spoken and role exhausted, plop into the moat.

I wouldn't be an adolescent again if you paid me. It still seems to me that my early life's book was strangely and perversely written. That I behaved like an idiot with every fresh turn of the page is beside the point; the tale itself was told by an idiot with a mean pedantic streak, the plot devices were niggling in their pettiness, the humiliations pleonastic, the scenery glum and the cast of characters, of course, insufficiently cosmopolitan.

TO SUM UP the principal point: knees structurally weak: not good joinery: digressing from the vertical, they do not represent the principles of good design. *Architektur ist überhaubt die erstarrte Musik.*

I'd gone to my usual chiropractor a couple of times but the usual crunching assault had not turned the trick: I'd walk out the door feeling fine and in thirty seconds of Manhattan sidewalk the knee pain would kick in and I'd have to sit down on a piece of car, gasping and slackjawed.

Fortunately Nick Prestigiacomo patronized physical healers as well as the psychic kind, and that year's hero was Richard Hirsch. Nick swore, really swore, that Richard should, could, would . . . Yeah sure, I told him, but having no other options and finding myself within six weeks of a bought-and-paid-for departure I hardly felt fit to undertake, I gave this Hirsch a try. The first visit was nearly three hours long and the guy did a complete diagnostic job on me: it was like being worked on by a piano virtuoso fresh out of the conservatory, Richard working my keys with blinding speed to dazzling tonal effect but uncertain expressive efficacy: one second he was pushing down on my arm while pressing a series of points on my acupuncture meridians, the next he was placing a drop of my own blood on my tongue—oh man, is this really necessary? I asked him—while placing bottles of herbal and homeopathic remedies on my—Richard, c'mon man, cut it out: I appreciate the primal zonk of the blood voodoo but will you please get that bottle off my belly-button?

It seemed, not for the first time, that my life was hanging by a farcicle.

But I hung in there for the diagnosis, and it wasn't a lot more encouraging than the procedure. *Of course* your chiropractor couldn't make his adjustments last, Richard told me.

It turned out that transmission between the hemispheres of my brain was impaired because of one of those systemic yeast infections every hypochondriacal chucklehead I knew had discovered in himself that year. My right-side-of-body/left-side-of-brain were afflicted by the yeast-lings and by the way was I having any trouble—you said you were a writer?—any trouble creatively speaking? okay, since it's a matter of your hemispheric problem we'll fix that . . . In short, Richard Hirsch sounded ready to cure me of everything this side of cancer—which of course my uncle Avram could have handled with cold water gratis and for nothing.

But in for a penny in for a pound, and I had six weeks in which to get roadworthy and there was no other game in town while a wad of inherited money burned a hole in my guilty pocket.

It was a month's worth of brain and yeast treatment, two or three visits a week at a hundred bucks a pop, before Richard would consent to fiddle with an actual knee, but, you know, once he fiddled it stayed fit for days, and when my body finally told him, as he put it, that it was okay for him to address my elbow the results were as impressive. If I could have stuck around another month he might have had a go at my creative problem, but the ticket was paid for and untransferable and off I flew.

Richard's juju had worked until I hauled my baggage over that Jersey check-in line, but even if my tendons had taken the load, I had to face it, arm and leg were not the heaviest weights in that year's burden.

To speak plainly, I was not in my perfect mind, I was leaking pain all over the place and they'd have me for breakfast, those English, starting with my buddy Tash, from whom it was folly to expect simple kindness at the best of times and who, a dozen drinks or so down the day, turned into the most lethally percipient mean drunk who ever pissed away an evening or a life.

I was fragged and ill-equipped for travel.

At least I wasn't self-involved. At least heaven had spared me that.

What was I doing on this plane, sleepless above the summer ocean? And what, fixed in my rented seat, the rented muscle in my rented head flexing and unflexing to no purpose, could I do about it now?

Just as an English traveller flying in the opposite direction must prepare himself for an unrelenting atmosphere of sentimentality and violence, so I made a series of inner preparations that in the end, of course, would do no good: ritual motions, a series of perimeter defenses, an attempt to fine-tune myself for the more intricate and elaborate social coding of Britain—in America we communicate by grunting and shoving each other; occasionally we point at objects, if they're large.

What would my English friends make of the new, morose me?

Delphine Seyrig. Claude Jade. Michel Lan*ford*?

Humpty has another drink. Dumpty tries to take a nap.

2

O N A REFLEX BASIS and groggy from lack of sleep I assessed the quality of the light and cultural climate change as the train from Gatwick to Victoria ticked me past dozing fields, then a series of classbound British brickvilles under hazy morning sun: row houses humbled by their rooftops into uniform workaday slumps, other tenancies with otiose knobs of castellated gesture out front trying to deny the featureless brick, slot windows and narrow pens of sunless grass at the rear: a lot of English residential architecture tilts between the poles of the pompous and the penitent and sometimes manages to achieve both at once. It was the true, familiar English drear—Bampton, Bumpton, Bimpton, Slough—a mingy, resentful tidiness suggesting the weight of labor, the tattiness of home, and a million inconsolable kids with runny noses wailing *Mummay!*

But what New Yorker has the right?

Approach my fair city by train and you pass through a world of industrial hulks and deadgrass tractland, undisturbed by even failed aesthetic touches, that looks as if a weather system of skyborne garbage had passed through and let a blizzard of scripscrap loose from its clouds; or as if a glacier of waste had receded from the land leaving behind a moraine of fishwrap, newsprint, rags, bottles, cans and an inexhaustible strew of ex-white plastic bags, half of them snared in the branches of starving trees. Factories dumpsters bulksters bridges houses yards and the ebbtide of trash over all, ancient seabed of a rubbish sea, the epic carelessness of America.

As we clacketed nearer London I noted thickening commercial and residential accumulation, more densely ordered swarms of brick, an increasingly cramped and fortressy architectural style, all walled and curved enclosure with bright corpuscular traffic zooming down the arteries and clotting at the lights. A tall spotty kid of twentysomething bestrode the rocking aisle of the traincar, his salad hair dyed and tossed like Johnny Rotten's, wearing the clashing plaids of Johnny Rotten and complaining loudly to a smaller friend hunkered in a seat but also broadcasting to the car in a voice like Johnny Rotten's what a shit Johnny Rotten had turned into down the years, a fucking corporation now, innee.

"Fuckim," said the gloating Rotten-impersonator. "He's just another fuckin capitalist *noww*, mate. Public Image, Limited. Too fucking right."

I was now old enough, I understood, to witness the death by exhaustion of a younger generation's cultural revolution. I'd met Rotten—the one rock feature of my jazz career—and had liked his quick peremptory mind, though I didn't think his recent music was up to much.

"Fuckim, shit." The underkid cowered in his seat and the carful of working people pretended he wasn't there, while he pretended he was.

Michel . . . Michel Lom . . . some trick to his name . . . something not entirely French to it . . . gone.

City thickening, amassing its stones and smokes, London the most material of cities, pleased to seem ponderous if need be, as if moral weight accumulated with the stone.

Our train descended into a gully, brick canyoned us and we rolled in, slowed, stopped: couplers shunted home: fact engaging fact: you're here.

In the likeable high wide pleasantly ugly barn of Victoria Station, I bought a copy of *The Guardian* and consumed it at a counter over a cup of overbrewed English tea while giving Tash and his household a chance to wake up. Good old *Grauniad*: they were running original installments of Krazy Kat. Seven-thirty. Eight. International coverage thinning out, though.

Taxi time for the last of the Zabors. Could an insatiable Mercedes be far off? Father forgive me, for I know not what I do.

When the rounded black taxi pulled away from the flank of the station, lightly grinding its diesel—a distinctly English music that further notched my sense of place—the morning had gone brilliantly sunny. The train had trundled to the city beneath skies of diffuse, apparently sourceless light, but in town a rain had come and gone and scrubbed the air. The cabbie had come from Ealing Studios. Redfaced, whitehaired, big smile, he bunged my bags into the floorspace beside him: "Mornin' guv, welcome to London! Staying with old friends in Islington? Right then, welcome back!" It was hokum, but the timing was good. He wheeled us through the glistening town—rain and now the unaccustomed sun lent a jewelled shine to a freshly minted London: a few last pearls glistened on the shopfronts and the flanks of cars. I pulled my window down and had the momentary impression of travelling in an open carriage, bathed in light. The long curved wall of Buckingham Palace Gardens swayed past, and on the other side gleamed the squared, decorous spaces of the shopfronts, the freshly painted doors of townhouses—life continued, thrived.

Soon we were heading north toward Islington along Theobalds Road. I sat back in my seat, no longer the panting American dog of travel: settle in: relax. At length the cab turned left before Sadlers Wells and ascended the hill of Amwell Street, grinding past the dark brick complex that housed the pumping station for the underground river Am.

"Over there," I told the cabbie.

On both sides of the street, modest flat-fronted three-storey buildings caught the rainswept light and only a scattering of shops—greengrocer, newsagent, corner dairy, laundrette—pressed pieces of the street-level view into commercial service. The driver handed down my bags, I overtipped him, and after a central-casting wave and "Cheers, guv," he drove off.

Tash and friends were established above a downscale neighborhood hair salon, its dim front window framed by pillars painted a once-bright red—a diminished echo of Tash's past: a couple of decades back he'd been part of Swinging London and had cut important hair: Orson Welles, Goldie Hawn, Carrie-Ann Jagger and various Rolling Stones: a keen eye could find him at the edge of photographs chronicling the period.

Tash would be a world of trouble, of course. What was I doing here? Fidelity to old friends could be taken too far. At least I won't be around long. Running late for the Turkey trip. Say hello to the gang, get a lead on a car, and book.

For some reason I failed to notice the Mercedes parked almost directly in front of the building.

I hoisted my two soft suitcases and a shoulderbag already chocked with an anxious profusion of books, staggered through the building's open door to the right of the hair salon, banged into doorpost, wall, corrected for drift, hit other wall, and began a cripplecrab ascent of the creaking wooden steps. Flimsy stuff: cheap London buildings, so unlike their heavy-footed New York equivalents. The place reeked of parsimonious gas heaters and rented television: so many grades of architectural sadness in the world, so many nuances of insult for the instruction of the poor.

After one turning of the stairs then a second struggle upward, I achieved the landing and hefted my bags through the open door into the sitting room, a generous space—the walls and carpet still in tatty shades of pea-soup green, same white trim and random furniture: English Provisional. Two tall windows faced the street and let in the day. The windows were unimposing despite their height and had white frames and interior shutters that needed a coat of paint, but they would get something very different. First they would be smashed to pieces and then, two weeks after that, although the street outside was treeless, a couple of trees would burst through them into the room.

I dropped my bags, retreated to the landing and shouldered open the kitchen door onto a familiar friendly shabby place, full of shelves and cheap appliances, with lino warping in the center of the floor, clocked the remains of breakfast and saw, by bulge of curtain and rise of mist, that someone was taking a shower in the plastic stall in the room's far corner. "Tash?"

David Banon's face poked around the edge of curtain, his hair half-lathered with good shampoo. Careful of his unlined looks, David always used expensive stuff and had advised me to do the same. "Hi Rafi," his lilting voice having passed through French and whichever Indolanguage they spoke in that dot in the eastern ocean, Mauritius. "Lovely to see you. Tony's upstairs. Have some tea. There's a pot on the table."

David's face withdrew into an issue of domestic steam.

I bypassed the offered tea, shouldered my bookbag, hefted one suitcase and continued my ascent, one storey up the three tidy rooms in which David lived with his younger, pretty blond English girlfriend Sandra and occasionally with his son and daughter Justin and Miranda, then one more upward slog until chaos and decay began. The coherence of the walls fell away in gaps of busted plaster with laths showing through; elsewhere waterstains assumed the shapes of undiscovered continents, beams exposed themselves amid rinds of paint, the carpet underfoot ceased, then resumed in a different color, and at the top of the stairs I was offered a choice of doorways resembling metaphysical alternatives in a dream: off the landing to my right a room of miscellaneous rubbish and quasi-industrial discard, which I opened: in a shambles of upended porcelain, disconnected plumbing and scattered ladders, sacks and tools, a big black Gretsch drumset, stacked rather than set up, dominated the ruins. "Tash?" I asked back on the landing.

"Coriolanus," came the voice—I'll explain later—and for a moment it was a comfort to hear: how many people in England knew Lord Buckley riffs and could press their lips together and do Gil Evans' French horn intro to *Sketches of Spain*?

Tash strode into view in the doorway facing the stairhead, fixing me with his eye, the left one, from beneath a brow whose archery was always potentially lethal. He'd put on gut, I'd noticed, and his jaw seemed to have lost some definition. Yes, he was losing his looks, when once upon a time every facet of him was an instrument of charisma, alternating charm and command. Guinness may be good for you but there are limits. He was about my height, beardless some years now but retaining his entire black thatch of hair. His large irregular nose and jut of jaw still managed self-assertion through the slurring of his features, though beneath the jaw a bellying sag of throat had begun to flesh out a critique of pride. Nothing, however, had dimmed the acuity of challenge in those soul-assessing eyes. "I never liked you," Tash said first off.

"I'm not wild about you either."

"Fuck off. Morning."

Abrazos, then Tash snatched the suitcase and led me into his precincts. Through the doorway two deep narrow rooms faced streetward, the first a dumpery with most of its ceiling gone—blackened beams and a discolored underside of roof on view, a half dozen pots and tins set out on the floor to catch the rain—and stacked against the walls traces of Tash's stray professions: paintwork, construction tools, and items, here and there, of street-found machinery that he might learn to use one day or give to someone gratis: outmoded lathe, busted industrial drill, a veeblefetzer needing only a rearguard flopstock to be right as rain.

I followed Tash through a right-hand doorway into the bedroom: orderly but rundown, and almost every packrat object in it shabby. Pleasantly familiar though: my low narrow bed by the entrance at the foot of the room, Tash's on the far end below the street window, and between them a collection of tables, breakfronts, shelves, half-stereos, hotplates and hodgepodge. Hanging nearer in the room's sole place of honor on an unstained patch of wall was Tash's elegantly minimalist red-and-green prayer kilim—the prayerniche *mihrab* suggested only by a jagged green border at either side rather than fully delineated, a small black-and-white glyph afloat in crimson space to receive the bowing forehead. Bulent had picked the carpet out for him years ago in Turkey—"That one's yours," he had directed, and Tash obeyed.

I gave the ruin a once-over and suddenly it came to me. "Mahmoud West," I said.

"You only sussed that now?" asked Tash.

"I'm slow in the morning." It may have struck me then that those of us who had loved Mahmoud were if anything too much like him, and that the time for memorable characters and impoverished adventure had passed: we'd started hitting forty—Tash a few days earlier; I'd follow in three weeks. We were early and late Leos from the same year's crop, and the factfulness of life was laying a progressively heavier paw on us: we were partial beings who had left vast tracts of life untended. Tash didn't give a shit about what we had and hadn't done and perhaps he never would, but for me it was the year of feeling shaky, and the unsteadiness of our position troubled my wake and sleep. We could whistle a decent tune but had never swung the orchestration. It was entirely possible that we had blown the basic project and things were positioning themselves to take their revenge.

"Tea, squire?" Tash squared his shoulders, washed one hand with the other and rose lightly on his toes. He had an established repertoire of parody gestures. This one was either a waiter or Mine Host.

"Up here?"

Tash described an arc with his right hand and at the end of it dunked an imperial thumb at the floorboards.

"David's taking a shower," I said.

"Fuckim."

"By the way, I brought you—"

"Later." Tash dismissed my offering of bootleg Dylan tapes with an absolutist wave of arm, performed a brisk quarter-turn and marched back through the doorway. I followed him down the complaining stairs, watching his T-square but not very wide shoulders, ramrod back, and the military-parody gait that turned his knees out at every step. The narrowness of the passage prevented the full parade-ground treatment, the eyes-right eyes-left regard Tash turned upon the passing world to keep it in line. My appreciation of his hup-two operetta sergeant-major, which I'd first taken for a sharp-eyed satire of punctilio in all its forms, was only slightly diminished by learning that his father had been an army man.

The kitchen table radio played inane music and madly cheery voices yammered in British about weather, traffic, pop effluvia, irritating foreign nada. David passed through a few times and Tash's brother Mick dropped by. Everyone acted happy to see me and I was genial and dopey with travel. Tash behaved very like a human being and domineered only as an occasional flourish. I drank more tea, stumbled down the stairs to the building's only toilet just indoors of the scrawny back garden, peed tea out, and I climbed back to the kitchen. More tea and time untamed.

Tash, I noticed with small shock, seemed to be dyeing his hair: a piss-yellow patch peeked partway through his thatch of black: how come? For one thing I'd supposed him beyond the tidal pull of normal vanity—of supranormal vanity he had a paranormal supply—and besides, as one of London's former kings of hair he shoulda been able to swing a flawless dye job if he wanted one.

"It's about the Masons," Mick seemed to be telling me. "They've got all the work in town locked up, man." This had to do, as I was able to reconstruct, with the trouble Mick was having getting his light construction and painting business on its feet—wife and six kids back at home in . . . where was he living? Someplace monosyllabic not far outside of London. Hull? Husk? Hask? Hake?

Hard to stay focused. Gedding sleepy.

"C'mon man, you're shittin' me," I said. "Masons?" They'd lent Mozart money when times got hard and were good for a laugh in the Monty Python architect sketch but here was Mick tryna tell me . . .

He laid a finger alongside his nose and gave me the wink that was as good as a nod to a blind man.

"Really," I said, using the moment to turn the radio off.

'Too right, man."

The three of us did versions of international musicianspeak because we were musicians, part-time and sort of, but musicians nonetheless—Tash and Mick did pub dates with a cover band they tried to call The Heavy Light Band but the pub owners insisted on billing as The Booze Brothers—and it was remarkable how alike the three of us looked, all about five foot nine, with longish faces, big noses and dark hair. Tash didn't have his beard anymore but Mick and I had our neat-and-trims. Black Irish? Brooklyn Jew? Mox nix. Hakkı Bey would have made a smaller, darker fourth. Sid used to call us all the Mafia.

Tash lit a cigarette that was not, I noticed, one of his accustomed el cheapos but a Benson & Hedges Gold—Bulent's brand. How much was he getting on the dole? or was he pulling in outside work despite his well-known penchant for picturesque debacle? Once a master painter had made the mistake of letting Tash in on the secret of restoring elaborate ceiling rosettes: mix beer in with the paint. The sequels were local legend, and had produced a thinning of the ranks of those who still called Tash friend or would hire him for anything.

In the old days we used to smoke rollups of Golden Virginia and when we were feeling especially flush a pack of Sullivan's No. 28 from Sullivan's posh shop—fat numbers with near-transparent paper through which the topmost curls of high-quality Virginia could be seen. I'd had to quit but I took one of Tash's cigarettes and lit up in comradely fashion, no danger I'd inhale and restart the cycle: a skill picked up in Turkey, where to refuse an offered smoke can be an insult. After three puffs this one tasted lousy and I left it in the tray.

It was cozy sitting around with my English buddies but at that moment my mother's first madwoman cry broke through the scenery, not loud but eerie and unearthly as she sat beside me in the car and I put it into gear and pulled away from our house: unable to process the world shunting so inexplicably into motion she let out a high wavering cry of utter lostness, and in the rearview mirror my father went roundmouthed because, as he told me later, it was a shtetl sound: he knew that fearful music from of old.

I played with the cigarette again, but it was one of those moments, the solidity of the world draining away and an annihilating void assuming its tenancy inside each emptied object in view. I rounded the ash against the heavy glass of the ashtray, held it up for contemplation and wondered how many miles it would take for this to stop happening.

I woke to find Mick demonstrating a series of intricate hand gestures he wanted me to understand were coded Masonic mudras.

"The Masons," I said, agreeing with him now. "No shit."

"None whatever, mate."

As usual when talking with Mick I was irresistibly reminded of our friend Ivan—big, blond, knife scar down one cheek, a Viking out of the north London streets, what Nick Nolte would look like if he was really a roughneck and not just an actor with habits—telling me that Mick was the loudest fucking snorer in the universe. One night Ivan, stuck bunking with him once, couldn't take it anymore, and tiptoed across the nighttime room, a matchbox held between his fingers, waited for the perfect moment in the cycle of Mick's breath, then made the drop. Fast for a big man, he flashed across the dark as Mick woke up gasping and was under the covers suppressing laughter before Mick was conscious enough to remove the matchbox and look around.

"Where's Ivan these days?" I asked. Last I'd heard he'd managed to stay out of jail on the dope and housebreaking beefs and had gotten a job selling burglar alarms.

"He's head groundskeeper at Newmarket races," Mick told me.

"What happened to the burglar alarms?"

"They asked him to scare the clientele," said Mick, "and he wouldn't do it."

"Told them he didn't think God would like it," Tash said. "Then Newmarket came up and he took it."

"We oughta go see him there," I said. "Take in a race, put a couple of bets down, say hello."

"Could do."

"Ever been?"

"No," said Tash.

David reappeared in the kitchen, back from errands upstairs. He turned the hot water tap on at the sink and the wall-mounted gas heater said *poff* and a trickle of heated water issued forth. Primitive country, what? Why can't they waste natural resources on the same grand scale as grown-ups?

David didn't look like the three of us and had the best manners in the room. Even while fiddling at the sink he had polite questions for me and some actual interest in the answers. His East Indian coloring was a dark honey shade, his longish wavy black hair had gone past halfway grey, though his moustache had remained dark, and his soft-featured face lacked our trio's irregularity of feature.

He rinsed a pot of tea and reinfused it, brought new clean cups to the table and joined us. "So Rafi," he said, putting the accent on the first syllable, which is not where I preferred it, "how long will you be staying with us?"

"A few days. Just passing through. Trying to get to Turkey before . . ."

Had Tash made a noise? Tash seemed to have made a noise of which the vanity of human wishes was the subject.

". . . going to Belgium and buying a car . . ."

Tash definitely sarcastically cleared his throat.

". . . so I can get to a few places in Turkey I haven't seen yet, and my knee . . ."

"More tea, vicar?"

"Yesplease."

"Toast?" asked David, rising. Whomp of matchlit broiler.

And somewhere in there I thought I'd like a shower and the kitchen convocation politely decamped.

When Tash and Mick and I hit the street fifteen minutes later, the morning had dimmed and a rectangular mattress of grey cloud leaking tendrils of its innards at its edges floated over Islington. No rain down here, however. For some reason, we were standing not on the sidewalk but in the street.

"Quick quick, he's coming down," I was incomprehensibly urged by Tash and Mick, who were pointing, who were indicating I should, "Stand over here, no, here, he's been impossible since he bought the thing, just shake your head and look miserable," and seeing David emerge from the building, the brothers went into theatrical tut-tut poses, shaking their heads and applying a hand to chin or brow. "Oh dear what a shame, oh dear oh dear, just look at that . . ."

I was slow to understand the point of this as David was joined by his edgy intelligent adolescent son Justin—where had he been hiding?

"Oh dear oh dear," Tash and Mick continued in rough unison, tutting here, headshaking there, and gradually it dawned on me that I was being encouraged to mourn the streetside flank of the car separating us from David and his son: a roughly ten-year-old dark-coral-orange Mercedes.

"Oh dear oh dear, someone must have run into it in the night," Tash announced, sounding like a landlady lamenting the weather. "Looks bloody awful, don't it Mick."

"Bloody awful gash that is," said the brother. "Paint's totally fucked."

David hardly bothered to laugh as he waved their antics away. "What a pair of asses you are," he said. "Ready, Justin?"

"Got to give his leg a pull now and then," Mick confided to me in an aside, "he's been such a prick since he bought that motor."

I snuck a glimpse around the back of the car and saw the number on the trunk lid: 200, no E, a low-end Benz two models back, with a slightly dumpy, baffled look by current standards. "Good car?" I asked David as he keyed his door open and Justin came around to our side to climb in.

"Great car," David said. "Love it."

"Whadjou pay?"

"Three and a half and worth every penny."

"Really," I asked, ignoring the bathroom noises issuing from the brothers.

David eased himself inside, and Justin, ignoring us completely as he came around to our side of the car, opened the door and climbed in.

"David's been a cunt about that car," said Tash, backing his brother up.

"Has he?"

"Fuckin' unbelievable. A man of property now," Tash said, and though David seemed unchanged to me I wondered if I went ahead with the project would I be seen to . . . "The Grand Illusion," Tash concluded.

Mick and Tash and I made way as David steered his after all rather modest-looking barge off the curb and into the general swim. Bit too much blue in the exhaust, I thought as I waved goodbye. Burning oil.

"How come David's not working?" I asked Mick, who might give me a straight answer.

"Bank holiday innit," then, "Feel like a pint?" it seemed he had asked his brother, and I wondered two things: was it so late already that the pubs were open? and why would Mick of all people make so dangerous an invitation since who knew better than he that the pellet with the poison was in the flagon with the dragon. Tash drinking up most of its wine cellar had certainly helped kill their undercapitalized restaurant project seven years back in Oxford. Tash's other *specialité* of that *maison* had been strolling amid the diners playing softly upon a guitar or a drum and, once alcohol had perfected its work in him, collapsing backward, cruciform and unconscious in the center of some innocent strangers' four-course dinner; a pause would follow for the effect to sink in and then he'd slide to the floor and bring the table down. This at least had been funny, if you weren't losing your family savings to the act, as Mick had. Scarier by far had been the conscience-free insouciance with which Tash had charmed and hauled in a series of semi-rich acquaintances to refinance that rolling catastrophe in its declension from fancy French joint to kebab house to let's sell the fixtures and get out before the police turn up; several small fortunes were consumed in the process, and I didn't see Tash blink once as he reeled another sucker into the orbit of its collapse. It was possible that he conceived of himself, if he still bothered to conceive of himself at all, as something on the order of a force of nature, like high wind, high seas, a high opinion of oneself, or perhaps an impersonal instrument of God's redistribution of the wealth of nations. Tash had a certain roving, raider, Mongol contempt for all settled peoples, and if he could not command a Horde he could manage some small pieces of good even if he had to do it without actual horses and rapine.

My own last memory of Tash in his cups was set in a local pub so serious and esoteric that it chalked on a blackboard in descending order the specific bleedin' gravities of the beers and ales they had on tap. Tash sat there on an edge of stool from which some unknown force prevented him from toppling even though he'd downed ten pints of whatever sludge had been elected to poison our night, and growled at me, "You cunt. You cunt, you miserable fuckin' cunt." He had passed beyond the subtleties of character assassination by then and taken up the bludgeon of insult, although he hadn't yet started calling me Jew, which usually followed Cunt on his rolodex of wrath. Why had I sat there? Why did it always seem to me, when I should have known better for eons already, that if you talked rationally and in friendly fashion to him he would relent and return to human form?

What made Tash so lethal a drunk is that the alcohol corrupted and distorted his faculties without weakening them: in older, more sober days he had been the most eerily perceptive person I'd ever met, and even then his insights into one's character weren't particularly kind. Now drink may have turned him vicious but his aim was still acute, and when he wanted to hurt you, he could always find the spot.

And yet it was still there in him, a quality, a subtlety, a something he possessed . . . beyond anyone we knew . . . as Hakkı Bey had pointed out . . . on a good day . . . or year . . . when you could find it . . . ah Christ . . .

"A pint," Tash replied to Mick, "would be just the thing."

Ack, I thought. Tash picked up the wave of worry I had sent spinning through the aether, and favored me with an admonitory flash of eye. I glanced at Mick for guidance, but he returned me no meaning look, and seemed placid at the prospect of pints all round.

So we headed diagonally across the intersection for the corner pub, then ordered pint pint pint and drank them down. I heard a few minutes' further testimony to the insidious solidarity of the Masons—they'd as soon starve us—then Mick was saying goodbye he had to go and—hold page one—we exited the pub without having ordered a single additional beer. A miracle of sorts. After a round of handshakes on the corner and a reminder about an upcoming pub date for the band, Mick got into a worn blue van and drove off to look a property over.

"You know," I said on the way back across the intersection with Tash, "that pint might have set me up perfectly for—"

"A kip?"

"Two three hours tops or I won't sleep tonight."

"I'll wake you."

"Hey, how are Bulent and Sid?"

"You'll see them tomorrow. We're going to Sherborne."

"Are we? How come?"

"Trustees' meeting at the House," Tash told me. "You'll see all the old friends you never had."

This unexpectedly quick chance to see Sid and the Bey startled me a bit—no time to prepare a self in advance—but as we trundled up the stairs I felt my London burden lightened by the new, essentially friendly, one-beer Tash. It was almost like keeping company with a human being.

"I had a rough couple of years out there," I said, essaying a confidence to my new pal. "My folks had a hard time dying and I was in the middle of it for the distance."

Tash began to laugh hoarsely. "Something I've got to show you," he said. At the top of the stairs he swung into the sitting room. "We put on a bash for my dad's birthday this year," Tash told me, still laughing softly as he rummaged through a miscellany of curling papers on the mantelpiece over the gas fire whose interior was a chalky grid of reconstituted dinosaur bones and not the artificial log-turd model popular in some of your homes, O England. "We took this photo of him," he said, beginning to go a bit wheezy on the laugh as he handed the picture over, a color shot, and not only did Tash's father look so much like mine that depending on the pose you could have taken one for the other, but this picture, which had been shot in a garden with the stone wall of a house in the background, lawn beneath, and a border of flowers, featured Tash's father stumbling in mock horror beneath the burden of a paper skeleton whose arms someone had tied around his neck and draped over his shoulders.

Tash was wheezing with helpless laughter while I rocked in disbelief at the blatancy of the signifier. "Some picture," I said.

Tash was laughing too hard to reply, and he leaned momentarily on my shoulder to support himself. "Wha' a pisser," he managed at last.

"I'll say. How old is he."

"Seventy-eight."

My father's last age exactly. This was very unsubtle workmanship, I thought. Chekhov wouldn't touch it with a bargepole.

Tash kept laughing and wheezing at the photo and I kept goggling at it and that was the moment and it took a nice long time for it to finish and go.

Naptime. I hauled my sagging body up the stairs on its one bad and one good leg, reached bedroom, shucked off shoes, clothes, crawled gratefully under the covers of the narrow familiar bed—forgot to call Sara and tell her I was in town: fix that later—and just before the recent pint eased my plunge into unconsciousness I felt a tiny electrical impulse in a left rear quadrant of my brain make the leap it had been stumbling over as some doughty neuron shouldered its message over the synaptic fence and at last it came to me, a tiny connective dose of bliss adding its dollop of relief to the promise of sweet sleep:

Michael Lonsdale.

I'D BEEN EXPECTING Tash to wake me with a word or a touch on the arm, but a noise did it and judging by the quality of the light in the room it was later in the day than I wanted to have slept. There came that clunk or clank again and I grogged up onto one elbow to see what was up besides me. Tash was sitting crosslegged midway down the bedroom floor and he had dropped the bottle again. I felt my eyes widen and jaw drop as if I were an actor who couldn't do better. The noise had come from a pint of Scotch he kept dropping and redropping, most of it, I noticed, already gone. I'd never seen him drunk on hard liquor. Mere beer had been bad enough. His slowed-down heavy head swung my way.

"Time for lunch," he said.

"Lunch?"

"We're going out."

"Are we?"

A snort for retort, untwist the cap and a slosh from the bottle. Here we go, I told myself. How far? Where?

I dressed, splashed the features, brushed my teeth from the trickle at the drumroom sink and followed Tash down the stairway as he only lightly caromed left to right between the walls. He left the bottle in the kitchen with a couple of inches left. He smelled of sweat and Scotch.

Out on the street Tash seized my left, thank God unpained elbow, locked it in his right and we were walking bonded arm to arm across Amwell Street, my knee hobbling me, the ache swelling: I dragged behind and dipped with each step my right foot took. What did this remind me of? Dostoevsky? Dickens? Oh no, I wasn't getting off easy with literature: it was worse: it was life: I was my mother, that day on the boardwalk when her legs had died beneath her and, trailed by my father in his oxygen rig, with a lot of old Russians watching from the benches, I dragged her by the arm across the herringbone slats of the boardwork, a roiled slate sea behind us and a chill wind coming on while I insisted in a hiss *There's nothing wrong with your legs.* After that the day got steadily, remorselessly worse. Now the replay, every cruelty returned to me on schedule, a trick done with mirrors, as only Tash could manage it.

"Tash I can't keep up with you."

Another snort. "You never could."

"Yes I know but that's not what I mean. My knee's messed up. For Chrissake let go."

Derisive laugh as he locked me tighter and hauled us ahead. No half measures or passing truths. Yes, I told Hakkı Bey doggedly in my mind, I get it, I remember what you told me, but that was back in the day when Tash's faculties were undistorted and his act so convincing he sometimes seemed like Truth in all its confounding ruggedness, whole. He has his hooks in me from the old days and can still wring a piece of the old fealty from me but, Hakkı, take a look at him now, willya? There is definitely something wrong with this picture.

We passed the stone church set in the center of its placid square, then left the quiet of the stonefaced residential neighborhood to emerge at the busy junction opposite the Angel Underground. Soon we were laboring armlocked and slagfoot through the shopping crowds east along Upper Street.

I felt so self-conscious I didn't even notice if we were stared at as we shuttled past the queues at the ranked bus stops and along the shore of shopfronts—chains like Dixon's and McDonald's, I saw, had begun moving in although the cluster of antique shops and the antiques arcade persisted across Upper Street's multilane tangle of cars and tilting tall red buses. Scraps and rinds of market litter strayed underfoot from adjacent finger streets of shops and stalls, traces of London's complex commercial blood, where local differences persisted and country ways seeped into town: market days, regional and class accents, prices going down as evening neared.

"Tash please let go of my arm."

He grappled me tighter and began speaking nonsense Turkish: *"Sus tané."*

In Turkey, whence Tash had derived the gesture, walking joined at the elbow was common among normal statutory manly men but here it jarred; Tash seemed unbothered but to me it was nightmarish to be dragged crippleknee'd through the weave of people. That was Tash for you: just when you're half-prepared for a night of slowmouthed mean-spirited knifetwisting obscenity between barstools, another long ugly scene with Tash grinding the lens of insult until the clarity of pain was achieved, he outflanks you with a move you are unable to imagine in advance or, strangely, free yourself from in the event. Psychotic boozers can be canny bastards, and when they run their outrageous line of shit on you, inflate themselves and loose a tide of contempt upon the lesser souls caught in their all-clarifying view, they often have a fine-tuned sense of just how much the market will bear: they understand how to craze the air with a perfectly calibrated threat of metaphysically final violence: try to cross me and worlds will collide, primal chaos break forth and you will be hauled into experience impossible for you to endure and weather you cannot survive; so you cave before the prospect of confrontation and the moment stretches like some hideous moral taffy which nothing seems able to break; the air gets sucked out of the cabin, the laws of probability vanish to windward, your normal worldly gyroscope topsies, turvies, totters and veers you heartsick on that sea until you wonder will it ever end. Add to that Tash's sharknosed scent for the blood of hidden crime and you'll have the present picture pretty clear.

"Tash let go I'm in pain here."

"Sus tané," he said again, mangling two of the five Turkish words he knew. *Sus,* anyway, meant shuddup.

"Tash my knee hurts I can't keep up."

"Sus tané."

"Where are we going?"

"Sus," he said, hauling me along.

So, for my sins, I was lashed to the wheel of a mad captain's ship plow-

ing through fathomless seas of *al kahal*. It was still an open question
where we were going or in what unseemly shipwreck it would end, but on
the internal plane Tash's weather eye was eerily accurate: fuel him with
whiskey, double your image in his sight and blur both pictures into smears,
and he'd remain God's scourge writ just your size.

The angel of psychosis smiled on him still.

I tried to pull away from him but it was no go.

Tash's rolling eye regarded me, unanswerable because insane.

"Where we going, Tash?"

"Turkish place."

"Good."

We'd put the thickmost patch of crowd behind us and were approaching an overnamed wedge of treelined lawn between Upper Street
and a road angling right: Islington Green. The cinema, left across from
the Green, was featuring *The Color Purple*. The street-level storey of the
tan brick building past the Green and across from the theatre housed a
signless restaurant windowed on three sides. Tash dragged me there,
then pushed open a set of double doors in a swaggering cowboy-movie
entrance that commanded a modest Turkish eatery in beige, a few innocent diners seated at a scattering of tables.

"Tevfik!" Tash called out, and a greying thickset man nearing sixty
emerged through an archway from the kitchen at the rear.

"Ya, Tash," the man said in a voice part lifted in an arc of welcome,
part declining as he gauged Tash's current alcohol content with a practiced eye.

"*Kahve?*" Tash asked me, then confirmed the choice with an assertion
of his jaw. "*Kahve!*" Relinquishing my arm he marched off to the kitchen
to make the designated coffee, Tevfik trying to divert him with a blur of
hands that had no effect on his trajectory. A fortyish Turkish woman with
black hair appeared in the kitchen arch, her face falling tired and weary
as Tash strode past her.

I pulled out a chair and sat my body down, a moment of bliss and ease.

The succeeding scene remains a merciful blur in memory, from
which a handful of particulars wave hello.

When it became clear that Tash was insufficiently armed to demolish the restaurant—although once he got started on the coffee he made one dramatic backstepping appearance in the proscenium of the kitchen arch brandishing a longhandled brass Turkish coffeepot like a cutlass, as if duelling with a scurvy insubordinate stove—Tevfik heavied his way to my table to introduce himself, and with the Turkish solicitude for travellers that is a relic of nomadism long gone he established a zone of comfort and shared discourse that welcomed me, acknowledged Tash's booze-madness and one's abiding affection for him anyway. He accomplished this in a few words and an eloquent minimum of facial semaphore and checked to see that he was understood. It felt good, being back in Turkey. "Tash: a stone," Tevfik said, translating the name into English for me.

I nodded.

"We don't know. Maybe a diamond, maybe a lump of coal."

"Maybe both," I said.

"*Sus tané!*" issued from the kitchen, followed by the darkhaired woman raising eyes to the ceiling and washing her hands on her white apron of all further involvement with the impossible *madjub* let loose in her dominion.

Tevfik ran his hand through his wiry grey hair and shrugged the weight of fate away. My very limited Turkish sufficed to get me halfway through telling him I was heading for Turkey and halfway to saying I was hungry, but there I stopped—use the wrong *i* sound, *achiğim* or *achığım*, and you might appear to be inviting buggery, and I'd forgotten which vowel was which. Tash came to the table flourishing two delicate white china cups of coffee on a cheaply damascened brass tray and ordered food for us both before I could indicate what I wanted. I arranged a number of breadcrumbs on the table in a diamond pattern, placed a single crumb in its center, then looked out the window and read: The Screen on the Green. *The Color Purple.* The Screen on the Green. *The Color Purple.* The Screen on the Green. *The Color Purple.*

Tash insisted that I appreciate the perfection of the coffee he'd made and I told him that I did. It was good, with just a highlight of sugar brightening its depths. Then he asked me to admire the coffee again, and

I did. After that he didn't have to ask, only indicate the cup with his chin whenever either of us took a sip, and all I had to do was nod back yes, it was good.

In my weariness and under the lowering stormcloud of Tash's behavior, throbbing and pulsing with its internal electrics, the eventual oval platters of kebab, rice and a little salad eventually appeared and were almost infinitely welcome, but if I'd expected the simplicity of food to provide respite or even, as Tash began working his portion down, for it to soak up his alcohol content, I was mistaken, although the weight of his drunkenness did not fall on me this time. Somewhere in the middle of our meal it emerged that Tevfik's son, a roundfaced toddler five years old at most, had hardly been out of the restaurant that busy day—the wearied woman in the kitchen nook was his mother, and Tevfik's wife—and Tash, stirred to God knew what unhinged sense of gallantry, clattered his fork aside, seized the boy by his pudgy hand—the kid's large black eyes registered a soulful depth of unexpressable protest—and insisting on the immediate necessity of a healthgiving walk yanked him through the doorway into the rush hour crush of Upper Street. Tevfik, rehearsed in the ways of fatality, let it happen to the accompaniment of a stoic sigh and continued with me at the table as I ate, and in a mix of my Tarzan Turkish and his better English he asked after me, my family—dead, I told him; he sympathized, and we shared a depth of feeling, impossible between Western folks of comparably short acquaintance, that was part theatrical convention, part sentimental male bullshit, and part authentic communion—until his wife, whose attention restaurant work had consumed until then, registered the fact that Tash was out there with her kid in tow.

As in rapid Turkish and gathering fury she discussed the point with Tevfik, my attention was tugged awake by the uncommon chorus of automobile horns outside. I craned my head away from this after all unintelligible conversation to notice the clutter of cartops immediately outside the restaurant, then, following my ears to the epicenter of the tumult down Upper Street beyond the Green, my eyes widened when they saw, across the beetlebacked carapaces of the cars, Tash's torso thrust furiously forward in the crush, aiming a laser-straight arm and finger down the windshield of the offending machine that had screeched to a halt in front of him. His mouth was giving the driver a piece of his mind, and it looked like a large piece, and a loud one. Tash's left arm slanted down along his side, and he looked down it to speak more softly, confirming that the kid was still anchored to its end. Then Tash bellowed quickly up at a car that had made an unconsidered move, and the carhorn chorale worked its way toward free-form polyphony out of late Charles Ives. Tash swept his arm in a commanding arc across the cartops.

Looking back at Tevfik and his wife, I experienced a classic silent-movie moment—the word within a word, unable to speak a word, my mouth open, wide eyes blinking—and then, without, I think, taking in the full sweep and implication of the panorama outside, Tevfik's wife flung a glare of bloody murder at Tevfik and tore out the doorway into Islington. The double doors swung shut behind her, swept back inward, rocked a few times, settled.

Tevfik and I sat there in her aftermath, and among the things I thought in this caesura, one was particularly galling: Michel Lom*bard*?

I didn't see the rescue of the child. It took perhaps two minutes for Tevfik's wife to find the heart of darkness, extract her son intact, tow him back into the restaurant and sweep past us, too furious for even a passing glance, into the safe harbor of the kitchen at the rear.

The other patrons of the place minded their own business, peeked when they dared, and thought about finishing their kebabs before that lunatic came back.

Outdoors Tash was still conducting traffic and issuing damnations but the scale seemed diminished, and Tash even sidestepped, arching his back like a bullfighter's, to allow a car to pass.

Had it come to this? It was such a classic alcoholic trope, haranguing traffic, the last alcoholic flailing of a famished will to power. Is this what we'd worked for, broke our hearts and gave up the points of our compass of judgment for love beyond thought and circumscription? It was a long way down from the eccentric heights Tash occupied, once upon a time, in the days of gold.

It only took a minute for Tash to return quieter but unabashed, his jaw lowered not a jot against the gravity of dispraise, for Tevfik to refuse all payment for my eaten lunch and the one that Tash had barely touched, and to allow Tash and me back onto Upper Street with early evening coming down. Awfully, Tash grappled my elbow to him again, this time the right one, and we blundered homeward as magenta began its fall over London.

Tash seemed precisely as drunk and nuts as he had been en route to the restaurant, a demonstration perhaps that he used alcohol as a key to the energies of psychosis, and that once he entered that state, obtaining his relief from gravity, additional drinks were not required.

We had wandered from the mainstem of Upper Street into the remains of the market day on tributary lanes of shuttered stores and stalls, where rinds and papers tangled underfoot on hosed-down asphalt. Just before reattaining the junction at the Angel we proceeded along a narrow sidewalk between a brick wall on our left and cars parked bumper to bumper to our right. A duckboard shipping palette lay in our path, two levels of slat nailed together over a frame of solid lumber four or five feet square, and Tash, my right arm still pinioned in his left, stooped without breaking stride and as if momentarily invested with the strength of Uncle Avram grabbed the palette by its corner and spun it into the air out of our way. A brand new bright red Fiat Uno was parked in the arc of its fall, and the palette hit the car on the hood with one of its corners, which skidded so that an edge of wood produced a convincing dent about a foot long in the sheet metal and a protruding nailhead tore a gouge through the paint. The palette then bounced, and when it came down a second time its flat edge hit, slid off above the headlight and performed a second feat of damage I was unable to see, although I heard glass or plastic crack. Without the slightest backward glance Tash hauled us onward, and hobbled alongside what seemed a locomotive of pure destructive force, I was unable to come up with a *Klaatu barada nikto* sufficient unto the day, only whinge again, as ineffectively as before, "Tash slow up my leg is killing me."

I felt something like despair: the world was a chaos and your friends were insane. It was fusillade without respite out here, the hope of shelter a torn poster on a wall.

We got back to the house without further incident. Tash picked up the flask of Scotch en route to the top floor and when we got there I sat crumpled on my bed. Tash teetered, holding an edge of a folding wooden chair, then swigging at the remains of whiskey subsided to the floor as if down the cellar steps of the poor man's refuge, the beaten man's bliss, cheapest counterfeit of transcendent experience out there, for Christ's sweet sake you can buy it legal in a store.

"Coriolanus," Tash said in a softened voice, and waved me over.

"What." I wearied myself to the chair beside him, sat.

"You wanted to see your friend Tash," he said in a broken voice, uncharacteristic because he never copped to weakness, didn't believe in it, wouldn't have it, it wasn't there, "and Tash is a mess."

What followed was an appalling, cross-purpose conversation of which the details are lost, so that all I can offer is a reconstruction, which might have been written for "quality" television in the fifties as an object lesson in the rote conception of "the problem of communication," a ubiquitous trope in the culture of the day. What I do remember in shaming clarity is my vocal tone in the duet: it was the second time in about a year I had gone mealymouthed in the presence of psychosis, and I did it so broadly it would not get by in a film or on stage, where the actor would be rejected for overdoing the nonentity bit. My jaw had lost its talking muscles, my voice its chest notes, and my tongue had gone spineless. It was the voice of an abdication so blatant no one would employ it except in the artlessness of life.

"You wanted to see your friend Tash, and Tash is a mess."

"I've had a rough few years myself," was all I could manage, in a voice I was unable to alter. "My mother lost her mind and my father couldn't breathe. It was a small apartment."

"None of them can stand me," Tash said of the people we knew in common. "No one can stand me anymore."

"I was there about three years," I told him, "and even after my mother died and I was alone with my dad it was rough because we were both so exhausted."

"I go up to Chisholme and those cunts all hate me."

"I thought the time with my father was gonna be easy because we were so close but it wasn't and all he'd talk about was money. All he wanted to tell me day in day out was don't spend it."

"Those cunts can't take me anymore. None of them can take me anymore."

"We both knew he was going to die that year."

"And David's worse. There's an offer from the Council to buy this building on the cheap but he won't go in on it with me. Twenty-five grand's all they want and the cunt won't do it with me."

"After all we'd been through and looking death in the face, can you believe it, my dad and I found things to argue about."

"David can't take me anymore. None of them can take me anymore."

"So even that was rough."

"The Grand Illusion. They've all gone for the Grand Illusion. Fuckem."

"So I'm kind of shot, you know?"

"Life is like being invited to a wonderful party and they're not enjoying it? I don't have any time for that. They can all fuck off."

"I'm hoping that maybe on this trip I can get back some, you know."

"The Grand Illusion."

"Well, we'll see."

"Fuckem if they can't take a joke."

"Could I have some of that whiskey?"

"I've said it all and they don't want to hear it. Zum zum. Zum zum zum. That's all. Everybody out."

"Would you give me a little sip of that."

"Zum zum zum. The Grand Illusion."

"Thanks."

"It took you long enough to have a drink with me, you miserable cunt. Zum zum. Fuck off. 'Koff. Ha. Don't waste a syllable on 'em. 'Koff."

It ended after a few more pages.

We sat around.

Michel Lom*pard*?

Eventually went to bed.

Where I tumbled into a deep, throbbing hum of sleep, a time and motion study in folds of heavy black, mumblemind through blur and texture, a stunned ruminative fall through curtained dark. Long time last such. Last long such time. At longlast eversuch.

Wounds fleshed over. Fortunate fall.

Drooled a little on the pillow.

A crash woke me at four in the morning and I whirred up out of the depths—a light on in the room and Tash, naked, with his back to me, had toppled sideways into the breakfront on the left-hand wall, righted himself with a shove and wobbled on toward his bed, steps thudding on the floorboards: back from a visit to the can—old paint can in the neighbor room or maybe a pee in the drumroom sink. Someone—who was it? Aaron—had once pointed out, discussing Tash in the light of his triple-Leo natal chart, that he was in fact built like a lion: the narrow shoulders, ribs showing under the skin of the back, the sagbelly sack shown in quarter-profile as he stumbled rightward, and between his legs, rear view, beneath the narrow arse, hanging low at the end of an absurdly distended scrotum, a remarkably large pair of balls—it lacked only a cartoonist to put in the one or two finishing touches of mane and fur and fang, but there was Tash without them, an aged lion, half-pickled and doddering but still a recognizable king of the beasts, for as long as he could put the act over on the pride.

He almost tipped over sideways but a steadying stomp of his left foot saved him.

And what I thought at that moment, once I had gotten over the improbable size of those balls, was, We're in deep trouble here. All those changes of country, crossings of oceans into continents of new experience, heights and depths of visions seen, braveries wrung from the flesh of normal unwilling human hearts—all the varied orbits and motions that composed our lives may only have served to set up the final pitfall and sharpen the waiting blade. Tash was a mere wreck of the former ruin of himself, Hakkı a lesser alcoholic dabbling his way into a smack habit that would probably rear up full size one day, and yours truly—"Necks!"—

looking as if he lacked the bottle to survive in any essential sense the routine passing of mom and pop. Maybe these were the last flips and wriggles before the critique was writ large upon our impercipient brows and our doom made legible to all.

Tash got the lamp off on his third pass at the chain and fell sideways into the sack, yelling *Fuck!* as flesh and bone hit bedframe. Something fell, something else rolled across the floor in the dark. Tash shifted, reshifted, cursed, settled, and after licking his chops for a contemplative minute began churning out a sequence of tunnelthroated ripsaw snores that would bear him, like a fallen warrior supine upon his bier, through all the pitch-black wide-eyed hours I spent before mercy and remission drifted in with the dawn. I made some noises and threw my shoes in his general direction but it didn't do him any good.

The angelheaded hipster division was hitting the beaches differently damaged at forty and it did not look good.

3

TASH PARTED THE VEILS of humming numbing sleep
made of lack of sleep and woke me at nine in the morning—cold
sober, no sign of booze-fatigue, and speaking in what I liked to
think of as his Spiritual Fog Voice: his normal instrument lightened,
lofted, aerated: his register of innocence: "Ah, good morning Rafi," he
said when I surfaced, and pushed a white mug of tea with milk and sugar
into my face. I could smell the sugar. "I hope you had a pleasant sleep."

"Uff," I said. "Rh. Wgg."

"We're out the door in half an hour."

"Fuhhh," I said, the only one in earshot worse for wear.

"I'll be downstairs." Tash sauntered off and I sipped at the tea.

The Spiritual Fog Voice meant that we were probably safe for the
day. Once he had pulled that stop on the organ all his music would be
harmonious and serene. I had Bulent to thank for this change of tune, his
ample proleptic sphere of influence summoning notes of classical decorum and placing them clear and ordered upon the stave.

I sat up, swung legs, eventually stood and was amazed, but didn't want
to think and jinx it. Bent the knee, stressed it. Sip the tea. Not a word.

We caught the 190 Red Arrow Express bus for Oxford. At no time was
there in Tash's demeanour the least whisper of back-reference or tremor
of remorse for yesterday's chaos and abruptions. He was cool and unread-

able as a Sphinx, and I was still too unschooled in the shades of *al kabal* to realize that he might have no memory of yesterday at all; but more amazing among the day's remissions was the fact that my knee was no longer of a mind to attack me: tested it on the stairs, sidewalks and in the enforced fixity of my seat on the bus and the pain was gone, though, true, there was still a thrumming in the fibers of my cricket elbow. Amazing. I sent a beam of thanks to Richard Hirsch and his blood-voodoo magnetology.

In Oxford we cooled our heels in the lot behind the Welsh Pony Inn without, wonderfully, dropping in for a pint, until the departure of a country coach that wound the local roads westward through the green world, jouncing on an old suspension, some of its windows open, the smell of land and occasional manure breezing in.

"I ever tell you about the first time I met Bulent?" Tash wondered. We were sitting across the aisle from each other in the mostly empty bus, giving our legs a stretch in the brown interior.

"Some Beshara get-together?"

"I was sitting in the kitchen of Marianne Faithfull's flat with Lennon and McCartney—"

I burst out laughing. "Aw c'mon man gimme a break."

"I was sitting in Marianne Faithfull's kitchen with Lennon and Mc-Cartney," Tash persisted. "The Rolling Stones were sitting in a circle in the sitting room with the head of the London constabulary—"

"Waitaminnit waitaminnit. A black magic circle?" Years back, Grenville Collins had told me about asking Bulent, What's this I heard the other day about you sitting in a black magic circle with the Rolling Stones? My dyah, laughed Collins in his rendering of Bulent's voice in answer, there is *no* better way of breaking up a circle than from inside it.

"Wasn't any black magic about it," Tash told me. "The Stones were sitting in a circle and we were all so wrecked on opium none of us could move or talk. There was a police car out front with its blue light spinning so no one would bother us, and the head of the London police was as stoned on O as we were. We fucking ran London those days, man. We ran the fucking town. Then this enormous man walked in. I'd never seen anyone that big. It was the Bey. This is before anyone had ever heard of Beshara. And right at that moment everything changed."

"What changed?" I asked.

"*Everything,*" Tash pronounced, indicating major cultural transformation but blocking the view of its particulars, and as he clocked me snooping for them he palpably chilled and withdrew from all exchange. Although, "This was when Bulent was working for the Kray brothers," he added.

"Whaaaat?" I asked him, the elastic of my disbelief-suspenders snapping and my pants falling down. The Krays, twin psychotic rulers of the underworld back then. "What are you trying to palm off on me, some ridiculous sixties cartoon?"

He gave me the familiar dismissive look but answered anyway. "Bulent worked for the Krays when he first came to England. They were illiterate. He wrote letters for them. They liked him. They wanted to set him up in business. If you wanted to buy a refrigerator those days you went to the Krays, mate. They wanted to set Bulent up as a front man in one of their businesses but he didn't think God would like it, and he left."

I decided not to quarrel with the absurdity of the story and to get that last detail. "What do you mean everything changed."

"Everything," Tash said from beneath an arched eyebrow: a door slamming shut.

The bus eventually dropped us in placid Burford, Gateway to the Cotswolds.

What I can't remember is how Tash and I got from Burford to the tiny target of Sherborne eight miles west. I possess a reel of mental film in which Tash and I are standing on the roadside with our thumbs extended, but this may not be a documentary feature, only fiction, since who would have picked us up? Two Mafia types with countercultural emanations? We didn't walk all the way. Did someone we knew motor by and open a welcoming door?

It's a blank, but at length we achieved the intended roadbank in Albion. Ralph Vaughan Williams had composed *The Lark Ascending,* the homegrown English transcendence in excelsis, not three miles off in a cottage in Bibury, and the local fields still showed the richness of his influence: the gently swelling breasts of green pasture across the road were English music composed in chorus-lengths demarcated by grey walls of rusticated Cotswold limestone or a line of trees, overarched by blue encircling sky with sailing fleets of cloud for expressive context: fields you would swear breathed as you watched them, an ordered rise and fall, a respiration of mothering earth. To an American eye there was too little forest left in hemmed, enclosured England, but this landscape made a music that overwhelmed its walls.

We were running late, and walked away from the view, on balding tartop that ran between stone abutments to the town of Sherborne, the tree parade on either side thinned by the Dutch Elm plague of recent years—a broken straggle of tall survivors raised flittering heads into the breeze. We encountered no houses until we reached the junction that began the town.

Grey limestone walls lowered their shoulders and simple wooden gates appeared in the gaps, opening paths to stone cottages and their working gardens: Lord Sherborne's outriggers for landservants in the days when he owned everything in sight and we strangers hadn't shown our suspect city faces yet. The feudal echo barely was audible now beneath the egalitarian anthem of the National Trust.

"What time's the meeting?" I wanted to know.

Tash favored me with a snort for answer and picked up the pace.

Your narrator is experiencing a difficulty, for a change.

This is the moment I have been trying to put off for over two hundred pages. The reader will have noted the appearance in this narrative of characters with odd, foreign-sounding names attached to their heads like thought balloons and still odder, more foreign-seeming behavior, and has seen me leaning aslant in a doorway at the margin of the action, taking up the pose of the last sane man in a roomful of loonies. But it is time to confess that when I was young I ran away with the circus. Or rather at a certain point in my life the clown corps came and got me.

When the information is squeezed out of me by the juice-press of conversation gone awry, I usually say yes, I am in fact loosely affiliated with a sinister death cult but we only kill a child once or twice a year, on special occasions. Then, looking evasive beneath the weight of further inquiry, I might mutter something about oh, Snufism and then, like a good shepherd, I get the flock out of there.

I've run out of evasions now, so it's onward into the maw of an underrecorded subculture—it's usually written about either satirically or devoutly, in a bracketed manner—eyes wide open and no lies allowed along the way.

We turned right at the crossroad and walked along the roadside verge beside the high grey wall until we reached the main gate of Sherborne House, where J. G. Bennett had run, in the years immediately preceding his death, the ten-month courses of his modified-Gurdjieff school. He had met the formidable Mr. Gurdjieff on the Bosphorus in the immediate aftermath of the Great War, but had gone around the block many times since then, and had incorporated the results of his researches and adventures. Installed in our Sufi funny farm across the fields, our troupe—Beshara, to give it its proper name—sometimes used to call Sherborne House the Bennettentiary; Bennett's riposte was to dub us the Beshara Lovies, but some of his inmates, having little inkling how unsparing a demiparadise ours could be despite all the kind words and kisses of greeting and farewell, used to flee Sherborne over intervening hill and dale on free Sunday afternoons and, only half-joking, beg us to hide them in a hayrick before nightfall, take us in, please don't make us go back there, nooo . . .

The Bennettry and Beshara, *via negativa* and *positiva* respectively, were located a convenient four miles apart as the rook flaps. At Sherborne, Mr. Bennett was very much the omnipresent spiritual-teacher-figure on his courses, intellectual, rigorous, robust, and a wonderfully convincing figure: if there weren't enough British customers to fill the House, a short speaking tour of the States would easily provide the remainder; whereas if Bulent was behind Beshara, as some people whispered was the ruling fact of the place, he would not let himself be called a teacher or spoken of as anything like one, and was for a long time less visible, to Beshara's proletarian population and the outside world, than Damon Runyon's Seldom-Seen Kid. The visible running of Beshara at Swyre Farm was given over to Reshad Feild, a charismatic redbearded Englishman of forty years, likewise capable of speaking-tours of the Colonies and even capable of playing the guitar. Beshara seemed to run on the oxygen of high aspiration and high-wire acts of transcendent hope, while at Sherborne House—despite the free license given to sexual shenanigans among the inmates—stone-cold rigor and even, in the unremitting wintry middle of its courses, a sort of holy terror held sway, at least until the last three months, when a measure of paradise regained was permitted and even encouraged.

Glimpsed piecemeal through the gate as we passed, Sherborne House remained, for all its brightenings and evolutions, a wide, ugly, misproportioned near-Gothic stretch of stonefaced boys' school four storeys high, a grim grey church and steeple tacked onto its left extremity like the threat of final judgment. No doubt it had been an awful enough place in its boys' school years, though it should not be confused with the better-known Sherborne School in Dorset that had helped disfigure the childhoods of half a generation of English novelists—you keep running into this piece of history in biographies and book reviews and, disguised, in their fictions. During its Bennett years the Cotswold Sherborne House had scared the shit out of any number of people from England and America and a scattering from other lands, and in the process had even raised a few ancestral spooks: when Elan Sicroff turned up there in '71 from his round-the-world trip via Asia to visit his German girlfriend and get laid a little before heading back to the States, he found her crawling into the big bread oven in the institutional kitchen and telling the cooks You must turn on the gas please because I deserve, I must to be burned, *ja*, for the terrible crimes. I don't know what happened to the girlfriend—no one baked her; I would have heard—but Sicroff did one of those ten-month courses of daily spiritual nerve-scraping and mortal exposure without intervening anodyne, then stayed on for three years as house pianist and even thrived there, in his fashion.

Mr. Bennett—John Godolphin Bennett, who as an usually young Army man after the war was put in charge of British intelligence in occupied Istanbul and had the power of life and death in his hands, and is said to have exercised it—by then a vigorous massive gaunt craggy grey tweed Englishman in his mid-seventies topped by a small chaos of stray white hair and looking slightly mad about the eyes, died in the fourth year of the six-year run of courses he had proposed from 1970 to '76. His school survived him for the duration of the cycle. When the time came to sell the property there was just one credible customer. My gang of visionaries, feeling they'd outgrown the cozy farm across the hills that could house thirty-five, forty pilgrims, tops, and then only on the weekends, felt ready to host, like the formidable Mr. Bennett, coherent courses nine or ten months long attended by seventy-five or eighty aspirants and, under Bulent's laissez-faire supervision, they plunked down cash and a mortgage on the enormous property intact—woods and pasture, tillage, house, outbuildings, gardens, nurseries, potteries, workshops, all: the nearly endless sprawl of enterprise and demesne that had once lorded it over the village and still more of its adjacencies and surrounds—and set up shop. This incarnation of Beshara breathed for a few years. Once most of the old crowd had been cycled through the increasingly serious and substantial new courses—I never attended, and only kept in touch via my almost biennial trips to Turkey in search of solo visions—the place ran short of young inductees and the outsized schoolhouse went moribund; without the income from the flock of newies they were unable to attract—the problem wasn't just the new, more serious and recondite bill of fare but, with Reshad's sudden disappearance from the scene, the lack of a star performer who could tour the States and entice fresh wanderers inside the tent: Bulent certainly wasn't up for anything that public (though he did make a few trips to America so discreet that I, for one, only heard about them by historical report), and none of the kids had the stuff or a taste for the limelight—they had to sell the House and withdraw the esoteric presence to the stableyard at the rear, there to conduct what business they could with the outside world and the handful willing to come in and have a gnaw at the abstruse, sometimes impenetrable texts of Muhyiddin Ibn 'Arabi: over seven centuries dead and still going strong, for those who could handle the arabesques of syntax and the dazzlement of all worldly coordinates and perspective.

History had done its stuff. Once upon a time Beshara was foaming at the crest of a great unstoppable wave—Western Sieve's next inundation— and now appeared to be dabbling on a deserted beach, the strays and stragglers of an alleged elite, amid a scattering of its buckets and shovels.

In the interim Sherborne House had been done up as luxury flats for which most of the buyers were rich crackers from Mississippi who had made their pile in the pylon business and liked to come over for weeks at a time and lord it over the scenery, though they'd stopped short of scattering hired darkies in glyphs of noble labor across the lawns. My friend Sid, whom the receding flood had deposited solo on these shores, did occasional work for these new tenants, taught them how to buy antiques and paintings, on commission, tended their Mercedes, collected their flight-racked bodies at Heathrow, pre-heated their damp and shuttered flats and stocked their massive fridges. Kith and Kin—went the name of the company, business cards and all—never developed into the full-paying gig Sid hoped might save her from more skilled and tedious seamstress labor, but the you-alls kept telling her how darn *quaint* she was—those cheeky cheeks with the rosy blush, that pert upturned nose, and her knockout combo of proper manner and saucy looks—and some of the menfolk paid her the final compliment of chasing her around the furniture she'd bought them for a tidy fee. The House's facade had been shriven of its ancient soots and sediments, a surprising taupe now that the grey was gone, though the ghastly church retained its gloom and the place still looked like a prison builder's notion of country splendour. Since the Snopeses were in residence Tash and I didn't enter by the main gate. The stableyard was slated to be ceded the following year, and esoterica farewell, but Beshara still had possession of its gate, that year.

"Tash, are we early, late, on time, what?"

"What's your problem, Rafi?"

"Forget it."

"I would if you let me but you don't," Tash said.

The trees thinned to our left to open the view upon a scattering of sizeable greystone houses for successful locals or interlopers from without, then rich green pasture descending to a stream, the Windrush, in the pool of which, below the little weir, who knows, five wild swans might have been making a show of themselves at the time. Across the stream a line of trees was succeeded by farmland ascending to eventual hills. Tash and I almost certainly would have heard the local mantra of dovecall by then: hoo HOO hoo hoo-hoo: everywhere and inescapable in this green and pleasant patch of world.

A bit farther, across the road from the little country graveyard in its shade of oaks, just as the row of lowbuilt council houses shuffled up to the houseback humble cap in hand, Tash and I took a sharp right cut up the fanshaped drive past the gatehouse and came in at the rear of the property. The back of the House, like a dragon departing over a hill, showed us its intricate spine and tailwork of chimneypots and interslanted planes of lapped slate roof and leaded seams: a miscellany suggesting haphazard additions to the original mass or indifference to the disposition of the servants' quarters; maybe both.

As we approached the stablehouse I saw an increasingly thoughtful sky in which some ideas of cloud had begun to build and gather, then Tash and I passed beneath the stable archway into the yard. Our architects had really done the joint up since I'd last seen it. In Mr. Bennett's day the place had been a bare cobblestone yard with blind walls that looked cinematically perfect for lining up a straggle of innocents and dispatching them by firing squad—to be perfect, that bygone plaza lacked only a busted colonial clock over its entrance arch and a scattering of straw to whisk away the blood.

Under its current stewardship the stableyard was an ordered paradisal garden in which souls might take their ease and living water purled—a square formal garden quadrisected by gravel walks into grassy portions of lawn banked with rows, spills, nods and dazzles of flower and blossom: a lush nearly Turkish profusion of color in the center of which a multi-tiered white marble fountain twirdled its spumes and streams.

Tash knew the layout and I didn't. He trotted us through an unexpected doorway, up a narrow staircase with white walls—you could hear the solidity of the structure in the echo of our steps, and the place was spotlessly clean—down a hallway to a white enamelled door with a bright brass knob. We went in and encountered an uneven palisade of tall wooden chairbacks and heads half-turning to clock our entrance. We found an open bit of floor and sat on the carpet. There was a lot of daylight coming into the room from windows on two sides, producing a bright diffuse effect in which I found it difficult to select and focus upon a backlit, sidelit lot of people, maybe sixty of them, sitting closely grouped in chairs, and a supporting cast scattered at their feet. A familiar face emerged from the brightness here or there, and I even recognized the backs of a few familiar heads before my eyes, finding the center and Hugh Tollemache's lofty chin and almost too noble knight-errant's profile beneath its black cliff of hair—starting to grey now in backswept featherings along its sides—then picked out in a chair beside Hugh—known *en famille* as Halim, and sometimes Tolley—looking large and somber and darker than I remembered, his face a great though now sagging sack beneath who knew what weight of experience, Bulent.

He sat heavily, a portrait of gravity bearing a massive earthly body down, though he seemed a source of some other gravity himself, a collapsing star, a broad brown mountain folding in upon its mines, veins of ore returning to original secrecy, the light upon their silver fading, and unaugmented earth reclaiming its dominion. He looked bad, but I didn't yet see in him the harshness of line that had been death's signature on my father's face. Bulent seemed asleep, or nearly so, large head bent, eyes shut or nearly shut inside their pursy nests above their bags. It was almost a month since his seventy-fifth birthday had passed and he looked at least his age; but early in the 1970s, when Bulent was barely sixty, Mr. Bennett, fifteen years his senior with only a year or two left to live himself, used to call him the Old Man; and in fact there was always the sense, especially on seeing Bulent for the first time after long absence, of coming upon something uncannily heaped with the sedimentary sands and silts of time. He was a physically enormous man, and if he still resembled Rembrandt it was only the last self-portraits now. He was a mound of humanity in his chair, a pear-shaped hillock of flesh, his neck long since vanished in a bellying gullet of underflap, his middle girth still ample despite his evident illness—although this impression was in part a trick of optics: in attempting to come to grips with the sense of existential size you encountered in Bulent—of that unaccountable elephant in the room—one fumbled at the dimensions of his belly and chin.

There is a color photograph of him of which I would love to have a copy, set on an English lawn in the late spring of 1973: an also rounded ample fellow, but younger and built on a somewhat smaller scale—an English Buddhist sometimes called Shamseddin—is holding forward by its stem a lone red rose, and Bulent, wearing, as I remember it, a blue-grey velour blazer and a mauve shirt with a bit of scarlet silk puffed about his throat, a faint smile crumpling his lips above his wisp moustache, has bent to sniff it: he's enormous in the shot, but he appears to descend upon the scent of flower like the flight-defying bulk of a bumblebee, and his body seems to hover at the lip of the rose with a hummingbird's poise and loft: the effect is subtly comic and captures much of the man's charm.

He seemed more earth-weighted now, and his complexion had darkened—his normal coloring was European, the greatest part of his ancestry being literally Caucasian, with perhaps a blush of the Mediterranean in his cheeks, and only the merest visible trace, if any, of the Levant—and his general manner might be described as French: it would be easy to imagine him, in a simpler life, strolling the whited sea-descending lanes of some French town, wearing good linen clothes, leaning heavily on his cane and puffing slightly through lips pursed with the pain in his hip and the effort of his descent over the uneven cobbles; recognizable as aristocratic, retired, a man of learning and culture likely to be capable of excellent conversation about his interesting past, *un homme peut-être un peu plus que moyen sensuel* and something slightly exotic, perhaps not entirely European, about him besides. Had he really darkened? Perhaps his skin tone had dulled. With astounding dimness of mind I remembered that, oh yes, he'd had stomach cancer and its attendant surgery in the three years since I'd seen him. In repose, as usual, he seemed someone who had endured the full catalogue of human sorrows but this again was partly a trick of optics: once he spoke and acted, once you began a social interchange with him, his conversation was so wittily airpuffed that your impression changed: he was deep but not sorrowful: he was large, but light.

Or was that an illusion too?

In the room they were talking about . . . what? Some practical matter. Tree-planting, drainage. Several people put their oars in, and then Bulent raised his heavy head and added to the discussion some small conclusive remark on the order of, "We shall replant the forest first, and after the planting drain the slough and install the new water pump." Exciting, esoteric stuff, all referring to Chisholme, a property in the Scottish borders that housed Beshara's principal current school. The greenhouse, cost of renovating same. Health of ducks in pond. Condition of Steading Cottage and the Bothy. Which part of the old forest to coppice next. Two or three items of this kind were summarily dealt with, and the meeting adjourned. All rose in a rustle of cloth and rumble of chairs. Tash and I, intrepid in our race across the landscape, had arrived just in time for the finish.

As other, more miscellaneous bodies parted, hurrying or dawdling this way and that, Bulent hauled himself diagonally across the room on the disproportionately slender support of his cane, and it was a blow to see how painful his earthly progress had become, his body pivoting partway around the stick as he bore down with each step, the effort showing in his face. I winced for him as his features contracted, felt a moment's shock, and saw that yes his skin had darkened, a definite tint of grey in it now, an unhealthy undertone of charcoal. Just then, having given no previous sign of seeing me, he looked my way, raised his left hand and shook it with a pivoting motion to show me the watch on his wrist, then continued through the room and out a door. Ah yes, the moon-phase watch—I'd forgotten it.

Bulent was not much given to superstition—he had a fine distaste for mystification generally—though he had a few folksy touches charming in someone of such lofty culture. The most prominent of these was his regard for the moon, particularly the wary eye he turned upon it on the last Wednesday of each lunar month: a bad day, a black rock, a time of ill omen to be treated with the proper caution: avoid big decisions, start no major projects: sweep your day clear of consequence, clean house, see a movie, take a nap.

Here in the solar, rational West, the day marked down for the new moon is the one on which there is no moon at all, but in a lunar-calendar culture the first day of the month begins when you can see the first fingernail-paring of light curled around that suggestive bulge of dark, and you don't declare the month or fast or feast begun until someone reliable comes down from the hilltop or the roof with the news. The preset calendars are unreliable and the weather's iffy. The best thing you can do is buy a moonphase watch, set it correctly, square the thing with observation every few months to check for drift, then sail through the cycle with your mind at ease.

When moon-phase watches first hit the market a year or so before, I'd thought Let's buy Bulent one before someone else does, and had quickly enlisted Hakkı Bey and Ria Eagan to split the cost with me. They said fine and I bought it at Fortunoff's, bypassing the intended hundred-buck model as soon I saw the hundred-fifty that had a bevelled brass bezel around the crystal with Roman-numeral hourmarks etched into it and was waterproof besides. Getting the watch to Bulent proved complicated. Natalia Neville, who had spent a brief, tremulous time at Beshara in 1972 but had never met Bulent, was passing from California through New York on her way to England at just the right time, and I'd handed the package off to her—as part of the gag, I'd written Bulent a note to the effect that if with the moon now safely on his left hand he could bear the sun on his right he'd really be in business. Natalia did luminous translations of Lorca but got so flustered en route at the prospect of meeting Bulent that she blew the chance of delivering the watch personally, arriving in Scotland just as he left it for England, then repeating the maneuver in reverse, and in the end had to confide the object to the uncertainty of the mail. But here he was, wearing it: cool.

I'd wanted to buy one like it for myself before leaving New York, but when I went back to Fortunoff's fat with my inheritance, that model had been discontinued and the standard sans-bezel model lacked panache. I was sporting blue plastic Swatch that year.

Everyone was leaving, the room stale with the echo of official doings while bright air beckoned outside. I waved at some familiar forms but everyone, hustling on stiff limbs or stretching them, was busy being gone. A nudge, then a nod from Tash and we joined the dispersal, down some stairs then back out into the dayblazed colors of the formal garden, framed in its square of white.

SOCIAL WHIRL is not all metaphor: I seemed to spend a lot of time spinning to greet first this passing face then that one, pinned in place by serial social obligation to a region in and around the kitchen doorway. Bowls of multicolored salad had already appeared upon the boards, freshly homebaked loaves were going under the knife, and a coordinated swarm buzzed about the stoves and ovens, tending this, checking that, brandishing oven gloves, towels, utensils, and whisking lolling salivators out of the way with the flick of a tea towel or an imprecation. Pleasant crusty scent of good food upon the air.

Bright flitterings in and out the doorway, and women's voices saying things on the order of, "Oh Rafi, helleau. Haven't seen you in yonks. Been shut up in America all this time? How boring for you. Must run."

I remember feeling especially dull and stupid, but years later I learned that I'd impressed one woman there with my "New York energy," so I might have produced a stray moment of vitality or charm, and in fact I ended up doing a few choruses of duelling Bulents just outside the kitchen door with a guy named Razi Martin.

I got hooked up with Razi—a tall wide shambling reddish lantern-jawed mildly shamefaced specimen originally from Northern Ireland—on the pebbled verge of the garden. He wanted to know how things were going in America, and I would have sputtered about Reagan, I suppose. As memory kicks in, a third party standing with us says, "Oh really? Razi does Bulent's voice too," and I reply with complete confidence, "My version is betttah."

A brief competition followed.

"How good it is to see you, my dear," Razi attempted.

"The same wind that blows me here, my *dyah*," I said, "has brought you."

Although Razi had had far more time to study his subject, it seemed to me that he had bypassed some of the finer points. "What a lovely day it is," Razi said.

"I'd like a banahnah," I told him, pulling out all the stops. "A nice spottted one, please."

Razi just didn't have the ear for it. There's a sort of gurgling in the throat—it sounds grotesque but it's charming once you get used to it—and while this obstruction keeps the voice tenorish there's a large bass-baritone chest resonance beneath it, and it was this combination, I felt, that Razi failed adequately to reproduce; he also hadn't understood that most consonants had to be articulated by the flat of the tongue full against the palate, which broadened them. His rhythm was all right, with ample float and languor, and he had a pretty good take on Bulent's humorous-lyrical lilt.

"Indeed He is beautiful and He loves the beauty," Razi maintained.

"*All* the prophets were shepherds in their youth," I confided. "And do you know why?" I cast a glance over the people buzzing about the garden and rolled my eyes. "*Only* a shepherd could have the patience." I suppressed a yawn. "I think I'll go upstairs Andropov."

"You win," the third party told me.

"I *kneau*," I said.

When I'd whupped him vocally Razi asked around for something that might pass muster as a cane—apparently he did physical shtick; Bulent had once walked in on him performing said shtick for a local audience and it was good enough to have pissed Bulent off—but this gambit came to nothing, and the conversation dissolved and reconfigured elsewhere, with different participants, according to the laws of the hive.

AFTER LUNCH I seemed to be in demand, fastened in place at a plain wooden table just inside the kitchen door, pivoting to engage passing interlocutors while regaling a clutch of mostly female blurs straightening the kitchen with who knows what specious string of anecdotes—might have been doing American oddity or New York horror, stuff that always plays in England. I found myself, as so often in the Somewhat United Kingdom, tugged upon by a thousand social strings to which I was trying to respond with some grace without turning puppet entirely. My spoken idiom was drifting progressively eastward across the mid-Atlantic and I had begun to misuse bits of British idiom. The women were making a small fuss of me, plying me with tea and cakes that would keep me at the table, chatting away, including me in the music of the moment, and sometimes even commenting about me: how I looked, how I sat, where I'd been for so long. I was probably being flirted with, but I felt so unsexed that year I thought they were making fun of me.

Long about then Charles "Aziz," the future Lord Locke, came in.

"Now *there's* the man I'm looking for," I bellowed happily when I saw him, in some narrative midcareer, and yes, it seems I'd begun gesturing broadly, waving my arms and announcing rather than merely relating things: what generally happens when we dead awaken.

"Well I should hope so," Locke said.

"I would've been in touch," I told him. "Just got in last night."

"Well that's all right then. This man—" he began fake-vehemently. "This man—" Aziz seemed about the same, although now he was dressed for country life: a good-looking upper-class English guy with rosy cheeks, wavy black hair, the full kit, though cut on a less knightly scale than the son of Baron Tollemache. "This man," he tried again, clearly less than satisfied with the quantum of attention his first two invocations had amassed. His third attempt was quickly defeated by the entrance of a bicephalous creature close behind him saying, "Helleau everyone, and can you budge out of the doorway for a minute, Charlie, so we can get inside?"

This two-headed person soon resolved itself into a flushed cuddle of woman and baby swathed in country clothes and overtopped by a spill of red hair tumbled all awry.

"Certainly, certainly," said Aziz. "Rafi, have you met my wife?"

"You're kidding!"

Followed a celebration of wife and baby and congrats, best wishes.

"You must come visit us," Aziz told me, "while you're in the area. We're in Clapton."

"Clapton?" A huddle of a half dozen houses at a road junction two miles uphill from town. "Somebody actually *lives* in Clapton?"

"Well, erm, *we* do, actually . . . This man—" Aziz began again, awakening from these distractions. Immediately, all innocent bystanders walked away, and even Mrs. Locke felt the baby's bottom and hurried off. "This man," and when he'd roped in a passing hapless kitchen slavey he continued, "this man used to wake me every morning by rattling his bloody vittamins. Chakachakachakachakachakachakachakachakachakakachakachaka," he explained, shaking a phantom bottle vigorously in his hand.

We'd been barracked together for a few months in Scotland.

"Every morning! Chakachaka! Every bloody morning!"

"I didn't shake them, Aziz. I merely tipped a few into my hand. There were two or three bottles and they rattled slightly when tipped."

"What are you doing this evening? You must come round."

"I'm at Sid's. I just came up here with Tash and—"

"Good Lord. Tash. Still walks among us."

"Some of the time. Anyhow—"

"Which reminds me. There's something I'd like to ask you," he said, and sat down across the table from me, his slightly fuddled handsome features flushed. "In fact you're the perfect person to ask."

"Anything, Zeez."

"By the way how is America?"

"How is America what?"

"Because it struck me, it struck me the other day that America, not being either European or exactly non-European—I've never been to America, you know. Must go one day. We all should go to America."

"Count me out."

"Because it's neither European nor non-European, and because it has its own . . . unique . . . By the way what are the plane fares just now? Reasonable? Not that I could go at the moment—"

"Your wife and child."

"And we're broke. Utterly flat." This was no figure of speech. Future Peer of the Realm he might be, but the Locke family mezuma was long gone and well out of the picture. "It seems to me that culture is a kind of pattern. And a pattern is not in itself uniform. A pattern can be realigned. It can be related to other patterns. It can be fit to other patterns. Do you live in a house or a flat?"

"Flat."

"Do you own it?"

"I rent."

"And what is a pattern really? Is it a form? or is it a form of forms, or, how to put it, a thing according to which forms find their form . . ."

If there is anything I regret about the cancellation of hereditary seats in the House of Lords it is that the future House will not find itself wrapped in the interminable wool of Aziz Locke's rhetoric. When he gets a train of thought going he becomes, in effect, the little engine that decided to see what it might be like to run alongside the tracks rather than on them. I think he will be called "dear boy" well into his seventies. In his case the "dear" will not only be parodic but sincere.

"And a culture is not a form but a pattern."

"Absolutely," I told him. "Right."

One afternoon in Scotland, after Aziz had favored a meeting with a typical peroration, thereby ending it, on leaving the room Bulent nodded to the person sitting nearest Aziz and said, "Strangle him." Ivan obliged, and Aziz played along, but Ivan didn't stop.

"Which reminds me," said Aziz.

Wife and child made their reentry at that point all abustle. "Charlie, we really must go," Mrs. Locke said, and the Lockes were out the door with a parting "Chakachakachaka" for good measure.

"Come round back for a smoke," Tash, coming out of nowhere, said to me, prison-style, out the side of his mouth.

An indicative jut of jaw lifted me from my seat and through an unremembered passageway into a geometric garden, sectioned by paths and hedges and alcoves, outside the stableyard square. If Tash had something to tell me he never came up with it, and presently we heard the sound of a car grinding its way over coarse gravel just around the bend of stableyard wall. The stilling of the engine and the clashing closed of a car door produced a redfaced man in at least his sixties, in buttoned blazer, shirt and tie despite the August warmth. He was walking with apparent sense of purpose, head thrust down, eyes intent on the path.

"It's Gerald Green," Tash said.

"Yup."

Tash quickly assumed the aspect of one escaping and I followed his lead, although oddly we did this in a ritualized freeze-frame fashion that caught and held us, in profile and with arms geometrically akimbo, like figures in a Hittite or Assyrian frieze, even before Mr. Green's "Hellooo" assailed our flanks and seized us by the conscience.

"Hullo Gerald."

"Mr. Green!" I cheered.

First dutiful, then cheerful, that was the sequence of our greeting. Then mutual approach. I noted, as we switchbacked down to him, by descent of flagstone path, amid the hedges, that since I'd last seen it Mr. Green's face had altered. With the loss of still more hair his cranium seemed to have bulged forward, giving it the look of a helmet clamped down upon a foreshortened face which the brow and nose assembly were compressing by main force. His mouth seemed to be receding, and his face appeared to be reddening under the stress. I was, as usual, glad to see him. "Rafi Zaborrr," he said in his Gloucestershire accent. "I heard you were soon to be among us. How are you, Mr. Rafi Zaborrr."

"Good to see you, Gerald," I said, and shook his hand.

"Oh what a character he is," Mr. Green said of me to Tash. "What a character. And you too, Tash, to be sure. What two characters you are, Tash and Mr. Rafi Zaborrr."

"We're all characters here," I assured him. "I trust you've been well?"

"Well enough, well enough." These words seemed to issue from a grinder. "And what news might you have from New York of that great character Hakki Bey, and Mr. Nick Prestigiacomo, what a character he is, and have you any word, now you're in England, of that American woman now living in London, Miss Sara Berrrenson?"

"I hardly know where to begin, Mr. Green," I told him, thinking, Call Sara before dinner.

"He's a great character, is Hakki Bey. You must tell me all about him, and Miss Sara Berrrenson, I've gone to call on her, but for some reason, heh, hmm, she doesn't want to see me. I don't know what she's got into her little head about me."

"She doesn't appreciate being pursued, Mr. Green," I hinted.

"I went round to her flat on Elvaston Place in South Kensington, and ha, hmm . . ."

"I think Derek Samson told you to buzz off over the intercom," I said.

"She's irritated with me for some reason, Miss Sara Berrrenson. She's got something into her head about me, she has, I don't know why."

"She doesn't want to see you, Gerald," I said, which at least was clear enough.

"Look we've really go'a go," glottal-stopped Tash, extinguishing his cigarette.

"Where are you off to then, Mr. Tash?" Mr. Green wished to comprehend.

"Upstairs, see the Bey," Tash said.

"Well off you go then," Mr. Green allowed us. "Will you be staying over at Siddiqa's then? I'll come and look you up there. You must tell me all about your recent adventures when I come to visit you at Siddiqa's."

"They don't really bear telling," I said. "Not this year."

"I'm sure you underestimate your powers, Rafi Zaborrr. I'll let you go off then, shall I."

Then, just as we began to pull away, Mr. Green delivered himself of the one sentence of his I can vocally reproduce in all its English country-accent particulars. "I shall never forget the way you two greeted me," he said.

Fixed ritually upon a frieze, in bas relief, guiltily, caught.

"I shall never forget the way you two greeted me."

Ask me when you see me. I can do that voice down to its final dot.

4

UPSTAIRS, see the Bey.

I was expecting a few people in armchairs sitting around sipping tea, share a little cake, casual and familiar. Tash led me to
some new facet of the stableyard square, then up yet another stairway to
a shut white lacquered wooden door with an entirely too populous rustle
of voices behind it. We entered to a blast of people in a long deep
crowded room, most of its occupants sitting on the floor and Bulent, I
don't like to use the word but he was pretty much enthroned in a large
high armchair less than a third of the way in. He appeared to be performing, which surprised me, since Bulent was usually a skilled and subtle avoider of the spotlight of mass attention; yet here all eyes and ears
were turned upon him and he appeared to be thriving in their radiance.
Tash and I found some floorspace approximately in front of him, roughly
three rows back, the windows behind us giving onto the stableyard,
where much of the gold had gone from the day's light.

The absolute beginning of what I heard Bulent say that afternoon is
lost to a preambular shimmer, but the scene snaps to clarity with Bulent
saying, "I *eaunly* care for the Sheer Beauty, the Sheer Being, now." You
have heard of pear-shaped vowels. Americans with their simple syllables—flat, efficient, leached of variation except in the South—don't speak
them, and the better sort of English, whose vowels begin in one place and
blossom before ending in another, do. Bulent's speech was a voluptuous

enlargement of the English manner, his vowels goblets plumped with the fruit and color of rich red wine: claret, judging by its depth of purple. "I *eaunly* love the Sheerness now. Do you know, I don't see people anymore." He gave us all a vague once-over. "I don't see people. I see meanings."

This was new to me. The Sheerness, which seemed to have become more prominent in his conversation since last I'd heard it, was a discreet way of referring to the Absolute Ipseity, the Itselfness before it clothes itself in attribute, universe and aspect; and even this discretion was daring, since Bulent almost always, in my admittedly limited experience of him, spoke in a way to deflect attention from whatever his own state might be and from the presumptive quality of his own person or attainment; speaking so familiarly of the Sheerness alluded to a high station of gnosis. Still, this was casual-lyrical self-expression, mere effusion, playful conversation, ease; but Bulent was usually a master of impersonal inference and a subtle elider of the personal pronoun. Now he buddied with Sheer Being in public and—something tugged obscurely at my attention—saw not people but meanings? What was up? What had changed?

Now I cringe at my thoughtlessness. At the time, it didn't even occur to me that in nearly dying of cancer, then enduring a slow recovery after surgery, over the last three years Bulent might have been through, um, at least as much as I.

"For instance, Ibn 'Arabi is not a man. He is a meaning."

Well, fair enough. Ibn 'Arabi. Anything was possible with him. Once, when he had attained a particular station, he let out an involuntary shout and everyone within range of it fell unconscious, some from second-storey windows unharmed. He'd inherited the mantle of Khidr, and all the Prophets in history had turned up to meet him when he was still quite young.

"No, I don't see people anymore." Bulent gestured foggily at us.

Again something tugged at the hem of my notice. Some recognition, some hint upon the stone of which my acuity sharpened, the blade not knowing why; but it was about to rend my garment.

"It's as if there were a swamp," he gestured nebulously, "and *meanings* seem to bubble up in it."

Suddenly I found myself thrust halfway out of my seated position on the floor, a loud involuntary "Yes!" having just escaped my throat and all my nerves on end atremble. If you were filming the moment and if I were the point of it, you would need to dial the room noise swiftly down and have your camera perform some variation of Hitchcock's *Vertigo* effect, simultaneously tracking backward and zooming in so that foreground and background were elongated or compressed to isolate my face midscreen as I dopplered out of phase with the surrounding world and its coordinates.

I hadn't intended to speak; in effect I hadn't spoken. Some deepseated recognition had leapt out of me unsummoned, shouted "Yes!" and left me to deal with the scatter of faces instantly spun my way. An American had arrived again—must we have them?—the priceless Ming vase of the social moment wrecked in the normal course of his unconscious, sprawled intent. In response I took the path of least resistance and trusted to the almost infinite power of British decorum, pretended that nothing had happened—so, seamlessly, did Bulent—and settled back on my haunches. But in fact something had happened, hadn't it, and after a moment or two I knew what it was, and that its nature was double.

When Bulent had mentioned the strange essential invisibility of people to him now, and this swamp in which significations bubbled into view, he had described my current experience of the world with staggering exactitude, and although likely everyone else in the room assumed that he was speaking only of his spiritual state, I knew in an infallible flash that he and I were both halfway over among the dead. For me, in my continuing state of shock these last few years, the world had indeed been wiped clean of visible significance: I was looking at an insufficient scrim from which the essential substance had been drained: it was insubstantial show, shadow puppetry, untenanted ghostworks, a shell game essentially unalive, although I was not freed from its enactments. In naming this peculiar condition, Bulent had told me two things: that whatever the height and breadth and subtlety of his spiritual state he did not have long to live, and that my weary familiar sense of being stuck halfway in the land of death was less metaphorical than I'd thought—a result no doubt of excessive unskilled empathy: "You have taken on *too much*"—and that my literal job during the course of this stumbling journey I'd just begun was to haul my mortal self back among the living and inside the borders of their land. Did Bulent know how soon he'd be going? The cancer had nearly taken him, and he was barely, only provisionally back. He might well know, but was he aware how baldly, even granted the indirection of his speech, he'd been saying it aloud?

The moment, a long one, continued to shake me. In the moment all things stood literal, clear: I saw the work I had to do.

I looked up at Bulent, his center of gravity, like mine but for different reasons, over on the other side of the divide and, although this was the cruel natural calculus of youth and age, I didn't belong there and he did. He probably had no idea why or from what world I'd cried out, and in fact it wasn't his concern. As ever, he was sailing regally by, full-bellied with the wind that breathed him, keel cleaving seas I'd only glimpsed once or twice myself.

A second chill ran through me: in the old days Bulent used to enjoy saying, "I live only for the Absolute and my stomach," and his second, nearly fatal bout of stomach cancer raised the phantasmal prospect of a niggling, beancounter, jealous God who couldn't take a ribbing, even from a friend. Then again, when Bulent was off the high metaphysics he used sometimes to chat about God as if He were a kind of recording idiot: "If you ask him for Mercy too often, well, what can He do, He doesn't like to refuse you anything, so if you already have Mercy He will put you in a position in which you are in need of Mercy, so He can give it. That is why you should not pray for patience. No, it is better that you should be impetuous. Want Him *now*."

The soundtrack was picking up normal breath and chatter, depth of field racking back to true, time ticking back to its accustomed motion.

"Ulrlp," Bulent had said, although it was not an actual belch: something had bubbled up out of his belly uncensored into the middle of a word. "You must pardon me," he said, in a seeming fluster of mild embarrassment. "Since my surgery . . . how shall I put it. Along with the bit of my stomach they removed there went a little valve between the stomach and the esophagus, and things just bubble up, you must excuse me, it's not in my control. Do you know? When I was recovering from the surgery and was able to eat again, all the tastes had changed places with each other. Chicken could taste like chocolate. Chocolate might taste like asparagus one day and lemon custard the next." He laughed, shrugged.

"*Ne hosh,*" I said. In Turkish: how pleasant.

"What?" said Bulent, puzzled for an instant. "Oh, *ne hosh.* Yes, very pleasant. Tea might taste like beefsteak."

Good Lord, I hadn't finished speaking yet: "If you live long enough," I seemed to have said aloud, "you get to see everything." Where had that one come from? Again a hundred outraged faces whirled my way.

Bulent sailed on regardless. "A cup of tea might be fish soup. And fish, my dyah, fish could taste like anything at all."

The room chuckled with him, although mindful of a queasiness at the core.

For years, in a special lugubrious-ironic tone he reserved for this purpose, Bulent had purveyed a peculiar line of comedy based upon the routine humiliations of his outsized mortal form: his leviathan capacity for after-dinner gas, the necessity of pre-establishing the availability of a sit-down toilet somewhere on the road between Istanbul and Edirne or he would have to cancel the trip—if forced to use a Turkish squatter, "my dyah, you'd have to leave me there, I'd never be able to get up again." Now here was a new, still more mortal adjunct, although Bulent's tone was still ironically amused.

"Thank God my taste has returned or I would never know what I was eating. I would have to *look.* Tea? How kind of you to ask. I'd love a cup of tea." He used this natural lacuna to fuss about in his seat, primping the cushion, reassuring himself as to the location of his eyeglass case. "But what about all these people? They will be jealous of my tea if they have none themselves. You must get them tea, or I will be attacked."

A crew rose out of undifferentiated mass, coalesced, departed on a clarity of mission.

For the first time I realized that Bulent wasn't smoking, must have quit. Unthinkable. Usually he smoked, well, like a Turk, or in Tash's felicitous old phrase, like a . . .

"Hello, my dyah," he greeted me. "How good to see you. What has brought you?"

"The usual, Bülent." I gave his name a version, at least, of its true first vowel. According to the principle of what Daniel called Vowel Harmonu, front and back vowels ordinarily were not spoken in the same word. "I'm off to Turkey again."

"Where will you go?"

"Istanbul, Ephesus, Konya, the usual hotspots. Your brother's grave . . ."

"You won't find it," said Bulent. "It's not marked."

I smiled without speaking, smug that I had vibed the location of Mahmoud's grave on prior visits to Kanlıca. I had already half-decided not to tell Bulent anything in advance about my plan to buy a stone, and to deal with the family in Turkey when I got there. In any case this was hardly the time or the place to raise the subject.

"You must come see us in Scotland before you go," said Bulent.

"When will you be there?"

"We leave tomorrow. Come."

"I will."

I was about to ask how long he would be up there when, excuse me, what? Tash was getting up, clambering past me, untypically awkward, hey watch that elbow, man.

"I've brought you something," Tash said, leaning over the intervening rows, extending the book, a large one, handing it to Bulent and adding some extra mist to his Spiritual Fog voice, "two weeks past your birthday."

"Oh dyah," Bulent said as prologue, acknowledging the book's heft with a weighing gesture, then paging it open on his lap. "*No*," he said, looking through it, "this is far too good. Habib, how can I accept this? It's far too fine for you to give away." Bulent appealed to others near him. "Look at the quality of these engravings."

Tash had shown me the book earlier, on the bus: finely bound, over-size boards of dark maroon, ridged spine with faded gold embossing, published late in the nineteenth century, *The Beauties of the Bosphorus,* with a number of fine engravings of old Istanbul and the Ottoman provinces smattered through the long body of text, their precision safe beneath gentling intertissues of diaphanous paper.

"You put me in a most awkward position. How can I possibly accept this book?"

"It was meant for you," Tash told him. "It's yours."

Bulent did a small silent theatre piece of deferral, submission, consent, followed by a mock hardness of eye to forestall further such extravagances in future.

Tash had a good touch finding things; even so, this book must have cost him. "It's my pleasure," he told Bulent.

"You must all look at the engravings." Bulent passed the book to someone near him, accompanied by a softened backhand gesture to indicate that it should be passed around the room, then turned back toward Tash and favored him with a last admonitory "tsk" and a Turkish upnod of jaw to indicate his sham displeasure. "An impossible person," he said.

Tash settled back down, pleased.

Bowls of fruit began to circulate in countercurrents to the book. Eager customers partook, then began to wonder what to do, in this mix and press of squat humanity, with seeds, pits, core, this curl or strip of peel.

Two teacarts were rolled to the edge of the crowd and people slid to make space around them, quartets of china cups were unnested from stacked saucers, shortbreads arranged, braiding spumes of tea poured forth amid arising forms of steam, and the numbering of sugars began. Darjeeling or Earl Grey? One? Two? Milk or lemon? Biscuit?

My attention drifted.

WHEN BULENT RESUMED his discourse after tea it seemed to me that he had turned to an inferior text. A large square book with a black-and-red glossy cover and many illustrations had found its way into his hand, its subject and title Chinese Astrology. "The year of the Dragon," Bulent read. "The year of the Dog. I wonder what I am. Table on page two ninety-seven." He flittered his way to it, resettled his silver-rim specs, pursed and moistened lips, frowned down. "Nineteen hundred eleven: the Year of the Baww. My dyah: I'm a Baugh." A boar, a bore: unkosher and *haram*. "Let's see," said Bulent. "What are the qualities of a Baugh? We must look them up. Page one forty-two."

It seemed to me that this was comedy unworthy of him, but he seemed determined to pursue it.

"One . . . forty . . . here we are, one forty-two: The Baugh. 'The Baugh is gregarious.' I ask you: could I possibly be gregarious? No one is more solitary than I. But it also says, 'The Baugh must not fall prey to the temptations of his sensuality.' But I *always* fall prey to the temptations of my sensuality."

General laughter, and he marched on into the bristly body of the chapter.

"The Baugh has a good sense of humor . . ."

I was mildly embarrassed for him, but understood at least that he was taking a breather, wouldn't keep it up for long.

He kept it up for long. It seemed he was prepared to keep it up for the rest of the declining day. I cast an eye over my shoulder several times and watched the edge of shadow advancing on the courtyard garden, colors going under the axe of the hours.

"The Baugh . . . 'may enjoy good fortune in a political career.' Have I missed my calling? The Baugh . . ." He named another quality of the Baugh.

I could only blink at this.

"What next? The Baugh . . ." Another boarish quality.

"The Baugh . . ." One more time.

"And the Baww . . ."

His audience seemed to be enjoying the routine, but I felt the richness of the day wasting and niffed an encroaching odor of decay, a pitiable sense of human limit. If he was too tired to engage in actual conversation, why didn't he just wave his hand, excuse himself and send us back to barracks?

"The Baugh . . ."

On the other hand he didn't look fatigued at all, whatever the weariness of the material. He seemed an enormous happy baby self-surprised by a pure capacity for play, a tinge of wickedness in his ability to pull everyone in the room into his sphere of fun. I remembered Tash telling me that the top of Bulent's skull had never closed, that when you were cutting his hair you could see the skin over his fontanelle rising and falling with his breath, quite a large gap, inches across.

"And the Baugh . . ."

He still reminded me, both in girth and in the theatricality of his grip on our attention, of Samuel Johnson, who was one of the very few people or things toward whom Bulent would admit to a hearty dislike. The others were Japanese culture—"Food is meant to be *cooked*"—and the sign of Scorpio—"Please get me away from that person"—and he was playful about those. He was not playful about Johnson. Bulent actively loathed the Doctor. ("I was made to study Johnson at New York University and again at Cornell." A shudder. "A perfectly awful man.") Yet here he was, more ponderously like the Great Cham than any other man imaginable even if he was working well below his accustomed level, a crowd thriving in his company as if fed by the fumes of his conversation, the aura, osmazome . . .

"It is furthermore true of the Baww that he . . ."

I, who adored Samuel Johnson, had shared Boswell's *Life* and the great "Preface to Shakespeare" along with selections from the *Rambler*, with Bulent's brother Mahmoud at his house on Küçük Çamlıca in 1975, and we'd feasted on those banquet sentences. "The irregular combinations of fanciful invention may delight awhile, by that novelty of which the common satiety of life sends us all in quest; but the pleasures of sudden wonder are soon exhausted, and the mind can only repose on the stability of the truth."

It made sense of course. If one brother Rauf couldn't stomach Johnson the other would find him to his taste. Fat and Skinny had a race . . . Following our reading of the *Life* Mahmoud took to calling me Sir—

Good morning Sir, Would you like some tea Sir, Did you sleep well Sir. He kept it up until I left.

"'The Baugh is subject to diseases of the kidney.' It's possible. By now this body is in such disarray that may happen too . . . Let us see what else." Turn of page. Might there be, as between Lear-hating, tragically Learish Tolstoy, some fearful symmetry between Dr. Johnson and the Bey? Johnson's dread of death wasn't in it, that was sure. "Ah. Good. The Baww . . . should the Baww really have that much fresh fruit in his diet? I suppose he must. Then pass me a bananah. A spottted one."

If nothing else, his stamina was impressive, and if I was not mistaken he was playing, with these repeated mock-ponderous inanities, upon the possibility of being, so unlike his usual self, a Bore. If so, this was a turn upon a turn upon a turn perhaps too many for the joke to pay dividends, though the punters still seemed to be buying it. He had them wrapped round one fat Turkish finger.

A gleam of turning brass, the unsticking of white lacquered wood from its jamb, an opening door. Who was coming in?

Our rescue from the all-consuming Baww began with the entrance of Avraham Abadi, who for a moment took stock from the doorway of the inland terrain and the disposition of its troops. Longlimbed Avi, with a waterbird's arch and awkward grace, stepped his way to the other side of the chamber as if traversing a perilous and uncertain pond upon thin stalk legs. "My dyah," Bulent asked him in mid-career. "Did you know that I'm a Baugh?"

"Rrreally Bulent," he trilled, his *r*'s rolled more emphatically than Daniel's. "I hadn't the least idyah." He was a Sabra but his mother's family hailed from Smyrna, as it once was called: Turkish Izmir now.

Avi stepped, stepped again, successfully passed to the room's far side, subsided to a windowseat someone had cleared for him.

After a very few moments Tash's gift book settled in Avi's hands. "Oh look," he said, standing up to show, a characteristic flush flaring across his articulate cheekbones, hollow cheeks. "These are the wonderful illustrations of the Englishman David Roberts in the 1830s. Here are the old

Byzantine walls near Edirnekapı, here the Prince's summerhouse amid its
gardens on Büyükada as viewed from the west. This one shows the great
kiosque we have all seen outside Hagia Sophia before its last restoration
but one . . ."

"Tash brought it," Bulent told him.

Avi's grey eyes flashed across the room. "This must have cost you—"

Tash waved this away with an imperial backhand topspin lob.

"This one is particularly lovely," said Avi, showing the book again, the
tissue shield lolled aside. "Bulent, do you see the way he has rendered
Rumeli Hisar in the background? It is so French of him. Most of us have
seen these things in situ, but do you know, if the British had taken Istanbul by force at the end of the First World War much of this would now
be gone—either destroyed by force of arms or carted away to the British
Museum by the ton."

"Yes," said Bulent, roused to fresh interest from the trough of Baww-
dom. "And do you know why Istanbul was not taken?"

Remarkably enough, Avi had no instant comeback for this, and I
thought for a moment of inserting myself into this pause because I did
know why. Having read Lord Kinross' near-hagiography of Atatürk, I
knew that the British had been so bloodily defeated at Gallipoli, and
hence barred passage through the Dardanelles into the Sea of Marmara
and the undefended capital beyond, because Mustafa Kemal Pasha, the
future Atatürk, had served during the Balkan Wars in the hills above
those narrows and knew precisely which ground must critically be de-
fended and which commanded naval passage through the straits. This
knowledge, which he enforced with Turkish troops sent running by the
sacrificial thousand against numerically superior forces—"I don't order
you to attack; I order you to die"—made him the only victorious Turkish
general of the war and catapulted him to the eventual head of the reborn
nation.

But perhaps I had spoken twice too often already. I bit my tongue.

And in fact I was in part mistaken. Months later in Israel, when at
Daniel's urging I read David Fromkin's study, *The Peace to End All Peace*,

I would know the more peculiar truth. When British warships made their first exploratory probe beyond the Dardanelles, their officers, assisted by vast diplomatic misinformation as to Turkish intent and strength, seeing some batteries and fortifications thought them heavily manned when as it happened only a tiny token force lay behind them short of ammo. The British ships might have sailed on unimpeded, crossed the Sea of Marmara and taken the ancient seat of Empire with a few theatrical booms of cannon in the bay. But, misinformed and daunted, they turned tail and went back for more. By the time a British expeditionary force returned, the straits had been massively reinforced and wholesale slaughter ran amok among the Anzacs, blood ran down stone like black Cimmerian wine and darkness closed their eyes, almost within shot of ancient Troy.

"Shall I tell you why Istanbul was not taken by the British?" Bulent asked the air, and responded without intermission. "_____," he said, naming a bygone dervish, "Shaikh of the _____ Order, said in 187– that Istanbul would never fall to outside force; when it fell, he said, it would fall from within. And so it did fall out, in time."

The room said something on the order of a hushed Aha.

In the context of Bulent's sophistication and sensibility this pat prophetic shaikh seemed to me a primitive and *völkisch* reversion, for all his mysticism; but might not the advancing shadow-edge of age and death, I wondered, be leading him all the way home to the humble ground of his mother patch of earth and its wisdoms?

"Do you know," said Avi in his room-commanding Israeli-officer voice, "I saw Gerald Green outside just now."

A ritual groan throughout the room, coda of laughter, slow fade.

"I brring him up because of his connection to the Middle East during not the First but after the Second World War, and because of the story he *insisted* on telling me, so that I arrived a full twenty minutes later than I had planned." Acknowledging chuckle from all points of the compass. "Mr. Green was stationed in what was then the British Mandate in Palestine, and when the British proconsulate finally departed from the port of Haifa, leaving behind it the certainty of war, he was on board one of the ships. And what he told me," Avi laughed in soft amazement, "he told me,

'Arvi, there was this little Arab chap, ooh arr, and he liked us, he liked to spend a lot of time with us, he did. And do you know, Mr. Arvi, he wanted to come onto the ship and leave with us. He asked us, Oh take me with you to England, I like you English people, I want to live in England. And Mr. Abadi, we couldn't take him and he was terribly upset he couldn't come. He liked us, you see. Now here you are, Mr. Avraham Abadi, living here with us instead.'" There was a polite chuckle: the crowd had missed the story's point, but Avi quickly noticed this. "Can you believe," he asked the room, and spun a long, sculptural arm into the air, "can you believe the man? He thought 'the little Arab chap' pleaded with them to take him along because he *liked the English,* when it is completely obvious that 'the little Arab chap' *had been an informer for the English* and would be killed immediately the British were gone, whether by the Jews or by his Palestinian brethren it hardly matters! Can you believe it?" Avi wanted to know, and in response to this the sound of the unrustling pages of a hundred Mr. Green stories began to whicker about the room.

Bulent put a halt to this with a commanding gesture. "He has been very useful," he said of Mr. Green. "He has been very useful to us, over the years."

As Avi might have put it, it was true what he said. When Beshara showed up in this stretch of country and acquired a piece of property—small Swyre Farm, in Happy Valley, as it happened—it might in its strangeness have been denied every kind of official cooperation, but Mr. Green in his capacity of licensed land surveyor expedited permit and imprimatur, enabling construction and demolition, roadworks, deepened wells, improved power, and the customary flexibility of code among good neighbors. The place might have been impossible without Mr. Green. That he also may have informed his old superiors in Army Intelligence about Beshara's goings-on mattered less than a gnat's wing and was a good bargain besides: a few years down the pike, some Besharanik in government got a look at the Beshara file and saw that the organization had been termed, correctly, "harmless."

A voice, issuing from a crowded corner of the room that obscured its origin, added, "You all like to have your sport with Mr. Green, but if you search your feelings you will find that you like him quite a lot."

Bulent seemed to nod assent to this.

There was a momentary lapse of narrative, and Bulent resumed his study of Chinese Astrology, finicking his spectacles atop his nose.

"Do you know, Bulent," Avi's voice arose. "There is something I have been meaning to ask you. Immediately after the Ottoman conquest of the Middle East following the fall of Constantinople, there was the most extraordinary renaissance throughout every aspect of the region's culture: the arts, sciences, medicine, agriculture, architecture, construction, all."

"Yes, and do you know why?" Bulent asked aloft.

I knew that the Ottoman conquest of the Levant was necessitated by the Sultan's assumption of the Caliphate—the leadership of the Islamic world, the mantle of the shadow of the Prophet on earth—and by the inconvenient fact that in his enlarged empire the Muslim population was a minority, hence the advisability of a rapid consolidating conquest of the Muslim territory nearest to hand; and I was about to say as much in the hope of provoking a discussion, but once again Bulent was prepared to answer his own request.

"Because the Quran says that among the things God hates is that a slave should become king. And the Mameluks and all their dynasty were former slaves who attained to rule through successful rebellion."

Let's hear it for the Mameluks, man, was my immediate American response, and would have been Dr. Johnson's: he applauded slave rebellions in the Caribbean and everywhere.

"That is a most interesting point to me personally, Bulent," Avi said, "and shall I tell you why? As it happens, in my family . . ." Then he and Bulent were off into a thicket of regional-historical twig and branch, and a certain restlessness began to shuff and twitcher in corners of the room. A few folks got up to find the loo, and some more public-spirited souls began regathering empty teacups and bits of pith and peel.

I followed Bulent and Avi in a general way, and began to see why Bulent liked him so much when there were so many who did not—even Avi admitted, under typically implicit English pressure, that he was an abrasive Israeli army officer, but I knew the type, and had seen worse. All that afternoon we had sat hushed at Bulent's feet, and he had graciously agreed to stuff that silence with whatever anecdotage fell to hand, and we took it, laughed where indicated or appropriate, and in general acted like an ideally docile herd of acolytic sheep; but Avi expressed his thirst for knowledge the way his throat felt it, unimpeded by the self-protective cautions most of us erected as needless palisades between ourselves and the boggling immensity of Bulent. As Bulent had said of Avi one day, in a *yalı* whose Osmanlı windows opened on the sunbright, diamonding waters of the Bosphorus, while trying to entice me to come visit him in Scotland—he didn't have to work too hard—"Avi is in Scotland with us. Do you know him? Avi is good. Not superficial good. *Deep* good." Most of us were content to waste Bulent's time in politesse. Avi's unambiguous avidity for knowledge, I saw now, was an ample piece of what Bulent liked in him. Why wasn't I more like that?

In any case, this Avi-and-Bulent duet spun the day to the end of its rinse cycle, and eventually Bulent said, "Well," and may have turned his hands palm up then checked his watch, which would have summoned up the desired rustle, stretch and stalk of mass departure.

Tash and I hooked up and after a round of goodbyes were heading across the village past its Social Club—not a pub, it was closed to out-landers—and row houses to the T-junction, then left, then up the steep ramped driveway.

5

A S SOON AS we reached Sid's everything was in a rush of
course. Tash absented himself in the can and I hardly had a moment to tell her how nice it was to be back in Lobstershire before
she said Fuck! or more nearly Fock! I've got to get to Bourton before the
butcher closes I've got fuckall for dinner and what time is it? stuff me
with little green apples it can't be that late where are my keys where are
my fucking keys PHIL! have you seen my keys not the house keys for
fuck's sake the keys to the car oh here they are right in front of me where
I left them sorry Phil I swear if my head weren't on my shoulders I'd
bleedin' Ada where's my bag I beg your pardon Rafi what? you want
to come with me? we don't need wine we do? it's you that needs the
wine Rafi but do remember Tash is here and I *won't* have scenes like
that in my house you're right he doesn't like wine well are you coming
or are you not? yes it *is* so nice to see you, helleau dahling we're off then
right?

I was then treated to a bout of English country driving in Sid's burgundy Ford Sierra—"I sold my Granny," Sid not very helpfully explained, meaning, as I deduced only when the rush was done, her old
silver-grey Ford Granada—hurtling at insane speed between grassbanks
down roads wide enough to admit about one and a half cars into suicidal
curves of homicidal blindness without so much as a hornblast of annun-

ciation, whacked by treebranches and lashed by long grasses nodding their seedpolled heads over the road in the heat of day, skittering on the switchbacks while Sid asked the landscape Where the fuck's my and started rummaging in the glovebox or sticking her head under the seats to find her bleedin' whatsit.

We missed demolishing half of Clapton when that small junction was achieved, screeched dogleg left then battered right onto the main road to Bourton on the Water where for a careening moment downward and to our right the shrubbery and perspective fell away revealing towns nestling in tree-thick laps of land, checkered field and pasture assembling their green and gold ideas across the hills, lanes of crops, bobbin spools of sheep. A plump tawny panicked pheasant flew up into our press of air in a rush of feathers.

"If you'da hit the bird," I told Sid, "we wouldn't need the butcher."

"It's past the hour we're late he'll be closed," her Valkyrie profile dramatic above the wheel, still gorgeous at forty-five though nowadays her crested heap of dark brown hair benefitted from a chemical assist.

"I think your dashboard clock's ahead. My watch says—"

"*Look* out," said Sid of the head-on car crash looming instantly before us as an old dark green Morris Minor 1000 emerged from the bush brandishing its spear. There was no room for the two cars to get by, so without retarding her lethal rush Sid passed a portion of our Sierra collisionless through the body of the Morris and whooshed downhill upon the unsuspecting town. A mild chicane through residential accumulation slowed us—"Awful bloody place," I learned—and then we had to wait before the scenic little hump of greystone bridge over the scenic stream with the scenic grassy banks, the town before us in all its shoppy bustle: three southbound cars crossed toward us over the bridge, glassy headlamps open eye to eye. Funny English cars with everything wrong side and all.

"Sid," I said, with our animal still halted, growling and panting, "the wineshop might be closing too. Why don't I get out here and—I'm opening the door and getting out, don't step on the gas till I'm gone, okay?"

As she motored off I stood on the wayside and saw that Sid had managed to transfer the bumper sticker from her old Granada, or had found another or kept a spare:

KEEP BRITAIN TIDY

KILL A TOURIST

The little wineshop was just down the twisty streamside lane to the right. I bought two overpriced bottles of lower-mid Margaux and a third of random plonk just in case, paying with the new money-green American Express card I'd only had a few months—my first venture into plastic money and crucial to buying a car and my travel plans ahead—then ambled over the bridge into the small boutiquey busy town. Hey, I thought, feeling my nostrils flare a bit, Wake up, you're on the road again and life is full of interest, maybe.

After I'd met her at the butcher's and we were ambling back to her car through Bourton's clutter and beneath the whispering above us of dusk's first rumors, Sid proposed an interesting thematic variation. "Would you mind coming with me to the House? I've got to pick up the Chasteens' Merc so I can take it in for a service before they get back from the States."

"Can I drive it home?"

"In your dreams, Rafi. You drive mine. I drive the Merc."

Sid's accent was improved East End, what some Americans might think of as corrected Cockney: crisply enunciated, bustling with demotic vigor, a long way from the languor of her betters and more flavorsome than the odorless decorum that was most middle-class speech; all told, one of the liveliest idioms the language has, although to my ear the best English was still spoken by Irish tongues.

Her family hailed from Barking.

Then are you one of the Barking Casses? I'd asked her once.

Watchit Buster, Sid had explained.

"This Merc a nice one?"

"Very nice," Sid clucked. She was mad for Mercedes. Best car made. Good the Germans can do something right. "An estate."

"A station wagon."

"An *estate*. I might be able to have it from them cheap when they get a new one next year."

"Really? What color."

"Gold."

"Gas or diesel."

"Petrol: 280E. You're not driving it."

"I know. So how's the curtain bidness? You still underbidding on the jobs?"

"Look, I'm covering most of it, Rafi, and Mum's been helping with money a bit. And when Aaron goes—"

"He's going?"

"—not yet but when he does I'm having his bedroom for a workshop. Meanwhile I've cleared the middle bedroom for Tash tonight. You can have your regular room down the end."

"Thanks," I said.

On the way back to Sherborne there was no need to rush so we killed only a few pedestrians and bagged a brace of hikers, but when approaching Sherborne House up its curve of drive we slowed and grew more respectful in our progress. We crept around back, tacked around a hulking wing of House, crackling over sand and stone, found a yard in which the rear ends of five Mercedes had turned their near-identical tushies to us beneath a lee of august wall: their racked ridged tricolor taillights, status flags of red and clear and orange.

"I'm buying one," I said.

"Not one of these you're not," Sid warned me.

"Of course not. A used one. In Belgium. Take it to Turkey, maybe Israel after."

"You're not."

"Well, maybe. Depends on the price. I'm squandering my estate—"

"You're not."

"I hope I'm not. Five grand tops for the car."

"Pounds or dollars?"

"Dollars. Let's say an eight-year-old 230E. By the way, do you know what the E stands for?"

"*If* you can get one at that price, it will be a money pit. You'll always need money for parts and repairs. It'll eat you alive, Rafi."

"But the idea is I'm not keeping it too long and I should be able sell it at the end of the trip for almost even money."

Sid drilled me with a one-eyed gimlet glare but kept her pursed lips latched. The insufferable thing about Sid was that she was always right— not that she thought she was always right, but that her weather eye in fact was so unerring that next year's sun or rain would almost infallibly bear her out. To her infallible eye I opposed counterfeit good cheer and my usual hopeful desperation regarding the cash-down fuck-you material world.

"So you're driving one of these home?" I asked her, to get off the moment.

"If you can drive mine. It's right-hand drive, Rafi."

"Is it now? Why sure it'll be the end of us entirely."

I got behind the wheel and waited for her to start the gold Merc wagon. As she backed it out of the spot I admired the seeming decisiveness with which its front tires moved when steered, unlike the random tread of lesser cars, and wondered if this was foolish misperception. Of course it was foolish misperception, though it also had to do with smart wheel-well design, deep-greaved rubber, and vented matte aluminium wheels: in short the color of money.

I let her take the lead, and we made our ordered pilgrimage back across the village to her home.

Sid rented an ever-increasing portion of yet another limestone house once belonging to Lord Sherborne's estate and now administered by the National Trust: essentially a council flat that had started off as two rooms upstairs, two down, since expanded to a slightly discontinuous four-up four-down after years of unceasing charm directed roughly quarter-blast at the estate manager, and the death of Mr. Smith, a working countryman who had lived in an unwatered one-up one-down adjacent, which still had a separate entrance: Sid's son Aaron was living in it now. It was this winglet we approached, once we'd parked the cars in a nook beneath trees off the driveway, along a packed dirt path, Aaron's lit upstairs window regarding us, monocular in the grey breadth of stone. The building was a wide H which stretched off left containing other flats, but by now Sid possessed it almost to its midpoint. A peaked slate roof ran across its breadth, and the large rectangular blocks of body stone were faintly watered over by splotches of lichen, some yellow-gold, some tinged green, some awash of frost-grey. Coalsmoke from the chimneypots had darkened all of it over the years.

A snitch of dialogue overheard in the Brooklyn subway the week before played its tape that moment in my mind.

—Dat was a smood manoova. He's a smood manoova man.

—Uh-huh.

—Yeah I couldn't deal with it so I had to blow it up.

Each with our share of wine and grocery bags, Sid and I walked around the right-hand wing, the patch of rucked potato earth at its front, past hedge and vedge garden to the rear, where a semicircle of flagstones, flowers, shrubs, herbs and an old stone owl about three feet tall clustered between the entry and the back lawn, which rose in a low mound that was intensely green, especially where . . .

"Good Zord, Sid—"

"Zord," Sid laughed.

"—the grass is still coming up greener where Ali Bey's buried."

"Is, isn't it."

"How's Rula?"

"Getting old, poor ratbag. She might last another year."

We entered by the kitchen door. Inside, even before we found a note saying that Tash and Phil had gone off to the Social Club for a few beers and a game of pool, Rula sauntered into the kitchen to say hello. I put my bags down, looked into her big brown eyes and bent to let her lick my face. "Roo!" I told her happily. "Hello Roo! How's the world's most neurotic dog?"

"She *is* the world's most neurotic dog," said Sid, unpacking food from plastic bags and conical wraps of thick white paper. Rula's eyes flicked briefly sidewise to see what might emerge, then back to me. "Aren't you, ratbag."

"You think she remembers me?"

"Of course she remembers you."

"Oh Roo it's good to see you sweetie," I said, and worked her head and ears. She was fine for a moment, but then her eyes went anxious with the suspicion that this affection was a put-on and I was setting her up for a fall. "Let me get a look at you. You're still a pretty girl, old thing."

Rula had the general shape of a border collie but was leaner, more foxfaced, all her body fur black except for featherings of brown and white about the withers, chest, and long, tassled tail. She was a Gypsy dog with a hipswitching walk and the inbred Lurcher habit, when she chased a rabbit in the field, of running just past it and twisting lithely back to nip its neck for the kill.

Back in the days of Beshara Mark One there had been a young lad named Lew Cleverdon who lived a tinker's life, slept in the fields a lot and would turn up at Swyre Farm so filthy Reshad would order him immediately dunked in the bathtub, if necessary, as it usually was, by force. Tash was usually one of the enforcers, and I'd been conscripted once and it wasn't easy. Lew travelled inseparably with a dog named Rye—later made semifamous, with Lew, in a BBC documentary about the time Rye went missing for a couple of years. Rye was a shaggy grey ghost of smallish Lurcher—part greyhound, border collie, shaggy with a sort of mohair—of quiet, focused intelligence who also sired a lot of puppies in his circuit of the Kingdom. Periodically Lew would shimmer into view with Rye at his heel and a puppy under his arm, saying, "This one's yours." Reshad's dog Ali Bey, later Sid's, who looked mostly black Labrador but more squared off, muscular and handsome, was one of these, as was smaller, leaner, neurasthenic Rula, whose tenure at Sid's had overlapped patient Ali Bey's last few years.

What was most distinctive about Rula was her quick overanxious mind and the mobility it lent her features, primarily those certain then uncertain eyes and the ruck of worry just above them, but also her tapered foxy muzzle, so prone to quickly gain and lose its smile. "Your muzzle's going grey, Roo, innit? Well so's mine," I said, and stroked my chinwhiskers, where the first words of silver script had been inscribed. Her tail had stopped wagging but now, her eyes briefly reengaged with mine, she it gave another, social toss to demonstrate that she was in fact happy to see me. "Man comin' for us all, petunia."

"Some of us sooner than others," Sid put in.

"I'm hip. But she looks all right to me, Sid."

"Her hips are going and her eyes are getting cloudy."

"By that standard I'm ready for a needle at the vet's myself."

At which point my peripheral vision caught a dark blur of motion past the side window above the kitchen sink. This was followed almost immediately by the appearance of Sid's son Aaron in the windowpaned door ajar on the garden: he lurched in stifflegged and looked to be unwashed after a day of manual labor.

He looked tall and shaggy at a thin six foot one or thereabouts. He was twenty-three trying to pass for thirty-five: three days past his last shave, a squint like Clint and dressed in denim, he was covered in grey grit and smoked a Golden Virginia roll-up with a certain vehemence to his puff and suction: overacting.

"Hi Aaron."

"Hullo Rafi."

Rock star or contract killer—which look was he going for? I couldn't tell. He was a year out of university and stuck living with Mum, but that wasn't all of it. It was the golden girlfriend in Edinburgh, the abortion, the fallout after. The world was grim judgment and stern challenge, now. I'd last seen him in New York, during his junior year abroad in Philly; which meant he'd last seen me in the middle of the turmoil with my dying parents, often failing badly to stay sane and help.

With Tash and Hakkı I was one of his three godfathers and he'd seen us all fuck up, but I had fucked up on a more serious moral plane lately, it seemed to me.

"What the hell you been doing, Aaron, working in a mine?"

"Putting up drywall with Wahid McDonald."

"How is the old goat?"

"Pretty goaty."

"You look like a man of the earth. It's good to see you."

Aaron almost broke a full smile loose from the rockface of his scowl and said it was good to see me too.

And to think when I first met him I was new in England and he was a Dickensian nine-year-old with upturned nose coming across the lawn at me with a squeaky 'Ello, 'oo are *you*?

"Aaron," said Sid.

"Yes, Mumty," he said in parody politesse.

"Did you take the washing in?"

"Yes, Mumty."

"Dig up the potatoes for dinner?"

"I did."

"You might make up the guest bedrooms for Tash and Rafi."

"Can I do it later?"

"Yes."

"And would you like the cathedral built before bedtime, or will to-morrow morning do?"

"Watch it, Aaron," his mother advised him.

"So," I said, intruding upon this charming family drama. "Aaron, now that y'all been freed—"

"You can watch it too, Rafi," Sid told me.

"—shall we join Tash and Phil at the Social Club for a pint before dinner?"

"Give me a minute to wash," he said, and made what seemed a nervous exit into the sitting room.

Sid, busy at the sink with her back turned, looked over her shoulder at me and raised an eyebrow and a corner of her mouth in ironic tribute to her son, of whom no one could have been more proud than the lioness who'd raised him solo: in art school on half-bursary, scared shitless but good to go, no money, tiny flat, a time with perilous few public single mothers, the world unknown and wide, with the sixties going into gear. She made clothes for various Rolling Stones and stretched canvases for John Lennon when he decided he wanted to paint, though he never thanked her and McCartney made it up by being nice when he paid the bill. She hung on for dear life, and mother and child got by.

"How's Aaron doing?" I asked her.

"I'm a bit concerned. He's got this car his granddad left him. A Renno."

"A what?"

"A *Renno*."

"Oh, a Renault."

"He drives it much too fast and he's crashed it twice last month alone—"

"What?"

Sid nodded yes. "He's not really working."

"Drywalling with Wahid."

"It's very kind of Wahid but come on, Rafi. He's adrift. What I'm working on . . ." Sid screwed up her mouth, a characteristic pucker-twist.

"Yes?"

"Bulent said he'd like Aaron up in Chisholme on a bursary . . ."

"A scholarship."

"There's no other way we could afford it, but you know Bull." No one else called him that. "It was a remark."

"Dropped offhand."

"You wouldn't hear it if you weren't paying attention, and I'm not sure anyone else did hear it. And I would like to get the hierachy, the . . . the heyarachy . . ." It was a word she often choked on. "I'd like to get the bloody *hierarchy* to take it seriously and for Aaron to get in line: it's tricky. I'm not entirely mad about that lot up in Chisholme—"

"I know." She'd raked me over the coals when I finally went there for half a term, and there was a heap of messy history behind her unease.

"I want Aaron there before he kills himself in that bloody car."

"Can I help?"

Sid thought about it half a mo. "Best leave it. I've got to nudge *them* and push *him* along too. He's not particularly keen on going."

"Just out of school and all . . ."

"It's rather tricky on both sides. He's in . . . what's the word I want."

"Jeopardy or danger."

"Both, and I don't just mean the car, Rafi."

"You sure you don't want me to kick in?"

"Let me think about it."

"Done."

Sid had visited Brooklyn too, in the middle of a flying visit, especially to say hello to my father, my mother already gone I think, and his subsequent "Oh, she's such a beauty, you didn't tell me your friend Seed was such a beauty" may have begun the late-life shift in which he decided that my oy-vey spiritual friends might not be a uniform bunch of addlepated ay-carambas after all. "Such a beauty, Joel," this longtime aficionado of the form said one more time. "You didn't tell me you had such a friend." It wasn't just Sid's looks that had impressed my father but the energy and integrity of her presence, the unmistakable sense of Someone Definitely Home inside the package. She'd been especially charming and attentive to my dad, had liked him right off and sussed him comprehensively and correctly on the first impression, which was no surprise to me.

When I returned from these mists of time, Sid had unwrapped from a packet of butcher paper our dinner's centerpiece: a rather stringy bony wedge of roast with most of its meat gone brown. On a favored part of it I saw a faint array of the color spectrum, an oilslick rainbow where the flesh had declined toward the next step of its decay.

Sid had observed my observation of the roast. "Meat isn't any good until it starts going off, Rafi," she said. You had to tell Americans everything.

"Costs less too, I imagine." I continued to look iffily at the rainbows on the meat, an iridescence in which pale green and magenta predominated but which also featured a hint of gold, reminding me for a moment of the highlights on the throats of the mourning doves that had put in their first appearance on my windowsill, an unexpected grace note, shortly before I left my prosaic patch of Broocolombe.

"You could talk to my butcher if you like. He *saves* these cuts for me. He can't help it if his other customers don't know how to buy meat."

"Yes, dear," I said. I'd been eating Sid's dinners for years and had never caught anything worse from them than nutrition.

The phone in the living room started ringing and Sid was busy with the food.

"You want me to pick that up?" I asked her.

"If you would, please."

The off-white dial-phone lived beneath a lamp on an ornate table, chocked with jade and turquoise objects and photos framed in silver, that shared a corner with an end of Reshad's old French provincial dresser, on which a piece of framed calligraphy read *Zord, make me an instrument of your peace*, then the rest of the prayer in smaller script, the words of St. Francis—*Where there is injury let me sow pardon*. The execution of the *L* in *Lord* was a hair eccentric, I'd always thought.

I picked up the receiver and said hello. I already had an inkling who it was.

"Ah . . . hello?" Reshad Feild said to my momentarily unfamiliar voice. He almost invariably called when I turned up at Sid's, the first day or the next, after which I could stay for months without him ringing and me picking up. "Is . . . ah, is *Janet* there?" he asked.

"Crikey, Reshad. No one calls her that," I said. "It's Rafi. Sid's in the kitchen. I'll get her. How the hell are you, man?"

"Oh *belleau* Rafi how *ahh* you," came Reshad's uppercrust voice, only slightly slurred, and as usual I heard it snaking around the enseamed surmise that I was sleeping with his former girlfriend.

"All right, Reshad. A little rocky actually. Look, let me get you Sid and we can talk after."

Sid was already standing in the doorway, one eyebrow raised and her mouth twisted sideways. "I heard," she said, and put her hand out for the receiver.

Sid's conversation with Reshad lasted awhile, but since she indicated that I didn't need to leave the room I hung around for long silences punctuated by Sid's occasional *Yes* Reshad, *No* Reshad, then a turn toward me and a rolling of her eyes and a *Look* Reshad it's not necessarily the way you— . . . *Yes* Reshad. So it went as Reshad evidently made his case against yet another someone who had failed to understand, to appreciate . . .

"*Look* Reshad," said Sid. "It may just be that he . . . *Yes*, Reshad, but . . ."

This seemed a long way from the days when Reshad and Sid, the most stunning spiritual couple in all of England, had the running of the Beshara Centre at Swyre Farm and exuded a dazzling mutual flash and sheen.

Those had been golden days, with golden apples frequently abundant in the orchard, before Reshad's expulsion from the Garden. Sid had been stuck smack dab between the opposing armies of the Civil War that followed the Expulsion—we tended to think in capital letters, for a time, about this apparent End of the English Eden. When the time finally came for Sid to be told that she was no longer welcome on the property, they had made Tash part of the deputation and asked him to speak the crucial line, and he had done it. Making up afterward had not been automatic. Aaron, now audibly taking a shower in the bathroom, had grown up in the middle of the best and the worst of it, and toward the end there had been friends who were no longer friends, and friends among whom former friends were suddenly unmentionable . . . Not so easy, but probably less of an issue than it had been for Sid.

"It may not be exactly as you *see* it, Reshad," Sid was trying to say. "It may be that . . ." she began, but it fluttered earthward with a ". . . *Yes*, Reshad . . . *look*, Reshad," and after a pause, "Of course he did, but you bloody well know what *he's* like."

I got up from my armchair and ambled into the kitchen to start the electric kettle boiling.

I was standing at the counter mixing a cup of instant coffee when Sid came back into the kitchen. "Gordon Bennett," she said. Her driving done, she'd moved on from her string of Fucks, Fuckaducks, Fuckableedinducks, and Stuff me with little green apples, into an oathworld less continuously obscene and perhaps more venerable, though I hadn't yet twigged that the first syllable of Gordon Bennett was the East End "Gawd" of which it was the nonblaspheming replacement, and I still didn't know where Bleedin' Ada came from or what it meant and neither did she: just something her father used to say. "Mr. Feild will speak with you now," Sid told me.

I took up my coffee and walked. "Hi, Reshad," I began, then, "Off to Turkey as usual. Might even buy a . . . what, Reshad?"

I don't remember the substance of this conversation, although I do remember his pronunciation liquefacting as we went along, even though I never heard him take a sip—the English don't use ice much—and he didn't come close to changing from Jekyll to Hyde.

"I'm sorry to hear about your parents' deaths," said Reshad. "I know that you truly loved them and how fine a man your father was."

"Thanks, Reshad."

I was happy Tash was out of the house when Reshad phoned. Tash wouldn't have spoken to him, but that wasn't the problem: he might have huffed angrily about Reshad for hours—he couldn't stand the thought of him anymore. Tash's problems with the current Beshara crew were of a different, less vehement order: back in the wild-eyed days of Beshara Mark One, with Reshad putting on the show, Tash had been unassailably superior to everyone there, cock of the walk, but under the new, more intellectual and orderly dispensation, people who had been intimidated by him in the old days were all too ready to use their newly validated rational grip on the spiritual life to climb out of the reach of his dangerous intuitive cognition. Tash's loss of place was doubtless one of the things that had helped turned him into such a bitter drinker, and his behavior when drunk had resulted in further social losses and given his former underlings more torque and leverage: they could tut-tut his drinking problem, sigh compassionately about his declining character and prospects, and by the magic of condescension experience a remarkable feeling of safety in the presence of someone who had once unnerved them just by standing there.

Tash further obliged them by behaving still more outrageously. Bulent kept opening the door for him and inviting him inside, but he never stayed long and usually departed in boredom or a huff. He had lost his niche in the world and it hurt him plenty.

"Have a nice chat?" Sid asked me when I rejoined her in the kitchen.

"Not bad. Yours?"

Another arch of brow, twist of mouth.

"Well he wasn't pickled," I told her.

"Close enough."

"Be fair." I still had hard feelings over the time I'd spent in Colorado with Reshad in the late seventies, when he was invested, for a time, with the leadership of the Mevlevi, or Whirling Dervishes, in the West; and his visit to New York in the middle of my parents' illness—the last time I'd seen him—had been no picnic, but there were things he had done— most of them in the old days, it was true—that I would never forget and would always love him for, at least.

AARON JUDDERED BACK into view, perceptibly cleaner, though with his clothes still workworn and dusty. What had he done, I wondered, to win Tash and Hakkı and me as godfathers? He had picked us out, seemed to have known on first sight what he'd wanted or needed in that line.

"Let's go," he said.

Once outside we walked back down the path and past his separate-entrance domicile. "You got the drums upstairs?"

"They're in Aldsworth at a friend's. Have you met Jules? He's built a small studio in his house and I go over there to play."

"We should go and jam while I'm here."

He had picked up most of his godfathers' vices: played drums, wrote, painted, but had worked up his best-matured talent on his own. I'd seen him onstage a few times in his teens and once in rehearsal up in Edinburgh, and he seemed to have it all: knew quite young how each square inch of stage could be worked, and how to scale word, stance, gesture, and facial hint to expressive purpose and the size of the given room. He was good-looking enough to play the lead, sufficiently skilled and funny for character roles and possessed the voice and chops for Shakespeare. As a writer his young work had always seemed a lot like mine at the equivalent age, a gift of gab but nothing yet to say, a musical line and a decent set of descriptive chops but no sense of narrative, no ear for other people's voices, nor any clue how to write dialogue; and in fact we had styled ourselves after many of the same writers. Occasionally and as he got older he'd bash one into his own patch of the outfield: when he was given a copy of the two-volume photoreduction of the *Oxford English Dictionary* for his twenty-first birthday he told me about it in a letter: Of every word in the language in a row he had written: "What the seventh day of creation would have been like had there not been love." That electricity was his own. As a drummer he had an adequate natural gift and good enough hands and ears but little sign of an original style, his idiom somewhere between the jazz I'd schooled him in and the rock that lay everywhere around the landscape. He would have given his eye teeth, once upon a time, to play like Tony Williams in his Miles Davis or Lifetime days. Painting, his mother's onetime art and Hakkı's, seemed a tertiary talent, and he knew it: adequate for a stageback scrim and the occasional poster, but his sketchy sense of anatomy showed.

"That your car?" I asked. At the bottom of the drive an old brown Renault huddled against a roadside wall. It had been blunted here, baffled there, and must have pranged part of its face into a tree. "Why isn't it up the drive?"

"Must make room for the Yanks' Mercedes mustn't we."

"I hope you'll remember that in future, young man. I'm buying one myself."

"Are you?"

"Taking it off to Turkey. But when I get back, make way."

We turned right into the elongated course of the village, the houses on the right behind their wall and gardens, a larger spread of farm at our left and up the rise: blockshaped barns, open fields, machines standing idle. Even though it was a summer evening, rumors of smoke rose from chimneys here and there about the town: coal in Raeburns heating house-water and maybe the evening meal. There was still plenty of light left in the declining day and the local doves were busy at their hoo-hoo.

"Really?" I asked Aaron, dropping from my observations with a thump.

"A mistake."

"The whole university shebang?"

"I should have skipped it and gone to drama school." He nodded in grim judgment.

"Well. Hmph. You're good. You would've gotten into Rada."

Aaron raised skeptical eyebrows at the height of my estimation. "I would have got in somewhere, anyway."

"But all the stuff you studied in Edinburgh . . ."

"I'd have read Blake and Lowry on my own." Head down, voice level. "And Rilke. I didn't need to be there."

"You sure?"

"Yes." His acting was so persuasive it didn't immediately occur to me that so heavy a dose of Too late, it's all too late, was fairly ludicrous at twenty-three. Not that it had prevented me from beating my breast at the time, but still. Now forty, forty, when you're forty it's all too credible that the jig is up.

I peered sidelong at his downcast face in the hope of reading it or finding a helpful clue. It was an actor's face beneath medium English rocker hair, and for all Aaron's unshaven attempt at roughness of effect it remained a pleasant and essentially likeable construct; neither was it smooth milquetoast: the eyes were forthright in expression and quickly lit by any spark that passed behind them, the cheekbones gave sufficient crag and male assertion, the chin was delicately tapered but the thrust of jaw held it firm, and the fortunate nose bumped the face away from prettiness. Something of Sid had been traceable in him when he was a kid, but that was gone once his face lengthened in adolescence.

"I'd've been be'er off not going."

Aaron elided his consonants when at ease, and went glottal in mid-word even though that was an accent he'd only lived around in early childhood, pre-Beshara.

"You doing any gigs with Gordon?" Gordon was an older guy with a near-impenetrable country acccent and a working-class anarchist axe to grind, rock 'n' roll down to his shinbones, and a blues-based trio called the Roadrunners.

"Now and then in Cheltenham."

Gordon favored covers, but I remembered him grinding a good, Graham Parkerish original full of class resentment into the microphone once or twice. When you're on the outside looking in, went the lyric.

"It'll only ever be the odd gig in Cheltenham," said Aaron, stymied.

Rhythm and Blues in genteel Cheltenham: where was the future in that? Aaron's best inventions were no use on the drums in that band but at least he was learning steadiness; occasionally he came front on a slow one, a ticking triplet blues, played some harp into the microphone and yowled out a vocal.

"I might go up to London with you and Tash when you leave," Aaron told me now. "See if there's anything I can . . ."

"Cool. Great. Tash'll put you up."

"I know." Small throttling ring of contacts: you could hear the constriction in his voice. It wasn't all abortion, but the hospital smell was part of the mix: all you dreamed you were, then fact fact fact. Aaron was hitting his early twenties about as hard as I had, but I hoped that his wider experience of the varieties of human nature would kick in and help bear him up.

And Sid might get him up to Chisholme.

"We'll get around a bit in London. Have great times." The demicorpse speaks.

"Right," Aaron said.

The Social Club was unmarked: no pub sign, and nothing to distinguish it from the other houses off the road but the smallish car park up the asphalt drive around the right, and on the inside it was plainer than any pub, not providing much more than walls, a few tables, scaled-down coin-op pool table and a sparsely stocked bar with its beerpulls. A cirrostratus cloud of cigarette smoke, chest-high, planar, provided the remaining decor, and there were just a few habitués getting mildly stupefied come twilight.

Tash had meanwhile cleared himself of Spiritual Fog and was back in cocky-bastard body set. Leaning on a cuestick beside the pool table and raising his pint of bitter, he eyed our entrance and spoke up. "Who's up for a game then," he asked the evening.

THE LONG TWILIGHT at last gave signs of night's arrival, and over Sid's back garden the day's last swifts and martins were wheeling through the air, circling down the day's last dole of flies. I stood outside her kitchen door, stemmed glass of plonk in hand, watching them circle cheeping in the sky, performing their routine magic of turning midges and skeeters into forktailed bird: their virtuoso flight a miniature Battle of Britain up there made diminutive and strange by their tiny, tuneless peeping. I saluted them with my glass and sipped, remembering the family of swallows that had made their nest above my door upstate and were frightened out of it at every entrance, every exit.

And—ah Dad—remembered you telling me in response one of the last of your stories from the old country, unforgotten after what, seventy years? The swallows you had loved, how you watched them peck bits of straw from globes of horse dung in the gutter to build their nest beneath the eaves where they'd beget their brood, and how some slackmouthed crude and cruel *grubyann* had laughingly bashed their world to bits with a broomstick and they flew peeping piteously up and down the street above their devastated nests as if their grief could fill the horizons pole to pole. Which for you, in your instant, Dad, it did. Ah Dad. Had I dreamed of him again, sitting with his back to time's river, the water flowing by?

"Peep away, sweeties," I told the birds. "Heaven help us all."

I took a last sip of outdoor summer wine and went inside, where Sid was busy in her kitchen, another nest in the overwhelming world, its light electric under darkening heaven. She didn't enjoy cooking but was extremely good at it, and always turned out something impressively multiform when guests had come. "You need the table laid?" I asked her.

"If you like, but it's not urgent yet. Fock!" A burnt or sliced fingertip flashed into the air. "Fuckaduck. Bleedin' Ada."

She had the oven going for the roast, carrots and potatoes, two pots steaming on the stovetop and a third asimmer on the yellowed-ivory lacquered iron Raeburn wedged squat in the corner beneath its black chimneyshaft.

Tash and Phil and Aaron were in the sitting room with the TV on but I hadn't seen Sid in a couple of years and it was time to pull one of those tallbacked chairs askance from the table and sit down. She declined a glass of wine.

"Not yet or I'll be bloody useless. How were things at the House?"

"Tash and I just made the end of the trustees meeting and didn't hear much. I thought Bulent looked pretty bad, but upstairs later he, uh, held forth for an hour or so and seemed to revive, though I'll tell you . . ."

"Yes?" asked Sid, her posture perking.

"Well, it seemed to me he was playing to the crowd a little cheaply." I told her about Chinese astrology and the unending Baww. "He seemed to be basking in it, and it surprised me, it's not, you know, what he's usually about."

Sid's overshoulder face flashed teeth and eyes, then she turned to tell me: "He *likes* it. He has a weakness for it, dear. He's not supposed to be the center of attention but sometimes he can't help himself."

Of those who loved Bulent, eagle-eyed Sid was among the firmest and fiercest, and what's more, since she was hardly part of the Beshara crowd anymore, her love burned without the polluting grease of self-interest common in other kitchens—you'd think her hope of getting a bursary for Aaron might have smudged her eyelight, but Sid was as uncorruptible as they come—and so, perhaps uniquely, was not much conditioned by what she imagined she could get from him. Since Bulent's official position on himself was that he was not the leader of a spiritual school or even a teacher, still less a shaikh or quasi-guru figure—a deferral central to Beshara's activity and intent—Sid's eyeflashing pounce on this alleged weakness of his touched what others might have thought too critical a vein to talon with.

"Yes, well, maybe," I said, backpedalling mostly in ignorance—I only passed through every few years—but also cowardice. "I suppose . . ."

"Who else did you see today?" Sid, impatient with my inability to engage with her on the issue, wanted to know.

"Well, let's see . . . At lunch I ran into . . ."

And here followed a sequence of me naming names and Sid serially saying something on the order of Now *that* one's right out of her tree, or Jesus he's *completely* cracked, or *That* one needs a sharp knock on 'is head, or Bonkers, *Completely* out to lunch, *Dreadful* woman, or sometimes just a shudder.

"Now *that* one," Sid told me as I sipped my gentling wine. "If I could get my hands on him for a month I'd soon straighten *his* willy out. And don't get me started about bleedin' whatsisface . . ."

"Jesus, Sid," I said at last, blowing air.

"I used to think I'd mellow when I got older," she told me, diminuendo for a sec, "but I haven't, so fuck it. Did you see so-and-so?"

"No."

"Well, he's all right," she sniffed. "Did you run into such-and-such?"

"No."

"I like *her*," she purred.

"Frightfully decent of you, Sid."

"Rafi, you've seen them. Come on. You've *seen* them, Jesus' sake."

"Sid, I'm just passing through. A man of peace."

A screw-eyed look. "You remember the crowd we had in the old days. Just look at them now. Halim's all right, but the rest of the so-called hier . . . higher . . . Have you seen the way they *walk*?"

"The way they walk? How do they walk?"

"They walk so bloody *slowly*," she announced as if pouncing on the living heart of crime, or the filet mignon, ideally rotted, of their essential fault. "They're so . . . so . . . what's the word I'm looking for."

"Languid?"

"They're all so fucking *languid*, Rafi. There's no *rigor*." Pronounced *riggah*.

"Because they walk so slowly."

"Yess," she hissed conclusively and, spinning, renewed her attack upon the stove. "And when they talk about the old days it's always about the Bad Old Days with them. Of course we were all out of our minds and hanging on for dear life, but if it weren't for those Bad Old Days they wouldn't be where they are now."

"It's small thinking on their part," I agreed. "Beshara had a florid youth, and needed it."

"And they should know better."

That Sid had fetched up, after the wars, on the other side of Sherborne from the remainder of the old gang was pure happenstance, if there was such a thing: she'd been living with Aaron in unsuitable digs in a bend of the road called Little Barrow under the snooping eye of a censorious landlady she also did work for, and when this little two-and-two in Sherborne came up she had snapped it up despite the heavy karma panting at the other end of the village.

Stalwart friends like Sue Collins dropped by, along with a straggle of malcontents with their regimental uniforms in disarray, and eventually Sid managed a renewed liaison with Bulent—they had never argued, and whenever he dropped down to Sherborne from Scotland or abroad Sid would dream his arrival, often including a chat with him before she woke—and by narrative time present something more than uneasy truce between herself and the unpronounceables had been achieved. I was a traveller she could blow off steam with. It was a work in progress.

"How are you then?" Sid asked me, the Beshara file snapping shut.

"Pretty rough," I said.

An indicative silence followed and I stepped into it.

"Do you remember the last time I was here I asked you about my mother falling out of the car on a visit to the cemetery? I asked you about the creepiness, the idea that—"

"I remember," Sid told me.

A couple of years before there was any unmistakable sign of my mother's senescence, she and my father and Aunt Rose drove out, in the tincan-patched blue Dodge Dart that had preceded the Chevy Malibu, to the cemetery on the Island for a ritual visit to my grandmother's grave. The visit completed, my father was in the course of driving the car slowly along the looping roads toward the exit when the right-side front door popped inexplicably open and my mother tumbled out of the car onto the asphalt. Despite her age she got nothing worse than a bruising but I remembered her lapsing into a saddened, dreamy state in the aftermath, as if a gap had opened in the certitudes by which she steered her life and defined her world. I'd watched the shadow grow on her and it was like a haunting. The first signs of mental decay followed not long after. I'd asked Sid about it three years back, on my last outing before the vault door clanged shut on the ramblings of my still-young life.

Sid had been admirably common-sensical on the subject. These things are only omens, she had told me, insofar as they connect with one's subconscious—if there's a connection, guilty or otherwise, through which they can gain entry. It creates a suggestion, she said. It expressed something your mother already felt. Realistically speaking, your mother had subconsciously left the door incompletely latched and then, on the emotional plane, had interpreted her tumble as exactly what it looked like to superstition's eye. Given that, it might have helped, a little, to set off a condition already latent in her.

Sid's explanation fit better than she knew. There had always been the suggestion that my ghostly grandmother—with her salty fingers, claw-like hands, sallow hollow cheeks, loose false teeth, tight bun of thin grey hair, and a personal rhythm out of step with everyone else on the scene—had killed herself in the Home we'd sent her to. She had lived with us in our one-bedroom apartment until I outgrew the crib in the corner of the bedroom, and had slept on a foldout bed in the foyer, and although I was not much aware of the drama that attended shipping her off to the Home, I'd felt relief at her departure—her strange unhealthy smell, her accent, her neurosis, the fact that once, the most outlandish thing she'd done, when I had trouble peeing she had rushed through the open bathroom door and seized my penis painfully in her crooked fingers, a moment I later associated, inevitably, with the painful emergence of my adolescent bloodclot—only lightly inflected with a sense of triumph over her, since her presence, like her absence, was a simple given of my childish world and she came and went as inexplicably as a season. But. There'd been a muffled drama attending her death in the Home, a whisper, a suggestion, a stifled word, a look in the eye and a hand covering a torn mouth on a yellowlit evening of slashing rain outside the streaming walls of some Brooklyn institution as seen through the windshield of the black family Dodge. My grandmother might have taken her life inside those exile walls.

So that when my mother tumbled out of the car departing her mother's graveside on the cemetery road did it seem to her that primal guilt had seized her with a crooked, bony hand and pulled her down to earth?

Sid's no-nonsense take on the spookiness had been an effective clarifier.

"I feel like I've been yanked halfway into death myself these days," I told her. "I saw my parents destroyed piece by piece and it was unlike anything I've ever . . ."

By a stiffening about Sid's back and shoulders I could see a frost of nonreception setting in, and I checked my recitation.

"It was pretty rough," I said in a less consequential tone.

"I'm sure it was," Sid said.

Sid was strong but could be brittle. Essentially unsentimental, she was as uncompromised a spirit as I'd encountered in this world, and was British to the core. When things got grim she clenched her teeth, stiffened lip, pulled her finger out and got on with it. We don't grow Jews like that in Brooklyn.

"And *your* dad's death?" I asked anyway. Hard as it was to believe, other people's parents had died those last few years. Sid's dad, a big grey man with a beaky nose, had been a fireman and flirted with Mosleyan fascism before the war. Sid knew him for what he was and had loved him anyway. Her mother, of French descent and delicate, presented a more complex engagement, and was still alive. "Did he . . . did he suffer badly?" I could hear the morose and sentimental compromise in my voice, but fell into the question anyway.

"It wasn't easy," came the clipped response.

"And how're you doing after it?" I seemed condemned to ask. I was a grief-seeking missile whose aim had been ratcheted tight the last three years and set on automatic. "Are you all right?"

"I'm fine," said Sid incisively.

She popped a stack of dinner plates to warm in the oven cabinet of the Raeburn and began uncloseting the serving china. "You could lay the table now if you like," she said.

Phil's timing was excellent and his tone well judged: he appeared smiling in the kitchen doorway, washing dry solicitous hands, his large curved nose emerging from center-parted sheaves of dark blond hair, and his eyes alight to the evening's possible amusements. "Shall I make you a Bloody Mary before dinner, my love?"

BY PLYING SID with strong drink, Phil had hoped to get her going at the dinner table, but she only went red-faced and laughed more than she otherwise would have done at the dinner patter, and left a second crimson glassful untouched as we tucked into the roast and gleaming veggies.

After dinner and the dishes done, with Rula gnashing bones in a roasting tin by the Raeburn, we withdrew to the sitting room. It was so smartly appointed, with upscale items Reshad was not getting back but also with standard-issue comfy chairs and the puffy loveseat tucked beneath the slant of stairs, that at first you didn't notice the patched unpainted state of the walls or the snooker scores pencilled beside the kitchen doorway—Tash was slated to do a paint job tomorrow but pull the other one it's got bells on—and once your eye had found its way past the furniture, throws, jade *objets* and gleams of silver you felt that you had landed in the most stylishly appointed bomb shelter that had ever protected friendly souls from encroaching night.

The talk ran to the Good or Bad Old Days—

"Where's that cunt Hakkı Bey and why isn't he here?" Tash grumbled from a corner but otherwise behaved.

—and Phil, since he had met Sid more recently and off the Beshara circuit, assumed observer status. That left me, primed by overpriced wine from Bourton, seated in the old Eames chair, its busted black leather leaking its stuffing and strewn with compensatory sheepskins, working in high narrative mode.

It was only as I was finishing up a Hakkı Bey story—"I must have gotten really shitfaced, Rafi, because I blacked out wide awake and the next thing I knew it was three in the morning and I was standing out in the hallway in my underwear with the gun in my hand and I'd just shot three holes in the wall because that asshole wouldn't turn down his fucking radio"—that I realized from the appalled expressions around me that I'd been a trifle indiscreet.

"He has a *gun*?" Sid finally asked.

"It's just a little twenty-two automatic."

"And he was standing in the hallway with it?"

"Yeah, but after the rum and barbituates the pain in his back was completely gone!" This information didn't seem to fill the gap, and with nervous sleight of hand I managed a transition to the story of Mahmoud and Bulent and the umbrella mender, the best-known, most often polished tale of Bulent's global mysticism and Mahmoud's insistent rejection of it.

I'd already noticed small implicit tussles over ownership of the tribal narrative, and Mahmoud was the only unjealous patch of ground between us, the absent elder whose friendly shade guaranteed peace in the circle.

"The umbrella mender?" Tash asked.

"You know that one. Bulent and Mahmoud and a few of you were sitting on the, whattayou call it, the balcony, the veranda of Mahmoud's house, Istanbul west across the Bosphorus, and Bulent said, 'If you say yes to Him only once you will be given everything you need,' and Mahmoud ground his teeth, got up, went back into the house and came out waving a busted umbrella. 'Now, what I need is an umbrella mender. Will He send me an umbrella mender if I say yes to Him?' You don't know this story?"

Blank looks around the room.

"I only know it in Latif Shelley's version and I think it's been buffed a few times," I said.

"Will you just tell it, Rafi?" Sid said, a bit snippily, I thought.

" 'Kinell," Tash put in.

"Mahmoud stands there waving his broken umbrella and Bulent rolls his eyes. 'My brothah is an impossible person,' Bulent says. 'Pay no attention to him. He is the Misleader. What can you do with such a man?' So they were sitting there drinking tea, and after a couple of minutes they saw someone coming up the dirt road around the side of the hill, all the way down there, and it was hard to tell at that distance but it looked like he was pushing some kind of cart. They watched him come and when he came alongside of the house they could read the words on the side of his cart: UMBRELLAS AND ALL THINGS MENDED. Bulent only nodded. Mahmoud started yelling: 'Coincidence! Synchronicity! Jung has explained these things!' All Bulent would say was, 'You see how it is. Even when He shows them they still deny.' That afternoon they all went down to the harbor in Kadiköy, and every time they came around a corner they kept running into the old man pushing his cart. 'You see?' Bulent would say, and Mahmoud, 'Synchronicity! Coincidence! Jung!' You don't know that one?"

"Never 'eard it," said Tash.

"Aaron?"

Aaron shook his head.

"Bleedin' Ada," said Sid, her face midway between pallor and blush. "I was *there* and I don't remember it. Sidney's done it again."

"Anyhow, the umbrella mender," I saluted, raising my glass.

The umbrella mender's health was duly toasted.

On the far end of the sofa, to the right of the fireplace, Aaron was smoking his roll-up Hakkı Bey–style, flaring his nostrils out of sequence, occasionally glaring with experimental anger at the carpet: a facial ferocity that must have had more to do with the continuum of an internal monologue than with the particulars of the present. He was trying to struggle himself into the picture and find the frame, sifting personal history and moving figures who had meant a lot to him: working out the shape and scale of the man he might become. Or just trying Hakkı's face on for a moment.

Sid, the unaccustomed flush of alcohol faded from her, looked fatigued by the long day's work, her face washed pale and the cheeks gone saggy, but then at the passing of a friendly anecdote she'd revive with a signature flash of lightning in her eyes and her color returning for a minute.

At some point Rula tried to pass herself off as a conversationalist in English, as she sometimes did on such occasions—"Urlurlrulrlrulrlur-rruhh?" she asked during a pause, then went scatty with anxiety—dogface panic, misery, nervous whichway eyes left and right Did I pull it off? I did I didn't I did. I did I did. Didn't dammit didn't. Oh shit.

"*English*, Roo," I urged her. "You can do it."

"Come over here, ratbag," Sid told her, and rubbed her head free of worry the best she could.

EVENTUALLY OUR TALK ambled toward its close: the evening's oxygen frittered away in staler air, conversation emptied its ashtrays and the shambling evening followed suit. At length I was left alone in the sitting room, the rest having ascended to the sleep of the just and Rula, having been let out for a final wee, lay at my feet awhile, then slunk off to her scrap of blanket in the kitchen. She had been the evening's only speaker to essay something original and heartfelt in the present tense. The rest of us were lousy with nostalgia or regret.

I remembered sitting here at Sid's—which year was it?—alone late at night in this same highbacked armchair when I'd heard a faint tapping at the inset casement window and looked up to see a white moth with eyes like two black marbles beating its head into the incomprehensibility of the glasspane—the whirring wings, the headfeathers of its antennae and the miniature horror of its ghastly face and obsidian eyes, which seemed fixed on mine: it felt like pure undoing tapping with mad mechanical insistence at the casement glass.

World too heavy, brain not lift it anymore, I'd told myself, then written the phrase down in that year's notebook, but now it seemed to me that all my visits here in search of repair from the most recent of my misadventures were fraudulent in their neediness. Stale redramatizations, perhaps, of some fundamental unspoken story: a usual human waste of time. Uncleared subjectivity I should have taken care of years ago.

All right, the first time I'd come to England, before meeting these people, in 1972: that had been excusable: you need repairs after basic late-adolescent fuckup, fine. But since then? Too much acting out.

And there was a perhaps more serious worry. Bulent had not been doing one of his comedy bits when he called Mahmoud the Misleader—a Name of God, usually spoken in a whisper, if at all—and it did strike me that we outlaws and failed artistic types holed up at Sid's were in sadder, far more perilous shape than the True Belongers at the other end of the village. Sid would be all right, of course—to live outside the law you must be honest—but the rest of us in the band of outsiders?

I sent a threadbare prayer aloft, then fossicked through Sid's bookshelves of heavy esoterica and lightweight murder mysteries, but nothing grabbed me, and eventually I had to go upstairs to bed.

I HAD THE END BEDROOM above the kitchen, Sid and Phil down the other end and Tash snoring in the middle. Aaron was in the top half of the one-down one-up around the other side of the building.

The lamp on the bedside table had been left on for me. At the head of the bed, nearly as high as the ceiling and as wide as the room's west wall spread a densely convoluted Indian screen carved of darkened wood, all twining leaf and vine and peeping wooden bird. Across the room from the bedfoot stood a tall dark wooden closet in which old suits and coats were hung: a vaguely haunted object. There was one small casement window in the middle of the right-hand wall, over which heavy curtains with a floral pattern echoing the Indian screen were held open by braided cords. In the corner past it hugging the wall was the wide grey box of one of those English storage heaters that emit a gasp of warmth only when you're not looking. On its narrow top, above its row of teeth, sat a row of books including a uniform edition of the works of Hermann Hesse: pseudo-heat and the pseudo-spiritual: they deserved each other.

Then I got it: live long enough you get to see everything: Peter's father: that's where. I cringed at the memory of having said it to Bulent, then got over it in stages, the best I could.

I undressed for bed, noting the usual smell of smoked walrus meat wafting up from the underworks. I put on a pair of boxer shorts in case I had an especially happy dream in a bed not my own.

I was not at home, and this solid bedroom in the heavy stone house held no creak of father heard in every tock of the settling old apartment, and no sound in the hushes of the small hours that for a moment impersonated my father's footstep on the boards or my mother's distracted shuffle. One's parents are never quite departed, at home, but remain latent behind each small suggestion in which the mind can find a common touch. Sid's guest bedroom lacked an established habit of recent death, and the weave of leaf and flower behind my head wafted down a scent from an unaccustomed wood. The hushed substantiality of the heavy carpet softened the slow beats of time upon the air, and I could feel the body of night swelling around me, and by its steady weight I could measure the distance I had come from home. Farther east in that night the Mediterranean rolled its breast to the moon and lay back in the old lap of Empire and on Zion. Miles to go.

I had latched the window one notch open and pulled the heavy curtains nearly shut so dawn wouldn't wake me early. Wisps of country cool insinuated themselves through the gap as I read by lamplight—one of Sid's Len Deightons?—propped on my left elbow, then with my head laid back on three thick pillows. A few flickers of my heavying eyelids, dimmed persistence through a few more paragraphs or pages, then roll to put the book down, lamp to sleep and ride the moment down.

I SLEPT LIKE A LOG and woke, several times, in episodes, like the dead.

In the first salient instance I woke quietly to notice the slightest paling of denim night in the curtainslit at the window—if I'd gotten up, stumbled over, stuck my face outside and craned it left, no doubt Venus would have been brilliant in the east, a diamond set in indigo baize—and a solitary prophetic bird awake and singing the shape of day to come. To be exact, this solitary predawn song, an extended line of identical twitters that swelled in their fleeting middles and tapered in and out of silence at either end, sounded like the working of a pair of fine silver scissors snippeting a measured line along the margin of the dark: I opened my ears to it, shut my eyes and after not too long redescended the spiral path of petals to the blossom depth of sleep.

In my next waking moment the day was shifting from last grey to early silver, and a morning chorus had started up in country earnest: a thicket of chirps as dense and intricate as a thatched roof or wattle wall, and behind or above it a higher more intermittent peeping that might have been the swifts and swallows casting themselves in circles for the day's first round of midges. This wave of waking birdsong rolling continuously across the world as sunlight finds fresh purchase on the turning earth—even at sea, as the leaden waves turn brighter metal: gull, tern, petrel, cry upon cry as the light comes on—an unceasing threading and fretting of the air as a million throats work open and let out their silver along an advancing band of daybreak, a rippling surge of song, many-grained and gleaming, proclaiming time's ride around the burning star that always speaks the same word out: day day day. I checked the bedside clock with one suspicious eye, my left, closed the shutters of my shop and said goodbye birdies, under and out.

Next time up I detected the finalizing of the day's contractual light and a subtle thickening or thinning of the texture in this or that section of the orchestra, the parting of one veil of birdsong to reveal some new detail behind it—the hooing of that ringdove there—and perhaps a few contract players losing their enthusiasm and easing up on the bow; all this accompanied by the occasional passing lurgle from the tank in the corner closet when someone downstairs tapped some Raeburn-heated water for a bit of a wash, though nothing, yet, so radical as the brute subtraction of an actual bath. Twitter, tweet, lurgle, hoo: you are getting sleepy. Your eyelids are getting heavy . . . You are carrying a large iron frying pan before you while out for a walk in the woods of Yugoslavia and although you are worried about missing your train the woman you are talking to is also a snowy egret. Then completely unexpectedly you turn around and see a lurrrr and what you want to say to it is muhhhh, and you're out of there down to the full throb of dark.

From which I was startled awake, perhaps only minutes later, into a wilderness of difference: amid the strings and piping woodwinds a sudden irruption of rattling brass: a rasping clarification of throat that reached down to the last crag of lung, a more abyssal bonescrape scrawk than anything their cousin crows could come up with back in Bkhraakkhlyn—who sometimes refrained from the mockery of their caw-caw to dispense upon the dreaming rooftops the mere derision of a sidemouth *heh*-heh—whereas here the whole shebang of sky and town, fruitful farm, country hill and full circumference of day were razzed and jeered by carbonblack scrawls that cracked the skin of curse to let something harsh and nameless claw a path to daylight: the raucous caucus: rooks.

And the tolling of a distant churchbell: thee?

The moment passed, the thicket of twitters raised again its scrim, the throaty doves resumed, and your reporter took another dive.

When I woke the last, definitive time it was after a deeper stretch of nap and I was back in character: the last one in the house up and ready for one more day of world, at my natural time, about eleven in the morning. The alchemical light at the window had drawn one element nearer gold. The birds had folded their music stands and gone severally off to the bird equivalent of work, occasionally sending back a factory whistle from the perimeter.

Now I had awakened to a countryside whose soundscape seemed to be ruled by some giant creature seething in its cavern. In my first visit to this part of the country I hadn't known who this throaty lord of the landscape was, and may have imagined something on the order of a badger sending out a perpetual growl of warning from the doorstep of his den. I was either very stupid or didn't give it any rigorous thought; but in my last stretch back home, mourning doves, perhaps lured north by the fruited air of global warming and, who knows, to my windowsill by the amount of dying that had gone on behind it, had begun fluttering into the neighborhood, by pair and cluster and clan, and of course they charmed

me: their shapely mottled dun bodies, one-third the size of the brute
gendarmerie of pigeons, the nearly seamless interleaving of their finely
wrought feathers, full breasts underblushed with rose, the iridescent pas-
tel patch of pale green and faint magenta on their necksides, their round
black startled eyes ringed with a fine line of peacock iridescence, their
timid manner and whimpering fantail flight: I was almost in love, although if I were God I would have painted their forked feet charcoal grey
and not that pinkish red.

When Daniel first saw the doves and the characteristic movement of
their heads, he said, "Ye-es, you can see the primal lizard in them." I bit
my tongue, and reminded myself that Daniel had grown up in Nazi
wartime and later on had seen the animal facts of the world up close. The
primal lizard was not what I chose from the range of available views. I put
out seed for them and those birds of peace began to fight each other for
it. Downstairs neighbors tromped upstairs to complain about the seedfall
destroying their vented air conditioners. I sublet the place, took a plane
out of there, and left no instructions for my tenants. I hoped the doves
were getting by.

Back home there was a ritardando in the last two notes, the broken-
backed fallaway that is the ametrical cadence of their mourning, but
British dovesong, I thought—actually, plump whitecollared wood pigeons were doing the work, and the ringdoves, near doubles of the
hometown mourners, only had a three-note ride beat—marched straight
through in 4/4 time: hoo-*hoo*-hoo hoo-hoo, hoo-*hoo*-hoo hoo-hoo.

Back home in Broocolombe the doves took up ceremonial roost,
notes on a stave in the candelabra branches of the ailanthus tree outside
my window and looked back at me when I looked out at them—got
food?—but here the ringdoves were timid to the point of invisibility, seldom seen: a generic birdshape up some distant tree, but vocally the countryside lay beneath the ferocity of the doves.

Lying there, I began assembling as best I could the bits and pieces of
my mind and readied myself for the usual sort of action: deal with traditional late-riser's guilt, and one way or another with the impossible Tash,
and Sid, seldom still, Sid was already at her work.

I could hear her sewing machine whirring on its appointed patrols—it's curtains for you, Sid—either directly below me in the kitchen or next door under Aaron's roof, and I thought dreamily of time's shuttle moving back and forth in the workings of the loom, the thump of the bar and the pattern slowly raising clear, as Sid's gleaming needle darted swiftly in and out of the oncoming cloth like the darting beak, deft and avid, of a bird feeding in flowing water—and as I lay half-dreaming in my last moments of respite, appreciating the smoodness of the manoova, time washed me back and forth, and my mind bobbined backward, spinning like a silver wheel.

PART THREE

They say he is already in the forest of Arden, and a many merry men with him; and there they live like the old Robin Hood of England: they say many young gentlemen flock to him every day, and fleet the time carelessly, as they did in the golden world.

—*As You Like It*

When the dervishes catch a white man, they cut off his nose and hang him up by his toes.

—JOHN BUCHAN,
Greenmantle

NORTH BARN

CRUCIFORM
BARN

MAIN
HOUSE

MEDITATION
ROOM

ACACIA
AVENUE

CAR PARK

SWYRE FARM

NORTH

R.A.W. 2005

1

BACK THEN OF COURSE, everything was dramatic and new. Everything was on the go. Even my parents had disowned me. Well, for about a week.

I hadn't told them about the loony-tune pseudo-Gurdjieff group I'd tumbled into and stayed with for a couple of years in California, so the spiritual thing came as a shock to them, and the word that I was leaving the Bay Area—especially just then, when I'd won myself a medium-high-level national job in George McGovern's presidential campaign as a sort of associate freeflying interstate troubleshooter, right after we won the California primary—while things still looked good, before there was too much trouble to shoot—to go to some kind of, um, religious school in England was the worst imaginable news; though God knows they'd watched their shining lad stagger through some dark years since he'd sailed honored out of college and almost immediately broken to bits on the rocks of a late-term abortion in Japan.

No memory of how I got from Burford to Aldsworth, though I do recall that the gas station guys eight miles back didn't know where Aldsworth was the way I pronounced it, and that in the event it was a pub and a scattering of grey stone houses and a steeple behind some trees, with a little asphalt road leading away from it south into grassy combers. When I'd phoned from Burford I'd been told to walk up that road and take the first left: there was no one around, no one to come fetch you certainly, just us cooks in the kitchen and everyone else gone off to church. June 18, 1972. I'd flown overnight via Pan Am on a one-year round-trip ticket. Must have been a Sunday.

Jesus McChristmas, I thought, why would anyone go someplace as duck and doornail dead as church?

It's like looking through the wrong end of a telescope to see myself walking up the road that afternoon, though I remember a breeze passing over me from left to right. How might that soft wind have read me? Did I trust? Did I fear? Did I think I was I walking into hopeful new adventure or crossing the last line between anything like sane life and classic coo-coo inanition? Either way, I'd flown to New York from California, calmed my parents down—they retracted their disinheritance—and fetched up on this blacktop English road between green fields right here.

Carrying a small brown softsided Atlantic suitcase, the kind of thing that now might serve me for a weekend, and an Army surplus mummy bag sheathed in a rain poncho slung on my right shoulder. Books in some kind of bag, most likely Army issue. Yes, it's coming into focus: an olive drab canvas musette bag with U.S. printed on it in faded black, snapped shut, with a pair of drumsticks passed ostentatiously through the closure straps. Heaps of not quite hippie hair, trimmish beard, and not just a lean and hungry look but a distinctly pale, cadaverous and unhealthy air. The eyes might have been bright, though: daylight caught by windowglass in the wall of a shed ripe for collapse come any kind of weather, or lit perhaps, beneath a darkening sky, by the electricity of panic.

But it was a brilliant day in a green world, my eyes soaking up that brighter English green. And the fatal tan boots with white rubber soles, was I wearing them or were they stuffed in the suitcase, with something sneakery and summery on my feet?

Knowing how I operated at the time, no doubt I was referring the day and its issues to the vibrational determination of my crown chakra, an ephemeral organ I'd discovered on the top of my head the first time I'd breathed, as instructed by Lomand—tunemaster of our flock of California loons—as if my in- and exhalations were passing through me on a line of light extending from the center of the earth to the pip of heaven. It granted me a mildly sexualized sensation and spelled me, a bit, from the prison term I seemed to be serving in my body at the time; but my real pleasure point in those days, if you really want to know, was a spot in the air about eighteen inches above my head: once I could sense that one, once I could get some figment of myself to swim its way up to that phantasmal outpost, ah, sweet release, a kind of bliss, and intimations of lasting and objective felicity. My body had for the past few years seemed a locked and shuttered house hardly worth the dark of living in, and once given the opportunity I made a beeline past its sheeted furniture to any exit I could find. There were reasons for this. I had woken up, in my twenty-sixth year, to find myself so strange and tangential a human being, wearing so tall and invisible a propeller beanie, for the soundest and most legible of dramatic reasons.

Oh man this was not the life I'd envisioned. This was not the life I had envisioned at all. I put the suitcase down for a moment and looked at my hands.

SINCE CHILDHOOD, I've enjoyed examining the backs of my hands. I still do it sometimes. Alone or in conversation I might at any moment extend my hands before me and look down at them for a contemplative pause. Sometimes, if circumstances or space restrict, I might make do with the right or left alone, the benefit's the same. What had drawn my eye there in the first place was a question that had occurred to me in early childhood and then persisted: where did this consciousness I called "I" come from? this locus of awareness, this eye and the seeing self behind it that experienced, sifted, analyzed, contemplated the swarming world that came its way—its skies and cities, bright air, gesticulating trees—and rose to meet it through the shape of its own swarm of thought and intuition, dream and surmise. Over the years I had learned, like everyone else around me, not to expect much of an answer to so fundamental a question; but as a way of focusing my regard on it, and on the particular reflective flavor that accompanied the inquiry, I would extend my hands before me and look down upon their backs in the simplest subject-object relationship literally ready at hand; and it remained a way of centering myself amid the press and rush of life, of touching a persistent essential spot that was always there waiting.

On the cross-country trip by means of which I moved from New York to California in 1969, two years into the abortion's aftermath, I was driving through midwest tableland and saw my handbacks atop the steering wheel. I lifted the right one and extended its fingers, and thought something on the order of Everything in my life has been spinning out of orbit since Japan and I don't know which end is up anymore, but look, there are my hands, the same hands I've known since childhood, grown larger, sure, and dark hair scattered on their backs but recognizable still, insignia and guarantors of the self that had always looked out through these eyes at them: we're still here.

In the course of the next two days, to my incredulous horror, the index and middle fingers of both my hands, left and right, warped out of true and, as if pressured by some inexorable invisible torque, curved themselves toward the unaffected ring fingers, and the pinkies, the innocent little pinkies, were pulled less radically askew and rendered indecisive above the knuckle, curving first slightly outward, then slightly in; and it was as if, above the roof of my westward-bound drive-away car—forty dollars' gas and burgers would get you right across America, you slept in campsites, or a motel if it rained—it was as if—though no doubt there was some perfectly reasonable explanation, as doomed secondary characters always say in the second reel of monster movies, for this small instantaneous deformity, still: my hands were twisted out of shape beginning the very day I'd framed the thought of their sacramental constancy—and it was as if some massed and coiled power had bent its ear to the tiny mumble of my thoughts, then crouched low and twisted my guaranteed hands out of natural shape and all but snickered the words in my ear: This is easy.

Alack and well-a-day, you know what I'm saying? I felt myself gripped, at the time, by a sense of inescapable Law grinding out its juridic syllables in my flesh and bone; and for all the adolescent melodrama accompanying the perception, was I so wrong?

Man, I should never have gotten Barbara Majevska pregnant. I hooked up with her my last year at Brooklyn College but had seen her the year or two before hanging out with the older poetry crowd and I'd been struck by her high Slavic cheekbones and the mad, inspired look about her eyes, one brown, one blue. Barbara's face was wide across the forehead and through the cheekbones, then tapered to an angular jaw that offered forward a fine chin, but she was not built on the gazelle-pattern that usually attracts me: she was buxom and combined somehow the slinkiness of a European movie star—she did a funny Monica Vitti impression, ideally while descending stairs—and the rough construction of a Russian peasant woman hauling cabbages in a basket. Throughout my summer in Europe, 1966, between my junior and senior years, I travelled as if with her face imprinted before me—a version of her diaphanous but detailed—and when entering some new place in the world or meeting people of an unfamiliar type I would sometimes say to myself, I wonder what the Girl With Slavic Cheekbones would make of this. I met her the following autumn, when my friends and I took over the college literary magazine— of our editorial board of seven, three would be dead by their own hand within fifteen years—and we were quickly drawn to each other. She reminded me of Nastasya Filipovna in Dostoevsky's *The Idiot*—a relevant title—and I was fascinated by the way her behavior ran wild beyond the petty compassings of reason, and how her inspiration flashed its lights beyond the rim of any world I knew about. She was mad, bad and dangerous to know, and I went into her as if into a new continent, eyes wide and ready for fresh education and unprecedented adventure.

At least that part of the project didn't fail.

This is what you get for not asking Abby Krowitz if she'd go out with you to Birdland when you were still in high school and from whom you might have learned, given her grace of character, how sane civilized human beings express their souls in love.

My time with Barbara conformed to the course of the college year: we started in September and she didn't get pregnant until springtime; but her lateness the month before—the reality principle in presto mode, romantic illusion swept away in a definitive instant—showed how badly I needed to get away from her, but not only did I not get out, in the hysterical scene that ensued after the hysterical scenes of the pregnancy scare itself had passed, I actually begged her not to leave me: a bewildering day on which I saw with frightening clarity the degree to which I was driven by impulses beyond my conscious control and consent. To put it mildly. Then came the afternoon in her upstairs bedroom when, thrusting madly, I slipped out of her on the edge of a mutual climax, saw the lambskin condom lying on the sheet, the blue elastic at the base that was supposed to hold it on, and Barbara, her legs spread, pulling her labia wide in exposed wings of veiny pink epithelial tissue with a hole in the middle, as, with both of us gasping, practically howling, I plunged into it up to the hilt, came, and never said a word to her about the condom coming off. Okay, that's youthful idiot error just barely comprehensible under the circs, though, really, I should have told her after, and she could have douched; but the big mistake, as I saw it, was not getting out when the earlier scare had revealed to me that this was life, not literature, a problem of pathology, not a glamorous, significant matter of Dostoevsky made real. After that it went from bad to worse—illegal abortionists, knives, hysteria, first trimester gone, Japan the remaining option, my parents finding out, walking dazed in Tokyo on Hiroshima Day and men running up to us to pull up their shirts and expose their scars and burns . . . At least it didn't end as it might have, with one or both of us dead, when I sat in a Tokyo clinic corridor a few days before my twenty-first birthday and looked down at the backs of my hands thinking, Here we are.

In retrospect it's surprising that it took so long for my circulation to begin its withdrawal. It shrank from my extremities, capillaries shutting down—little white spots of nonreception appearing on those same hands, front and back—then larger blood vessels picking up the theme and sensation retreating up the avenues of its established city, blowing past the barricades, burning the restaurants and museums, flattening the pleasure houses, sacking the few mansions left and tossing once-beloved bodies into the river, until I went an overall pale white with a touch of corpsey yellow. I was weak, mostly impotent, natch, with constricted balls besides, dizzy when I stood, slow of brain and thick of tongue: the grand tour, it seemed to me in my youthful vanity and inexperience, of sublethal punishment enacted on my body with no turns of the screw left out—not to mention a crude attempt on my part to withdraw from life before I could get into further trouble.

To be possessed, since the crime—which was not abortion, still less sex, but an inexcusable ignorance of the realities of life—of a conviction of sin was one thing, but years later, before the spiritual loonies came and collected me, in the wilds of psychedelic California, I had taken my sentence on and wasn't expecting anything from life except to suffer more deeply and minutely until, perhaps—and then only if I got lucky—I learned the crucial lesson. I wanted to find, or to invent out of whole sackcloth if need be, a new form of consciousness, objective, clear, uncolored by the hallucinations of subjective psychology, beyond the bubble of the self; but I wasn't getting anywhere. I wanted, perhaps, to find and drink down, amid all the bitter obligatory ichors of those years, the chrismal drop that might restore me to the sweet fields of life as originally given, but I didn't expect it. For all I knew, I was under purgatorial pressure for life; I had vowed not to shorten the sentence by self-slaughter. Adult suffering had been achieved and an objective moral landscape delineated. I had to do the time. Then, big surprise, from an unexpected quarter and despite all my intellectual objections to the sideshow nature of the cavalcade—first I met Nick Prestigiacomo, then a few lesser clowns, and at long last Lomand—came a glimmer of light and a whiff of air, even glimpses of a portion of human nature I hadn't ruined yet because, innately, it could not be ruined, even by me—along with the nagging suspicion that, whoopsy-daisy, I might have cracked and gone around the bend and entered Nutville proper.

Since joining the wacko contingent of the out-to-lunch bunch in California, I had gotten used to a new, disorganized kind of life, with some parts of me working as the instruction manual said they should, others clearly busted and still others in varying stages of purgatorial repair, but—and here was the crux of the change—with some tenuous filament of myself drawing life and nourishment from a notional taproot in presumptive heaven. The wreck of my life still slodged around me like a wreath of sickness, like an overcoat of ash over underwear of mud, but now, although weak in ligament and limb, I was inching my way forward on faith alone or something like it—some florid flawed distorted version, anyway, characteristic of its time—to a promise of greater life that just had to be there, hanging on its skyhook waiting to be put on. Right?

Back in Brooklyn, before moving to California, when I worked from time to time in my folks' liquor store on Caton Avenue, just off Flatbush, there was one intelligent young couple—slim, trim, dark-haired, he kind of Waspy, she either Jewish or Italian—living in a top floor flat of a four-storey walkup just west on Caton, and they'd come in for the increasingly sophisticated wine my father was stocking, although there was as yet little money in the trade, and for my father, his conversation, evident feeling heart, avid mind, and actual interest in people who came into his shop, some of them. I'd gotten to know the pair eventually too, friendly folks a few years my senior, late twenties, maybe thirty, and it came out one day in conversation that they flew to England fairly often, where they were involved in some kind of it's-not-really-religious-perhaps-we-should-call-it-spiritual sect, the Sufis: I envisioned people in white costumes attending nebulous ceremonies lit by flickering candleflame, and standing there behind the counter, I hoped with no visible modification of my business grin, I'd thought, aha: idiots.

THERE WAS NO SIGN at the turning to indicate the Beshara Centre or anything else, only a truckwide opening in the roadside line of stonewall, a small road leading in, and just inside on the left a house of medium stature, two storeys and an attic under a peak of roof. Immaculate white windowframes, tidy yard. My normal diffidence told me not to walk up and knock, so I stayed on the paved lane that, unseaming slightly at the crown, continued into the property. A few steps down it disclosed two domelike wooden thingummies—dome frameworks paved here and there with bits of colored glass—standing like visitors from another planet in the yard behind the house.

Okay, we're here: Beshara Centre: yup.

To my right a stream purled at the center of the valley, and past it the land rose in a green wave of hill with a straggle of trees along the top. Ahead, the stream curved to accommodate rows of crops and a stand of corn. The road forked ahead, and even though I knew I should go straight on I took the dirt path left through a gap in a wall to find a stableyard.

A small white trailer with a clamshell roof stood in front of me unhitched, and a shed stood beyond it joined to the border wall. On the left, a row of stone stalls stood empty under a long slate roof. Underfoot, grass and dandelion strove through walkway cobbles and greenery sprouted on open ground. Inside the shed, sacks of cement and sand slouched against a wall, shovels loitered by a dusty window, and a cluster of rakes gossiped meanly in a corner. Old pitchforks hung in a rack, baring workbright tines. I could smell months of hard work ahead.

Along the length of the yard, the stalls illustrated different bandwidths in a spectrum of neglect, some of their interior walls bare stone, others faced with waterdamaged plaster; in still others earth and rocks were heaped. The separate tops and bottoms of their doors hung miscellaneously open to suggest a pictorial chart of vowel sounds. The last few doors down the end were shut.

Past a derelict cottage I saw another houselet set crosswise at the end of the yard; maybe thirty feet wide, it showed signs of human habitation: clean glass in its windows, curtains pulled to either side behind them, a vase, perhaps even a flower, and its white Dutch door was latched back open against the stone. I knocked on the shut lower half of the door and called a timid anticipatory Hello? to the shade inside.

"Coom in," a voice boomed, and when I had pulled the half-door open and stepped inside I saw a heavy, nearly naked guy swing himself out of an iron camp bed off to the right and pull himself to a sitting position on its edge. He yawned, stretching thick workman's arms, righted himself, and looked across the room at me.

"Is this the Beshara Centre?" I asked him.

"It is that," he said. He was of a type I'd seen in films but not in life: the Saxon giant, although he wasn't particularly tall: a stout ball of power thirty-five, maybe forty years on, wearing only minimal blue jockey shorts, his brown hair, already receding from his broad forehead, pulled back to end in a short ponytail; a thick beard covered the bottom third of his face. Massive, rounded shoulders and arms, the sizeable belly a bulge of power, stocky legs strong on the floor. A weight lifter's look and heft. He was covered in a mesh of brown body hair. *"Aleikum salaam,"* he said, assuming a greeting I hadn't given.

If I'd been shopping for a religion this was the last one I would have taken off the rack and tried on. "You too," I said, then introduced myself.

"Hakim," he said.

I looked away from him to take note of the stained interior walls, the worn but swept wooden floor, the scatter of iron beds, three of them but only two made up, and what looked to be a sleeping loft on a shelf above Hakim's cot. A couple of small wooden tables seemed even then to be fading from sight. A blue-grey felt derby perched on the sill of a small square window set high on the left-hand wall caught on a corner of my notice. If the hat was Hakim's and he wore it, I thought, there'd be a sedulous-ape effect, and maybe a Look 'ere mate bareknuckled dustup at the end of day.

Then I watched, with a kind of mild disbelieving tremor as Hakim groped a bedside table, came up with a packet of rolling papers and a bag of something to smoke and began to roll with lazy expertise something that looked very like a joint. He twisted one end shut and stuck the other in his mouth, then found a small box of matches, scratched and lit up. I watched him inhale deeply and may actually have shuddered as the numbing certainty landed on me: oh shit, I'd come to the wrong place. In high-psychedelic San Francisco and environs I'd seen enough dazed and addled potheads, eyes wide on the infinite but glazed pan-flat in a failure of intellectual or any other focus, to furnish a lifetime's supply of busted-mattress dirty-window pubic-hair peace-baby hey-man wind-chime brown-rice rotting-vegetable cracked-guitar crashpads and oh-wow country farms. So on sight of Hakim's English spliff I knew my hopeful voyage overseas to this small stone hutch was zilched, and my cell was latched, as ever, shut.

Then Hakim blew, without long retention, a shape of smoke into the room and I smelled it: tobacco: ah, only tobacco: emphysema, cancer, death: okay: smelled a bit different from the American equivalent, an unfamiliar rot and acridity to it: blond? In fact I might have one myself. I unpocketed one of my packs of duty-free Camels from my faded blue chambray workshirt, shook one loose, then offered Hakim one, extending the pack: "Try one of these?"

"I'm fine thanks."

I must imagine uncomfortable attempts at conversation from me, laconic replies, if any, from Hakim.

"I'm from Lomand's group. Lomand's group, from California? Lomand's here, right?"

"'E's 'ere."

"Well that's a relief . . . His group from California, although actually I'm from New York . . . Here for a three-month course . . . By any chance do you know when the course begins? I came when I could . . . All gone off to church they told me on the phone . . . Church not your scene? . . . Not mine either really . . ."

Hakim spoke with a Manchester or Birmingham accent—I couldn't distinguish between them, and he didn't give away much. Eventually, though, he said something about the Shaikh, and the Woon. It's all about the Woon, luv. And the Shaikh. I'd do anything for the Shaikh, bluudy anything for the Shaikh.

This large strong man was serious about his smoking and serious about the Woon. But as to this business of the Shaikh: was this the accepted mode of discourse as regards Reshad? I certainly hoped not. All I knew was that Reshad Feild, forty years old—a phony-baloney name if ever I'd seen one, with its fake Islamic startoff and a misspelled surname that was either a chunk of Saxon throwback or some arcane twist of artificial Druid jive—had the active running of the place, with the help of his girlfriend Siddiqa, thirty and a healer, and that behind them lurked the shadow of Bulent, otherwise known, a little scarily, as the Turk. So much Lomand had informed me by aerogramme and that was all I apparently needed to know. But were we to go around calling Reshad Feild the Shaikh? Hello, Shaikh. Yes, Shaikh. No, Shaikh. I really wasn't up for too much ooh-ah-let's-kowtow-to-the-holy-man rebop, and did he wear a robe?

"If the Shaikh asked me to kill someone, I'd do it," I think Hakim actually informed me that early in our relations.

"Would you really?"

"In a minute, loov."

I dragged the smoke of what would have been my second Camel down my lungs—Hakim had accepted one by now, we'd discussed its virtues as a cigarette, and I'd given him a pack out of the carton—and I would have felt the tobacco's inevitable effect: my circulation pinching further shut, and a deathly fume playing about the cells and circuits of my brain. I didn't doubt that my circulation problem had cost me the odd few million brain cells, and I wondered how much of the old intelligence would be left when finally I managed to quit the habit, as I'd been trying to do for the past four years. Once I'd been told that I had Buerger's disease—it was said to favor Eastern European male Jews, but I'd had an Irish classics teacher in college whose father had lost some toes and finally a foot to it: gangrene—and that I only had to quit smoking cigarettes to restore my circulatory system to the full flush of health, it seemed obvious I'd quit in no time flat. And I did, a few times in rapid succession, but maddeningly—huddled in my cell, I rattled my chains with diminishing conviction: this wasn't even melodrama, just pathology—I couldn't file through the bars or roll away the stone.

Is it possible I was the most screwed-up shank of bubbleheaded human being to stumble through the fields of grace to the Beshara Centre, Aldsworth, Gloucestershire?

Sheer twisted vanity, but you have to admit that my style of damage was idiosyncratic at least.

"So you'd . . . really kill someone for the Shaikh, would you?" I might have asked Hakim again.

"Absolutely, loov, if he asked me."

"Well, that's nice."

Oh what was I doing here and into Whose hands, exactly, had I conveyed myself? All my preliminary spiritual experience demonstrated one thesis, and led to one conclusion: whatever the prose of momentary circumstance, we were all of us living and wandering in a supernal state of Grace. The entire mass and stature of the universe was sustained aloft and in place by an aeration of grace and favor, and by a beauty beyond preconception without which the whole megillah would collapse beneath an insupportable weight of judgment before noon next Tuesday. So why was this wrestler-shaped individual, carelessly clad in miniature blue jockey shorts and puffing one of my duty-free Camels, telling me in an Ealing Studios Northern accent about the Woon and killing someone, anyone, for the Shaikh, if asked?

On the other hand I sort of liked Hakim and had a hunch he wouldn't be killing anyone soon.

At about this time, an assemblage or two of automotive iron rattled past behind Hakim's cottage wall onto the property and not long after that, in through the doorway came the king off the face of a pack of cards. At least that was the first impression everyone had on meeting him. He was short, a bit rotund, had the right beard and a mild brown center-parted mane, was about my age and was not flip-flop bicephalous but had legs and everything, amused intelligent eyes and an easy, friendly smile—"Hel-lo," he said, in two notes—and a pleasant English voice to go with it.

"We've got woon more," Hakim told the card-king. "From Lomand's lot."

The card-king smiled at this. "I'm Shing," he said.

I had entered the world of people with funny names. Good Lord I was wearing one myself. "I'm Koren," I told him. Merciful reader, eventually I'll explain.

"Shing for short. It's Shing Tao-Mao in full, I'm afraid."

"Doesn't sound very Arabic," I perceived.

"It's Tibetan."

"Funny, you don't look . . . um, that's cool." It comforted me that Shing Tao-Mao didn't look like the kind of guy who would kill someone, even if the Shaikh said pretty please.

Then again death can assume a pleasing form. From behind Shing, a cat flowed into the room through the open door in a longfurred luxuriant grey swell with a lush whitetipped plume pennanted at its end. This very pretty cat, grey inquisitive face with a white V-neck collar of contrasting fur beneath, stood against Shing's legs, looked up at him with a mild expression, said "Mao," and stepped back a pace.

"Hello Govinda dear," Shing said. "What have you been up to then?"

"Mao," the cat said again, took an assessing look at me and a delicate step in my direction across the floorboards.

Yowtch, I thought. I put out my hand, palm forward in the interspecies sign of Don't Come Near Me, and the feline stopped and thought about it.

"Allergic?" Shing asked me.

"Almost to death," I said.

I contracted inwardly at this threat to my respiration: and yikes, what if the whole of Beshara Centre Swyre Farm Aldsworth Gloucestershire England United Kingdom Planet Earth was cat-infested, room by room, mattress by mattress, mote by mote of dust by dust? Used to be only little old ladies kept the creatures, but now the counterculture was slinky with a near infinity of felines. What if purring squads of cats insinuated their way through every building, every room, leaving a fine deposit of dander wheresoever they passed? What was I thinking? I hadn't popped the cat question, maybe trusting Lomand to tell me, since he knew how bad it could get for me if the place was loaded. I'd sneeze, my eyes would swell and finally shut, my lips puff and bleed, the inside of my head start to itch and—an innovation only two years old—my breath dwindle to a wheezing dotswidth, my father's terror: the actual inability to breathe.

Funny I hadn't felt the telltale itching at the back of my throat and inside my middle ears, sitting there talking with Hakim. I'd sat in a plain wooden chair, and aside from the beds there was no upholstery: the room was spare: that had helped.

"I just came in to drop this off," said Shing. "This" was an indistinct provisional object, now deposited on his bed beneath the blue felt derby window. Then he stooped to stroke his cat, who had put one small white-booted foot forward, to restrain it from further exploration of the new-comer. "There's a meeting with Reshad at the House," Shing informed us.

"How was choorch?" Hakim wanted to know.

"Lovely." And to me: "Would you like to come along?"

"Uh, sure."

"Is that your bag? Let me take it. All right, your shoulderbag then." I looked up again at the derby on the sill. Definitely not Shing's.

"I'll come oop for dinner," said Hakim.

"Thanks," I said to Shing, who had my bag.

"It's nothing to do with me," he said.

Shing and I set off. As we passed through the gateway between Hakim's house and the stablerow the property opened out, to our left a hulking stone barn and before us an expanse of land sloping from left to right to a small unpaved parking lot with half a dozen cars. We took the path past the parking lot, past small greystone buildings to what I sensibly concluded was an entrance to the House: built of the universal local stone, two tall storeys plus bits of attic under outcrops of roof. At the left of the path stood a rudimentary wooden structure about as tall as a guillotine. In lieu of a blade at the top an old bell with a pullrope hung beneath a circumflex of roof.

We went into the House and were looking at a corridor. My fate was sealed.

"Leave your shoes here," Shing advised me.

"I guessed." There was a door just inside the entrance on the right, and to this door a pilgrimage of footwear had beaten a path before falling by the wayside and giving up the ghost. City shoes and country shoes, leather polished to a gloss or sneakers smirched with mud: all had come here, their laces now undone, tongues aloll, socks stuffed in their heads, and had offered up their feet.

The corridor had walls of forest green and was floored with large worn flags of smooth grey stone. I put my baggage along a wall past the heaps of shoes, unlaced and unshod myself. I kept my socks on.

The door's paint had been stripped and its pale old wood left unstained. Shing opened it against the momentary resistance of a body, then we edged our way inside and tiptoed across the room to an open spot through vari-colored folks on pillows or the clean tatami matting of the floor.

The walls within were forest green, the room about eighteen feet square. There were two windows either side of a polished stone hearth, and two more on the left-hand wall through which before sitting down with my back to them I saw a broad well-tended lawn sloping gently to the stream behind an informal palisade of reeds. A centrally placed white wooden footbridge spanned it.

Reshad Feild, for obviously it was Reshad Feild, sat on the floor at the head of the room beneath the right-hand window, a spill of afternoon daylight falling over his shoulders. He looked up to register Shing's entrance and take in my new face—his smiling eyes fixed me for a moment and moved on—then returned to his discourse with those already in the room. My own regard passed quickly from him in search of Lomand, whose California smile and beaming peepers awaited me when I found them almost directly across the room, against the wall: freaky intellectual-looking guy in steel-frame glasses, a mathematician in fact and appearance although by no means small and spindly—six foot and a bit, strong shoulders augmented by a small hunch on his back—with a wavy mane of center-parted mid-blond hair reminiscent of the Cowardly Lion's, and what I still thought was a silly-looking longish beard that rimmed his face without the matching dignity of a moustache: a vaguely frontier Mormon Farmer-Jessup-has-come-in-a-cheerful-mood-to-kill-you-for-sound-doctrinal-reasons look. He also bore an odd and I think intentional resemblance to Hanuman the Monkey God of Hindu iconography. "Interesting" and "amusing" were his two favorite adjectival characterizations of life's rich pageant, and at the moment he looked both interested and amused. What fresh entertainment might my appearance usher onstage? What new evolution of sense might now unfold before him? I nodded hi to his long pale blond wife Mea beside him—she returned my nod and mimed a big affable laugh—settled myself, and prepared to examine the scene and its primary figure, the anointed Shaikh of the Woon, Reshad Feild.

It was obvious right away, or should have been obvious right away, that he possessed more than merely adequate theatre sense. Although seated on the floor like everyone else in a room without furniture, he was easily the most imposing figure there—a good-looking man, well-formed shoulders, large, sunny, appealing face—who had used the falling daylight behind him in a way that was both lyrically evocative and added to his aura. At forty Reshad was bald on top, and the rich red-fox color of his fringe of hair and fullish beard—it didn't follow the line of his chin, which might have been weak, but ended in rounded fashion a few inches below it—framed a handsome face whose ruddy features suggested a blend of strength and warm expressive heart, this last suggestion emphasized by eyes almost as overfull of expression as they were of socially cognitive light. They also had a lot of twinkle in them. His mouth was soft within its shrubbery without seeming an effeminate flower.

I'd be lying if I said I remember more than a specific flicker of his speech that afternoon, but I'll tell you when that flicker comes.

"Remember," he might have said after the mild interruption of our entrance. "What you are is a compound manifestation of a moment in time. And as St. Francis said, What you are looking for is what is looking." He paused to let the jagged aspects of these statements not so much coalesce as jangle unresolved.

Although he did not necessarily seem on the con, the association was irresistible and immediate: Reshad: Renard: the Fox: a trickster: an association everyone must have made as quickly as I did, given his manner and the coppery hair and beard. It helped that he was wearing brown. He almost always wore brown. Despite the season he might even have been wearing his usual rig of brown turtleneck, open brown sheepskin vest with a ruff of brown shearling along the collar and every edge, the outfit finished off with pressed brown slacks. If he'd been wearing green we'd have been thinking Robin Hood, but in brown he was a fox in the forest, clever, wakeful, brighteyed, neat. There was a gold thingummy hanging from a chain around his neck, the outline of an eggshape with a sort of spiral unspooled inside it.

In my attempt to orient myself I had lost the soundtrack. Someone had spoken, and Reshad had listened, nodded yes, but now laid on a balm of gentle caution: "Be careful. Be very careful. If we condition our prayers with our personal expectation everything can and I'm afraid often will turn into its opposite. A man once said to me: The world is full of your prayers; now all we need is love. Now all we need is love. And we might well ask, why don't we have it?"

Rather actorish tremor at the end, I thought, and although his voice was native upper-class without a trace of reformed demotic I made the association immediately, as I'm sure many Americans did: Cary Grant. A similar dancing lightness alert to the shifts and flexes of the social instant.

His physical bearing indicated authority and purpose and might have been imposing on its own, but his animated facial workings—his easily raised eyebrows, smiles, tilts and deferrals of the head and brief aversions of the eyes—decoded as absence of animal threat. His speaking voice had good chest notes but no boom.

Here's the part I remember clearly, although it may have come a bit later:

"But if I were enlightened," a young man seated before him said, "if I were enlightened . . ." and went on to say something about what his thoughts and actions would be like, were he enlightened, and as for his prayers . . . would he even pray, would he need to pray, if he were enlightened?

Hippie kid with a gapmouthed grin and some kind of multicolored hat-and-tassle arrangement covering a sloppy blond haystack, a gawking, lost-it smile with large uneven teeth—brainwaste, hopedash, clatter.

It's useless, I thought. We're not getting there from here.

And certainly his prayers, he continued, if he still needed to pray, and certainly his love, would be different, wouldn't they? Wouldn't be colored by his personal . . . He couldn't pronounce his *r*'s well, and sounded the fairly hapless perfect fool.

Reshad made shapes with his large, well-articulated hands. "But, my dear boy," he said. "How could 'I' ever become enlightened? Do you see? How could 'I' become enlightened? It's not possible. Do you see?"

And this was what caught on a corner of my mind and stopped me short. Here was a piece, if only a piece, of something new. In any circle I'd shot the breeze with, the spiritual life had never been conceived as anything other than a fairground test of one's strength with a cosmic hammer on the pad life had placed before you: you boffed it, enlightenment was the bell at the top you aimed for with all your mortal strength, and the rare contestant rang it. But "I" could not become enlightened? This was new information, a shard of picture seen from an unfamiliar perspective. Wasn't it?

I've lost the audio again, but at the time I must have listened with freshened attention to Reshad's next few sentences to see if more of that perspective would emerge and assemble—and there was a powerful sense of such a picture latent in what Reshad was saying—and then I ran into what would become Reshad's familiar brain-confounding signal-to-noise ratio: just when the broadcast was at its most vital point and coming in clear a wall of static would wipe the foreground and a foreign yammer shear in from outer chaos or a neighbor station with a ripsaw sound that tore a page of your brain away. The number of the Perfect Man is nine, the Virgin Mary's number is six, two is not a number it's only the doubling of one and the first number is three, therefore according to the diamond body all the prophets are contained within your armspan. If I showed you where Moses is you'd lawff.

Was this a conscious technique for slipping the noose, the grasp of greedy reason, or was Reshad a goofball?

"My dear Twinches," said Reshad to the gapmouthed lad; and the girl beside him, holding his hand, set up a twitter. The twittering Twinches, subset of the finches.

"Look my dears, and I do mean all of you." Reshad renewed his conversational ambit with a sweeping survey of the room. "You can do all the huffle-puffle you like: fine . . . but it won't get you enlightened. You can meditate all you like. You can meditate atop an ant heap"—or did he say antique?—"and if you *do* meditate atop an ant heap you can be sure that *something* will happen"—here a wavelet of laughter rippled through the room—"but it isn't, I'm afraid, going to get any of us enlightened. As we know from Ibn 'Arabi, it is the nature of the divine guidance to bring us to the point of bewilderment. If we think enlightenment is something 'we' can achieve we're in cloud-cuckoo land, I'm afraid, and—please don't create a thought-form or a fear around this, my loves, but it must be said—if we think enlightenment is something 'we' can achieve we are heading for what could be quite serious trouble, I'm afraid. It's about service, as we know. It isn't about anything else, loves. But do we know what service truly means? We may think we do. But in fact we cannot think a thought. In truth a thought thinks us."

Yada yada, I thought of this rehashed Gurdjieff, but the word "service," though spoken without clarifying context, had rung a bell in me, and the reverberations hung between my ribs and I rocked a moment with them: some forgotten piece of me recognized the sound and could almost understand it.

But Reshad had again veered into language I couldn't follow, some of this due to my inexperience and some not. Reshad's pronouncements were often inspiring and at the same time slightly off the mark. When you tried to find the actual man or pin him in recognizable place, he used a magician's sleight-of-mind to cast his image so quickly here and there about the room it could not be seized in any spot; although, if he was ostentatiously mercurial at times, there was also a certain tactfulness in that, a modesty and a drawing back. He danced away from portentousness, and sometimes from plain sense; but this might not be an evasion, I thought, and could be mystically de rigueur: much Zen discourse was designed to take you beyond the limits of rational mind. Reshad's scattershot manner could be the right, the necessary thing. But there was also, it seemed to me, a hint that he was afraid of something. He thrived on the

spotlight but was of at least two minds about being out there, and he performed a come-on while dancing toward the wings.

On first sight I found him inspiring and encouraging, with a quizzical
aftertaste.

"I hope that those of you who are leaving today"—huh? I didn't get
this; had a course just ended?—"I hope you will take with you into the
world some sense of . . ." It had been a privileged time, this time we've
had together, he said. "And as we go on, into the next phase of what we've
experienced, we take with us the Ariadne thread of remembrance . . .
Since the lesson is often learnt long after it has been given, what has been
given here may go with you without your quite knowing yet . . . And as
Rumi says, Come again, come yet again, come. Even if you have broken
your vow a thousand times, come."

Reshad often seemed on the verge of giving the St. Crispin's Day
speech from *Henry V.* Just now, as his eyes filled, as his cheeks seemed to
grow more generously rounded and his forehead to bulge with the
wealth of the inexpressible, you could almost hear an echo of the lines:
We few, we happy few, we band of brothers . . . It was all very dashing
and romantic, and you felt it might even be true. The moment was
swelling, heightening, rising into an approximate Empyrean . . . And
gentlemen in England now a-bed shall think themselves accursed they
were not here and hold their manhoods cheap . . . Well, maybe.

"And now in gratitude for what we have received in these past few
days we will do thirty-three yashakoo . . ." Thirty-three whut? Yashah
who?

Settling of hams, straightening of spines.

Some legs tucking into full or demi-lotus.

A rosary or so coming out. Thirty-three yashah well we'll see.

Some eyes open others shut.

Ahem ahem and sniff.

Long pause then voices joining on the single note:

YAAAAAAAAAAAAAAAAAAAAAAAAAAAAAAAAAAAAAAAAAAAAAAAAAA

Yeah already got that part.

SHAAAAAAAAAAAAAAAAAAAAAAAAAAAAAAAAAAAAAAAAAAAAAAAAAA

Okay here's the . . .

KOOOOOOOOOOOOOOOOOOOOOOOOOOOOOOOOOOOL

Kool?

YAAAAAAAAAAAAAAAAAAAAAAAAAAAAAAAAAAAAAAAAAA

SHAAAAAAAAAAAAAAAAAAAAAAAAAAAAAAAAAAAAAAAAA

KOOOOOOOOOOOOOOOOOOOOOOOOOOOOOOOOOOOOOL?

We're gonna do this thirty-three times? It's gonna take . . .

YAAAAAAAAAAAAAAAAAAAAAAAAAAAAAAAAAAAAAAAAAA

It took a long time, man.

Still longer pause when it was done and, especially if you peeked and saw the faces, a silent music of souls striving upward or, receptive, straining to inhale the last motes of grace from the thriving air. A couple of folks looked relaxed and supercool—that character over there with the jutting jaw and bandito moustache for one—but who knew?

Long exhalations. Long inhalations. Peace?

"Oh there's no business like soul business," came Reshad's voice to break the moment.

And then the Donkey Laugh.

Reshad's donkey laugh was a long English "eau," one note sounded on the inbreath through the vocal chords and into the chest in the baritone range. Starting softly, swelling, pear-shaped, then gone: at first you couldn't tell where it was coming from, until you found Reshad blushing beneath it, eyes focused somewhere above the room or shut in pleasure, mouth mildly open . . .

Here came another one. "Eeeaaaaauuu."

And a voice, American: "Oh no not the Donkey Laugh."

"There's *no* business like soul business," Reshad said again.

And it seemed that following Reshad's lead we were all getting up.

"Tea will be served in the dining room," a voice aloft advised us, "for those who would like a cup before they go."

A blur carried me through the press of room to Lomand and Mea, where I was welcomed and what's this? Lomand usually didn't hug—and then he pulled back: Reshad was standing there, at my left. I turned to him, was held at arm's length and sparkled at extensively.

"Welcome," he must have said, or something like it. Then serious: "Come see me, half-nine tomorrow morning, in the Cottage." (This is the Village. You are Number Six. I am the new Number Two.)

Lomand stood at the ready.

"You'll look after him till then," Reshad instructed.

"Tea in the dining room everyone. Tea-ea."

And Reshad, accepting and shedding suitors, was out of there.

Lomand: "Come upstairs with us. Ah, Mea, could you get a pot of tea and bring it up?"

2

L OMAND AND MEA had an attic room, bright but crimped by downslants of ceiling. The walls were white, the simple furnishings clean and shipshape. The single window that overlooked the lawn and stream caught a reflux of afternoon light and brought it indoors to us in advance of the tea. I sat in a small wooden chair and Lomand faced me in a larger one.

Like Reshad, Lomand had his own characteristic laugh, a short, wooden hah-hah that was at best a mildly aggrandized chuckle. One thing you didn't get from Lomand was a normal human emotional tone. Pleasantness and clarity in plenty, but not the sense of regulation human contact. Not all of it could be put down to math, and besides, math was a long time back. He'd spent more time as one of San Francisco's major acid dealers than he ever had as a pure mathematician. Busted, but served no time: it was in acid's early days, and Lomand had been a pioneer. He hadn't abandoned numbers, though: for years he'd maintained a day-gig, on and off, as a computer programmer, and was exceptionally skilled and highly paid.

"So," Lomand said. "You made it. You're here."

"Looks like."

"Hah. Hah."

"Interesting?"

"Amusing too."

Lomand was an easy prompt sometimes.

As to this matter of tone: on the day of Lomand and Mea's wedding I was on hand at the front door when his family came to the house and he greeted them. Hadn't seen them in a long stretch and here they were, up from southern Cal, his father at the head of the column. The dialogue went: Hello Lawrence: Hello Dad: then they shook hands like gentlemen meeting at a business lunch. I'd never seen anything like it, not even in parody. It was so bland it was almost extraterrestrial.

And in fact I had long regarded Lomand as a late-psychedelic version of My Favorite Martian. If antennae had risen from behind his head in mid-conversation I might have blinked but wouldn't have keeled over.

As for me, I looked like a Russian madman of course.

"I brought that Dr. Seuss book you wanted." He'd been oddly insistent about it. I unsnapped my musette bag and pulled out the copy of *Horton Hears a Who* I'd been so careful with in transit. "But I don't get it."

"Wonderful. Thank you," said Lomand, took the book from me and leafed happily through it. "Hah. Hah. No, you wouldn't get it. But in a day or so, we'll see." Looking up from the book he gave me one of those unsettling quasi-Mormon smiles.

Lomand mildly adjusted his glasses on the bridge of his nose. I'd come across a few highly intelligent people in my life, but not one of his stripe. The sort of mind I was most familiar with, first through owning one and later through acquaintances, showed its stuff by streaking its way through a thicket of possibilities and ringing a bell when it had found the gleam. Lomand's mind didn't seem to have a pace at all. He appeared to see the objects of his thought, or the constituents of a problem, as coexistent in an open field and steady state, which he could then pick through at his leisure. If "interesting" and "amusing" were his favorite adjectives, "clearly" was his signature adverb, used most often to preface a statement delineating the component parts of a complex situation on which he seemed to direct a constant and impersonal light.

"I've also got a message for you from Nick," I told him. "He wanted me to get it to you as soon as I got here, but maybe we should wait until Mea's back."

"Ah, Wotar," said Lomand at this mention of aka Nick. "How is Wotar?"

At this cue I had to laugh, however it was I laughed those days. My range ran from a burble to a shriek; this one would have been dealt from the middle of the deck. "I saw him in New York on the way over," I began.

"And how is Plafsay?"

"Her name's changed to Plafsaï now—"

"Ah."

"—but Nick has taken to calling her the Greater North American Speckled Plaf. That or H. Judith Wonderbunny."

Wotar, Plaf-whatever, even the relatively more moderate Lomand, Mea, Koren: the names sounded like they'd come out of a cereal box, but actually it was worse than that. *Karmic names from a Ouija board.* A cute blond Lomandine named Nina, when she'd been given the name of Aumy and noticed that our new names tended toward the exotic, opined that God's karmic name was probably Sol Feinstein. Somehow, even on slender contact and brief acquaintance, I was already sure that whatever the Beshara Centre had going in the way of silliness, it wouldn't be giving Lomand's old Gurdjieff group serious competition.

"Well, you know about Nick's job with the Lindsay administration."

Lomand nodded to acknowledge that he did.

The route by means of which Wotar, accompanied by his beloved Plafsaï, came to be an aide to the Mayor of New York City, Planet Earth, had in fact been fairly simple and direct. A couple of years earlier, in the Bay Area and utterly broke, the young man—unassuming, innocently penguin-shaped, a bit vague in manner—then known simply as Nick Prestigiacomo, had taken on a job of emptying bedpans and mopping up blood in a San Francisco hospital. Led by his bumbling but operative radar in these matters, he happened to chat up and impress a post-op patient who had a couple of his fingers in the area's radio pie. In short order, someone now known as Nick Preston turned up on the progressive

rock station KMPX, with Creighton Churchill and the politically connected lawyer George Dunlap, as the third wheel of a truly bad broadcast
news team aping the free-form slash-and-edit style Scoop Nisker had in-
vented up the dial at KSAN. (And I do mean bad: an early story on Native American rights was read by Churchill with Nick chanting a
B-movie Hey-yuh Hey-hey off-mike; they improved as they went along,
as they probably couldn't avoid doing, but never achieved competence on
the Nisker scale.) The trio quickly parlayed this coup into Pacific Management Associates with an office on fashionable Polk Street, funded by
Churchill seed money—yes, those Churchills, and, small world, I'd met
him my first full day in California. For a while PMA's biggest coup was
landing its secretary, the beautiful but inaccessible Sacheen Littlefeather,
soon famous for delivering Marlon Brando's nonacceptance speech for
his Oscar as *The Godfather.* The Associates also got prematurely involved
in promoting something called Computer Imaging—it was alleged to
have a future in the movies—and managed the Indo-crossover band
Shantih, which lost them a midrange chunk of money. This track record
somehow landed PMA the gig as campaign managers for the presidential
campaign of New York's tall, charming mayor, Gentleman John Lindsay.
Once the campaign folded a couple of states into the primary action,
Nick, by now known in some circles as Wotar—which even he admitted
sounded like someone with two bolts in his neck and a tendency to smash
furniture and small buildings while announcing "I AM WOTAR"—had
angled himself a spot as media adviser to the Mayor, and even though
by then he knew that he and Plaf, the former Lena Zellweger, Swiss,
were destined for Mr. Bennett's Gurdjieff Academy in England that Oc-
tober, Nick picked up a fashionable brickwalled sublet from someone
else in the city's employ and took the task on like the man of the moment
he was.

"They gave him a good salary—he's got some bread socked away by
now—an office, even a City car with a red flasher for cutting through
traffic. Did he write you about the brass plaque idea he had? He proposed
that the city put a brass plaque on the side of the Empire State Building
that read KING KONG DIED HERE, then the date, 1930-whatever—"

"Hah. Hah."

"—and it almost came off but I guess someone higher up wasn't Fun enough—you know they're trying to sell New York as Fun City, right?— and it got nixed."

"Pity."

"I think so too."

At this point, Mea came in carrying a tray.

"Koren's been telling me about Wotar in New York," Lomand informed her.

Mea laughed. I did the King Kong story for her while she poured tea and I accepted lemon, declined milk and sugar, examined a cookie, took two.

". . . and after a fundraiser at a restaurant Bella Abzug chased him into the street waving a chicken leg yelling, 'Nickee, you sure you got enough to eat, dolling?' I think Bella kind of adopted him."

"Yes," said Mea, and with her appetite for farce now freshly whetted asked me, "and what's this we hear about all this work you did in the McGovern campaign?"

"Well, when I went down there I lucked into a guy named John Steiner out of the San Francisco Zen Center and we organized the financial district, put some sign-up tables on the street, opened a local office, put on a couple of arts events, then started opening neighborhood offices around town and troubleshooting generally. Put together a big rock event at the Family Dog. The Joy of Cooking headlined. We almost had Neil Young but the city office fucked up."

"Hah," and an accompanying peal from Mea.

"Then there was the time Jack Nicholson walked in on us when we were sitting there with a table full of cash—thirteen grand in bills and we couldn't even count the coins."

"Wait a minute wait a minute wait a minute," Mea said, flinging a blur of hands into the air.

"What." She was lanky and longjawed and a couple of years my junior—Lomand was, like, pushing thirty, man—with a peaky nose and an uncoordinated physical act, big on knees and elbows, very American in its gracelessness, with a bit of shame mixed in: one parent or the other had disenfranchised her, which one I couldn't tell. Vocally she had a tendency to blurt. I thought she was a pretty nice kid.

"Wait a minute," she said again.

"Yes."

"But how did you get into the McGovern campaign?"

"Through Nick for starters—"

"Ah of course. Through *Nick*."

"But, but, wait a minute—" My explanation wasn't getting across: yes, Nick had been working for Lindsay's presidential run and met someone in the McGovern campaign who turned out to be an old poli-sci-major semi-chum of mine from Brooklyn College, but all Richard Berke did when I went to see him was suggest that I go lick envelopes, and I had to dodge the mailroom a few times, but almost immediately upon meeting up, Steiner and I made the grass-roots organization of San Francisco up as we went along, starting with the financial district then easing into Chinatown and moving onward and upward from there, Steiner the brains and me the hustle-muscle doing most of the nuts and bolts: see, I'd made my own way and swung myself a spot.

"Ah, so it was Wotar."

"Good old Wotar."

"Wotar the Motar."

Buzz buzz, trundle trundle, smash smash. I AM WOTAR. The stricken city burns.

Smiles and nods exchanged. No point trying to alter the discourse.

I gave up. "Anyhow, we won the California primary and a couple of days later Steiner and I were offered jobs as a freelance team in the national campaign. Your letter telling me I could come here showed up a day later and it took me like a whole quarter of a second to decide which way I was going."

"And what did you decide?" Lomand asked.

"Hah. Hah," I said.

A moment's pause while we turned our cassettes over: dead air.

"Hm. You said you had a message from Wotar?"

"He wanted me to get it to you right away and word for word and I promised him I'd do it." I then told Lomand and Mea a racist joke, because a promise is a promise. The punchline was, "We doctors done studied dis question fo another year and we still don't know why de dick stands up even though it got no bone, but we thinks it got something to do with de fack dat de asshole bites off de shit even though it ain't got no teeth."

Lomand laughed heartily and Mea was polite.

"Okay, so tell me," I asked them, "what the hell's this place like? Aside from interesting and amusing, okay?"

An exchange of looks and grins between them: where to begin?

WHAT I KNEW SO FAR was that Lomand, after taking leave of the pseudo-Gurdjieff group he'd originated and leaving it to its homegrown devices if it chose, took off for the general direction of India, the regulation address for further spiritual study at that time. It was also, I should note, characteristic of Lomand that when it dawned on him that he knew roughly jack shit spiritwise and had no business running any group, his first response was to send his roughly dozen acolytes out on a membership drive in order to raise enough loot to jet him and Mea to the Ganges, though his dutiful dozen hardly knew his planning at the time: he'd only told them, hm, he thought it might be a good time for the group to expand. There were about forty pilgrims in it by the time he split; I was on board for only its last four months and I am proud to say that when he left I owed him dues money. I suppose technically I still do.

Lomand and Mea's first stop in their journey toward the dawn was England: they quickly went to have a look at Mr. Bennett's operation in Sherborne, then in the first year of its envisioned six, and elderly Mr. Bennett diced Lomand into mincemeat—"Oh look everyone, look who's come

to visit us: a *teacher*"—after which Lomand wrote everyone back in California that if they wanted to get on with the Work they should raise the
money and attend Mr. Bennett's ten-month course beginning next Octo-
ber—the fact that I was incapable of getting $2,225 plus plane fare to-
gether explains why I had fetched up early at Beshara. What puzzled me
in Lomand's account of Bennett was his praise of the speed with which the
old boy washed a slew of dinner dishes: he had a lot of energy, Lomand
wrote us, and really knew about service. Well, uh-huh, sure, I guess. After
hanging around London a little and sampling segments of its mystic circles they headed for the visioned Orient, and since they were passing
through at about that time, in Turkey in December it might be a good
idea to take a look at the Whirling Dervish festival in, where was it,
Konya, because it had something to do with Sufis, and once they were in
this Konya place they almost immediately ran into Reshad Feild, whose
Sufi meetings they'd taken a couple of looks at in London, and Reshad
said Oh you must come and meet Bulent, and he led them into this hotel
and upstairs and there was a big Turkish man with baggy eyes and they
suddenly felt their knees go weak and their hearts go sunder and Lomand
wanted to say something on the order of Take me I'm yours. Bulent said
he didn't know what to do with them and Reshad said he didn't know what
to do with them either, so why shouldn't they go to India and after a time
we might write you a lettah, my dyahs, and perhaps you'll come back to
visit us then. L&M went to India, and among many swell swamis there
was one who lived in a treehouse and placed his bare foot on Lomand's
head so that Lomand felt the heavens open, but when the note finally
came from England Lomand's head turned with the changing of the light
and followed the logic of the day toward its sunset in the West and that
was pretty much *et voilà*. Eftsoons came a letter from Britain to California
informing the old group that Lomand and Mea had come to the Beshara
Centre at Swyre Farm and that while the old group was still encouraged
to attend Mr. Bennett's ten-month course at Sherborne House, Lomand
personally had given himself over to Sufism and the Path of the Heart—
there was a cornball Valentine-shaped heart with wings rubber-stamped

onto the envelope—which involved this oddly spelled Reshad Feild person, forty, his wife or girlfriend Siddiqa, thirty, a healer . . . uh-huh . . . and back of them someone called Bulent—which sounded more like some kind of food than someone's name—also known as the Turk, which sounded sinister and exotic and maybe kind of deadly. Also: taffy, carpets, towels.

Such at least was the sauté Marengo of half-truths and divertissements anyone was willing to serve up at the time, and of which Lomand was spooning me a last few morsels now.

The working facts of the matter were a mill less whim-driven and more gristy: with the nostrils of unassisted intuition, Lomand had whiffed the heavy body of Bulent behind the busy scrim of Reshad's presentations at Portobello Road—"It was pretty clear," Lomand told me only later, "that this Reshad dude didn't know what he was talking about, but there were pieces of something larger and apparently coherent you saw bits of here and there and, hm, it seemed to me there was probably someone real behind it"—then, having confirmed Bulent's existence by means of persistent Q&A, he was importunate in his desire to meet the hidden man. But Bulent would not be met, was not available to public view, was wrapped in mystery and mantled, maybe, in depths and folds of dark reclusion—back then Reshad sometimes referred to Bulent as "He whose name we must not mention," which is as hooky a come-on as can be—or Reshad was in esoteric fashion fucking with his head. Reshad finally told Lomand that if he came along in mid-December, en route to India, to see the Whirling Dervish festival in Konya with the rest of the gang, Bulent would probably consent to see him. When all that followed and fell— with Bulent, likely doing nothing more dramatic than lighting a Benson & Hedges with a slim gold Dunhill lighter, making the overwhelming impression he usually did in those days—Lomand said please teach me, Bulent said I'm not a teacher, and at length it was suggested that Lomand and Mea go on as planned to India while Swyre Farm went through an interregnum between a construction-and-overhaul phase and its true inauguration as a spiritual school, and that they should afterward return there to work and study with Reshad. This prospect interested Lomand almost exclusively because Bulent was in it. What was in it for Bulent was in part the fact that it would keep Lomand away from him. *My dyah, he thinks I'm a* teachah. *He* wants *me.*

When I wrote Lomand, then newly installed at the fully opened Beshara Centre, a fairly desperate letter from California about how I couldn't get the bread together for Bennett but didn't want to be left behind—I'd been brushed by the angel's wing and did not want to be exiled back to chickenfeather earth—there was a long pause with some Lomand notes in it about how it rained all the time and they were both sick a lot, and finally the calloo-callay about how I could come over for a three-month course if I could raise five quid a day above the plane fare.

Yes: definite exchange of looks and grins over there now, and the thought between them: how much to tell me.

"Well . . ." Lomand began, and here incipit a tale treated as a light comedy of unmet expectations, as all of us involved in spiritual stuff, Lomand implied—a new note in his discourse—should expect our expectations flipped like pancakes on a regular basis because that's how it is. Even so, some of it had come a little hard. There Lomand and Mea were in India with gurus in the trees and heaven's flag unfurling, great weather, groovy ashrams, lots of curry but the letter from Reshad that was essentially from Bulent resulting in an immediate flurry of tickets and visas, a winding of the way from the jungle to the airport and from there to months of unending cold wet grey seeping creeping dripping oozing underheated condescending—

—here Mea broke in upon Lomand's lightly ironized narrative with: "They said they didn't have a room for us so they put us in what they call a caravan but was just this dinky little trailer standing in the wet and cold—"

"I think I saw it coming in. A white one. Small."

"The caravan of despair," Lomand nodded.

"Excuse me?" I asked.

"Ah. Hm. Local joke. There's a poem by Rumi that gets quoted a lot around here. 'Come, whoever you are: wanderer, worshipper, lover of leaving,' then some other stuff, then, 'Ours is not a caravan of despair; even if you have broken your vow a thousand times.'"

"Heard a piece of it downstairs. Nice thought."

Mea was tapping her foot on the floor.

"Hence the caravan of despair," said Lomand, completing the equation.

Mea resumed. "Nobody came to see us, we were both sick, stuck in bed with flu, some days they didn't bring us food, we couldn't get to see Reshad, the roof leaked, Reshad was away, the electric heater didn't keep the trailer warm, the power went out, we ran out of stuff to blow our noses in and I finally got this lung thing and they said we couldn't use the van to go to the doctor because it was needed for some damn hauling job or other . . ."

"It wasn't California," I hazarded.

"Some of it was interesting," Lomand ventured, and cleared his throat.

To which Mea responded with an explosive "Ppphhhpphh," and turned her head aside in extravagantly disgusted profile.

Lomand did one of his understated entrances. "So, ah, it got pretty unpleasant for a while, hm, but I figured we were being tested, and there might be some use to this and maybe there was something we could learn from it—"

"Everyone was *horrible* to us," was Mea's take. "They didn't talk to us at *all*."

"Hah. Hm. Well, it's true these folks could've been more friendly." Now that he was in England Lomand fell back on American country cadences more often than he did Stateside, where he occasionally used it to deflate his usual tone of high abstraction. He played the autoharp. He owned every Doc Watson record. He knew a lot of country gospel songs and sang them, unsyncopated, with affection and a detached sort of cheerfulness. It's me it's me it's me O Lord, standing in the need of prayer. Not my father not my brother but it's me O Lord, standing in the need of prayer. When he was feeling raffish he would raise and lower his eyebrows a few times, smack his lips and say to Mea: Woo-woo, honey. Hello Lawrence. Hello Dad. He was white folks. "We weren't having a real good time in the trailer," he conceded.

"Finally, one especially cold, awful, horrible, dripping day," Mea said, "when we'd had it up to here with all this intentional suffering jazz—" Intentional suffering was a typically sobering nostrum one was supposed to ingest as often as possible according to the bylaws of the Gurdjieff dispensation, but Lomand had long subtilized it into something almost unrecognizably cheerful—subtilized and not a little sillified, by his characteristic nouveau-cornball sense of humor: in Lomand's group, if you were spotted expressing a negative emotion you had to sing a Disney song about Johnny Appleseed. I'm not kidding. Gurdjieff would've barfed.

"The wiring wasn't strong enough for the electric heater," Lomand particularized.

"And the paraffin heater they gave us filled the place with fumes—"

"They gave you a heater that ran on wax?"

"Paraffin is English for kerosene," Lomand let me know, "and it wasn't meant to be used in a sealed environment like the caravan—"

"We were lucky it didn't set us on fire or gas us to death," said Mea. "And did you say sealed? There was water running down the walls all day, all night."

"That was condensation."

"Condensation phphh. Face it, Lomand, they were trying to kill us."

"Hah. Hah," said Lomand. "It was kind of rough. I was down with bronchitis and Mea was tired of slugging it out with everyone, including the kitchen staff. Finally one day—"

"It was absolutely the worst," Mea interjected. "The worst day at the end of a long bunch of cold wet dripping days . . ."

"Hm . . . There was a knock at the trailer door. I was in bed, not breathing too well, I hadn't seen anyone except Mea for weeks. Mea got up to open the door, and two of them came in. I wasn't breathing well enough to get out of bed . . ."

"The water running down the walls," said Mea.

"... and this dude we'd never seen before was standing there and he said, 'I have a message for you from Bulent.' Ah, I thought: *Finally.*" Lomand was brightening even in recollection. "The dude holds up his index finger, says *Service, service, service,* wheels on his foot and leaves."

"It was just the worst day at the end of a string of . . ." Mea said, but the moment had been achieved, and she let it go.

"Hm. I said to myself, well, this service stuff is kind of confusing to me and it might be a good idea if I found out what it was. So I asked Reshad if there was anyone around here who was particularly good at it so I could take a look at them and get a better idea. He mentioned a couple of people, and ah, well . . . let's just say it didn't clarify things." (I got the drift at the time, but years later, in a public talk on the subject of Service, Lomand would characterize Reshad's two exemplars with a firmer sense of line: "One of them behaved like he was running for Flying Asshole of the Year, and the other was a psychotic barber.")

"Well, Lomand, what can I say?" I asked. "Thank you for inviting me to this wonderful place."

"My pleasure, Koren. It's better now. For example we've got this lovely room."

"It's nice."

"We got *some* of them straightened out anyway," was Mea's version. "And Lomand's in charge of the work rota."

"My health's a lot better and I've been given a few things to do," Lomand admitted.

"And now," said Mea, "whenever anyone wants to get anything actually done around here, it's *Leau*mand, oh *Leau*mand."

"Seriously, Koren," Lomand told me. "I think you'll find the place extremely interesting. And as they say around here . . ."

"Good grief," I said, unconsciously taking on one of Lomand's locutions: he did an occasional Charlie Brown. "I meant to ask: Mark. How or where is Mark Adler?"

"He was here awhile, and should be back in not too long."

"But how's his arm?"

"He's recovered some use of it, and he's working hard at getting the rest of it back."

I'd first met Mark in Berkeley maybe two years before, in the communal house across the street from placid Ho Chi Minh Park. I'd gotten a room there, found through Nick, whom I'd met not long before and who had quickly become an inseparable buddy. Then Nick moved in on me because he owed Lomand past monthly dues for this ridiculous spiritual group he was in, a hundred a month and he owed four, so couldn't afford rent himself. I kept wanting to meet up with this Lomand character because of what I thought of as my hip ironic interest in con men but which actually went little deeper than an early-adolescent partiality for *Maverick*, but Lomand never seemed to turn up where expected or announced. Hey, you just missed him. All I got was some of his group dropping by after one of their weekly séances or whatever.

I received a few of them in the living room, smoking a cigarette, offering them a splash of Almaden red or white and wondering why Nick, who'd invited them, hadn't shown.

Among them, Mark Adler was obviously one more smart sweet Jewish guy mislaid by the whims of character and culture and now out there in the wilderness with the rest of us. With his bushy beard and commanding nose he had the face of an Old Testament prophet, only, at six foot something he also had arms and legs that may have seemed disproportionately long only because of the awkwardness with which he disposed them—big feet too, in big shoes, splayed out there at the end of the legs as he sat there—and, at the focus of his face behind his blackframe glasses, a pair of eyes so tender and unguarded he never could have cut it with a message in the hardness of the desert.

I was snug in an armchair, he was out there on an ottoman. He batted his brown doe eyes at me and after only a few preliminaries flexed his soft Bahston accent and wanted to know, "Haven't you ever wanted to save the world?"

Oh Lordy. Where to begin?

Not five minutes earlier, Linda Lundy, a dark somewhat exotic woman seated on the floor to the left of my armchair, had told me that in Lomand's group she had finally found what she'd been looking for all along. What's that, I asked her. "The superhuman," she said, with shining eyes.

Lord knows what I might have looked like in this little scene. Here's a guess: a stick-thin bloodless cadaverous fella squinting ironically back at Mark and Linda from depths of purgatorial fire.

Another thing I remember about Mark that evening was his gift for farting in mid-conversation, loud and prominent and unashamed—Mark seldom farted during a speech, but usually found a pause to accommodate him—then blinking lamb-eyes innocently around the room to signal the social acceptability of this after all perfectly normal function: what I later came to think of as farting with a California accent.

Months later, when Lomand had left us in the lurch and taken off for eventual India, and the remains of his assembled fruitcake had crumbled on for a spring and a summer, Mark surprised us by striking out on his own, and in adventurous fashion. Perhaps for the pleasure of it, perhaps to further slip the chafes and binds of his mild temperament and Harvard background, he had long gone in for martial arts and mountaineering, and rode around the People's Republic of Berkeley on a motorcycle—one granular dusk, when a bunch of us were motoring alongside him in a car, we gawked at him in subverbal puzzlement until Bob Mooney nailed the archetype and said of him, indelibly, "Snoopy"—and now, while most of us were content to huddle in Lomand's aftermath hoping for further instructions from above or beyond, Mark decided that the time had come for him to realize his long-nurtured dream of climbing a few choice peaks of the Himalayas.

Armed with a new karmic name fresh off the Ouija board—Dualon, three syllables, accent on the first, alleged to mean the Road to Light but sounding like the latest set of steel-belted radials from Firestone—Mark attained the Indo-Pakistani border exactly in time for the beginning of the Bengali War of Independence of 1971. While fleeing its onset in a crowded taxi with his arm hanging outside the window, Mark watched in strange fascination as a donkey loomed out of the wartime chaos and multitude of the street and seemed to careen his way, saw the crash coming but was unable to do anything to avert it or to pull his arm inside the car. The donkey hit him and tore his arm off. At least that was his first impression as he saw it lying beside him on the taxi seat in a pool of blood. His second impression was that it was still very tenuously a part of him, and drawing upon God knows what reserves of consciousness and will he managed to get to a doctor who was not himself in full flight from the war, corral him into doing some preliminary work—Mark had to bargain for the price of an X-ray—and then managed, arm in hand, to get himself onto not one but two plane flights, the first local and the second to London, where more surgery was performed, but his arm wasn't given much of a chance either to last or to swing very freely.

"I think he may be climbing Mont Blanc with Fattah at the moment, as we speak," Lomand said.

"Whaat?" He's climbing Mont Blanc with the *PLO*?

"Either that or he's in the States for a visit before he comes back."

"But-but his *arm*."

"Mark's been very determined about it and the Good Lord seems willing, so he appears to be proving the doctors wrong."

Lomand must have decoded my amazement: "I think you'll find that whatever you thought was spiritually possible in our group . . . I think you'll find that everything's substantially accelerated . . ."

"That'd be good."

"And as they're always saying around here, the effect of the divine guidance is to bring one to the point of bewilderment."

"Hey, I'm good at that."

"Hah. Hah."

"I'm already there."

"I don't know if that's exactly what's meant—"

"I'm telling you. I got championship potential in that area."

"We'll see."

"If there's one thing I do well . . ."

Mea broke into this two-shot with: "Lomand, we should show him those pictures of Bulent."

"Good idea."

Someone must have risen, gone to the mantelpiece or the bureau drawer, because soon I had some color snapshots in my hands, outdoor photos of a fleshy oddly smiling man apparently in his middle sixties, with longish thinning crinkly greying hair afly in the breeze that blew across those sunny grasslands. If there was a gleanable vibe in the pictures I didn't pick it up. I'd been expecting someone darker in most senses—a Turk—with theatrical power and intensity to his look. This guy seemed . . . surprisingly genial I suppose . . . I didn't quite know how he seemed.

Lomand and Mea were chuckling, and Lomand was the first to tell me why. "He told us not to shoot him in profile—"

"Not to shoot pictures of his *stomach*," Mea meant.

"—or he said he'd crack our lenses. And as it happens a couple of cameras jammed, and none of the pictures we shot of that in profile came out—"

Mea was laughing about it. "Total blanks. All black."

"Uh-oh," I managed to say. Was this the real deal? Power over cameras?

"Hah. Hah. Don't worry, Koren. We'll fill you in as you go along. We'll look out for you."

I heard the tolling of a bell. Must be the one on the guillotine outside. One, two, three. For thee?

Lomand signalled a change of chapter with an expansive stretching of his arms. Then, "Woo-woo, honey," he said to Mea, and raised and lowered his eyebrows. After that to me, "We'll get you installed in your room later, and now Mea and I will get on with our ablutions."

"Uh-huh." Ablutions. I'd never heard the word used in conversation before and figured it was a gag.

"And remember," Lomand's envoi began, "as Mr. Gurdjieff put it"—he still pronounced the name with its last syllable accented and a rhyme of "thief"—"only two things have no limit, the mercy of God and the stupidity of man."

I knew that one and had pinned my only hope on the last part being as true as the first.

"And I've seen nothing to convince me that things are any different here," Lomand said.

I WANDERED DOWNSTAIRS and thought about checking on my luggage, while everyone seemed to be rushing purposefully in several directions, then narrowing it down to fewer directions, finally maybe to one. Someone asked me on the run, "Coming to meditation?"

Well, okay, I supposed I was.

I followed a few people out of the house past the bell on its gibbet, beneath which someone stood with his hand on the rope looking about ready to pull it. A collection of mildly hippified people, mostly men but a few women too, were converging from a variety of directions upon a small stone building ahead and on the left. I followed, climbed the exterior stairs to the low second storey, removed my shoes and left them outside the door, entered a dark room under the slants and beams and saw that people had seated themselves either directly on the floor or in kneeling postures atop diminutive benches and wooden T-things; one or two may have sat legs in lotus pretzel but the knees seemed to have it. I selected the simplest-looking T-biz—slat nailed atop a barky chock of log—from a bunch in a corner, found what I hoped was an inconspicuous spot of floor along the left, plonked myself down and waited.

A few last people came in from daylight, squinted, sat.

A tall thick candle burning in its sconce on a clothed altarlike bench at the head of the room, and sticks of incense. More a smell of stone and folks and clothes than that.

At the head of the room and its two informal facing groups left and right, sat a dignified but unimposing figure with his eyes closed, a guy a few years my senior: harmonious face beneath a sweep of mild brown hair, the mouth crested by a suavely tonsured moustache. He looked unassumingly serene, and may have been wrapped against the damp in a swath of blanket.

Lomand and Mea came in and were seated.

A smallish Arab-looking guy rustled in with an air of intensity and drama, accompanied by the larger character I'd noticed earlier with the black bandito and forethrust jaw, whom some charisma of dignity, even pomp, attended.

A few last arrivals, throats discreetly cleared, bodies settled: less than twenty of us. Then the bell: once: and the ringer didn't come in after.

The fellah at the head of the room began an invocation, and the room's voices took it up in rough unison. "Towards the One, the perfection of Love, Harmony and Beauty: the only Being."

Then a prayer. I followed along as best I could. Nice text. Ecumenical, unexceptionable stuff, to which an underbreath of devotion added warmth.

A long moment's silence in which, as usual, I found myself maladroit at sit-there meditation: whirl of thoughts, unsorted energy, tight spine, stiffening shoulders, and little idea of why it might be worth my while to watch my breath.

Then the guy at the head of the room spoke alone, an English voice, a good one, not brittle, well modulated, soft: "Imagine a line of light extending through you from the top of the sky to the center of earth . . ."

Oh, right. Knew that one. So I got a little swoony and let a vapor of myself pass through the top of my head and back and felt pleasured by the rub, as if against a membrane, of that figment's passage in and out. Did I sense a local turbo-boost? Occasionally, on my guard, I peered around: what were the others up to? Intentness, quietude, blissness, marking time, inscrutability, repose; and an occasional eye gleaming open, like mine, to sideline-check the room.

Then the soothing, dignified voice took us back to the line of light and its doings: we were to send it up, down, attach a sound to it, circulate it inward. We were talked all the way through the meditation, if that's what this laden train of mental imagery was. We were, ultimately, to imagine all this busy light centered in our hearts. My heart: that bramble, that boxed-up bomb.

After perhaps ten, fifteen minutes of imagery ending with all that light radiating out of our hearts into the world and the limitless beyond, on the breath, we were left to the silence and our loaded respirations. I prayed or daydreamed, wished for love, felt it, gave it, rambled, relived the bus ride and the passport line, worried about my suitcase or my feet, consulted my inner clock.

Upon departure, some hand-over-heart bowing salutes, a few hugs, and once outside some casual chat, and part of that a deliberate meditation blowoff, a back-to-life shucking of the sanctified manner that may have risen to a backslap or a laugh. Some new faces for me: a tousled blond head here, a dark one there, must have said hello to me, sounding friendly, with a normal human sense of welcome, then off elsewhere to business.

Someone took charge of me and bags and led me to a room situated in what he said was the North Barn, the ground floor of it a wood workshop, tools bracketed and hung, rack of lumber down the end; up the stairs a narrow corridor of recent wallboard panels led to a room offside the stairs, two beds in it but I'd have it to myself for now. A bedside table and a lamp, a small bureau. Pillow, quilt. Little window facing north.

My caretaker told me about dinner coming up and where the plumbing facilities were. I unpacked, tried the mattress. Felt alone and quiet. Felt noisy, curious and uncertain. Indulged in my customary sense of odd man out. May have unpacketed a Camel and smoked it. In the attendant lightness of head and dimming of mind I might have thought, as so often, that one of the virtues of the tobacco habit was that, if God or some guilty phantasm of your own misdream should burst through the ceiling to ask you what you were doing with your life, the answer was ready at lip and hand.

Hey, you mind? I'm having a smoke.

Checked my watch and looked around at the walls.

MEMORY RACKS into focus just before dinner, which was served at seven. Perhaps a quarter-to and having clocked another bell I drifted downhill to the house in a change of clothes through the early evening light that was still that of a long late afternoon, and in the entrance corridor ran into the character with the turned-down bandito moustache, assertive jaw and challenging, tigerish eye. I was intimidated but asked him his name.

"Anton," he said.

"Koren." Then, trying to decode the social order: "And how long have you been here?"

The left eye opened a degree, worked its crosshairs, fixed. "Long enough," he said.

"Then I'll see you soon enough," I said, and eased around him down the hall wondering if I'd scored a point or been marked down for later.

In the dining room I would have avoided the whirl of tablesetters at their tasks with white plates and serving mats and flatware, and loitered at the edges hoping for a familiar face or two but if I found one my files do not record it. What I do remember is the mental snap with which I caught the fact, as people assembled before grace and sit-down, that of the maybe twenty people seated sociably on benches around the squared U of three long varnished plywood tables, a dozen of them were wearing some silver version of the eggshaped thing that had hung from Reshad's neck that afternoon.

Some were cast silver duplicates of his, others less regular handtwists of silver wire, but all I could think was: uh-oh, *Star Trek*. Us and them. Beam me up. A cult.

Dinner was a team of oxymorons hitched in tandem yoke and harness: good English vegetarian cooking: a deep-dish, crusty, multivegetable pie, parsley potatoes and salad besides, virtually all of it picked that afternoon and tasting like it. The food at Beshara's was superb. It would be months before they figured out that the cooks' fantasias were bankrupting the joint.

Sinister cultish whatsits aside, table behavior seemed normal enough, haircuts and demeanour conventionally countercultural but not over the top. About two men for every woman, the men above average handsome, no great beauties among the lasses. Folks seemed to like each other well enough, a knot of conversation here, another there, and unless I missed my guess there was a more than representative sampling of Jews on board. That guy with roughly the same hair-and-beard set I had, and his ruddy girlfriend with the froth of curly black hair. That longnosed tall guy there. And I wondered about Shing, sitting over there with Hakim. The Arab-looking guy sat with Anton and they looked like the hipsters of the house, riffing in semi-secret language, but once or twice the Arab's voice raised up, deep, with musical phrasing and an unlocatable foreign accent that excluded him from the hipster circuit. At the head of the table, a gauntly handsome aristocratic knight, sociable but reserved, nodded hello and made a grin. The meditation guy, sympathetic, sidled to his place near the head of the table. His name was Paul Finegan, alias Kushnazib, I was told. I must have been sitting with Lomand and Mea, clinging to safe harbor.

Once or twice I caught some sidelong eye looking me over.

After the main course and before dessert and tea, glass ashtrays were placed around the tables and about half the population lit up, some with pocket boxes of wooden matches, scratching, others with slim gold Dunhill lighters, like the knight, whose name Lomand told me was Hugh. He seemed at ease in conversation but there was a crinkle of reserve in his eyes, amid the mixed smoke: rollups, Benson & Hedges, Piccadilly Sixes, my own Camels. I handed the pack around, for those who were interested. The Arab took a couple.

Feeling awkward, I didn't join in washup, though I may have cleared a stack of plates.

There would have been a meeting in the front room later, some sort of freestyle mystic jam session, rambling talk with occasional dabs of poetry, and it would have ended with a bell at ten.

Up in my room after washing I undressed for bed, and carefully peeled off my white cotton socks. My feet were a sight: it was as if their topskin had been flayed from the juncture with my calfbone to the roots of my toes, and atop the remaining pink lay a gluten of lymphic exudate the approximate texture of vaginal secretion. It didn't hurt much, but now and then an irrestistible shiver of itch would work its way to the surface and I would tear the flesh freshly open with my nails or, when shod, work the heel of one shoe into the forefoot of the other and dig, dig, dig. Usually when I woke in the morning the mess would have jelled over and dried, and if I could keep my feet bare it might stay that way for an hour; but once the socks went on the flow resumed.

I had long drawn supplies from both wings of my parents' somatic repertoire—been bothered by skin problems from childhood on, particularly on my feet (my mother's problem was with her hands), and recently my polite ambient wheeze had escalated to deathgrips of bronchial paralysis roughly once a winter—but I had acquired my current foot problem in a personal and quite literary manner. In the autumn of the year that followed Lomand's departure for the East, his quondam sublieutenant Larry Dancey—sometimes known as Agaf, one of the least felicitous karmic names to come off the board—called me up to ask if I'd like to join in with him on a night-and-weekend job he proposed to get going, hauling and hand-delivering oak and cedar firewood by the cord in his big orange Ford pickup. I said okay and he said he'd supply work gloves but advised me to buy a good pair of boots; so it seemed entirely providential one day not long after, as I stumbled across the drygrass hills of upper Oakland in an even greater daze of addled intellect than was my custom at the time, that when, after a last savage altercation with a chickenwire fence, I descended from a hillside to a civil street, the first of the world's overhanging signs to greet my eye was one to my right reading GOGOL SHOES.

Gogol Shoes?

The place drew me as irresistibly as you'd figure, and when I got there it turned out that its front window was full of boots. When I entered the shop, of a Russian dimness that swallowed at the window every outdoor photon of California bright, the man behind the counter, a long bald stringy individual somewhere in his sixties with wisps of hair fluttering above his peaky ears, was blessed with a nose of extraordinary elongation which itself received the crowning benefaction, just aside the tip, of a wart or wen on which three or four long grey hairs depended for their living. In short, behind the counter of Gogol Shoes stood a man of such exemplary Gogolian caricature that my disbelief suspenders had snapped and the pants of credibility fallen around my ankles.

The emanation behind the counter raised overgrown Gogolian eyebrows and smiled to signal that he awaited only a specific request in order to do his best to help me. The seagrey eyes behind his specs seemed friendly.

"It's lucky I came in here," I wheezed at him, winded by the hills. "I just got a job hauling firewood and I need a pair of boots."

"You came to the right place," Gogol assured me, and if I'd been hoping for a comic accent I didn't get it. He gestured at a shelved array of boots stage left. A small grey moth fluttering out of a boot top would have been a nice touch, but I didn't get that either. "You need a high boot? Ankle boot? A color?"

I thought fondly of the pair of high off-black Lincoln Boots that had served me so well on the baking backroads of Holmes County, Mississippi, but the hightopped items Gogol had on show seemed too massive, too bolted and bracketed in brass for anything short of Armageddon. Still, clearly I was buying my boots here and now, no other place would do, and I'd have to choose from what Gogol had. "Ankle boots, I think, with a hardened toe."

"Do you think you need steel-tipped?"

"I don't think I have to go that far."

Mr. Gogol strode to the shelf and lifted an ankle-high tan-cum-orange boot with a thick white tready sole. "This is the boot you want."

Actually I didn't like the look of it. "Do you by any chance carry any Lincoln Boots?" I wondered.

"Never heard of them. This is a Red Wing."

"Any good?"

"These are the best boots in the world," he announced.

It was an admirably Zaborovskian formulation, and by it the magic was made complete: all other options vaporized in a categorical whoosh. "I'll take a pair," I said.

"What size?"

"We should measure."

The rest was mere formality. They cost thirty-five bucks and I had it on me. Upon departure I paused for some last Russo-literary flourish but it was no dice.

Almost immediately Gogol's shoes began to play havoc with my pedal extremities, weaving a tapestry of rash on the topskin that soon gave way to an overall flayed near-liquid state, but such was my fealty to the Gogolian day on which I'd bought them that I kept on wearing them. I passed a fearful midnight or two sniffing the discharge, considering my retracted circulation and the possibility of gangrene, but now I'd brought them to England, where the story—"The Boots"—awaited an appropriate denouement to match the one in "The Overcoat" or my special favorite, "The Nose."

I swabbed the tops of my feet with toilet paper I'd taken from the loo down the hall, patted them dry—one good thing about this little affliction, it had no smell, and the bottoms of my feet were unaffected, so I could walk—and applied Bacitracin from a tube. Got into bed and marvelled what an unlikely mess I was.

I was all too aware of how easily my manifold debilities might render me a piece of classic cult fodder, ready to cling to any passing fiction that might seem solid enough to save me, and for this reason had adopted a set of standards for spiritual experience that excluded dreamy emotionalism from serious consideration, and which I hoped might keep me from confecting some cloud-cuckoo land—to use Reshad's phrase—to live in because honest earth was just too hard: no, the thing had to be objective before I'd budge my essential self a millimeter in its direction. Faith and hope were fine, but I needed empirical fact or I wasn't buying.

The remarkable, no, the amazing thing about Lomand's cockamamie group was that for all its misappropriations of Gurdjieff and its other, still more unripe audacities, and despite the patent, daylight fools we were and the distant orbits of oddity we flew to—and this narrative has yet to nick the gleaming surface of that implicit sphere—there was something serious working through its follies, and its fools, that connected us—is there really no other way of saying this?—to something greater and we hoped more true than anything we had known. That redemptive possibility could stoop to such cartoons as we'd become was a kind of miracle, a revelation maybe even worth the fucking up to get in line for and, who knows, the signature of a larger grace that circumscribed the whole of life, the sky above it, earth beneath it, all.

Very little in my background had prepared me for such a thought, or such a faith, but there I was, my bet placed, my marker down, and all my life's curious capital laid upon the line. Still, the question hovered: could you get this screwed up and make it back to life?

My parents would have been appalled: before sleep I read my small-ish Bible—bound in black faux-leather, nubble-covered, boardless, pages with their corners rounded, edges gilt—as if it now contained letters from home: some passage in late Isaiah or a favorite Psalm in which mercy floods the covenant and inundates the dispensation, inclining itself to man in his poverty, husk and shell—*Fear not, for I have paid thy ransom and called thee by thy name. When you pass through the waters, I am with thee; and the rivers, they shall not sweep thee away*—and then the Psalm—*Thou hast beset me behind and before, and laid thy hand upon me. Whither shall I go from thy spirit? or whither shall I flee from thy presence? If I ascend up into heaven, Thou art there: if I make my bed in hell, behold, thou art there. If I take the wings of morning and dwell in the uttermost parts of the sea; Even there shall Thy hand lead me, and Thy right hand shall hold me.* And a passage that had special resonance for me: *Thou hast covered me in my mother's womb . . . My substance was not hid from Thee, when I was made in secret. Thine eyes did see my substance, being yet imperfect, and in Thy book all my members were written, which in continuance were fashioned, when as yet there were none of them.* Then listened to the foreign night outside: hushing shushing winds, reposeful land, tread of come and go till throbbing quiet, like a breast of feathers over a still-damp hatchling, settled, huddled, held.

Or was I just another poor dumb cluck.

Dropped out of last rush and beat of airplane flight into nest or web of newfound dark.

3

I WAS AT THE COTTAGE DOOR to see Reshad at half-nine on the dot, and knocked in a flutter of anticipation, only to have it opened by a dazzler of a woman in tight jeans and a colorful blouse—swirls of blue and green, flitterings of gold—with a sweep of brunette hair, a cheeky face and upturned nose, brilliant grey-green eyes set in dramatic flares of blue cosmetic shadow, and what were certainly too many silver bracelets about her wrists. "You must be . . . Siddiqa?" I ventured. A lot of silver and turquoise on her fingers too.

"Just call me Sid," she said. Siddiqa. Not what my expectations had led me to expect: what even my repressed mother back in Brooklyn would call a sexpot.

"I've got an appointment to see Reshad at . . ."

"He's upstairs." I had the brief impression of being subjected to a silver-brilliant, lightly frosted examination beam, then a gleam of smile as she beckoned me indoors and indicated the way.

The place seemed too big to be called a cottage: if this wasn't a house, what was? I walked up a narrow creaking stairway between wall panels, then left, as directed, past some lesser doors to the corridor's end: I knocked, got a "Yes?" and entered a large, mostly bare daylit whitewalled room with tan carpeting on which Reshad already seemed to be in motion, much on his mind and his body active, pacing. His "Hello" was partly concentrated on me but seemed to have been abstracted from a multiplicity of ongoing concerns. He was wearing a different set of fine brown clothes and the same gold thing on its chain. By then Lomand had told me it was called a Hu, *Hu* meaning Him in Arabic, referring esoterically to the most inward and intimate aspect of God that could be named at all.

"Come in, come in . . . Koren, is it?"

"Lately, " I admitted.

"Yes, well, come in, sit down . . . would you like tea?"

"I'm fine."

The setup, as I remember it, was me sitting rather helplessly in the luxurious leather lap of an Eames chair, and Reshad alternately standing over me, striding about the room, sometimes peering out the window toward the rearward bulk of the property, then sitting beside me on the Eames' nearby ottoman for a time. During these less animated stretches his face was a map of intelligent interest and concern, with an occasional ruck of worry between his eyebrows.

"Well then. You've come from Lomand's group. Extraordinary fellow, Lomand. We've had one of his people here already. Mark Adler. I liked Mark Adler. Liked him very much, and now there's you, ah, Koren. By any chance are you Jewish too? Yes, I thought you might be. We're about half Jewish here, as it happens. I was circumcised by a rabbi myself. As are the Royal Family, you know. We have so many Jews here I finally asked Bulent, Can you tell me what we're doing with all these Jews? and he told me, You need them, my dyah. But Bulent, what on earth *for*, I asked him. *Devotion*, he said."

"Yes," I said, and my inner trout rose to the surface of its lake and rippled the water. Devotion. It was probably the last good quality I would admit to. "Devotion. We manage that."

"Good." A lift of eyebrows. "Comes in handy here, you'll find."

I nodded, breathed, thought something on the order of Lucky me. On the other hand, Reshad seemed rather pleased with his Jewish riff and entirely unaware that it was borderline gauche at best, but this little error of judgment and taste was paradoxically endearing, perhaps only because it momentarily showed him as a fellow fuckup, under the suavity and the skin.

"Do you know what Bulent told me?" Reshad asked. "It's not about Lomand, he said, but what will *come through* Lomand." He looked at me meaningly.

I nodded, or shrugged, or managed to do both without tipping over.

"But I'm afraid we have a small problem." He got up to pace around the room, then came back to face me, slightly bent in concern. "We may not have room for you at present."

My heart did a little tumble-and-fall routine by means of which I discovered that, for all my wealth of anxious doubt, I had already attached my hopes to the place. "Lomand wrote that there was a three-month course and I could come over for it. And here I am."

"Yes, well, it's summer you see, and . . . is there someplace you could possibly go for a few months and come back to us in the autumn?"

"I haven't been thinking along those lines, and . . ."

"No, of course you haven't."

"I've got a little money with me." Very little. "Is Spain still cheap? Maybe," I said with no great certainty, "I could go to Spain until there's room." This was all wrong, I thought, but I was willing to go if I had to. It didn't occur to me to go back to the States, though that would have been cheaper and easier—hang out in Brooklyn, work for my folks, save my pennies. No, I'd crossed the water and wasn't going back until whatever this was was done.

"Give me a moment," said Reshad. He closed his eyes and seemed to consult the air, may have raised a sensitive-seeming hand to further measure its conjectural waves or held his breath. The rounded eyes beneath their lids echoed the rounded cheeks, the dome of forehead, harmonious. It was an expressive face even when its lively eyes were shut. He came back, then reached into his pocket and came out with, good grief, a small clear crystal on a silver chain, and dangled it like a pendulum for a moment, watching it closely before palming and repocketing it. "Right, you're not going to Spain. There's a bit of a space problem at present but perhaps we can make do. I'll be off to Turkey shortly. You stay on and we'll see about it when I return next month."

"Okay," I said, which was about all I could manage. He was going off to Turkey. But hey, what about the course? Man, if I was only here for three months—and maybe I wasn't—I wanted him around and teaching.

A knock at the door.

"That will be the tea."

And it was, tubby teapot, china cups, brought in by Sid with a nod before departure. She and Reshad were easily the most glamorous couple I'd ever met, movie stars. I felt like some subset of earthbound *zhlub* by contrast, but these glamorpusses were being so extravagantly *nice* to me, so gracious and considerate: they seemed to see through me but without a critical edge, as if meeting me was one of life's little privileges. The automatic alpha-dog dominance action you always found Stateside was not in the script—was this an English thing or was it because they were spiritual and enlightened? Could they read every trembling letter scribbled in my anxious little mind? If so, they didn't let on. I felt as if I'd entered an atmosphere of finer air, subtler cognition, friendly if unnerving social light.

Reshad hardly touched his tea, or sipped it once for cordiality's sake. I drank mine and watched him, waiting for the next item up.

"So," Reshad said. "You have a Gurdjieff background. I see you're self-remembering. Very good. You can stop now, if you like." In a light and tactful tone, with an amused lift of the eyebrows for a finish.

Actually I was doing some of my lightweight out-of-body shtick, sending points of my presence or at least attention to disparate corners of the room, locating myself in a matrix of space and at the same time feeling lightly freed from it—which was the paradoxical point of the maneuver— but Reshad's light dismissal of this bit of business trumped me flat. As for a Gurdjieff background, it was doubtful I had much of one, and almost alone among the members of Lomand's bunch of bananas I hadn't invested very deeply in Gurdjieff's laborious ethos of building a soul against the cosmic odds and the common flow toward mineral nullity. As for the

old boy's prescription of Intentional Suffering as the statutory means of
getting on, I felt my beaker was already full, thank you. The way out was
up, Lomand liked to say while wearing stretched full-flag across his face
his discomfiting American smile. It was an alien perspective, but after being rocked by a few apparently objective experiences that confirmed it, I
had signed on, and still hoped the way ahead might be easy. I didn't have
the strength for hard.

"Our work here," Reshad seemed to be telling me, "as I think you'll
see once you've settled in, is rather different. What we do here is quite
beyond form, you see . . ."

Uh-huh, but what did that mean? Spooks of gossamer meeting up in
fields of mist?

". . . we do nothing for ourselves here . . ."

Uh-huh.

". . . attribute nothing to ourselves . . ."

Ah hah.

". . . it's not about us, you see . . ."

Oh hoh?

In the next clip available to memory, Reshad has crossed the room to
peer through the blinds back toward the rest of the property, then has
turned to me, come back, sat.

And here followed, relieved perhaps by various comings and goings
about the room, the points of our colloquy that I can no longer call with
sufficient exactitude to mind. Representative samplings fill the provisional soundtrack . . . Some of you will have to know Him, and some will
have to know Him *and* His ways . . . Here we go straight up, without intermediary . . . The most direct route, therefore also potentially the most
dangerous . . . Tibetan Buddhism . . . the Naqshbandi Order . . . Bulent
attached to none of the dervish *tariqats*, you see . . . hidden masters . . .
the Uwaysi, named after Uways al'Karani who lived at the time of the
Prophet, they never met, and when the Prophet died he instructed that
one of his two cloaks was to be sent to Uways . . . the Uwaysi are those
who have no physical teacher, they are outside the traditional lines of
spiritual teaching and transmission, their guide is Khidr, also known as

the Green Man . . . green . . . blue . . . the number seven, the number nine . . . As Bulent says, there are many ways to Him, but the way of Mary is the sweetest . . . Do you know the children's prayer, Mary, wrap your blue cloak around me? . . . Mary is water . . . Work, Study, Meditation, *zikr* . . . You *must* meet Rosemary Russell, the loveliest imaginable lady with greyish-purple hair and a dear friend . . . radionics . . . black box . . . long-distance healing and of course she doesn't really need the box, you know . . . although as it happens a new black box is in the works that will register all the subtlest aspects of the . . . matrix, pattern, all you need for sample is a lock of hair, and in fact a snapshot will do as well . . . the encoded subtle human form . . . Trust, Certainty, Patience, Resolution, Veracity . . . And according to the Diamond Body, you know, all the universes are within your armspan . . . *and* all the prophets . . . quite a bargain come to think of it . . . would you like me to show you where Moses is? . . . you'll lawff and lawff . . .

It all flew past me like the lit windows of a train of thought I'd fallen from miles back, and I sat on my rear too stunned to even dust my clothes and watched the serial windows flash past, the unending clacket of information, wondering how I'd ever get back to town from these fields, so late in the day.

". . . because, you see, what we're involved with here is revolution." Back at the window and stooping slightly in his survey of the demesne, eyes looking up from beneath a brow furrowed by the cares of supervision, Reshad had said this in an aside and lightly, but the schoolboy bravado throbbing beneath his tone was obvious to me even then. "They don't take me seriously when I say it, but it's true. *Quand c'est fait, c'est tout fait. We are* involved with revolution here." Well, he was pushing it now.

There are any number of things, many of them later understood to be essential, that Reshad probably told me in the middle of our meeting— about service and how there may be no essential difference between the ambition for spiritual development and an ambition of any other kind, since both were conditioned by the eggo, as he called it, and therefore Service was our central means of avoiding the impasse—this made complete sense to me, and came as a relief—Mr. Bennett saying in a recent talk that we had not to expand our consciousness, which might only enlarge the prison, but to go *beyond* consciousness: which sounded stirring but what the hell did it mean—all accompanied by the admonition to "keep it light," for which in my frail state I was grateful.

Reshad tended to direct his heaviest avowals out the window or around the room, and took care to gentle his output when speaking up close. Something about me seemed to pain or fret him, and place again that pleat of worry between his brows.

As now, with a freshened concentration of intent: "Do you know what my job is here? I'm not a teacher, you know. I'm the front man. Do you know what a front man is? He's the one outside the tent, putting on a show to get the people to come inside."

Ye-es, but wasn't there something too dutiful about this pronouncement? It chafed him. He'd been told it. He had eyes for a bigger role. I was sure of it.

"'Reshad' means He who initiates again and again. It's my job to stand at the door and bring the people in. I may not be able to go in myself, you see. I may not be able to go in there with you."

"Uh-huh," I might have said to this Moses note, watching conflicts parade across his face. The camera liked him and the way his inner dramas played: you could watch the troops march past, feel stirred by feather, flash, and drum, experience a tremor for him as a rumble outside the gates announced the odds against victory. It was a noble battle, nonetheless.

"There are no teachers here. Even Bulent is not a teacher. God knows what he is. I certainly don't. We have no teachers here. Life is the teacher."

After that avowal came a moment's pause, then a modulation down from drama to brass tacks: "I'll give you some practices to get you started."

The first of these was given with some ceremony. "This is the *dhikr,* or *zikr,* of Hasan Shushud." I'd heard of him: old frail man in Turkey, Mr. Bennett's teacher. "*Zikr* means the remembrance of God. It's central to what we do here. You can do this particular form of it in private and also as you go about your work during the day—some people have been known to do it all day long and even in their sleep. I have to transmit it to you in a special way. Ready? Good. You're not to give it to anyone else, please." He took one or both of my hands in his and led me through it until I had it right. It was a repeated invocation of the name *Allah* hammered breathwise in the heart in a particular way, and could be done audibly in private or in the relative silence of the breath when with company—there was a third, still more private form in which *Allah* was implied, and not pronounced—with intermittent retentions of air worked into the sequence. (All it ever did for me, as Reshad gave it, was produce a tense congestion in the workings of my chest. Other people had a similar experience. Only when I was shown it again, seven years later, by Hasan Shushud in Istanbul, did it lead, thanks to a slight but crucial variation, to anything more worthwhile. Mr. Bennett himself transmitted it to his many students in truncated form, as a breathing practice detached from the pronunciation of *Allah*, presumably so as not to start the kids projecting. There seems to be a persistent tendency to not get these things right, from which your reporter cannot be immune.)

"Good," Reshad told me, when I appeared to have the rhythm down. "There are some other practices I'd like you to try. I'd like to give you a few *wasifas*. You're to take some time during the day or night, do your ablutions, and find a place to do these practices in private. Aloud or quietly on the breath, either is fine." *Wasifas*, as Reshad explained, along with *zikr* essential Sufi practice, were invocations of the distinctive Names, or qualities, or aspects, of God, such as the Merciful, the Compassionate, the High, the Powerful, the Self-Subsistent and so on: conventionally there were said to be a hundred of them but of course their number was infinite. Ninety-nine acknowledged Names were available for invocation although some, the so-called negative Names, were avoided—"There are certain times in Turkey they have to do all ninety-nine in sequence, I've seen it, and when they get to *those* Names their voices get very, very quiet: they whisper them"—and the hundredth Name was secret. In sounding the names, with one or two exceptions I was to begin with the syllable *Ya*, which was the vocative O, therefore O Merciful, O Compassionate and so on. I was to do each Name according to its proper number, which was derived from its letters. The meaning of each Name, Reshad said, was powerfully inherent in its sound. "For example the Name *Hakim*, the Wise, begins *Haa*, in the chest and ends *keeemm*, in the third eye," Reshad asserted this with a fingertip, "fixed there by the emmm. The *Hakim* refers to the discriminative wisdom—it also means the Judge—and you can easily hear that it is quite different from the All-Knower, the *Alim*. You do see that, don't you? Good. Before starting your sequence on each Name you are to say *Bismillah ar-Rahman ar-Rahim:* in the name of God, the Most Merciful and Compassionate. It's rather like crossing oneself before doing anything important, or for that matter doing anything at all—do we actually know what's important? Everything is important, or nothing is." Reshad wrote down the *Bismillah* and the *wasifas* I was to do, with their corresponding numbers, on a slip of paper and gave it to me: *Ya Hadi*, the Guide; *Ya Hakim*, the Wise; *Mu'min*, performed without the *Ya*: "I'll show you how to do this one. People think it's pronounced 'moomin' but it's *mümin* and must be done in a special way." Seated beside me, Reshad closed his eyes and began chanting something with the syllables of its repetition strung together in a high, piercing tone that reminded me of a high-speed drill. After he had me try it and was satisfied with my rendition, he told me what it meant. "Some people think it means the Faithful but it's the Guardian Who Leads the Faithful to Belief. I'd like you to finish the sequence with *Ah-Salaam*, with its proper number. *Salaam* of course means Peace."

I looked the Names and numbers over, and it didn't seem impossible: there was only one I had to do more than a hundred times, and one of them needed only twenty repetitions. I think Reshad also gave me thirty-three or a hundred-and-one of the Forgiver to do—which would have been astute of him—and the Grateful, which turned out to be *Ya Shakur*, the syllables of the day before; apparently I didn't have to pronounce any of these Names as slowly as they'd been done then, but at a normal pace, which was one thing to be grateful for already.

"You are *not* to pick other Names and do them," he warned me, though where I would have picked them from was a mystery to me, "which might easily produce an unforeseen result and an imbalance. Neither are you to pass them along to anyone else. *Wasifas* are prescribed for a specific person at a specific time. I'd also like you to practice the turn."

The what?

"The Turn of the Mevlevi Dervishes. The whirling dervishes, as they're called in the West." *Shazam.* This was an unexpected pleasure: I'd been fascinated by the whirling dervishes since I was a kid and read the Landmark book about the fall of Constantinople: the dervishes, whipping the soldiery to a frenzy—although it was never exactly clear to me how you whipped an army to a froth by whirling at them. Like most kids, I'd tried it a few times and gotten dizzy enough to fall down laughing, but that was it.

"It is *not* done in a frenzied manner," Reshad told me.

"No of course not," I agreed.

"It's done simply and rather slowly." Reshad stood up and with ceremonious deliberation folded his arms across his chest so that each hand lay atop its opposite shoulder and the arms formed a V, or perhaps a W, across his chest. His legs were pressed together with an at first puzzling primness; then I saw that the foretoe of his right foot was placed to cover its leftmate. "We stand this way in tribute to the humility of Mevlana's cook, who as it happens was a very great saint. I'll tell you about him later. Watch me. As you turn, the left foot remains in place on the floor at all times," he said as he began to turn, "and you push along with the right. After a few times round, you unfold your arms," which he did gracefully, the arms opening in a smooth curve that sweeping upward from his shoulders looked structurally strong and naturally tree-branched. Reshad's right palm was held aloft, the left palm turned down. "The right hand receives mercy from above," he told me as he turned, "and the left dispenses it below." He turned for perhaps half a minute without speaking. At six foot two or thereabouts Reshad was a dramatic figure in a room made smaller by his elegance of motion. The ceiling seemed to have drawn low, and in the natural breeze that emanated from the turn I also seemed to sit in some other, less material wind before which the husks of established precedent shook a little—I was less aware of anything mystical coming at me than of the sheer volume of surprise, but my gyroscope had taken a funny, vertiginous tilt all the same: here was this impressive baldheaded redbearded guy turning in front of me in a cozy English room, cloaked in foreign echoes but in a way I couldn't place it was strangely, powerfully moving, and what the . . . Reshad torqued his turn abruptly to a halt, refolded solenical arms across his chest and bowed gravely from the waist, foretoes lapped. When he resumed his seat beside me his face was flushed, and his eyes seemed additionally brightened.

"The Turn is done anticlockwise only," Reshad resumed. "When done clockwise it is called the Knot of Manifestation and it is done only under specific orders and only when circumstances have made it necessary. I saw a man in Turkey who decided to try it on his own and he gave himself a heart attack, silly tit. In short," a demi-wink, "I don't advise it. Remember to keep your left foot in place, and above all, above *all*, you must be centered in your heart. Center in your stomach or your solar plexus and you'll get dizzy. Possibly sick to your stomach as well. And for God's sake don't *expect* anything. Expectation is the red death."

I would have nodded, or something. Things were definitely getting out there, but how far had I travelled really? Compared to my father leaving the old country at thirty with the wave of war coming on and his parents in its path unless he could get them out, well, compared to that it wasn't much at all. I was on vacation around the bend, and the people here were funny.

"The Mevlevi Turn is *not* done quickly, as you've seen. There *is* someone here who has been trained in the Qadiri Turn, which is done very quickly, with small steps. Have you met Jafar? They call him the White Tornado."

We chuckled over that one.

"Being Jewish, do you have any reservations about, ah, using Arabic?"

"Oh no." I was pretty ecumenical by then, and thought it well enough established that the total buzz of mystagogic foofaraw referred to one fundamental Reality which all traditions and names addressed overtly in a general way but intimated, in subtler sotto voce, a more direct and private path to those elect who came upon it or, like me, fell face first and and flopping like a flounder on its stones. "Well, then," Reshad said in a summarizing tone, "I think I've given you enough to work with for now. Is there anything you'd like to ask?" *Ahsk*.

I probably said that I was glad to be there, and would have indicated a readiness to learn: sounding eager, dull, innocuous and conventional to a tee while inwardly trying to be receptive, open, clear, but my busy, wheely mind whirring for all its worth in a search for intellectual categories that might clamp a conceptual armature around all this jumping data: a mug's game, but the organ plowed on regardless. Cartoon the picture and there'd be a sizzle about the eyes, wisps of smoke emerging from my ears, and the smell of burning insulation in the room.

"These practices may seem a lot to do, but as I've said we try to keep things simple, and as far as possible without fixed form. The intent is to go straight up, which is the most direct path, and therefore it is also the most dangerous. So we do need to take care."

Yes, I saw. No, I didn't, but straight up sounded fine to me, and as for danger, hah, I laughed at danger.

"No questions then?"

"Uh, what about—" I pointed at his chest, where the golden thing hung. "What about the, the Hu?"

"You can have one whenever you like," Reshad replied, "but it would be better later, when you've grown more familiar with what it means. Literally it means 'him,' any 'him'—him over there, oh you mean him—but esoterically it signifies the internal aspect of God, the highest we can know, just before any manifestation begins. The Hu is implicit in the *h* of *Allah*, and—see the design of it?" He made a spiralling figure with his finger in the air that sketched it out. "That's the Arabic script for 'Hu,' but it's continued to suggest the completion of the cycle. You can have one whenever you like. We don't charge for it—how could we charge for it? There's no charge for the teaching either: how could there be? So, ah, Koren, is there anything else at all?"

I SAID NOTHING about my real concerns.

My silence was pure cowardice, the continuation of a long policy of secrecy about all essential things, and the momentary preservation of a last crippled leg to stand on, but there was a smidgen of precocious intelligence in it too: an early recognition that I'd come for spiritual reasons and not for lesser therapy, that properly understood the spiritual englobed the personal and would address it in due course and, best sign of all, that I had sufficient control of my pathology, and enough tact, not to heave it in a bleeding heap at Reshad in the hope that he would guru it away. It was cowardice, yup.

So there was no mention, although the imagery was playing vividly in my mind, of an earlier self of mine sitting in the spotless corridor of a Tokyo clinic shortly after a series of increasingly large balloons had dilated the cervix of my once-beloved, in a private room just up the hall, to provoke a premature birth. The cheerful doctor, educated at Johns Hopkins, came out to tell me that the abortion had succeeded and to ask me, since the creature would have been nearly five months old, "You want to know sex of baby?" Once the immense Hokusai wave of relief that Barbara was not, as I'd feared, going to die there had drenched me—I probably would have snuffed myself in response; if not, the physical and moral task of carting a dead woman back to her Brooklyn family from Japan would have done it—I sat there wreathed in the consequences and made an oath, a vow: antique words I never would have used seriously before, but times had changed. I swore to deprive myself of every gilt and plated pleasure that had brought me to this hallway seat and distracted me from the reality of the things before my eyes and in my hands. I sat there and crumpled up, like a sheet of paper on which I'd written an especially bad first draft, the organ of my greatest pleasures: my heart and everything that had once enlivened it—my sense of life and humor, the intellectual pleasure of the creative burst, the breakthroughs of vision out of partiality into bliss, whatever it would take: every single pleasure or perception that intervened between myself and the bedrock substantiality of the finally real: all those gems and toys, since none of them had produced the molecule of simple knowing that might have prevented this abortion, its balloons and the further ruin of a desperate young woman I had taken or mistaken for the object of my love.

The shockeroo for me in this—and it was something I had never articulately suspected until, after all the rush and horror of getting myself and Barbara alive to that corridor and that room, I had a moment's leisure to chew and swallow down the day's grisly contemplative placenta—was that it had been a central but unwritten law of my life, for all the callow cynicism I'd learned from books and the street and then had affected, that I would never bring suffering into the world—it was a mystery: where had such a conviction come from, and in such strength?—and the stinger was that in the world of plain fact, suffering was precisely my productive sum. So: that's it, I told myself sitting there: no pleasures or distractions for you till you find another basis for human life and a way out of the bubble that has blinded you. Let every green stalk of yourself wither until you learn.

At the time I'd had no idea that such an oath, or the storm of adolescent melodrama that gave it wind and strength, could have such severe empirical consequence as, to say no more, the blood withdrawing from my grasp and use. I had landed in a world too new for me to know anything about, and although I was already straining to hear past the dry rattle of its fields for an answering echo, I had no real expectation of my bid being taken up. There was at first a certain grim, unfledged pride in having achieved adult suffering at last, of feeling the moral weight of all existence bearing down for real.

When the doctor let me, I went up the hallway to see Barbara, pale and sweat-drenched in her bed, one eye grey the other brown, her Russian face, its high wide cheekbones, soaked hair strung all awry, still in mortal panic: I comforted her the best I could, sentimentally and no doubt Hollywood-inflected, and thanked God, I think, for the competence of the place and the doctor's expertise, and when evening came I took the crowded subway under Godzilla's Tokyo to Frank Lloyd Wright's Imperial Hotel—a masterpiece of just proportion, a model of the intricate earth and its breadth of welcome, in which I felt a measure of serenity even on that grim day—and sent a telegram to my sleeping parents saying it was over. To my considerable surprise, they had wanted me to run out on Barbara and let her family take care of her, but I'd held on and stayed the course. There was that, and my birthday coming up in a couple of days: twenty-one. It's true, I tend to hit the given demarcations pretty hard.

"AND, OH YES, the bells," Reshad said as he began ushering me out. "There's always a bell going off, you may have noticed. Did Lomand or someone fill you in?"

I nodded.

"It's quite mad, you know. Entirely too many bells. Have to do something about it soon." He paused for a moment and shut his eyes. "But not yet," he said decisively. We were heading for the door, and Reshad might have placed a hand lightly on my shoulder. "Bulent's a great cook, you know."

"I've heard." World class, crowned heads, had written a book.

"We were chopping onions together one day and the tears were simply pouring down my face, I can be quite hopeless in the kitchen, and I noticed that Bulent wasn't crying at all. I asked him about it and do you know what he said? 'I know that it is this onion's destiny to be cooked and eaten and transformed by me. What is there to cry about?'"

"Ah." Obviously it was a parable about suffering, nudged in my direction with considerable tact, but I wondered if that knowledgeable cook Bulent had chopped his onions sitting down and let Reshad stand there with his novice face in the rising fumes.

One clear thought, though: Reshad is badly frightened of Bulent.

"Work well, then, and you're not to worry about staying on, we'll get you sorted out. I'll be here through the weekend, and Lomand will look after you I'm sure . . ." Reshad opened the door to let me out, and a large but still puppyish black wagging dog looked up at us with his busy brown eyes, then thrust his snout forcefully into my crotch and rummaged through its balls and sausage. "Oh do stop it, Ali Bey," Reshad told the dog uselessly, then held it by the collar and watched me as I went down the stairs.

I didn't see Siddiqa on my way out or on my way back up the road.

Behind me, Reshad had come to the conclusion I myself would reach over the next couple of weeks: I wasn't going to make it.

Sid on the other hand and sight unseen had already told Reshad when they'd got back from church the day before that another real one had shown up.

It was a clear and beautiful day. Its air was sweet, was nectar, was English air, and only the occasional passing puff of thought troubled the expanse of upward azure empyrean.

4

THE JOB I'D BEEN ASSIGNED beneath that sky required muscle and persistence but not a lot of skill. In the plot so far we had cleared the cars off and I'd been shown the apparatus: I was to be a one-man steamroller and flatten the car park. The roller had been rented for the day, and I remember it clearly enough.

It was a heavy black steel cannister five or six feet wide and about three feet thick. Its axle ends were linked to the prongs of an iron-bar U, which was mirrored by an attached upward U of iron with a band of canvas webbing strung between its ends: this I was to push against with my chest to make the roller go. There was an electric switch that set the roller vibrating but did not impart any forward motion.

The surface of the car park was dirt-road reddish sand and silt chocked with gravel grading up to larger stones, and seemed serviceable enough; I was to make it more serviceable still for the Open Day and Fête which on the coming weekend would celebrate the first anniversary of the opening of the Beshara Centre, although the actual, pedantic date was July 1. The public had been invited for miles around and old friends were also expected. An arcade of ringtoss games, darts, and something called a coconut-shy was being hammered together by more skilled hands, and musical entertainments were being devised and rehearsed.

Lomand had assigned me the roller job at the front-room work meeting after breakfast—we'd awakened early, meditated our way up and down a line of light, and during what a couple of people had called "brekkies" I'd made the classic American mistake of slathering a slice of toast with something called Marmite and learned on the spot the English exclamation *Faugh*—and I'd trailed a scattering of Beshara people and watched them move their cars, the big blue blunted van, a nifty Triumph four-seater ragtop and a sharknosed red BMW 2002 that belonged to Hugh. The Triumph was a cutish readhead's, about thirty, I hadn't noticed at last night's dinner: Fiona had a friendly grin and a jaunty air and appeared to have something going with the intense Arab-looking guy. Hugh said hello and welcome to Beshara and in return I tried and failed, twice, to pronounce his name as something distinguishable from You. Must practice, I told myself. Hhyoo. Hhyooh.

The last bit of business before going off to my meeting with Reshad was pushing what I was told was Bulent's old Mercedes off the lot and into the tall grass by the wayside. It was a dusty black 190 from around 1950 and it seemed a simpler, more stately version of those cool postwar Fords with the insinuating slope to their trunks and eye-slit taillights. Much dust had settled on this car. I peered in at its cracked brown leather seats and older air. *Bulent's* car. No one even tried to start the thing. There must have been at least three of us pushing, two from behind and one at the open door, managing the wheel.

We got the thing moving and pointed right, then came a certain degree of improvisation as we got it out of the lot and downslope off the road with its nose sniffing at the reeds.

Then Richard Waddington, a pale English item with a brisk efficient manner and an educated rugged look under a tousle of blond hair, showed me the workings of the roller—flip switch, push hard, flatten everything in sight—and I tried to joke about it without getting much back except a See you later and let me know if there's a problem.

By then it was pushing half-nine and I ambled up the road to the Cottage. (You are Number Six. We want . . . information.)

BACK FROM RESHAD'S, I stood there looking at the roller while the roller looked back at me. It presented my very first opportunity for physical-spiritual work at Beshara. I was ready. This was work. This was life. I could think about the sheer solid reality of it for hours. The great scything scenes in *Anna Karenina* . . . nobility of labor, the profundity of earth as given . . . whole human condition implicit . . . breakfast wasn't bad . . . powder blue Mercedes convertible they try to kill Cary Grant with early in *North by Northwest* . . . there's an Edsel in one of those Foley shots . . . Grant making funny drunken faces at the wheel . . . Glen Cove police station and Grant, drunk, pronouncing it Glen Clove . . . Sergeant Emil . . . Emil . . . James Mason Lester B. Townsend . . . wonder if that really was James Mason I ran into during the oilspill up on the cliffs in Marin last year . . . said he wasn't but I think he was . . . Emil . . . Jessie Royce Landis . . . soles of Cary Grant's shoes hardly worn . . . Sergeant Emil Klinger.

For example.

Eventually I must have gotten down to it, in my workshirt, jeans and Gogol Shoes beneath that flawless sky: flipped the switch to get the roller humming and gave the thing a push. It wasn't easy but it wasn't impossible either. I began running the thrumming roller over the surface of the car park and listened to the gnash of it atop the sand and gravel, the tread and push of my feet, Gogol's soles alternately slipping against the pressure of the work then gripping hold. Some drift of backwoods Mississippi rose up amid the small red dust.

The lot might have accommodated a dozen small cars, with barely space in the middle for maneuvers, so it was not a job of either Herculean or Sisyphean proportions. I started off down the southern edge along a waist-high grey stone wall. Over the wall tall grasses, the dozing Mercedes and, some distance off, the stream. The occasional offstage sound of hammering and power saws came across the summer air, sometimes laughter, and occasionally folks toiled by with lengths of lumber or carrying a wicker basket out to the vegetable field down the valley, but for the most part I was alone in the arena and I tried to work seriously and well.

And even managed it awhile, pushing my chest with all the solidity of Hemingwayan material fact against the rough canvas webbing, digging in and grinding forward in my Gogol Shoes, steering with serious Tolstoyan hands and looking down at the newly rolled surface as it emerged from beneath the steel to see what might have been accomplished; and there did seem to be a bit of compression there, a certain flattening of the rocks into the road dirt. I had a persistent problem of the canvas belt pressing a button of my workshirt into my breastbone, and kept shifting the shirt to get it free.

I started working in rows, then decided to circle in from the perimeter, and shortly the process assumed the characteristic pattern of virtually all the work I'd grunt my way through across the coming months: a mix of poseur's theatre put on for an audience of one, played alternately as drama and as farce, mumbleminding free-association, restorative bouts of *dhikr*, and finally a burgeoning feeling of uncertain competence as I began to wonder if I was getting anything, or the right thing, done at all.

Thanks to the months I'd put in hauling and stacking cordwood, I did get off to a decent start. After a time, though, the usual circus came to town, as the sun began to blaze upon me and with dramatic particularity I felt Eternity in love with the productions of Time and the sweat of that Love sheeting down me, and I was, for a conjectural moment and in a wavering way, a blazing iron bar fixed between earth and heaven, the sun replicated in the center of my mind as I . . .

I ran the gamut for as long as I could put it over on myself.

Should have marked the absence of birdsong but didn't.

"So they stuck you with the really good job," someone told me from behind, and I turned to see who it was.

"Oh, hey, hi," I said, and two Sufi roughneck types were stopping by to say hello and loaf for a minute. One of them was the short intense Arab-looking guy—Jafar, the White Tornado—and the other one I don't remember.

It seemed like a good time for a little break, and I switched off the motor. "What're you guys up to? Smoke?"

"Hey, you kidding?" said Jafar, idiomatically American but in an unlocatable Middle Eastern accent: Arabic, Turkish, Persian: he hardened and at the same time fluttered his *r*'s and had a deep voice for a small guy. "American cigarettes? Just give me the pack and I'll see you later."

But I gave each of them a single cigarette, and the English guy—he was English—scratched us alight with a wooden match from a yellow pocket box, sheltering the flame against the nonexistent wind.

"I see they've put you in it," the English guy told me, nodding at the roller.

"Welcome to Beshara," Jafar affirmed, squinting from behind a puff and scratching at his wispy, see-through beard.

I shrugged aside the suggestion that the work was maybe a little hard, or meanly intended, or that I couldn't take it. "What are you guys up to?" I asked again.

"We're building a fortune-teller's booth," said the Englishman.

"We're building a fortune-teller's booth in Shalla," Jafar appeared to say.

"Where?" I innocently asked.

Small laughter in response to this.

"Over there," said Jafar, and pointed over yon green hill south, "in Shalla." More chuckles here.

"I don't get it," I said.

"It means 'God willing' in Arabic," the Englishman informed me. "*Insh'Allah.*"

"Aha."

"We're always building things in Shalla," said Jafar, and picked a thread of tobacco from his lip. "Either there or in Schtook."

"Uh-huh." Didn't know the provenance but thought I could figure it out. "Thy will be done in Schtook," I essayed, "as it is in Shalla."

Jafar had a laugh at that one but I got a definite sense of uh-oh gone-too-far from the Englander.

"Well."

"Well."

"Thanks for the cigarette."

"Good luck with the job."

"Salaam."

I surveyed the perimeter, stuck the cigarette in the corner of my mouth, flipped the switch and resumed the push. Well, that was a hip little exchange. Nothing weird or eerie in it. I might fit in here yet. Funny how Jafar from Wherever . . . Wonder what his story is. And I learned a word. Two words. Schtook and Shalla, attorneys at law.

And then I had myself a normal human good-enough time on earth, although given how I've presented myself I wonder if you think me capable. I threw myself into the work and dug it.

A bell tolled and I checked my watch: eleven o'clock, meant it wasn't tea at 11:30 but one of the bells Reshad and Lomand had explained, so I switched off the roller, wiped my hands, straightened up, paused a moment, put my hands out before me palms up and let out a longtoned sotto voce *Allaaaaaaahhhh huuuuuuuuu* and offered skyward as much of myself as I could muster in the moment, then, outbreath exhausted, a moment's mortal stop and open myself, as instructed, to whatever might descend from conjectural heaven in response . . . and . . . well . . . yeah I guess there was redescent of a kind, a falling down out of air and through myself of some high ethereal who-knows-what that portended way off, could be, the sweet nullification of lesser self . . . sorta . . . kinda . . . aand . . . time to get back to work.

By teatime I had reached a point at which I could no longer tell if I was doing anything to the car park or if its surface was susceptible of being further flattened by anything lighter than the hull of the battleship *Missouri*, so I made another pass, then another, and examined the planetary surface as it emerged from beneath the wheel of law to see . . . if . . . maybe . . . that bit there . . . that flat rock pressed perhaps a measure further into the sand . . . was I doing anything or not?

Saved by yet another bell. Half-eleven.

Time for tea.

"HAVE A BICKIE?" someone asked me not three minutes later, extending the packet.

"Love one. Thanks." It looked a not-much thing. Out of a blue ob-long packet: McVitie's Digestive Biscuits: hence, by detestable diminu-tion, bickies. I accepted one, took a bite, contemplated, assessed, and Brooklyn supplied the syllable: eh.

A sort of butter cookie without the butter, crumbly to the teeth.

I sipped again my tea, taken straight, without milk or sugar, an in-fringement of local law that netted me a few gawks of incredulous judg-ment: from the land of brekkies and bickies, the socially unassailable stare.

I would have loved some coffee.

All this seething action took place in a spare small whitewalled room at the rear of the House's ground floor where one could sit on a worn-out stiffish leather sofa or an easy chair or a window seat or a shelf beside the large sooty hearth. It was called the Quiet Room, which was where everyone went to talk. And smoke. My duty-free Camels continued their popular stage career and I wondered how long the carton would last.

As an uncertain new inmate I had a natural inclination to seek the shade of Lomand's wingspan and huddle in it, and he seemed welcoming enough, asked me how things were going in the parking lot, grinned his grin, looked at me as if he were sizing up my aura, said "Hah. Hah," then brushed me off by pivoting into a conversation with someone else, and I sat there eyeing all the English-English chitchat without seeing opportu-nities for ingress. Heavy old upright piano painted white against that wall; wonder if it's any good or in tune. Sip sip puff puff, put my cigarette out in the tray, expunge the ash—the way my father used to do it before he quit: no mashing: a measured sidewise pressdown into the tray that detached the ember from the unburnt tobacco to leave a briefly glowing smokeless coal amid the cinders—and try not to feel lonely doing it. And then I heard the beat of a distant drum.

That was a drum, wasn't it?

Like a hungry wanderer amid unfamiliar islands who comes upon the scent of familiar food upon the foreign air, I followed the fume out of the Quiet Room, paused in the scullery to whiff the wind, then crossed the corridor's end into the dining room, where the sound strengthened, then ceased; but I'd heard where it was coming from. There was an open door directly across the dining room with an oblong of summer shimmer in it. Once passed through I had a view of the lawn's descent from beneath my feet to broaden streamward where, perhaps two hundred feet off, a young couple stood together on the white wooden bridge with their arms leaning on the baluster as they gazed down on what the water was dreaming up that day. On the expanse of lawn below me and to the right stood a rough semicircle of festival booths and stalls in midconstruction, a couple of grazing sawhorses, a lazy snake of extension cord and a gaggle of tools sunning themselves on the grass; but it was alongside the stone stretch of house to my immediate right that I saw, some distance off, Beshara's apparent bohemian contingent, its handdrums and guitars, and a couple of idling hangers-on. Mug of tea in hand I ambled over.

When I got there Anton, the warrior-looking number with the lordly manner and bandito moustache, looked me up and down from his seat on the edge of a worktable strewn with offcuts and a spare guitar, fixed me with an arrow from beneath an archery of brow, pursed his lips and blew, somehow, three fat French horn notes off Gil Evans' chart of Rodrigo's *Concierto de Aranjuez* from *Sketches of Spain*. Another character I hadn't really met yet but knew by name as Latif or perhaps it was spelled Lateef, hip name either way—a smoothfaced spiffy California-sounding cat in roundish silver-frame specs with a wisp moustache, a wisp beneath his underlip, and a nest of wavy light-brown hair up top; his stylistic signature seemed to be a puff of paisley silk tucked about his throat, even when he was wearing denim overalls and a T-shirt, as now—he chimed in, echoing Anton's phrase in a higher register with a buzzing in the lips that rendered a convincing impersonation of Miles Davis' harmon-muted trumpet on the cut.

How'd he do that?

Crosslegged on the grass cradling a smallbodied acoustic guitar across his lap—not your standard sixties regimental issue: beautifully grained honey-colored wood: maybe Spanish—Jafar waited for their notes to fade before spinning out a short flamenco turnaround—deeper, more fundamental song than Rodrigo's—with impressive tone and almost punctilious articulation, his hands, well formed but with shortish fingers, working powerfully up the fretted neck and sounding the strings with deliberate measure over the plectrum: not a casual player: a musician: as an Arab or whatever, he must have started out on the oud and switched. And the guitar: the elegance of its manufacture and its sound, the fine inlay work on the rosette. And there were handdrums lying on the grass, man, vase-shaped metal Middle Eastern handdrums lying on the grass all gleaming, and Anton had one, the biggest of the set, brightly chromed, tucked beneath his arm. I was dreaming, right? I was standing there with this big smile across my face and dreaming.

"Got another Camel?" Jafar asked me, and for a moment I wasn't sure what he meant, as if I'd just blown in on camelback out of the sands and dismounted at the edge of the oasis.

"Wha? Huh? Sure. Can I have a look at one of those drums?"

"You play?" Latif handed me a mid-sized matte-bronze drum—graceful waist, low golden burnish—and I looked for someplace to put my tea.

"Not one of these specifically, but drums in general, yeah. Jazz drums."

"Professional?"

"I have been, now and then," I admitted. Bizarre unlistenable avant-garde stuff mostly, but still . . . "Made a couple of records."

"See, that's what we need," Latif told Anton and Jafar, "a professional drummer, man, help us get our act together. We're just sitting around here magging readazines. We need professional input. That's what we've been needing here, a little help."

My widening smile expressed still greater incredulity as the beads ticked past on the rosary of Hip. Miles & Gil. Rindercella and her Three Sisty Uglers. Needadrummer. What next?

Anton didn't look too impressed with the new drummer in town, though, simply started a rhythm up and nodded coolly at the drum I was holding: show me. Your basic alpha woof-woof number. This was home turf here, with—how'd this happen?—an English guy, a California cat, and some kind of Arab or Persian or maybe Turk. My experience of Arabs was confined to shish kebab, of Persians to carpets, and my social interaction with Turks pretty much limited to the guys in the Turkish Taxi Drivers' Association who rented the room above my father's liquor store and sauntered down, some nights, in progressively more generous amplitudes of yaw for fifths of Club Rakı, and who repeatedly set fire to Dad's green canvas awning with the cascade of cigarettes they flicked with great bravado from their second-storey windows.

To sit himself more deeply in the rhythm, Anton hauled his legs up off the grass and pivoted himself through the sawdust to end up cross-legged on the plywood worktable top, the drum athwart his lap, its head canted, the drum's flared back end extending over his hipbone, and then, his profile imperious and aloof, he . . . hmm, I haven't heard *that* one done before.

What he did, he played this sort of medium slow, loping, camel rhythm, maybe a hair ahead of a quarter note per second, a deceptively simple thing in which his left hand kept a straight four going low-toned on the center of the drum and the fingertips of his right panged a very few accents and embellishments treble off the rim . . . a sort of *Boom* da-Bamm-dip *Boom* da-Bamm-dip feel, the drum tuned low but the tone holding, an index fingertip planting the *Boom* deliberate in the middle of the skin, and the Bamm—this was Anton's innovative lick—played with the heel of the left hand and held down, higher in pitch than the sound of the open drum but a flattened final sound that choked the drumhead shut then released it into the coming accent's upflick, which lifted, lofted the rhythm unexpectedly and dropped it into the belly of the coming down-beat: a mix, a balanced flux, of floating up and finding earth again, a way of getting on through air and light across the sands of time. Nice, I thought. A new one on me.

And done with so few notes.

Rough grey wall of house, inset windowfames freshly lacquered white, lawn of paradisal grass beneath an unflawed canopy of blue with cotton trim, a stream of living water purdling through the bottom of the gar-den: I stood there in my sweated workshirt, jazz professional, with my

slender-waisted shape of brass, and wondered where to start. I could put
three beats in one hand against four in the other, manage most of Elvin's
basic licks, had a lot of Afro-Blakey down . . . and . . . but . . .

With the drum held uncertainly beneath my left arm, I ticked an accent on its rim, tried the center of the skin—sweet tone, pitched a casual
third above Anton's instrument and a grace note mellower—put a couple
of notes together, see if I could work up a tangent . . . and . . . let's see . . .

Sat myself up on the edge of the table and placed the drum between
my knees, try it that way, play it like a conga though of course much
lighter.

Problem I had with Anton's little riff, it was so damn *simple*.

Beginning to have an awkward moment here.

As it happened, it was Jafar who bailed me out.

While I paused, less for reflection than in the hope of an idea, Jafar
did not so much lay his guitar aside as carry it to the worktable and place
it firmly in the blue plush of its carrycase and lap an overcloth atop its
body; this accomplished, he swept up the smallest of the metal drums
from the grass and sat himself on the table edge, his not long legs adangle, and dropped the drum between his denimed knees, waited for his
moment and entered with a cleanly played single-stroke roll—a string of
thirty-second notes, not so easy, a classic jazz move simpler to play when
aided by the natural bounce of sticks, but you had to articulate them all
when playing by hand—and then into a fleet commentary, built four-
square of sixteenth notes and corniced with accents, atop Anton's implacable unassailable cameling.

Which gave me something I could work with . . .

. . . though when I tried a drumroll intro too I saw at once that my
chops and muscle were not as tight as Jafar's: some overspill from beat to
beat and a tendency for my hands to splay aside from the efficiency of the
vertical. So watchit, Joel—I never called myself Koren *en famille*—stick
with the sixteenths and . . .

Jafar's basic figure on the little treble drum was to play *DUBbuhduh* on
top of Anton's *Boom*, *DAKkatah* on the rim over Anton's dampered *Bamm*
and tick his other notes precisely but without conspicuous accent, all in

all a tight and agile little riff; so what I wanted to find was a figure close
to his that still could slot itself between him and Anton, and what I came
upon straight up, on this midtoned drum in the set of three, was a sixteenth-
note figure doubling Jafar but with a *DOOM-Doom-duh-Doom* played res-
onant at the center of the head in the bass, a decent interlock I thought,
and it seemed to work awhile as I got used to the flex and reflex of the
skin, the interplay of harmonics implicit in the drum, the variety of its
possible rimshots, and began to learn its range of tones:

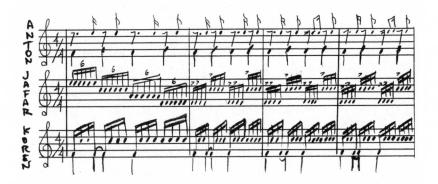

Latif stood there watching in archetypical assessment stance—weight
on left leg, torso canted lightly back, right hand cupping left elbow, left
exploring chin: he must have seen the rulebook—and the hangers-on,
whom memory has deprived of faces and number, although there were
not more than three of them, began bobbing and grooving as they sat
there on the grass, so I was okay, I was getting over, and this encouraged
me although I knew you shouldn't trust the audience but the best musician in the room.

Though who could read anything in the boxed shelved book of Anton
behind its pane of glass and its refractions? Outside his covers the dogs of
the moment barked but the camel of his caravan loped on: *Boom* da-
Bamm-dip *Boom* da-Bamm-dip . . . though check out the flex and bend of
beat he'd begun allowing himself ahead and behind the markers without
coming close to rupture and actually, listen to it, he was bringing the

tempo up now, and an imperial nod Jafarward acknowledged the intent: pick it up a notch. Made it easier for us actually, opened up a deeper groove.

I mirrored Jafar, swapped cadential drumrolls with him and when I missed the edge a bit exchanged a laugh and shrug with him as, oblivious of all else, the camel completed its acceleration and steadied to a trot.

To celebrate the event Jafar played one of his finegrained drumrolls in one smooth motion from the treble rim to his small skin's center. Two bars later I did the same and mostly pulled it off: my hands were getting up to speed, finding their rhythm, developing an ease and feel, but then . . .

But then the oddest thing began to happen: there came a kind of sliding off on my part that was not essentially musical but spiritual, properly so called: the showing of a certain unreality in my playing, a superficiality in its relation to motion on the earth of time as Anton's simple camel set it forth; and it was as if my intended music began decaying from the inside, and to die degree by inexorable degree. The blight took me intimately and unawares and confused me crosseyed. I had no idea, dismay aside, what had hit me or how far it had power to go.

Maybe, a little adjustment here, loosen up your back and shoulders, lose that tension in the wrists, and maybe this little shadow would pass and all would again be well.

Anton added a couple of new accents to his beat, heightened its implied contrarieties with a technically slight but dramatically syncopated complication of his rimshots—*Boom-ah* da-Bamm-a-dit—and by pushing the *Boom* just far enough ahead of the beat to open up a world of suspended implications and bring his entire rhythmic figure to the edge of dissolution in either outer chaos or greater benefaction—who could tell?

He lifted his head proud and apart from the actual business of handskin, drumskin, drum, fixed an eagle eye on yonder hill or perhaps beyond on Shalla and lifted his hands progressively higher as he played, as if they rebounded from each note to a new aerie from which they'd launch their next descent, his forearms wheeling down.

This guy, who I had begun to suspect, correctly, could only play this single rhythm and had zilch beside it in his repertoire, was some kind of master drummer nonetheless: there was more dimension to what he played than had any normal right to be there. My own posish got worse: my notes were slipping, and it was progressively revealed that they said nothing anyway, whatever I thought I'd inscribed upon their faces; several sweats were breaking out in panicky encampments on my body's failing field of battle, orders sent out went unreceived, and regimental flags were going down in smoke across the innocent hills. My act was dying on the air, and the very harmonics of the drum I played were splaying off astray.

My response to this small metaphysical insufficiency was to play harder, and as a result a kind of unregarding coarseness first crept then came galumphing in on whatever living music still issued from beneath my hands—and there was hair growing on the backs of them, I noticed: many individual tiny hairs, on the first joints of the fingers too, and their sweating flesh was pale, their veins unhealthily collapsed. Hey, waitaminnit waitaminnit: belay that and play the got-damn drum—but my *Doom* badoom-doom-doom was doomed, the day and the field were lost.

I'd had good nights and bad onstage and in the studio, and usually it was a matter of my chops not holding up or the conversation getting muddy, but this, it was as if my fundamental rottenness of soul had been exposed, or worse, the fact of no-soul-there. My body was locking cold and rigid. How and why was Anton doing it, or, a mirror trick, was it only me?

It's nothing to do with me, Shing had said. Lomand used the phrase too, and now it came to me I'd heard it spoken all around the place, accompanied by a smile: nothing to do with me. Anton wasn't smiling, but maybe it was nothing to do with him. Maybe it was in some sense this paradisal place massing up against my chosen interests and shaping itself as that old duo claws and jaws . . . sweet Jesus let this end.

Which in short enough order is what it did: just as I was coordinating rhythm figures with Jafar, who seemed disposed to help me out—his bullet-Arab head beneath its cap of hair turned my way and his almond eyes indicating potential welcome—giving me the nod, playing his down-beat more emphatically and reining in his rolls and syncopations so I could see it; just then due to lack of interest Anton faded out over the course of a couple of bars, laid his drum aside on the tabletop, pulled a couple of packets out of his shirtpocket and began to roll himself a smoke. He neither gave me a look nor didn't.

After lighting up and squinting across the lawn as if from his cliffcrag lair, flintlock sniper's rifle at his side, Anton turned his attention to a guitar that had been lying on the worktable top, not Jafar's treasure but a storebought boxwood thing with cheap nylon strings. He picked it up, began to strum some rudimentary chords he fingered home only with laborious deliberation up the neck. He wasn't a good guitarist. The guitar was out of tune. He didn't tune it.

Jafar and I had stopped playing a ways back.

"Ah, that camel I mentioned," he said to me down the table edge.

"Which camel what camel . . ." I wondered.

"That Camel I asked you for," he smoothed his wispy beard over the hinges of his jaws, "would taste awfully good right now."

"Oh, *that* Camel. Right. Of course." Recovering. "One hump or two?"

One eyebrow up and a screweyed look for that one.

Waitaminnit that was New York street idiom I'd used and he came from somewhere they maybe still had, actually, camels. Score one more foot in mouth for me. Though it looked like, thick foreign accent or not, he got the gag and didn't dig it.

"Here," I said, unfolded the foilwrap corner and shook the pack at him so a trio of coffin nails emerged. "You know, I bought a carton duty free, I could just give you a pack and . . ."

"I'd rrather bug you for them one by one," Jafar said in his rolled-*r* accent and surprising grasp of hipster idiom. Maybe he'd picked it up from travelling musicians.

Waitaminnit: my warehouse eyes my Arabian drums: funny thing: one strange afternoon while delivering liquor for my folks up Flatbush Avenue, a pint of VSQ brandy for some janitor on Martense Street, out of the corner of my eye . . . flash memory of the waxed-over window of a narrow shut-down florist's shop . . .

"So," Latif addressed me, stepping up to his tapemark. "You had a kind of . . . kind of *African* thing you got going there, huh." It was not a compliment. "Or North African," he allowed.

I gave him a Camel too. We all lit up: guys together but me in exile, Anton offside with his rollup and guitar and untuned strings. They buzzed against the frets, whined beneath his fingers' press and his lack of regard for me seemed about equal. Whereas . . .

Latif went on talking. "I don't usually play it that way," he told me, nodding chinwise at the drum. *Ah so, desu'ka*: it was his.

I handed him the drum. "First time I've ever played one of these."

"Uh-huh, I hear you. It was interesting. Yeah, maybe a North African thing," holding the brass drum lightly, smoothing the head with his right palm, checking the rim for injury, easing the brass with his hands. "Different."

It was transparent politesse but he kept working it . . . but that florist's window: I'd rounded the corner onto Flatbush, paper bag in hand, past the nuts-and-candy shop and must have been feeling drifty that day already—was this pre- or post-abortion?—aand . . .

Among the clutter of storefronts a slot where flowers had been sold, its windows whitewaxed to translucency, but through gaps in the wax I could see into the empty store, and as I passed, a little stunned, perhaps, by the heat of the day—it was late summer, and Flatbush Avenue was smudged by car exhaust and baking—my passing sideglance caught on some detail inside, and I seemed to see a number of drums of the kind I'd just now played—brass or bronze, longwaisted, urnlike—although almost certainly I was seeing something else, a pillar ashtray, a discarded vase, a piece of refrigerator unit: but the phantom drum impression shot a pain into my heart, a displacement and confusion that made no sense . . . Was it in some weird sense a forecast of this day?

My memory labored at the impression but I couldn't make it fit, or make its lack of fit make sense.

"I usually tune it a little higher too, you know?" Latif was saying. "But with the heat today I tuned it down and now that it's been played this much . . ." He gave the head a testing stroke, frowned at the harmonics. "Wish I had my drumkey here but I left it in my digs, you dig?"

"Should recover in a minute," I said.

"Of course of course," Latif assured me, though he was still squinting at the drum. "We didn't just blow in on the pumpkin here."

"Riight." The drums, the window . . . I tugged at them but got zilch.

"Hi, hi, that was great," a newfound voice was telling me. The couple who'd been on the bridge. They'd come across the lawn at the sound of the drums and stood a grinning distance off while the music lasted. "And as we haven't had a proper chance to meet . . ." He extended his hand for me to shake it, and his girlfriend nodded hi. "Morris Clark," he said, a name I later learned was spelled Maurice Clarke.

"And Lois," said Lois, from beneath disarrayed black curls.

Latif stood aside, as if not to mix with the unmusicals.

Maurice was an approximate English equivalent of me, longfaced, bearded, Jewish, lean and five foot nine, only more social, and Lois, a few years his elder I thought, maybe thirty, ruddy and becurled and also Jewish—more devotion, I guessed—spoke her obligatories in an accent I could not yet identify as South African.

We chatted. How I was, where from, my family from where originally, and was I a musician. He was an architect, I gathered, and she was in the visual arts.

I remembered the youngish Sufi couple up the street from the store on Caton, who went to England sometimes to join up with their . . . sect. After I'd joined up with Lomand's group I told them and they'd invited me up to their top-floor flat, played me some recordings of Jalali *dhikr* Paul Bowles had made in Morocco, and we'd laughed that early-mystic laugh together at how flat and narrow the rest of the world was.

And these: Maurice was designing some extensions to the House, an annex with showers in it, and plans had been made for the stableyard. Richard Waddington, he told me, had charge of the esoteric doings in the planning stages for the cruciform barn, but routine living arrangements were beneath his overall command. And Lois? Oh, helping out here and there, she said. Tidying up around the margins.

But what did I have to do with normal people? The musicians had abandoned me, sorta, or Anton had laid it down, and it stayed down.

These were my *friends*. These people were my natural friends, and I had been excluded from their essential company. How had Anton raised the bar and worked it? I mean, a few wrong notes, we shake our heads, laugh about it and work it out next week: the way it's done, ever was and shall be. It didn't seem to matter here, though . . .

Why was Anton's *nyet* the rule of Law? Even though Latif was acting ameliorative and Jafar was actually friendly, Anton got to determine the parameters.

I looked over at him plucking his untalented strings out of tune.

Who the hell appointed him Lord High Executioner?

I was in Schtook, when I wanted to be in Shalla.

What was I doing in England trying to join up with a bunch of Soofies?

When my father went up to the Turkish Taxi Drivers' Association to complain about the awning the morning after he'd uncranked it to find a hole the size of a roast turkey burned through the dark green canvas of Governor Wines & Liquors, he climbed the stairs early, found the Association's door open and entered an unpeopled room with card tables and chairs, a billiard table, and a tea-kitchen and samovar off in a corner. The smell of cigarettes and perhaps the anise hint of Club Rakı hung upon the air that early morning—my father opened at 7:30 a.m. after the walk past the Parade Grounds where, he said, every day he saw how beautiful it was the light, and he loved all of life again every morning. This was my father. "Hello," he said uncertainly, "is anyone there?"

His dismay about the awning was troubled into a sense of ambiguous responsibility: no one there and the door wide open: not the way things should be: the Turkish Taxi Drivers' Association was open to . . . what? Someone could make off with . . . the billiard table? It could happen. There was an old man, a customer of my dad's, who'd sat outside his building with his granddaughter one summer afternoon and watched—amazing—a crew of regulation moving men carry a complete set of furniture uncannily like his own out—which of his neighbors, unknown to him, had bought virtually the same bureau, the same settee?—pack it in their van and drive off. When it was time to fold his beach chair and go upstairs, he and his granddaughter were greeted at the door by an apartment swept bare of everything.

"Hello?" my father said again, in his new, half-custodial capacity. "Is anyone?"

And then, as he told me in amazement later, he heard a little shuffling sound—mice? a rat?—and a man emerged rubbing sleepy Turkish eyes from behind the tea-kitchen counter. "*Evet?*" said the man from his fog of the night before. "*Buyurun.*"

At this point my father had the oddest experience. It was like, he said, watching a Charlie Chaplin film. From behind a sofa, beneath a chair or from under a table that should not in reality have shielded them from view, emerged like genies from a lamp an assortment of dusty rumpled Turkish men, maybe a dozen of them from the dust to which Club Rakı and last night's gaming had laid them low. They brushed off their clothing—some of them wore rumpled suits—and blinked at the inexplicable apparition of my father.

Once the sight-gag had run its course, my father made known his complaint about the awning. It wasn't understood, and he was obliged to lead the presumed hetman of the Turkish Taxi Drivers to the front window and point down to the hole in the awning, through which a stretch of Brooklyn sidewalk was on view.

This indication did not communicate, and my father had to explain it all in words—there must have been interesting patchwork between my father's English and the Turk's—and finally asked the man, "Will you fix it?"

"I fix," the man assured him.

"How?"

"With paper. Piece of paper."

No, my father thought. He was going to have to explain the nature of canvas to the man. "How you fix with piece of paper?" my father asked, translating the question into Turkish English.

"Wait. I show you." The man shuffled to the tea-kitchen, busied himself there and returned with something as intelligible as an eye chart: CAMDAN DISARIYA SIGARALAR ATMAYINIZ, it read.

"What does that mean?" my father asked him, grimly aware that he had been reduced to straight-man in the sketch.

"Out the window don't throw them cigarette," his interlocutor reported.

Their discourse, although it lasted weeks, never succeeded in getting past this point, and in the end my father had to pay for the canvas patch himself. The Turks bought their Club Rakı elsewhere for a time, but eventually were kind enough to stumble in for two or three bottles on credit and my father, who knew the rites of small-time capitalism in even the least of his bones, couldn't or wouldn't tell them no. Külüb Rakısı they called it, with Atatürk smiling in a tux seated with his buddies on the label, but Külüb wasn't easy even for a Turk to say once his tongue had thickened, and this led to some interesting halts and interruptions. My father was like the merciful God in this respect, that he knew what they wanted before they asked him for it, and granted their request. The rain of fire resumed after a time, and my father entertained the hope that the Turks would burn the place down so he could collect on the fire insurance and retire—the business had gone bad when Governor Nelson Rockefeller got his balls caught in the wringer of a State Liquor Authority bribery scandal and took it out on the retail trade—but no such luck descended either from the Turks one flight up or from presumptive heaven. "It's *kismet*," my father shrugged it off. "The will of Allah."

Sitting there in England, it was pretty much the same thing. Anton was as unanswerable as the *taksicibashı* of Brükülün . . . and my first English teatime was ending up a drag.

"So when do you expect to get those showers built?" I asked Maurice. Behind me, Anton and Jafar were chatting, and Jafar had taken Anton's guitar and begun to tune it.

"Not for months yet," Maurice said, a bit sadly, I thought. "Other priorities, other plans."

"Aha," I told him politely, wondering what the backstory was.

Something obscurely familiar was shaping up in the chords Jafar was coaxing from Anton's cheap guitar, and the instrument's tone had improbably improved.

"Because we could all use a shower around here," I said. "I know I could, after steamrolling the fucking parking lot all day." Oops, the Brooklyn word.

"Other things to get done first." Maurice shrugged, and Lois gave him a little hug.

I think I know those chords . . .

As for the showers, it was odd, in a place that put so much emphasis on keeping ritually clean—ablutions explicitly required before everything but dinner, when it was expected anyway—that there was so little water available and so few places in which to wash. I'd seen the only actual bathtub in the joint, one flight upstairs in the House; the room also boasted a toilet, a basin, and framed photographs of Anton on the walls: professionally shot, judging by their chiaroscuro and formal flair, they captured him in the act of cutting hair, but not like any barber I had ever seen. The camera liked him, an impressive, almost solemn figure, bearded then, who wielded his professional combs and shears within an interhung complexity of apparently plywood hoops and orbits centered on the passive head of the haircuttee. Somehow Anton stood outside one last hanging orbit and inside another and managed to reach the encircled head to do his work, but he looked less like a barber than some avatar of a bygone culture, a mage who made a cosmos of a haircut.

I looked over at him in his huddle with Jafar.

The quality of Anton's silence, the gradual perception of a presence . . . he had an actorish charisma working for him, and although he didn't look or act like Brando he had a similar effect of simultaneously drawing you in and shutting you out.

Anton seemed to wield, even when he wasn't looking at you, the sword of some unmodified unsocialized truth it was threatening just to be around, the blade, even when it wasn't aimed your way, reflecting all your falseness back at you.

How were we supposed to get clean? Lomand had told me that the most important part of your ablution was the intention with which you did it. What was I supposed to make of that? And how, with the couple of little bathroom basins offside the Quiet Room and in the North Barn, were we supposed to wash the rest of us?

"I . . . gg . . . I *disown* you," my father said on the phone when I'd told him I was going to England and why, and the locution's twisted comedy had been apparent even at the time: hurt, he'd reached back to his adolescent reading list, some lesser nineteenth-century novel or other, some melodramatic Russian count hurling the family thunder, although my father's voice had been more confused than angry. That I'd hurt him was a two-edged sword that hurt me too, but disowning me, even if it were something a man of his heart could have managed for more than a minute, was funny in a painful, stagey way.

My mother, when I talked it out with both of them during my three-day Brooklyn stopover, had stared off to one side with a fixed blank look while my defeated father said in lambent *yiddisheh* notes, All right, all right. No, the only one who'd actually disowned a child was me, down a sluice in Tokyo and brought the broken woman home. How was I supposed to wash away the blood and slime of that? With a little English water and the intermittent trickle of my *intention*?

"Rain." That's what those chords had been leading up to. "Rain." And here it came, one of my favorite Beatles songs. Jafar and Anton had some finegrained two-part harmony going on it. They slowed the tempo nearly to a halt to sing the title word, really strung it out there. Curious. Half the speed the Beatles did it in. A performance, I guessed, they were working up for the Open Day, the fate, the fête, the next chorus up now.

Rai-ai-ai-ai-ai-ai-ain.

They could show me that when it rains it shines? They stretched that line out too, a little presumptuous, I thought. They could show me? Sez who?

BACK IN THE CAR PARK the sun blazed down much as before, spelled by transitory puffs of cloud—thickening up, it seemed, as the day advanced—and I took refuge in the fact I had a job to do, even if, um, the work was already done: I wasn't flattening diddly anymore: the level playing field had been achieved, within the natural limits of the ground. If I'd known where to find Waddington I might have sought him out and asked What next? Then again maybe not: I was hiding out in the unambiguity of work and not budging from its shade till lunchtime.

The press and crunch of the roller over sand and stones, the accustomed injury of the belt against my chest: it might have gone on for half an hour before Richard Waddington showed up, smudged with work and scratching the dust out of his blond coils of hair.

"That looks about right," he said, looking things over. "Good work. The thing to do next . . . aaah . . . perhaps not before lunch."

"No, I'm ready," I said, dripping happily with semihonest sweat.

"Best leave it till after lunch. Do you see those stones?"

I'd noticed them: grey rounded rocks the size of small melons in a pile beside the wall. "Uh-huh."

"It's about painting them white—I think you'll find some paint in the garridge here, and if not there are tins in the North Barn—and then arranging them . . . aaah . . . somehow or other to mark out parking spots, although frankly," he said, assessing the irregularities of the space, "I don't know what to suggest."

"I'll think of something."

"Perhaps you will. In any case, why not take off now, have a wash before lunch and get on to it after. This is fine."

LUNCH WAS SPLENDID. The tables and benches had been hauled out of the dining room onto the lawn and we ate in the sun.

After the meal and tea and smokes were over a few people kicked a soccer ball around the lawn. I was standing off to one side watching, my body's tubes and organs uncharacteristically flushed with the oxygenated blood of work, when this little Dickensian kid with a turned-up nose came up to me out of nowhere and asked me, " 'Ello, 'oo are you?"

"Uhh, Koren," I said. "And what's your name?" The kid was, what, seven? Nine? Where'd he come from? Whose kid was he?

"Erin," he said.

"E-r-i-n?" I spelled, unsure.

"No. *Aaron.* Double-a-r-o-n."

"Oh: Aaron," I said, giving it the American pronunciation.

"No," he said insistently, *"Aaron,"* still pronouncing it Erin.

I stopped short of telling him Aaron was a Jewish name and I should know. What I remember best about the encounter—which took me aback a bit: that anomalous Dickensian accent and manner—was the kid's simultaneous cheerfulness and fixed intensity; years later I told his sainted mother that Aaron had in some sense recognized me, could spot his sort-of father-figures and had homed in on me with a certain beeline cognitive surety. I'd felt the intensity of it without knowing what it was, I told her. Sid appeared to think about it.

I ran the idea past Aaron once, but he told me all he remembered was seeing this skinny bearded new guy, and he wanted to talk to him mostly because of those strange orange shoes.

AFTER LUNCH, as per instructions, I watered the paint thin and put a coat on the grey rocks, whose pores thirstily sucked the emulsion in. They dried quickly in the sun and I lit a cigarette as I waited for the consulting committee I'd been told would come soon.

Shing's cat came by in the middle of my wait, sat down about twenty feet off and looked at me unblinkingly for a while. It left just before the committee hove into view.

Richard Waddington the roughed-out working architect, Hugh Tollemache of knightly profile, Anton of warlike mien: the four of us took up stances with our backs to the garage and surveyed the car park as if we were old Confucians at this kind of thing. Waddington and I may have done some chin-and-hand business and Hugh might have shaded his eyes against the glare. Anton directed a level eyebeam left to right, then went impassive as a wooden Indian.

"I think what we *might* do," said Richard Waddington, "is mark out five spaces along the wall here," gesturing appropriately to his left, "and we might manage four where we're standing." His arm swept right, where the lot ended in an irregular border over uneven ground. "That could be a problem."

"Ye-es," said Hugh, in the tone of someone wondering why he'd been asked along. He did look executive, though.

I might have started to say something about the inconvenient, perhaps car-disabling bulk of the whitened stones. In fact I thought the whole project had begun to look unlikely. Flattening the lot, if indeed it had been flattened, was a good enough idea, but the painted stones, while they looked impressive, were almost certainly a wrong number.

"If we put the stones out now," was Hugh's opinion, "they'll be invisible by the weekend unless we keep the cars off."

"Good point," Waddington said.

"What *I* think," Anton piped up, and I noticed that his voice had changed: softened, lightened, mildly fogged. "I think we ought to arrange the stones in a spiral." He sounded completely serious. Pointing with his index finger he sketched a spiral upon the little parking lot, the cars driving up the by-road, coming in, then spiralling in successive smaller inward circuits until, poof, they either drove up their own tailpipes or disappeared in mystic air. "That way," Anton said in this new, aerated voice, "everyone will be received in the manner in which they really *are* received."

This did not appear to be figurative speech.

Neither Waddington nor Hugh appeared to react to it, but as the new hand in Dodge I did a long slow take in Anton's direction, and as slowly back, to accord sufficient time for the scales to fall from my eyes: ah-hah, I told myself redundantly: I see.

"Aah, ye-es," Hugh eventually said.

We tried delineating a parking place or two—try one stone there, ye-es, let's see, and perhaps one over there—before chucking the rocks into the long grass over the wall, where Bulent's Mercedes hadn't thought up any new tricks either.

5

RESHAD BUTTONHOLED ME ON THE RUN sometime
that evening either en route to meditation or dinner or when he
came up to the House at eight to talk to the collected inmates.
Our paths crossed outdoors near the bell in the beaten copper light of a
long summer sundown, where ephemeral insects spiralled upward, bright
motes in air already busy with swims of pollen and the vesper tones of
early evenfall.

"You worked well today," he told me with a tacit nod and his eyes
holding mine.

I raised my brows to that, then squinted off at the grey stone wall of
the North Barn atop its trodden slope.

"I have a very good view from my window, you see."

I knew that from the slitted window of his keep he couldn't see all that
much of the place and definitely not the car park, so he was indicating he
had Other Eyes and a certain Ooo-eee-ooo.

A brief squeeze of my upper arm and off he trotted into the house.

I joined the gradual accumulation in the front room, people arranging themselves on the high cloth pills of zafus or the matting of the floor
beneath the light in its ribbed white paper globe. I selected what would
turn out to be my characteristic spot in the left rear quadrant with a view
out one of the windows, where the softened sun had begun its play of
lengthening shadows across the lawn and a west wind was testing the

higher leaves of the taller elms and poplars. Reshad sat in his spot at the head of the room, offset right, quietly awaiting the hour and occasionally fingering someone near and leaning forward to convey a whispered confidence, perhaps accompanied by a wink, before resuming his seat of patience.

People came in singly or in groups of two and three, some casually, others in an anxious blur, still others flushed with the scullion steam of after-dinner washup. All soothed themselves eventually into place, settled, calmed. I thought the forest green wallpaint had been particularly well chosen, in this regard.

A single bell signalled the hour, and Reshad awaited the arrival of the ringer before he began to speak. There were, oh, seventeen or twenty of us in the room, and I confirmed with a routine presumptuous scan that there were no women there I was interested in—particularly comical in view of the fact that my rapport with women at that stage of my life was approximately zero.

Reshad cleared his throat in a polite way before beginning. A condensed impression follows. You'll recognize the one thing I remember with searing clarity when I get to it.

"As you know, I'll be leaving for three weeks and a bit," Reshad began, "the first time I've gone away for that long in this cycle of our Work here. Grenville and Sue Collins have been kind enough to say they'll look after the place while Sid and I are in Turkey, and while this may seem quite a simple thing, in fact it's the beginning of a new phase of our . . . Wurk"—this time he gave it a heavy American r and got a laugh for lightening the moment, but I had already begun to recognize the characteristic note of high drama he brought to his fireside chats—"and you should all be particularly aware of what happens in this time." Pause. "If not we'll have to ship you off to Mr. Bennett's school for consciousness." Got the laugh. "Quite seriously, if what we are involved with is an attempt to go straight up, and I do think that what we are involved with here is just that, it is or should be perfectly clear that our work cannot and indeed must not depend on my being here. How could it? It's ridiculous really.

For goodness' sake, I know perfectly well that Anton has a higher link than I do," most heads tried not to spin, and most succeeded, "but that doesn't make it about him either. And it's not about Bulent, whatever *he* is. As you know, he told me at the beginning that ours was not to be a guru-chela relationship. Beshara cannot be based on any person."

A pause with his eyes shut while he doused for the tune.

"In the words of Mevlana Jelaluddin Rumi, 'I want a heart torn by longing. I want burning, only burning.' Mevlana also said that in the end he knew three things only: first I was raw, then I was cooked, then I was burnt. And that's really all there is to it, my loves. And since Bulent is a very good cook I might easily come back from Turkey a tidgy bit singed." Rimshot.

Another measured pause to accommodate a change of key.

"'Arabi sessions will continue two mornings a week, or perhaps three," he nodded toward Latif, "and there will be *zikr* Thursday nights. The Collinses will be on board by then. In the meantime I can't sufficiently stress the importance of our preparations for the Open Day and Fête this Sunday. If we're not here for our small *s* selves we ought at least to be able to communicate with those who live immediately around us, don't you think? If we're incapable of that, then what *are* we doing here, if you get my meaning." A pause. "How is the coconut-shy coming?" he asked someone I'd learned was named David Hornsby but hadn't spoken with yet, a tall attenuated poetic-looking guy with a long neck, large Adam's apple, small chin, large expressive eyes, and a high brow above which, like an aura of high ideas, radiated an impressive fan of light brown hair; he gestured ambiguously in response. "While it's true that the coconuts haven't quite arrived yet," Reshad admitted, "as you know, the pyramids were built from the top down by means of music, so as long as we do our part it's certain they *will* arrive, always remembering *insh'Allah* . . ."

More small yoks. Can you run that pyramid metaphor by me one more time?

"Seriously, though . . . You have no idea . . ." His torso swayed a bit, striving for expression. "If you could see what I see . . . This Open Day, this opening of what we are doing here to those around us . . . is more important than you can possibly imagine . . . Do we have any real idea why we're here? Do we? Do you? Do I?"

And it's odd. You could feel it, shimmering up from the rippling surface of Reshad's shifts of tone and from the darker depth of his emotional persistence, a massing together of a choral sense of purpose, a knitting together of some immaterial gossamer muscle and fiber to weave something very like the evening's resinous heart; and although Reshad kept courting the edge of expressive excess and higher hokum, and went over it, and because we were young enough, it was compelling stuff whatever our flickers of misgiving. It was just about the coconut-shy and a few visiting farmers, but the hint and buried drama were beating in our depths: here was something worth heaving oneself into wholly, here was something that might speak from depth to depth the words the world had left missing from its lists and registers . . . There was a palpable gathering of warmth in the room, but it was about something unfamiliar to me and I worried about the Nuremberg effect, without the flags and torches.

Reshad played upon us as if we were the strings of a harp, picking out our individual notes in sequence by means of an implication here, a nuance or allusion there, or simply by a vibration of his own that set off a widespread or selective sympathetic resonance, and gathered us gradually into arpeggios that filled the room like the articulated spectrum of our youthful selves, overpacked with hopes, hopeful guesses, and unknowing . . . And even if, as advertised, the place was not about him, the way the evening was shaping up, the dynamic of it, the way it felt, he was the dramatic mote around which every drop condensed, the seed of whatever crystal might be bodying forth its indigenous geometry. If he was a front man, he was good at it.

Another unprepared-for modulation: "And you should all be on your best behavior. With Sue on board, things will be impeccably kept up. Sue runs an even tighter ship than I do, what-what, and you'd better watch your step. If not, she'll have you all walk the plank."

I looked aside to get my bearings: out the window darkening fingers laid soft chords across the lawn beneath a sky going purple.

It would have been odd if the evening didn't fractal off into color and number and unintelligible arcana from some half-tradition or an idiosyncratic recognition of Reshad's to me at any rate—the diamond body shows, the throat chakra is the higher harmonic of the second chakra, the Kabbalistic location of the Essence, the evolutionary and involutionary spirals converge, when we look up to Him we are actually in our second chakra looking up to our heart, we don't make love, God makes Himself love in us, I can't tell you what the secret hundredth Name of God is but when I learnt it oh how I lawffed . . . then: "Jafar Bey!"

"Effendim," came the deep reply from just behind me. I hadn't known he was there.

"I think we need the Call to Prayer."

I turned to watch: Jafar rose from his seat on the floor, frowning elaborately, almond eyes serious beneath flexed brows, nostrils flaring. Once he had stood, he seemed to compress his body into itself, huddling himself smaller, legs pressed together, feet pushed close, arms held in, shoulders down, and it was as if he had pulled his normal expressive aura into a penumbral condensation. He began washing his hands down the seams of his jeans and looking around as if for some small object he had misplaced. "I need a hat," he growled finally, and when there was no other response in the room I dug into the back pocket of my jeans to dig out the woolen hippy-dippy hat of many colors someone had knitted me in California and insisted was mine: an outsized, loose-knit skullcap with a concentric spectrum inside its circumference. I never wore it but it had seemed the sort of thing to bring to Beshara.

I tossed it to Jafar and he caught it in his right hand, then frowned still more theatrically as he encountered the remains of what had been the heat of my backside and glared at me as if I'd tossed him a piece of shit to put on his head.

He shook it vigorously clean, shot me a red look and excused his way through a few seated bodies to the left rear corner of the room, which he turned and faced, then adjusted his address a few degrees this way, a few degrees that, until, I guessed, he picked up the beam from Mecca.

He put the distasteful hat on his head and worked it down. Since my head was large and his small it gave him more coverage than either he or I expected and weakened the moment with the suggestion of earlaps worn against the cold.

He lowered his head, cupped his hands behind its ears, raised up and began the cry, his voice suddenly enormous in the smallness of the room:

> *Allahu akbaaaaaaar. Allaaaaahu akbar.*
> *Allahu akbaaaaaaar. Allaaaaahu akbar.*

It was as if a pillar of flame had appeared among us. *Akbar* was pronounced more like *ekber*, and it sounded to me for a moment like *Allahu hangman*, but even if it hadn't my instincts would have made me duck my head beneath this unexpectable onslaught from another world.

> *Ashadu'un la ilaha ill'Allaaaahhh.*
> *Ashadu'un la ilaha ill'Allaaaahhh.*
> *Ashadu'un Muhammed ar rasul Allaaaahh.*
> *Ashadu'un Muhammed ar rasul Allaaaahh.*

The sensation is indelible in memory: it was as if a Spitfire had burst through the corner of the room with machine guns blazing on its wings, and what scared me silly was not some Yikes at the thought of Here come the Muslims all teeth and scimitars but Yikes this is the fire Rumi was talking about, the one that demanded a heart torn by longing, and burning, only burning; and caught in the flame of Jafar's Call to Prayer I realized for the first time that Beshara might be the real thing. It was what I'd come for but it was more beautiful and terrifying than anything I had imagined or envisioned.

> *Hayu ala'l falaah. Hayu-uuu ala'l falaah.*
> *Hayu ala salaat. Hayu-uuu ala salaah.*

For a flash it was as if the world had returned to its origin in fire, in light, in fire, but at the same time I noted that there was something surprisingly jazzlike in Jafar's phrasing, rhythm, and sense of line: how come? In any case he was rounding it up with a repetition:

Allahu akbaaaaaaar. Allaaaaahu akbar.
Allahu akbaaaaaaar. Allaaaaahu akbar.
La ilaha ill'Allaaah.

The room sat there dusted back to primary particles. What had I been doing all my life? I thought I'd blazed my way to a sight or two but I'd only been sitting in the anteroom. I'd never opened the furnace door and stepped inside.

At length Reshad made a small ahem and spoke. "I think that says it all and we should call it a night. Perhaps someone will make tea. I might come up to the House for lunch tomorrow. Good night."

We remained seated until he left the room and then there was the usual brush and grunt and shuffle as people rose or began to chat or nod in Jafar's direction and raise their eyes ceilingward. Cigarettes were rolled and lit. Folks went out to make tea. Others came in with bowls of fruit. I just sat there and thought about it.

Eventually I creaked myself upright and beat a path to the door and of course ran headlong into Anton, who looked me coolly in the eye. "And that's when he saw the Bear," he said, followed by a buzzing mouthnoise right off the record, and there it was, the last brick of the prison of hipness morticed into place: the deferred Lord Buckley impression: Buckley's story about the guy who happens on a still in the woods and starts drinking moonshine until he wasn't just drunk, he was God's Own Drunk, with God's sweet lanterns a-hangin' in the sky . . . and that's when he saw the Bear, *vvvvp*, big Kodiak lookin' fella sixteen foot tall, and there I was eye to eye with Anton. The guy had me nailed and stapled, but didn't hold the moment past its beat: disengaged his eyes from mine, moved on. How'd he know what happened to me when Jafar did the Call?

Out beneath the skyful of stars and whatever moon, hushing wind in the border trees, scattered human sounds across the dark, a laugh, a door swung shut, the crockery sound of teacups from inside the House.

Okay, let's think this out. (1) How come that arrogant English bastard knows Lord Buckley routines in the first place? (2) How come he knows exactly what happened to me when Jafar did the Call to Prayer? (3) And how did he lay the riff on me and (a) know I'd get the reference and (b) I'd interpret it correctly?

It didn't play. Nobody could do that.

Look up, spray of stars, impersonal points of brilliant burning.

I looked at my watch. Time for ablutions and then my first turn upon the boards as a whirling dervish.

BECAUSE OF MY GOGOL-JELLY FEET I had to find someplace private in which to do ablutions—the upstairs bathroom in the House, where anyone might amble in and see, wouldn't do—and found a sequestered basin in a corner of the North Barn, essentially that old familiar spot the cold-sweat guilty huddle, in which to wash myself according to the book. First you wash your hands with cold water—soap is optional, but you use it if it's there—then sniff some water off your palm up your nostrils and blow it out, rinse your mouth thoroughly, wash your face, your ears inside and out, your forearms up to the elbows, and finish with your feet; all preceded by a *Bismillah ar-Rahman ar-Rahim*, in the name of God the Merciful and Compassionate, to clear the decks of lesser motive and protect yourself from unforeseen results. To be more entirely correct, which in those days we weren't, my genitals and bung should have been washed clean the last time I used them, and the day should have begun with a full-body wash, though none was available and you had to do your best at a basin with a bar of soap.

I washed standing at that nighttime basin, and managed to get my guilty feet under the tap, feeling edgy about Was I doing it right? and how was my Intention? and wondered Jewishly if these quasi-Muslims knew if the house soap—Cussons Imperial Leather, with an embossed label in the center that remained in place for the life of the bar—was made with lard.

I'd scoped out the Cruciform Barn and had decided that it was the place to turn: open space, high roof, fresh air, smooth tongue-and-groove floorboards underfoot. Sure it was dark but there was always a votive candle burning. Now if only I would find it empty.

It would have been about ten o'clock, and the Cruciform Barn was a hulking stone massiveness in the dark. I entered through the eastward face, its opening wide enough to drive a couple of wagons through now provisionally closed by plastic sheeting stretched over a loose but sufficient structure of wooden battens. A plastic-and-batten door with leather hinges was set at the right edge. I fixed it closed behind me with a loop of rope over a nail, took off my shoes on the flagstones of the entranceway and stepped forward into a plus sign each face of which was a twenty-foot span the walls of which also rose twenty feet before encountering structural oak beams and a slant of roof.

Cued by the social protocol of entering the meditation room, I may have bowed hand on heart before stepping up onto the floorboards in my twice-damp socks.

Despite the votive candle on the low altarish table across the floor, it was indigo dark inside, a downward intensification beyond the tones of dusk, the air made of swarming motes, then resolving as my eyes adjusted: rough stone walls ascending into beamwork, flowers in a vase down the table from the candle, an elaborately damascened columnar brass mosque candlestand five feet tall holding an unlit white candle about eight inches thick. The plastic sheeting set in the westward opening buckled softly in the breeze. Chinked stone walls closed the other two arms of the cross.

Time to die. I mean let's try this.

I walked out to the center of the floor, said a *bismillah*, overcrossed my arms and bowed facing the candle, then pushed off with a lot on my mind: left foot fixed, turn anticlockwise only, centered in the heart not in my belly or solar plexus or my head, right palm up to receive, left palm down to dispense, energy coming in the right hand and out the left, don't get dizzy, don't fall down, Jafar the White Tornado, and for God's sake don't *expect* anything, and . . . things went pretty much as an intelligent person, had one been available, might have predicted at the time. I performed a few solemn revolutions with my arms folded batlike, then attempted to blossom them outward and hoped they might express a sense and maybe soar of wings, but what I got was the overwrought monitoring device in my cranium trying to read the dials and meters and work the limbs. As the barn's darkness blurred past with the ping of candle-bright marking off each revolution, I felt a general sense of pulse and rush, an involuntary stiffening of my shoulders, the feel of a seam of floorboard beneath my feet tugging my socks sideways as my left foot spun beneath my weight, and worry worry worry . . . How long did I keep it up? Not more than a couple or three minutes.

When I spun myself halt and bowed with my arms recrossed on my chest, then straightened, there was none of the stomach sickness I'd been warned against, but my heart was pounding disproportionately fast and hard and I was dizzy enough to wobble on my spot and stand, shaking and slightly winded, pulses beating in my ears, until the room settled back in place. I don't know what, in defiance of the red death, I might have expected—certainly not an instant hookup to my childhood dervish dreams: whirling, troops, and frenzy around the fire—but it wasn't anything this prose-flat and uneventful. But that was cool. It was opening night, a tryout in the provinces. Did what I was sposed to. Try it again tomorrow.

Outside beneath the spectacle of stars the sky was extraordinarily clear, the galaxy spread in deep, detailed display.

God's sweet lanterns a-hangin' in the sky.

Where was Anton coming from with his tooraloom tooraloom and his higher link than Reshad? Reshad had laughed about that higher link jazz but the smile didn't go much deeper than his teeth.

Jafar's prayer made of fire.

And Reshad leaving a few days after the Fête: no protection there.

Lomand? Intelligent goodwill but always detachment, distance; to which one had to say Fair enough.

I didn't see how I was going to cut it at Beshara but having no alternative I was going to try. I'd been scared too sober since Japan to be anything like God's own drunk, and when he and the Bear were both drunk

on shine even he said, what was his last line before conking out? I
scratched in the dirt of my memory and finally got a claw on it—"I tried
to do the Bear Dance but it was so simple it evaded me."

THE NEXT NIGHT, after a golden day on which I don't know what
work I fumbled at, I was back in the Barn not long after ten—had to wait
for a solitary meditating shape to make its bow, back out and brush past
me nodding wordless into the night—easing my shoes off and readying
myself for a new attempt on the ramparts of Constantinople.

My ritual preparations were the same: the bow, arms crossed and
folded, the toes of my right foot lapped over their leftward mates, and a
respectful sense of wait and see, though tinged, it must have been, with
last night's sum, so issueless and routine.

Just before beginning, an innocent unpresumptuous question ambled
through me: what would it actually be like to be centered in the heart? I'd
heard a lot of talk about the heart in the last few days and I didn't know
what the word meant anymore, so if that ephemeral organ could be
found again, what might centering in it be like?

I began the Turn with folded arms, then after a few revolutions opened
them outward and after a moment or so of normal spin and without transition everything changed. With no as-if or metaphorical equivalence
about it, I found myself outside Time—something you know, when it
happens to you without ameliorative shading, as simply as you'd know
whether you were soaking in a bathtub or standing next to it dry—
standing perfectly still while my body and the barn and the encircling
English night revolved around me: all that was subject to rise and fall and
change in motion, but an imperishable center of myself free and clear.
On each revolution the votive candle ticked past like an instance of intellection in the big barn's darkened spin. It was an extended, objective moment wholly apart from the flux of life, simple as common sight and as
unmistakable.

Since that moment, in which I was returned to what seemed my inherent eternity, existed outside Time, there was no possibility of sequen-

tial thought, but this was not a limitation: cognition seemed huge, possibly limitless, all ordered and implicit, although I do remember a momentary amazement at watching my upraised hand go past me with each of my body's turns. I had no idea what eyes I might be seeing through: if my face and eyes spun around me with the rest of phenomenal existence, the stillness I inhabited contained within it essential and literal sight without benefit of material organ. Effort was impossible too: the moment was self-sustaining, and it was bliss to be there—though emotion had no place in it—and far more real than life. Whatever "I" was had been returned to a declension of overall eternity, and as for Space I could see it but was detached from its determinations. I retained physical sensation—my stocking feet on the floorboards, my jaw opened at the first shock of the experience—but they were secondary phenomena and I was on vacation from them: they had no purchase upon the self in which I stood.

The timeless moment and its cognitions consumed perhaps a minute of the mortal clock, and I was restored to the struggles of the physical turn, to which add a gasp of loss and a reflex striving in the dust after the caravan had passed. I spun myself silly in its wake for minute after minute, trying to wrestle my body back into the magic moonbeam or draw down again through the taproot fixed in heaven such holy water, light and air. Ours is not a caravan of despair! Don't leave me here starving in the dust of your extravagance!

In the end a mix of self-congratulatory exaltation and physical whirl-headedness overtook me and I ended it. Bowed, straightened, may have dropped to my knees, then head to floor, to grovel out repeated thanks. Without a doubt I addressed more words Upstairs to the tune of oh please please come again, or stay there and take me with you.

Later, in the reflective aftermath of that moment's privileged reprieve, there was again time for pennies to drop, and I stood there and watched the world radically revise itself down serial levels of concatenation.

IF I HAD WANTED an analytical demonstration of the difference between a self subject to and free of Time, respectively, I could have been shown no clearer better; and if one needed—as I desperately did—a guarantee of a self beyond Time's accidents, well, gotcha, Q.E.D.

And as it happened, the moment had its heralds and foreshadowings. Back in California, in the dark ages of Lomand's homegrown Gurdjieff group, at least two things had happened from which straight lines reached me in the Cruciform Barn that night. In the most prominent, though not the first of these, I'd been lying in my basement room the previous winter . . .

Seven or so of the people Lomand had left behind for higher ground had got together and rented a big white wooden house in Oakland—it had once belonged to the Hermetic Society, Hermites we called them, and we found crawlspaces in the woodwork beneath the big séance room out back that might have come in handy for drumming up phenomena—and took a room each in it. I was out of town when the house was found, helping my folks sell liquor on one holiday or another, and I came back to find that my partners in esoterica had allotted me a narrow dankness—with a private entrance, they hastened to point out—in the cellar. Anyhow, I was lying in it late one night while those in more blessed abodes above were hustling together their $2,250 fee to Mr. Bennett's school and I lamented my inability to do the same and my consequent abandonment in the dust; and then the strangest thing transpired.

What?

One instant there I was in my narrow iron bed in the lower depths, and in the next, without even the shimmer of a prologue, I was outside Time and Space contemplating my original eternality in the Garden—*a* garden in any case. Visually and experientially nothing was left of the material world and all its Oaklands; I had been whisked beyond terrestrial direction into a garden which apparently I had never left: the precinct, it appeared, of my innate eternal nature in which, wearing the face I'd had before I was born, I meditated, as ever, the resolved puzzle of my being both in and outside Time. I had never essentially left this place, had never suffered either a fall from it or the leastmost bruise in any mode of being: materiality and its consequences were one barely existent mote in the pauseless contemplation that was eternal being's activity and enjoyment.

And this contemplation took place, as it ever had, in a garden. I felt that there were other souls like me in it but I didn't see them, and deduced their presence from mine: I was one, but of a kind. All around me, trees greened and softened the light that fell—I understood this as a declension, as an ameliorative address to subjectivity from its higher origin—and the trees, of which I could see neither the bottoms nor the tops, were themselves metaphorical, were resemblances or analogies of some kind, beyond interpretative grasp for now; but ahead and a distance below me in a sort of clearing of my sight, in a pool of difference, I could see a single tree with bent branches and small leaves, behind it a bit of broken wall.

I was sufficiently my accustomed self for an astonishment at being there to form a sort of limit or meniscus to the inherently infinite contemplation of the involutions of pure being, and the lesson seemed to be: this is an essence and a beauty from which no happenstance on earth can damage you away.

When the hand of grace or whim redeposited me in flesh upon my seamy sheets in Oakland I knew a thing or two—although I'd had some generic suspicion of the unreality of the world as given—I hadn't really suspected before.

For one thing I realized that although almost no one took him at his word, Proust wasn't kidding about the real self and its abode outside the pendulum's narrowing arc, or that the sovereignty of art literally, not metaphorically, depended not on what the world called talent but from a native correspondence to a higher preexistent order of pure being. In fact . . . the only commentator who had not taken Proust's now obviously literal statement as some metaphorical subset of his aesthetics was the great naysayer against all transcendence Samuel Beckett, who alone among them had sufficient metaphysical cast of mind to compass the position and see it for what it was.

And one other French thing was settled—clear the café, kids, this could get ugly—Essence preceded Existence and not just by a nose in the backstretch.

Though perhaps after all my first thoughts were not of Proust—

alone among modern authors in actually providing a piece of useful information—because it was a revolution in like my whole like total notion of what we were up to wandering around down here. And—aha!— the dazzling complexity of the human brain—I was hardly in a position to deny the existence of the neuron—was primarily an interface with a preexistent consciousness it filtered and refracted in a partial and conditioned mode. And what the local folklore called the immortal soul is a fundamental fact of life of which one's subjective material self is an interesting precipitate.

I lay there in my cold-sweat basement bed and mulled over everything Western Sieve had lost track of in its smashingly successful ascent these last few hundred years. For one thing, the whole of physics, since materiality was a precipitate of consciousness—one might even say: of soul—was reduced to subsequentiality, and the entire machinery of evolution was permeated by a teleology. The mind reeled, more than a little.

Nor, for that matter, was one's essence what Gurdjieff said it was: a highly perishable subjective something the lightest hazard could stunt, distort or outright kill. Nor was it really, as most of my Lomand groupmates seemed to think, something one actually had to build, since it was already there.

You're missing a piece of the picture here, I told myself.

In any case, freshly stunned in the Cruciform Barn of the Beshara Centre, I'd been shown the same fact in another of its faces, indicating at the very least that the real, supernal self, should its lower counterpart clean its plate and learn its manners, might live here clear as daybreak in the axis of the whirl and change.

We might be learning something here in England. We might be moving on.

And what's more . . .

And what's more, this Beshara place appeared to be in line with whatever prior grace had seized me: it had continuity: I could trust it, should come all the way inside.

I was still, improbably and for all my fuckups, being looked after.

All right!

But was I a reliable witness? No blood, no feet, restricted wind and a harried mind: why believe anything this mess came up with? What if I was finally bonkers? It was possible. I was damaged, immature and wildeyed, a fevered fragment too eager to fly off on the first visionary gleam although or did I mean because my house had already collapsed around me . . .

But no: what happened in the Turn was real beyond all my capacity to confect it.

And there was that other, still earlier California thing, the year before I found myself in the Garden: Lomand had given us one of those perceptual exercises to do in the week between meetings of the cabal—there was a funky warehouse in the Mission District—only this time he'd told us the procedure was particularly powerful so we should do it only once and keep it up for twenty minutes max. And the exercise was . . .

"I'd like you to imagine," Lomand told us, grinning in his armchair like a cat who had dined on a particularly satisfying canary. What he asked us to do—only one other person in the group aside from me took him up on it and nothing extravagant happened to her—was to "imagine that every person in the world knows what you are thinking and feeling and doing."

"Including the people you know?" someone asked.

"Yes," Lomand said, "that includes friends and family. Mother, father, aunts, uncles, all your cousins. And all the people in the world you don't know."

"A six-year-old girl in a mountain village in Peru?" I asked.

"A six-year-old girl in Peru and Kirk Douglas and the Pope and everyone else down the line. Twenty minutes, once, everyone in the world seeing you in present time, as it happens."

"Oh Jesus," someone said.

"Since as far as we know he's not alive in a body on earth at present, feel free to consider Jesus optional."

Most of Lomand's exercises ended in dull insights or false ones—though he kept production up, whatever the result—and a stretch of braindead blather in the meeting room which Lomand would finally feel obliged to terminate with a lecture, dazzling in its abstraction, that balanced, in the end, with the exquisite simplicity of an equation. Occasionally, of course, the general population would turn up bits of actual insight—Nick Prestigiacomo was particularly good at this—although just as often someone would trip out on an exercise and come to a radically incorrect or even dangerous conclusion—likewise a Prestigiacomo specialty—from which Lomand would duly warn the group away.

There were nearly forty people in the group at the time and I have no idea why only two of us had a go at this particular mindgame, or for that matter why I was one of them: as a secretive and guilty Brooklyn Jewish guy I was scared silly by the prospect of transparency, but what the hell, I gave it a go, it was only play, it was just pretend.

I was crashing at a friend's apartment that week—must have been between rentals—about midslope on University Avenue, which runs like a zipper from the Bay up the front of Berkeley, ending at the buckle of the university. I emerged from Peter Tenney's sidestreet door in early afternoon, blinking in the light—he kept a dark apartment—and when I began my plod uphill I decided this would be as good a time as any to have everyone in the world look in for twenty minutes.

On what I was thinking, feeling and doing, huh? Well for starters I was walking in your typical California sunshine along with uphill traffic past housefronts and, increasingly, storefronts as I climbed. As for what went on intellectually and emotionally in the haunted house of myself, darker than Tenney kept his flat, okay, let's open up and throw some power of imagination into it.

I remember less the sensation of the exercise itself than my serial responses to an imagined everyone looking in: a cringe of shame at first for the usual shopworn reasons—greed and guilt and, worse, that fundamental feeling of existential insufficiency, the stink of botched project, leading to a general disgust at what remained of my soul—and I could take it, I supposed, as my poor parents looked in with their ageing worried eyes and, O Lord, the rest of the family ranked behind them—why should Gloria Agrin have to see me brought so low? Then came the kid in Peru, the entire sophisticated population of Paris, followed by loathsome Henry Kissinger.

After a turn on the boards before this swelling audience came the predictable flip: oh yeah? Enjoying the show? Well have a look at what I *really* am! And what followed then was a fanfare of unlimited egoism, a thirst for all the love and glory the world might have in it and dispense—a fucking exclusive on that, if you please—and recognition of my great wideflaring seafaring universal soul. Dig it, Universe! Take a look! Me me me me me me *me!*

This tune ran its course soon enough. I lost my concentration for a span of blocks, and began to jerk myself back into the assignment—checked my watch: ten minutes to go—only as I neared the major commercial intersection of University and Shattuck a couple of blocks before the UC Berkeley campus began its landscaped coverage of the hill. I had a southbound bus to catch on Shattuck, but when I crossed University right to left and reached the bus stop, I felt a hankering for a quick ice cream, and when the light turned green I strode across Shattuck past three lanes of growling car-faces to the other side, and just before reaching for the handle of the ice cream shop door I turned, still laboring at Lomand's exercise, to face the intersection. I began to see something unexpected, and forgot about buying that cone.

I'd like to get the sequence right.

First the thought occurred to me, based on what subtle unveiling I don't know, that in fact everyone in the world *could* see what I was thinking, feeling and doing—a thought that made no rational sense, but there it was, an established fact. What followed, my consciousness shifting into a higher, unrecognizable mode, was the recognition that I could also see what everyone else was up to—where was this stuff coming from?—and in the instant, as I scanned the assortment of humanity busy at this mundane intersection and its contending cars, I somehow began to see, like a mirage of heat refractions, or a shape made of water—it was either an objective, superior seeing, or a reality showing itself unmodified—in the form of a beehive or a hair-dryer's dome, everyone's individual enlightened eternal selves hovering above them while their coarser bodies went about the pretenses of the day. I might have imagined something similar in sentimental mode years earlier, but this was real and I was seeing it.

Out of the crowd I remember two people in particular: a black guy in his middle twenties bopping up the street toward me in some inner music rhythm—or rather this eternal enlightened Buddha-nature-being pretending to be this black guy bopping along the asphalt as he crossed University in front of me and passed, a transcendent being gracefully condescending to the individuation and its act—and across Shattuck a chubby middle-aged woman who had just run and missed a bus and her face flushed all pink and white, upset about it as a green shopping bag slipped against a white one and she had to clap both of them to her thighs—and it was the same damn thing: she was enlightened and eternal and hovered above herself like a transparent beehive hairdo in endless fascination with the humble prose and tiny pathos of terrestrial involvement. Missed the bus!

So Eternity really was in love with the productions of Time—but to so unaccountable an outcome! the whole machinery of heaven bent low to concentrate itself upon a single point so that unboundable omniscience might play at being a sweating panting lady flustered because she missed the bus!

The whole of life was like this always.

I stood there in front of the ice cream parlor and surveyed the intersection in a single sweep and, yep, it was true: every single one of these enlightened Buddhas acting out the roles of daydreaming bozos hovered above their earthly selves in compassionate contemplation—the strangeness of it!—so that the whole of earthly life, as people met and unmet or simply passed each other by, was shown to be the strangest, most intricately arranged ceremony: recognition and its apparent opposite elaborately enacted, by means of the most peculiar muggings and pretenses, between mutually cognisant spirits of immortal time and politesse—so tender toward each other's impersonations as never to trouble them with the rub of an unsought truth. There is probably no way to convey in words the refined, complex, ceremonial oddity of it. I gaped at these unearthly acts of courtesy—which would not, because they could not, cease come famine, flood or genocidal war! this was nuts!—like a greenhorn fresh off the barge at customs and immigration, and there was no rational world-perspective I either knew or had heard rumored that was capable of accommodating the sheer fact of what I saw before me plain as day.

But wait a minute wait a minute—wreathed in these first amazements, the thought was slow in reaching me—if this was true of *them*, it was also necessarily true of *me*, and what-what-what might that look like or mean? I tried to catch it in the light of the moment's flashing, but when the mirror spun my way I couldn't see, as all perspective skewed and scattered and I had no place to see from or in which to stand. In my sudden inability to turn the tables and become myself the object in transcendent view a confusion overcame me, along with an intimately painful roiling in my heart, and instead of ascending visibly into my higher Buddhanature beehive I felt, in my incapacity to go there, as if I were being torn apart from the heart outward, and what emerged from this bewilderment and disbranching was . . .

Well, was something very like, superimposed upon the daybright clatter of University and Shattuck, a clear but still diaphanous vision of, what to call it, some other, transcendent sun. Despite its transparency it bestrode or more precisely replaced the world down here and the little sun that daily shone above it. And . . .

And according to the dispensation of this supervening sun, there weren't any discrete individual Buddha-natures anymore, nor was I one myself either. Instead there was an all-obliterating something I couldn't tolerate standing in the presence of, something I felt it would kill me to see completely, and there was a tearing, burning, bursting in my heart I could not bear to live with—as if that sun had so obliterated the laws of space that it was also, unspeakably, located in the essential center of myself, and by its nature blew everything other than itself away and threatened to incinerate me where I stood—and although I wanted to disappear in it I yiked myself free in a reflex lunge at survival: I must have shaken my head or shivered my body to escape it, and for a moment the contradictions hung in me in a clatter of images that tore my perceiving self apart, and the sun shattered, or my ability to see it did, attended at the margins of my sight by what seemed crowds of snarling animals I quickly read as the fearful phantasms of my subjective nature thrashing at the sight and disappearance of that transcendent and intolerable sun.

Restored to the shreds of normal consciousness and soothing myself two minutes later with excellent vanilla ice cream—I can still taste it—I wondered What the hell was that? and in fact asked Lomand the same question in his armchair the next group meeting in the Mission District. I described the visionary run-up, the Buddha-nature stuff, then the supernal other sun and asked him what it was. "*I* don't know," he said, and grinned around the room like a cat who had signed a lifetime deal with a reputable canary supply firm. "Hah. Hah."

I thought about what I'd seen of course, and established to my satisfaction that I hadn't made it up—I might be screwed up but I'd never been delusional, and since I'd never dropped acid it wasn't a flashback—and moreover it was in line with a number of reputable precedents, not that I really cared: the veils of Maya, the shadows in Plato's cave, the River Lethe, the illusory nature of all existence, the voidness of all phenomena in the Noumenon, of which I appeared to have seen a phase. I even cracked a book and found a lovely passage in an Upanishad about twin birds on a branch, one descending to earth and the other remaining among the leaves, which pretty much said it all even if it didn't tell you why. What I'd seen might be a typical newcomer's gift, a lantern lifted clear of life's thicket, a star to steer by when the sea's unknown and the land ahead invisible in the dark.

Either that or a higher version of the dope dealer's classic tactic: the first one's free.

As Cardinal Newman had it and Lomand liked to say now and then, the trouble with mysticism is that it begins in mist and ends in schism.

And I did have one question left: why was life's dim game worth so bright a candle?

THE NEXT FEW DAYS until the Fête I did work of one kind and another. I remember digging in the dirt a lot, to lay new pipe they said, and the shock of encountering stinging nettles while pulling weeds at the base of the stableyard wall.

The Open Sunday came, and the Fête was festive. I didn't know what all those smiley English families in particoloured clothes were doing there with their kids and babies or why we had to be so friendly, solicitous and polite—so much for my transcendent sense of ceremony when put to the slightest local test—but hey, it was fun in the sun and it was all right with me.

Essentially I had given the place my dazed consent and had said in my flawed fashion, Into Thy hands I commend my spirit; but my secret wish was Get me outa here and despite all the hidden-intricate-beauty-of-manifestation jazz please make it simple and just take me back.

6

FOR THE FIRST THREE WEEKS of Reshad's monthlong absence, that consent made it seem as if I had entered the winds and involutions of a turbine and let it have its way with me. If I got too floaty I had my unsound body to remind me that life was also hard and had its heavy laws. I tried to quit smoking once or twice, but half a day into it, with my circulation opening up and my metabolism shifting gears, I wasn't ready, couldn't take it yet, and lit one up. It was helplessly autonomic and an uninspiring picture of human nature, and it wasn't even about smoking. It was who shall live and who shall die, and it looked as if I hadn't made my mind up yet.

There was one last blast before Reshad took off.

This was the *zikr* usually held on Thursday night but moved up to cheer him on his way, and there was both a stir of anticipation and an air of affected nonchalance, a casual breeziness about the prospect that was perhaps the clearer indicator of the thirst for what was coming.

Dinner travelled at a quicker pace, the talk turned brighter and more collective, people rushed to clear the tables and crowded the scullery brandishing tea towels, hoping to dry a plate. When this superflux dispersed, floors were quickly swept and mopped, large earthenware bowls were heaped with fruit, tea urns topped up, and the song of the Hoover was heard in the Quiet Room, where the furniture was also taking a beating.

Sets of extra-vigorous ablutions followed, with for once an efficient segregation of male and female queues. Freshly washed Besharites ran to their rooms and strolled out of them minutes later wearing their finest clothes and reeking, some of them, of improbably strong lemon cologne— garish Turkish stuff Bulent was said to like.

I'd asked a few questions about what to do and when, but distribution of intelligence data remained haphazard at Beshara, and I followed the rush the best I could and tried not to do anything egregious.

The only person who seemed unaffected by the change of tempo was Anton, who was seen strolling here and there around the property tuning his drum with a turnkey or tightening its skin above a fire, glaring down his crooked nose at almost anyone who crossed his path.

By eight-thirty we were headed in several streams for the Cruciform Barn beneath a soft bronze dusk. Inside, smoke of incense threaded the air and floodlamps mounted on the walls and in the oakbeams overhead chased the gloom from the far stone corners and shone on the central square of floor. A scattering of early-birds, kneeling on meditation benches or braving the floorboards unassisted, had begun to form a circle, at the head of which, west, a spread of fluffy sheepskins commanded roughly forty-five degrees of arc, with a dyed crimson skin placed in the center. Behind and offset a few feet to the right, Anton, Latif and Jafar sat cradling their drums, with Anton in the middle winning the posture contest, easy; and for a moment they reminded me of the Nairobi Trio that had cracked me up on television when I was a kid—Ernie Kovacs and a couple of accomplices in raincoats, gorilla masks and hats—and it took me several tries to loosen the impression and suppress the threat of laughter out of season.

I had no idea what kind of drumming they were gonna do for *zikr* but what can I say, I wanted to be in that number.

Taking the red sheepskin as noon, I found my spot at eight o'clock on the circle and put a meditation bench beneath me. Others found their stations among the hours, settled, stilled themselves, meditated or affected to, occasionally opening an eyeslit to look around. A few ahems, some rhythmic breathing and spiritual rumbles here and there, and a sense, perhaps, of the evening's air blowing lightly on the open strings of a large invisible guitar.

I'd already noticed—you couldn't miss it—the subsidiary position of women in the glamour of Beshara: they were more often seen than heard and sometimes not much seen either; even when, as in Fiona's case, say, there was so much sparkle showing; and Siddiqa didn't drop in on us very often. Tonight was different, though: the women seemed less cloistered and recessed, their place in the circle as good as any man's. Briar and Ruth—a pair I hadn't entirely distinguished from each other since I was an idiot but also because they seemed to be working, hiding or conspiring in the kitchen, even during meetings—were seated a few places apart either side of three o'clock, and wore a dignity I wouldn't have predicted. And long tall Sally, with the sharpish features beneath the tumble of brown hair, whose wit and quickness I'd had to deduce more from the brightness of her eyes than from the little I'd heard her say, seemed majestic in her ease of posture. Lois, socially buttressed by her pairing with Maurice, sat by herself tonight about five feet back from the circle at two o'clock, and I deduced, correctly, that it was her time of the month and her segregation was a matter not of an atavistic sense of uncleanness but a more up-to-date conception of "the energies."

At last Reshad and Siddiqa and what I assumed were our interim keepers the Collinses entered like a string of celebrities who had foremeasured the effect of their entrance and could be casual about it. They sat themelves in dignified fashion upon the sheepskins, with Reshad on the red one in the middle. After an accustomed pause for a meditative address to the moment, he acknowledged one or two of us individually with a nod and a hint of warming smile.

Grenville Collins—Ghalib was his Sufi name, I'd heard: the Arabic equivalent of Victor—was a languid number at least six and a half feet tall who seemed almost liquid in the disposition of his limbs, and when his eyes showed there was an equivalent fluidity to their gleam. Word was he had been the manager of the Kinks back when, and was the "well-respected man about town" in the song of that name. Doing the best things, so conservatively? I wouldn't have thought so. Sue Collins, seated beside him, was an unexpected chunk of woman with what I would have sworn was a stern expression on her face.

At Reshad's side Siddiqa comported herself with a simple dignity that muted, for the moment, the chromium shimmer usually attendant on her aura.

Aaand here we go: Reshad boomed out a hearty *Bismillah ar-rahman ar-rahim*, which the collectivity repeated in a mutter, and we were off.

We began with something we'd done a few times before meditation, a full enunciation of the first profession of the Faith, *La ilaha ill'Allah*, which had been explained to me in a number of approximate Englishings—There is no Divinity but *the* Divinity, There is no God but Allah, There is no God but the One God—but which had deeper esoteric significations that boiled down to the assertion that there was nothing in existence or beyond it other than the One Being, Absolute Ipseity, or Necessary In-Itselfness, and no reality other than that. Well, sure, went my first unthought response, everyone knows *that*.

This version of *La ilaha ill'Allah* was performed in a particularly dramatic manner. The *La*, meaning No, was begun with the head held erect, but it began a downward anti-clockwise motion that *ilaha* continued in a circle that returned the head to the top of the arc, from which the *ill'*—meaning but or except—thrust the head downward like a dagger with almost explosive violence into the heart, from which the affirmation of *Allah* rebounded, fortissimo on the second syllable, the head rising with it; the entire cycle embodying an annihilating dismissal of all existence other than the Absolute and the arising from that negation into the Absolute and Necessarily-So, the whole of it acted out, so went one's best intention, in body, heart and soul—Thou shalt love the Lord thy God with all thy Heart and Soul and Might taken literally and done straight, with each instance a fresh enactment, not the heathens' vain repeat.

There were no drums behind this.

I went at it with everything I had, occasionally opening my eyes for a quick gander around the circle to gauge the style of concentration, pick up a cue, and tell myself Uh-huh, here I am in this all right; but between the unfamiliarity of the practice and my own variable concentration I went in and out of the *zikr* as it progressed, and my experience of it was vigorous if not consistently inspiring. I remember treating this first invocation of the night's many as a sort of clearing of the throat of the heart, a blowing off of coarsest dust, though I tried to remember what Reshad had said about the sword of discrimination, on the *ill'*, sweeping down upon the store of illusion in ourselves and clearing the way for the self-revelation of the Real.

Or words to that effect.

After a few minutes, with an increase in volume and a momentary edge applied to his voice Reshad asserted a change of rhythm and we were into a straight-ahead *La ilaha ill'Allah* without the circular head motion and the halting accentuation it enforced, the invocations now strung together at about a quarter note per second and Anton's camel beat shaking the sand off its back and setting off. One or two people around the circle worked a bit of heavy breathing into the *zikr* with a hoarsened inhalation just behind the *La* and on the last syllable of *ilaha*. After a couple of introductory patterings upon the rim of his treble drum, Jafar started his sixteenth-note figures moving atop Anton's imperial lope and Latif, on the brass drum, insinuated his way into the midrange—sixteenths, but accented differently from Jafar's—with such craft that at first I didn't hear him. They were beautifully matched and meshed, responding subtly to the shifts and redirections of the *zikr* while leaving the leadership to Reshad.

Reshad eased the tempo up a notch and the drums came with him, smooth and propulsive, and you could feel the engine of the *zikr* building up its steam; even my own gauge, long rusted shut, began nudging the needle up the scale: I tapped the glass and squinted to be sure and, yes, there was action in the boiler.

There was an obvious sexuality to the gathering energies of the *zikr*, and I stole a quick look across the way at Lomand to see if he was into it and it seemed he was—Gurdjieff had pointed out, with emphasis, the misuse of sexual energy and the telltale hysterical emphasis it lent human activity and intellection, and Reshad had mentioned it a couple of times himself but hadn't characterized it except to imply a certain yuck factor—and I took Lomand's apparent absorption in the *zikr* as a go-ahead; and it did seem obvious to me that if specifically sexual energies were invited in, it was for the purposes of their transformation, a sublimation upward to whatever vision or illumination their higher use might yield. Since Beshara had already won my trust, and observation reassured me about the tradition and its spiritual technologies, I gave myself to the process the best I could, on such slim acquaintance.

There was a central excitement to the *zikr* that was akin to playing music when things caught fire—a recognition that caught you, led you deeper, through successive versions of yourself toward some more final revelation—but *zikr* seemed to focus this experience more absolutely in a specific address to the depths of oneself, an active, aimed engagement with the core of all you had; and it was as if listening to John Coltrane— all that time in Birdland or with a record spinning—had schooled me in *zikr* before the fact: Trane's progress through a solo incinerating in its passage the very materials of its making, along with serial versions of the man who played it: theophanies and annihilations whose goal was the exhaustion of the music and the man in the uncovering of greater means, life more lasting, and what he himself had called it: *A Love Supreme*. But this *zikr*, this was better than listening to a Coltrane solo—when I could forget myself and join it, this was like *living* a Coltrane solo. I'd never known there was anything the world out there had fashioned that could take on your essential self in so fierce, explicit and comprehensive a fashion and focus it this unambiguously on the Ultimate—a means of getting at the core of life as you had always intuitively known it to be—and because of Trane it felt like home. I thanked my lucky stars and took my chance with every wave that came my way.

Reshad nudged the tempo faster again and must have given a more general permissive nod: I didn't catch it, but there would have been some cue before the first person stood up and walked to the center of the circle, folded his arms across his chest, bowed in Reshad's direction, and began to turn.

About half the house was absorbed in *zikr* and didn't watch, or slit an eye open for a moment only, but I kept a lookout and wondered if folks in general had had the taste of eternality as I'd been given it, or had been given something else, or more, and did they get it all the time and would it show?

Everyone had his or her own style of turning, and I didn't learn much by looking. I remember that Maurice Clarke and Richard Waddington each had a go that night, and Hugh Tollemache, it's possible, might have taken one of his rare, graceful but rather stoic-seeming turns. Some turned for a minute before wrenching to a stop and bowing again before Reshad, and others took five; Lomand probably had a shot at it. A woman or two stepped forward, and I'd bet that one of them was Sally. The men surprised me, toward the end of their turns, by bellowing out "Allah!" usually with their eyes wide open, and I wondered with autonomic naïveté Were they seeing God? Was energy pouring through their hearts in such a way they must cry out? Or what? The experience of suprapersonal eternity, no, there was nothing to bellow about in that.

The tempo of *La ilaha ill'Allah* had increased as if along a hyperbolic curve progressively nearing a theoretical infinity of speed, but all this accumulating onrush of forward locomotion was brought not quite screeching to a halt by Reshad's sudden resounding imposition of another *zikr* that crushed the tempo flat with a thrust of his head down to his chest, left of center, bonded to a prolonged forceful *Huuuuu*, after which his head swung up to fling a loud *Allah* in heaven's rough direction over his right shoulder. Reshad had begun what I'd been told was the Qadiri *zikr*, central to the practice of the dervish Order that descended from Abdul Qadir al-Gilani, to whom God had licensed, about nine centuries back, the use of might and power. I knew in rudimentary fashion that *Hu* was the interiority of Allah beyond aspecting, metaphysically prior to Creation, and could intuit that the practice was meant to plunge that beyond-nameness deep inside ourselves, from which slash of descent we might rise to more unbounded worship, heated by an innerwork of flame—this *Hu Allah Hu Allah Hu Allah* became my favorite *zikr* on the spot. Let it burn me all away, I must have prayed, in those words or none . . . let this longsought love find completion . . . preexistent, foreordained, accomplished-in-eternity . . . let this love find due completion . . . With recurrent slow implosions the *zikr* picked up speed and the drums fell in with the rhythm.

This would be the time, I thought, for Jafar, adept in the Qadiri Turn—small steps, both feet moving very fast—to take a spin, but he favored the moment with flairs of accent and acclamation on his treble drum, and someone else stepped forward to perform a turn that seemed inadequate to the moment's energies. The *zikr* engaged me more completely and I kept my eyes shut for a stretch of minutes. When they opened, their lids heavied by my absorption—I hadn't noticed his subtraction from the drumming—Jafar was at the beginning of his turn. I had missed his entrance upon the boards.

His arms were still compressed across his chest, a hand atop each shoulder, as he turned with rapid shufflings of his small feet in white socks, his bullet-shaped head in its cap of hair bent down and canted left as if listening—all this strongly reminiscent of an athlete in preparation, and of a bat sheathed in its wings—and then, after a few more revolutions, Jafar opened, not with the slow unfolding Reshad had shown me and the others had attempted, but snapping his arms wide, almost audibly, with a sense of absolute orthography—no transition between the semaphore of one letter to the next and his arms unbending shafts extended either side, one palm down, the other as unambiguously up, his face serious, intense—he was a human propellor set for full speed ahead. I searched the air for signs of energy descending or a visible White Tornado but couldn't do it. He was cool to watch anyway: he went at the turn with a dynamic, I-am-there theatricality of presence no one else had managed, and from the projectile thrust of head to the small muscled shoulders down through his chest and narrow hips, short legs and diminutive feet, he looked as if he might either drill his way through the floorboards into the earth or take off buzzing for the empyrean. Not unexpectedly he belted out the night's most stentorian ALLAH! then wrenched himself to a sudden stop facing Reshad and bowed low, trembling with the end of whatever intensity had passed through him, wobbling slightly side to side.

He held the bow a beat longer than anyone else had, then shuffled, with small rapid steps, head and shoulders low, back to his seat with Anton and Latif, where after a pause he picked up his drum and resumed the rhythm.

Post-Jafar and after a pause there came a moment that might have had my name on it—a space at the moment's center in my shape, and I felt something like a nudge from behind but chickened out anyway, with my cowardice a probably visible blot in the center of the floor.

A longish stretch of *zikr* rose and fell through waves of who knows what individual and collective cognitions and then Reshad stepped up, his turn more graceful than anyone else's, with the smoothest motion and most beautiful curvature of arms, but lacking in excitement—because he was more knowing and refined than the rest of us?—but he managed a loud AL-LAH! before retiring anyway. Reshad's turn was the capstone, and the *zikr* ended about a minute later on a more or less climactic note. When the circle breathed itself nearer stillness, Reshad droned something sotto voce in Arabic, we all said *Huuu* in a descending cadence and flung ourselves forward in a bow, foreheads to the floor, and held it for at least a five-beat. There was no signal for us to rise but we managed something nearly unison, with one or two holdouts remaining prostrate for a further span.

We stood. Then followed something no one had prepped me for, a procession around the circle, begun by Reshad followed by those to his right in a circuit past those of us who remained in the circle, bowing each to each, hand on heart, saying *salaam*, and by the end of it everyone had joined the procession and said *salaam* to every other person in the room.

This ended the ceremonial portion of the evening. Then came kisses all around, given lightly cheek to cheek—everyone turning to his neighbor with a delighted look, bodies arched apart, and I found it predictably embarrassing: what expression to wear? how happy to seem? what to cover my out-of-placeness with and how? Anton, though courtly and impersonal, was a particular problem, and I felt myself seen through by Reshad and Siddiqa although their behavior was seamlessly courteous. I made no connection between this moment's ceremony and the exalted ceremonial sense in which, once upon a time, I'd seen the whole of life; which is how it goes a lot of the time, but I still wonder why not one spark of intellect or intuition lit up and jumped the gap.

After *zikr* fruit bowls made the rounds, and after that tea, tobacco and conversation were on offer in the Quiet Room for those who wanted it. I kept it up for as long as I could, then crept back to the North Barn and my box of Transylvanian earth.

7

MY YOUNG LIFE IN THE turbine of Beshara days and nights.

I gave myself to the place as wholly as I could and with all the hope I could muster but some force had sealed my jaw shut and I hardly spoke a word to anyone. Back in California I had tried, once or twice, to share my sense of predestinate felicity with a sympathetic friend or two in Lomand's group but had gotten puzzled looks back and some careful sentences about how our spirituality was something we had to build with main force and against the odds.

Now here I was, where the bravest hopes I'd dared were taken as simple truth, and our days and nights devoted to fleshing out that body of hope into fully functioning human form, and I could hardly speak a word. I felt dazed with privilege and at the same time terribly unworthy, and I still thought there was a chance I'd been put there by mistake. Oddly enough, Reshad's last word—there wasn't room for me, I could stay till he got back and then we'd see—seemed an irrelevant buzz. I was far more afraid of my own established and complex capacity for failure, and nerved myself up to say as much to Lomand one afternoon in the otherwise empty dining room.

"Man I feel so privileged to be here," I told him, "but I'm afraid of screwing up. I don't know how to live up to this. I feel as if everything I know how to do is . . . I'm afraid of doing something wrong, everything wrong."

Lomand recomposed himself on the bench and unnerved me with one of his math-wiz grins but came out with an arithmetically satisfying proposition: "Right now there isn't anything you can do wrong. At the moment you don't know enough to make a mistake. Mea and I have been here awhile and we've been given some responsibilities, and people like Latif or Hugh have responsibilities they might make a mistake about, but right now your job is to hang out, learn what you can and have a good time. There's no mistake you can make. You aren't at that level yet."

"You sure?"

"I'll tell you something else," Lomand said. "I couldn't put a group of people like this together in the States."

"No?"

"Don't you think this is a pretty impressive bunch of folks?"

"I suppose so. It hadn't occurred to me."

"Take a look, Koren. You couldn't come up with this wide a variety of personality and essence types in America."

"Aha." He had an odd way of putting it of course, but I saw what he meant.

"It's an impressive bunch. Take a look at Hugh, or David Hornsby."

Really? It hadn't occurred to me to be impressed by them. They were interesting, different, I didn't know their world at all and had little grasp of them as personalities. They were polite, I'd give them that.

"Then someone at the other end of the social scale like Hakim, with a heart like his and his capacity for devotion. And I don't know where in America I could find a Fool of God on the level of Anton."

"Uh-huh." Is that what Anton was?

"I couldn't find people of that calibre in the States." I noticed that he was still in proprietary mode. "Meanwhile, Koren, take it easy. If you're here, hm, it's probably because you're supposed to be, so enjoy the ride."

Aside from this confession to Lomand, an occasional Pass the salt please and some light conversation with Shing, I could hardly bring my-self to speak a word. All right, this silence had some history in me—I'd felt from early childhood that the most essential things could not be spo-ken, and here essential things were foremost—but my jaw felt unneces-sarily locked in iron.

THE WEATHER CAME and went. If I'd been expecting grey English misery I never saw it. Occasionally we had a spot of rain, and now and then a wash of clouds would veil the sunlit skies over Shalla, but this too would pass. It was a mostly golden early summer—in memory, much of it spent reclining on the lawn after lunch and watching fleets of cloud sail past—as I learned my way around the place.

The days went their appointed round of wake-up, meditation, meals, work and nighttime spiritual jam sessions with one significant addition: 'Arabi sessions every couple of mornings. I'd heard about them and had at first wondered if they were some kind of language course. In a way, they were. After breakfast and washup we'd meet in the Front Room for an hour, with Latif at the head, and read The Twenty-Nine Pages, which were, of course, more than thirty pages long in the wornout print of a foolscap mimeograph of a typescript. They constituted a précis of the thought of Muhyiddin Ibn 'Arabi, born in 1165 C.E. in Spain, deceased in Damascus 1230, and evidently considered the sum and summit of all Sufi metaphysical gnosis and discourse. The Pages were foreworded by a heretical-sounding quatrain—

> *My existence is through You*
> *And Your appearance is through me;*
> *But if I had not appeared*
> *You would not have been.*

—and the method of study seemed an odd one: each of us had a copy of the Pages and one by one we read from it aloud—typographical errors included: I will always regret the nonexistence of the word "arretion,"

which for us occupied a necessary niche between an assertion and an ar-
rogation: Ibn 'Arabi "cannot be contemptuous enough of people who
make such arretions." *Right!*—in a casual circuit of the room, a couple of
paragraphs apiece. If a question came up we'd talk about it before moving
on, and although we kept to the language when we could, it was less an intellectual discussion than a probing of the existential implications of the
text, most often in a sequence that defied formal logic. The method made
clear that Latif wasn't our teacher, although it was given to him to open or
close discussions as he chose. The language of the Twenty-Nine was not
for the most part devotional or metaphorical but abstract. For example:

> This is the Divine Essence, of which we can predicate nothing except
> bare existence. It is unknowable and incommunicable when regarded in
> abstraction and apart from any relation or limitation whatever. It is ulti-
> mately indefinable and, like a substance, it can only be described in terms
> of its "states" which, in this case, are the phenomenal world. Its nature
> admits of no opposition or contradiction (*didd*) or comparison (*mithl*)
> yet it unites in itself all qualities and quantities . . . This is the state of
> Uniqueness (*ahadiyyah*), which admits of no plurality whatever. As such,
> it is not an object of worship. The object of worship is the Lord (*al-rabb*)
> not the Unique (*al-ahad*). But such unity becomes intelligible once we
> admit the other aspect, i.e. multiplicity, for in Itself it transcends all mul-
> tiplicity. It is the state of "the One to Whom belong the burning splen-
> dours" (*subbuhât sl muhriqât*), that is, the One the manifestation of
> Whom would cause all the phenomena of multiplicity to vanish, so that
> nothing would remain but the Real. He [Ibn 'Arabi] says, "The veil of the
> Unity (*ahadiyyah*) will never be removed; limit your hope, therefore to the
> attainment (of knowledge) of the Oneness (*wahidiyyah*), i.e. the unity of
> the Divine Names." No one knows God as He is (i.e. His Essence) except
> God, not even a mystic, for a mystic belongs to the multiplicity.

Naturally, Ibn 'Arabi contradicts aspects of this statement elsewhere
in the Pages, in an apparent whirl of incompatible affirmations and de-
nials that seemed to delineate an underlying if logically obscure consis-

tency. The Twenty-Nine Pages often seemed to us a Zen koan of extraordinary prolixity and length that confounded the rational faculty at least as often as it led it onward.

Although Ibn 'Arabi had written about three hundred books, ranging in size from pamphlets to multivolume immensities, only one book by Ibn 'Arabi was available in English at the time—a spare, sere collection of reminiscences: *The Sufis of Andalusia*—and aside from a handful of quotes and paraphrases in other volumes, for his metaphysics The Twenty-Nine Pages were all we had. I had heard—as they say in comic books—the Story of their Origin from Lomand. It appeared, in the sfumato of the relatively recent past, that Bulent had been telling people in a general way that they had to study Ibn 'Arabi, a frustrating instruction when there was no way of doing this short of learning Arabic. Then one day Grenville Collins, so one heard, while browsing through esoteric London bookshelves, found a copy of *The Mystical Philosophy of Muhyiddin Ibn 'Arabi*, by A. E. Affifi, originally published in 1938 by Cambridge University Press, a volume that attempted a summary of the Shaikh's metaphysical discourse. Collins tried to read it but couldn't make head or tail of the thing, and took his headache and the book to Bulent's top-floor flat on Eccleston Square, not far back of Victoria Station.

There was an ancillary tale of someone who'd brought Bulent another such book on Ibn 'Arabi. Bulent took one look at it and flung it out the open window with a hauteur and unconcern beyond the reach of Turkish Taxi Drivers, Associated, back on Caton Avenue.

In the case of the Affifi, however, Bulent paged through it in a slow, considered way, then raised his sandbagged eyes to Gren.

"Of course you can't make sense of it, my dyah," he said, or so went the hieratic legend. "The man doesn't know what he's talking about. But why don't you leave the book with me for a few days?"

When Collins returned, Bulent handed him back the book. "Take it home and read only the parts I've underlined," he said.

This done, Collins came back and told Bulent it was remarkable, then wondered if he could show it around or, better, type up the underlined bits so that everyone could read them.

"What a good idyah," was Bulent's opinion. "Please do type it up and let me have a look when you're done."

The underlined passages, mostly direct quotation and close paraphrase of original text by Ibn 'Arabi, lacked complete continuity even after Bulent supplied some connective tissue and clarification, but they did manage to set forth, in the systematic fashion that Ibn 'Arabi himself usually abjured, and in concordance with Western philosophical terminology, a coherent beginner's summary of what the *Shaikh al-Akbar*—the Greatest Shaikh, as the tradition called him—had thought and written. In its first version the typescript was twenty-nine pages long, and although it had gone through some edits and emendations since, the title had stuck.

I heard this story early on from Lomand, but because of the haphazardness of communication at Beshara and then the vicissitudes of history, it would be thirty years before Jafar, for instance, heard the story from me, until which time he had been certain that The Twenty-Nine Pages had been written by Bulent from scratch.

Lomand also suggested that if I "wanted to check out this 'Arabi dude some more" I should read Titus Burckhardt's *Introduction to Sufi Doctrine* and Henry Corbin's *Creative Imagination in the Sufism of Ibn 'Arabi*,*— expensive, but there was a copy floating around that I could get a look at—but for the time being I let these suggestions ride.

Latif's style of 'Arabi-session management was both idiosyncratic and laissez-faire, with occasional references to magging readazines with Rindercella and her three sisty uglers and a tendency to say *Attention, attention, s'il vous plaît* if discussion veered too far off course or grew unintelligibly polyphonic.

As for the substance of the Pages, a great deal of it had to do with a question I'd had a snicker at when I'd first encountered it at the age of twenty in the pages of *Molloy*: What was God doing with Himself before the Creation? According to Ibn 'Arabi He had been beyond all description and qualification—and still was, despite the complications of the

---

*Now available in paperback as *Alone With the Alone*, with a quixotically misguided introduction by Harold Bloom. Then again, maybe Shakespeare *was* a Perfect Man.

sequel—and then, supratemporally, not in time, had seen all the possibilities of the manifest universes implicit within Himself and, struck by the
beauty of the project—"I was a hidden treasure and I loved to be known,"
He was quoted as having said, "So I created the world, that I might be
known"—had Mercy on these possibilities, allowing them to manifest
collectively and individually, first as forms or ideas in Himself, then in all
the complications and concatenations of space and matter, including
every single syllable of recorded time. Finally, the point of the exercise is
achieved when the Perfect Man, in his complete receptivity of the Essential self-revelation and manifesting all the Divine Names without excep-
tion, mirrors the Absolute Ipseity back to Itself.

I was particularly interested to read about what Ibn 'Arabi called the
a'yân al-thabita, or fixed potentialities. According to the Pages, everything that exists in the manifest order first has its being, already particularized, in a state of latency in the Divine self-knowledge, as forms of Its
own self-revelation; and although the Pages emphasized the *a'yân* as individuated forms and modes of the Divine Itselfness or Ipseity, under-
standably enough according to my experience I focused on the *a'yân* in a
more personal way. My vanity was especially pleased to take note of the
following passage: "Ibn 'Arabi holds that it is not so impossible for a true
mystic to obtain knowledge of the *a'yân al-thabita* themselves, particularly his own *'ayn* [the singular of *a'yân*]. He says, 'Or it may be that God
reveals to him his *'ayn al-thabita* and its infinite succession of states, so
that he knows himself in the same way that God knows him, having derived his knowledge from that same Source.' "

Well, I thought, buffing my fingernails on a nonexistent lapel, I
haven't been shown the infinite succession of states implicit in my *'ayn*
but I've certainly seen the thing itself. Just the kind of thing that happens,
it said right there, to a "true mystic."

I was less attentive to Ibn 'Arabi's insistence that at the end of the on-
tological day there was only One Reality in existence and no multiplicity,
not even of aspects, attributes or Names—because, well, everybody knew
that and it was kind of obvious, really. Even Latif kept saying it when discussion of details got confusing: "*Attention, s'il vous plaît.* Remember,

there is only One Being," obviously an echo of a burst of Bulentian thunder, and he sometimes turned the pages to read the bit of text that advised us to "base the whole matter of your seclusion upon facing God with absolute unification, which is not marred by any form of polytheism, explicit or implicit; and by denying with absolute conviction all causes and intermediaries, whole or part."

Only my obscurer qualms of conscience told me, faintly, that my rough heartfelt approximations may not have really added up to that.

And I definitely didn't see, since things were for all I could tell complete, harmonious and peachy in the pre-manifest, why in the presence of universal mercy and compassion and for the purposes of mostly comic ceremony why—it was the rebel angels' protest, I knew—why the hell we needed this stupid bloody fucking mess down here.

I said as much once, in politer terms, at tea, to someone in the Quiet Room, and was pounced on from behind by the unseen Anton:

"You were *begging* to come down here," Anton told me. "Screaming for it, on your knees."

NATURALLY ENOUGH I TOOK my cues less from Ibn 'Arabi than from the life I saw around me every day, where bliss seemed multiform and promiscuously available, as if upon one's least demand. All Paul Kushnazib Finegan, wrapped in the teepee of his morning blanket, had to mention was that line of light extending from heaven's linchpin to the inmost dot of earth and its passage up and down your spine on your breath and you were off on whatever flight the wings of morning might provide. All you had to do was sit there for celestial honey to pour upon you by the bucketful. Every door we knocked at opened, every window filled with its characteristic slant of universal light. Children unaccountably favored by fortune, we were free to play in the summer generosity of the Garden.

As such, we were perhaps only a topmost curl of seafoam riding the crest of the purest greedy gimme culture the world had seen so far, and we could hardly keep from helping ourselves to it by the handful. It was psychedelia without the drugs. It was what we knew.

"He was, and there was nothing with Him," The Twenty-Nine Pages advised us, "and He is now as He was then." This seemed to be our paradoxical, maybe inconceivable goal, and we set out to know Him as we were assured He was and in the grace of His favor. We were answered by a series of ecstasies and visionary states large and small, high and low, and I for one took that as the go-ahead: this is how we were to proceed, by revelations and experiences progressively more elevated, inclusive and refined through the aurora of His emanation until band by band of this spectrum we advanced upon the shores of primal light.

We were advised to offer our selves and problems up, and I did, and my difficulties seemed to rise from me like sheaths of mist, like silks unknotted and drawn one by one from within my sometimes trembling flesh, and were taken: one day, I felt sure, one day soon I'll disentangle the last of these secondary scarves from my essential core and be free.

My occasional reading of the Bible had begun to seem dips into my journal, the episodes only lightly recast as metaphor: the descent of the early, innocent Joseph of myself into the Egypt of bondage, time served and then, once a sufficient Moses had been achieved, the preordained return of Israel through the parted sea, the narrow passage between the solar plexus and the heart . . . though, okay, including forty years in the Sinai Desert and all one's lesser selves dying off and even Moses not making it all the way—but really, how long could a little detail like *that* take in a place like this?

In the meantime, back on earth, there was slavery enough. Trusting myself to the reign of grace I tried to quit smoking a few more times and still didn't make it; and the simultaneous feeling of luck and unworthiness remained, as did the lockjaw it enforced. All right, my uncertainty about acceptance, even of having a right to life on earth, derived from my problems with my mother and all that blahblah, and it seemed a shame, not that my mother didn't love me—and anyway, she did—but that given an overarching merciful Order we should have been given natures so susceptible of being warped out of true by such a basic bump in the road, perhaps for life: why? What purpose did it serve, that our natures could be skewed aside and kept there by the simplest flaw of circumstance?

What good was it to have such fundamental defects worked into the weave of us? . . . Okay, it kept the shrinks in business, but was it such a wonderful way to spend the precious pennies of our time? We were created wise, pacific, contemplative, loving, free . . . What were we doing down here with the bodkin, amid the blessing of a golden world freely given, still worrying To be or not to be?

I surprised myself by loosening up enough to say some of this in my interview with Grenville Collins, whom we were supposed to call Ghalib, though I had some trouble with the uvular diphthong at the start. As part of his tenure in Reshad's absence, Ghghaalib summoned everyone to the Cottage for an interview, or at least so summoned those he hadn't known for donkey's years. My name would have hovered near the top of the list, beating its anxious wings in the strata of the social alphabet.

Sue Collins noted my entrance with a measured hello and what seemed a disapproving look before pointing the way upstairs.

I didn't know who this former manager of the Kinks was to me, what to make of his size, his not-quite-effeminate-but-what-else-to-call-them manner, features, and flop of dark blond hair, or what to tell him, so I blurted out a portion of plain truth. "I feel incredibly lucky to be here. It's a community . . . I mean, if I'd known how to talk about God like this, or have such hope . . . I can't believe there's an actual place like this and that I'm in it . . . but at the same time I feel so low and fundamentally unworthy, so weighed down by problems I should have shucked off on my own, I don't know what to do or how to be here right."

Flung in a loose array across the Eames chair—he had moved it, and the ottoman on which I sat, beside the daylit windows—Ghalib seemed to think about it for a longish time, and while he did so I felt a palpable heat emanating from him as if from an oven. What the hell is this? I wondered. I half-expected all these people to possess super-powers of some kind, but this was heat, purely thermal, and not body heat either. What was *that* supposed to mean?

He must have told me to wait and see, and to be patient, and that everything would be clearer in time, as I went along. Without much transition, or after a transition lost to memory, he began telling me something about Bulent. "I asked him, Bulent, what's this I hear about you sitting in a black magic circle with the Rolling Stones? Bulent laughed and said, My dyah, don't you know that the best way of breaking up a circle is from the *inside*?"

Ghalib laughed in an accomplished manner while I chortled alongside and tried to work this new piece of the jigsaw puzzle into place.

"And just the other day," Ghalib resumed, "I heard yet *another* story about Bulent, and I had to ask him, What's this I hear about you in deep conversation with the Prime Minister? and Bulent told me, Yes, Mr. Heath and I did have a little chat—it just seemed to *happen*, but I don't know why: can you think why, my dyah, the Prime Minister should pay any attention to *me*?"

I didn't know what to make of this story either, but noted the self-delighted tone he'd lent Bulent's closing line: a grown man's playful version of an "innocent" child.

"You know," Ghalib said, in his liquid basso, the slowest pour of dark molasses, and by the sound of it I judged that he had reverted to my difficulties as a recent immigrant to Beshara, "in the traditional training of the Mevlevi dervishes, new initiates are sent to the kitchens. They stay there for months, sit in a corner and watch the cooks—cooks are very important among the Mevlevi—and every once in a while, they get up to practice the Turn, with a spike between their toes. They bleed, of course, and the cooks put salt on the wound to disinfect it." He lofted a hand into the air. "That's not practical here, but I wonder, do you cook? Do you like to cook? And more to the point, are you at all *good* at it, my dyah?"

"Not bad," I told him, though all I had going at the time was good spaghetti sauce and a rudimentary American sense of curry.

"There's always need for help in the kitchen. Why don't you volunteer to help with a meal once or twice a week?"

The wave of oven heat emanating from him seemed to reach its apex at that point, then faded, and I was set beside the stove to rest and let my juices settle.

"Sounds like a good idea," I told him. "I'll ask."

"Very good," said Collins. "And do come see me if you encounter any difficulties. Any sort of difficulties at all."

THIS BEGAN MY CAREER as the Pancake Fiend. I probably got through making lunch following orders like a good sous-chef—chop those, slice that, would you sauté these please—but Briar made the fatal mistake of asking me what we should make for dinner.

I thought Briar's question over for a long moment and then was struck by a sudden inspiration. "Pancakes," I said, and we were off to the garden with a basket. We ended up with a tottering multilayered gateau alternating cauliflower in white sauce and banana curry, with intermissions of chard.

Briar was a shortish reddish plain pleasant woman about my age, I guessed, with a potted cut of auburn hair, who surprised me—I'd made her as a member of the peasantry—with tales of the exclusive school she'd attended in the Scottish Highlands, where one of her underclass charges was Her Royal Highness Princess Anne, and how sometimes she would crack young Anne to order with a "Wind*sah!*"

Over the dinner preparations, begun at four, as we set to work in a medium-well-appointed kitchen too small to turn out meals for the general population of seventeen or so and double that on weekends—one four-burner gas stove with one or two of the burners usually out of commission—I relaxed enough to pry my jaw open and let a story or so out. Right away I found out that what went over best were tales of America as a half-savage wilderness, and these weren't hard to find, with Mississippi in the lead—hunted by the Klan on the Delta and cornered while laughing hysterically with Dinah Lopez was good—and Brooklyn for backup.

A couple of days later I was in the kitchen with Ruth West, building another tower of pancakes. Ruth was a sly conversationalist once she got going—her mother was a practitioner of radionics, that electronic voodoo healing done over great distances involving dials and meters on an impressively techno-looking black box—but before long I was cranking out manic

American gothic at increasing speed and volume, and when I happened past the small inset square of window on the panelled wood partition that separated the kitchen from the dining room I saw the top of Kushnazib Finegan's head as he leaned not so nonchalantly on the other side, listening through the wall.

Who knew this stuff would play so well?

OUTSIDE THE KITCHEN'S SAFE CONFINES, I was as silent as at least a couple of tombs. In part since I felt barred from the natural company of my own kind, I fell into hanging out with Shing and to a lesser extent with Big Hakim. Though it was not much of a fall: along with his own good qualities Shing possessed what I took to be the natural gentility of a Buddhist. Unlike the interesting Sufi egoists around, he seemed to have an actual interest in other human beings and to be capable of noncombative friendship. He had found his way into the wilds of Beshara in the wake of someone now named Shamseddin, whom he'd known in the Tibetan Buddhist monastery up in Scotland, Samye Ling.

There were a number of absent friends whose names were echoed about the place with special fondness and usually a laugh, though the expected accompanying anecdotes never materialized—there were a Khalil and Layla in London and a Ruhani and Helen in Edinburgh, and Fattah was mentioned often. Shamseddin seemed to be perhaps the first among these equals.

"Shamseddin doesn't know why he came here either," Shing told me. "It just seemed to happen to him."

I asked him for more detail.

"Oh, he's just this big orange Buddha—he doesn't wear robes anymore but always dresses in orange. You'll see," was all Shing would tell me. "What does Koren mean?"

"Grey-eyed." In my case the Ouija board had restricted itself to physical description.

Shing peered, squinted: "There's a little . . ."

"They pick up whatever's around," I said.

It turned out that Shing Tao-Mao, diminutive king of the deck of cards, had begun life as Michael Pearl, nice Jewish boy from London. "My mother calls me String," he said. "String, she calls me. Oh Stri-ing. Here, String."

Shing filled me in on the current state of esoteric Britain, the schools niched here and there, the foibles of this bunch or that: the folks up in Findhorn who talked to the spinach devas and grew luscious vegetables on barren sand, and how they'd got their start via R. Ogilvie Crombie, a wonderful old man who'd met the Great God Pan while strolling in Edinburgh's Botanical Gardens; the people who fetched up damaged by the Maharaji, the thirteen-year-old Perfect Master with acne, run as a family business by his mother and who had been taught, Shing told me, the rather easy trick of opening people's third eye, which produced enough of a spiritual sensation to fork the money over—Divine Light was the name of the Maharaji's outfit, and a lot of people had been damaged by him and needed healing. A lot of people came to Beshara by that route, Shing said. Others were still wandering around out there, lost.

Our conversations took on a heavier tone when Hakim showed up to express his unshakable devotion to the Shaikh and the Woon. Shing in his turn seemed quite devoted to Hakim. We would sit in the stableyard cottage Hakim and Shing shared, or outside it—I stayed off anything upholstered because of my allergy to Shing's cat Govinda, who was polite and kept her distance—and Hakim would brew up a pot of tea on a burner atop a gas tank about the size of an anarchist's bomb and we'd sit and shoot the breeze.

Hakim was welcoming, he didn't condescend or play at privilege, he was wised up about people but remained openhearted, he worked like a plowhorse and was not so solemn about the certainties of his faith as to lose his sense of humor.

Gradually, from him and Lomand and a stray of other sources, I was able to put together a working draft of Beshara's foundation narrative.

Bulent's portion of it was fragmentary and abrupt. Highborn in the Ottoman dynasty, as a young man he wore four new shirts a day but with the end of the Empire the money went too, although he later married into King Farouk's family in Egypt, and eventually became what he became outside the traditional means of spiritual transmission, at which point, in Latif's recitation of the tale, a certain man in Turkey shouted at him, "What are you doing here? You're supposed to be in England! It's all going to happen there!" then died practically on the spot, but not before telling Bulent that in the future many would come to Him by the Way of Science.

The Reshad story was contrastingly rich in anecdotal detail. Out of a busy miscellany of prior lives: pots of family money, Eton, officer in the Royal Navy (where as Wrong-Way Feild he maneuvered an entire fleet into the middle of an active minefield), then a successful folksinging career culminating with his years in the Springfields alongside Dusty and her brother Tom, "biggest thing in England before the Beatles," which was news to me, then freelance psychic who located the bodies of a few missing persons for Scotland Yard until it freaked him out, then a practice as one of the better-known psychic healers, which is how he met Siddiqa, and a parallel lucrative career at the top of the antiques trade, where without so much as a shop to keep up he could buy what he liked and sell it off to rich folks who respected his acumen, his taste . . . Charming, gifted, charismatic Tim Feild, as he was then called, lately toughened by some Gurdjieff work, was bound to find a big-name spiritual teacher who would want the use of him. This turned out to be Pir Vilayat Khan, whose father Hazrat Inayat Khan, a gifted poet and musician, had originated the explicitly ecumenical Sufi Order (an evolution of the venerable Chishti Order that continued its emphasis on music, dance and devotion) earlier in the century, beginning in his native India. In a poetic mode recalling Rilke, Hazrat Inayat Khan had left his *baraka* after his death to the yellow rose—a few specimens grew at Beshara, in a bit of well-tended earth along the wall beside the bell—and Pir Vilayat, whose aquiline features were handsomely framed by his sweeping white hair, tonsured beard, and the robes he favored, maintained the Sufi Order worldwide, except in those countries in which his brother Fazil, of whom one saw no photographs around Swyre Farm, had won his case for title in courts of law.

Tim Feild was established as a Shaikh of the Order and its official head in Great Britain. Pir Vilayat himself was international in scope, with a foot down in India, the States, Hawaii, and Sufi Camps up in the Alps in the summer. The Order paid elaborate respect to all the major traditions as enunciations of a single Truth, and the expression was long on sound and colors, angel-spheres and lines of light: it was floral, effusive, romantic lovely stuff that welcomed thousands of lovely people in.

It was at about this time, the story went, that Reshad browsed his way into a curio shop one day and came upon a large, older Turkish gentleman behind the counter who made an extraordinary impression upon him. Reshad quickly asked him if he knew anything about dervishes—as the opening pages of Reshad's book *The Last Barrier* relate—and Bulent replied, "What an extraordinary question. Why do you ask?"

Reshad gradually got to know him, and couldn't have been more pleased: this man was immense. In presence, knowledge, sophistication and apparently in power, he dwarfed any other spiritual teacher out there—Reshad had seen them all, and it wasn't that Bulent had More of what the rest had: Bulent was another order of individual entirely, not a difference of degree but one of kind: it was a fond dream come true: in the language of the day, he had found one of the Hidden Masters— Bulent kept telling him I'm not your teacher, I'm no one's teacher, I'm not anything, but that's just what he *would* say. Reshad alone of all the seekers had found one of the Hidden Great Ones: one of Them. Pir Vilayat is your teacher, Bulent said, and one last thing, please don't tell anyone about me.

This of course was impossible for Reshad, and at Sufi Order meetings, first in Reshad's apartment and later, as the congregation grew, in a church in the Portobello Road—at one point Reshad had a shaikh's robe run up for him by Pierre Cardin, blue exterior, white within, and eighteen buttons at the yoke to symbolize "the eighteen Sufi tests"—people started hearing about a Certain Someone, occasionally referred to as He Whose Name We May Not Speak. Sometimes Bulent attended a meeting as quietly and anonymously as he could, although he had a certain tendency to leave some of those who noticed him feeling splattered.

Eventually Bulent consented to meet a few of Reshad's people for an evening of conversation. He spoke simply and directly about religion as a necessary instrument of social order for the masses, and of the availability of essential knowledge of the Reality as It is for those who chose it: direct, without intermediary or mystification and with as little formal apparatus as possible: a possibility that had recently become both more available and necessary. When asked where he thought such a Path might thrive, he said Why here, among modern, evolved, Western minds, like yours.

Bulent and Pir Vilayat had never met, and their tandem tutelage of Reshad seemed free of conflict. In the signature story on this subject, when Reshad thought it was time for a change of name, he asked Bulent, who told him to ask his teacher, whereupon Pir Vilayat told him ask his teacher, and after a few yo-yoings Pir Vilayat finally said, Your name is Reshad, and he went to Bulent who said Hello Reshad, how good of you to come by, my dyah.

When it was time to establish a place outside of London where more than weekly meetings and meditations were possible, Bulent approved the property on a visit—it's to be called Beshara, he told Reshad, and when Reshad asked him what that meant Bulent said, Omen of good news; in the Quran it is what the angel Gabriel says to the Virgin Mary when she is startled by his sudden presence—but he had not been back to it since. It wasn't ready yet. The readiness, we gathered, was up to us.

In the meantime there were Sufi Order invocations before meditations at Beshara, Sufi Order ceremonies on Sunday, and from Bulent's side came an emphasis on Ibn 'Arabi, service, less music and dancing and emphasis on angels, and more rigorous and frequent *zikr*.

My own impression was that despite the sometimes elaborate practices and ceremonies and pictures of winged hearts about the place, Beshara wasn't essentially about the Sufi Order.

The Hu that most established Beshara residents wore was one of Bulent's few nods, or perhaps was his only nod, to a visible mark of affiliation. Originally it was one of a series of small charms Bulent had designed on commission for a one-off charm bracelet done in gold for a wealthy client of an associate; and the man who'd commissioned it was so pleased with Bulent's work that he took one of the dangles and made a large one for Bulent as a thank-you gift in addition to the fee. Bulent seemed to have taken this as a sign, and put it on. Like all but one of its eventual copies—only Reshad wore one made of gold—Bulent's was silver.

No presumption that Beshara was the one true church of God or that we were His elect.

It was a good romantic founding myth, all of it, I thought.

THE WORKING ORDER OF the Beshara Centre required far less explanation, and received less than it required. The population swelled on weekends, people with bedrooms of their own took on roommates, each visitor was assigned a personal minder, and every day, perhaps as an extrapolation of Reshad's time in the Navy, where there was always an officer of the watch, someone in the resident population was responsible, turn and turn about, for all the doings of his particular "day": make sure everyone woke up and porridge was ready in time, that work crews went off adequately staffed—although when Lomand rationalized the process with a rota this job became one of simply checking up—that the kitchen was stocked with the needful and the gas was working, and whatever else came up as the arc of day panned by. Monday nights in the Front Room there was something called a Moot, in which any frayed or forgotten practical details were brought up and we were threatened again with Mr. Bennett's school for consciousness: people, *please* see to the rubbish after washup; the hole dug in the North Barn slope is marked, but please pay attention and don't stumble into it in the dark; let's all try to be more aware; is there anything else?

With the Moot disposed of, someone might put a record on. David Hornsby's Bang & Olufsen stereo was stocked with precisely five albums: the Beatles' *Rubber Soul*, the first Moondog album on CBS, an excellent EMI recording of Fauré's *Requiem*, and two albums of Mevlevi music, one from the UNESCO series documenting the whirling dervish *sema* and the other a Turkish studio date mixing instrumental music with choral numbers. *Rubber Soul* was apparently never played and the Moondog album surprised me: I'd seen Moondog in New York, apparently living in a doorway on Sixth Avenue, a scary blind whitebearded longrobed man wearing horned Viking headgear, and I expected sounds of urban chaos and car exhaust; but it turned out that he composed music of charming innocence and polyphonic order, and that a haunting tune for alto saxophone and ostinato strings that had come and gone unannounced on jazz stations revealed itself to be his "Lament for Bird."

Hearing Mevlevi music for the first time was an experience of another order. The first piece on the UNESCO record was the *Na'at*, a setting of Jelaluddin Rumi's hymn to the Prophet, performed unaccompanied by a blind singer named Kani Karaca who had one of the most extraordinary voices I'd ever heard; four or five times in the course of the *Na'at* Karaca soared through an elongated, ornamented melody identical to the setting of the word "Rain" in the Beatles' song; which explained the slowdown in Jafar and Anton's version and disclosed the origin of the chorus in the Beatles' version.

The *Na'at* was followed by a solo improvisation for ney, the Turkish end-blown bamboo flute in the approximate range of the European alto flute. The throb of recognition the ney set off in me when I heard its breathy voice ascend through the stages of its song as if through the chambers of my body, was a doubling of what I'd felt the first time I'd heard modern jazz—This Is Your Life—but it was less about an identification with the music than a response to its breathtaking intimacy of expression, the sweet shocking beauty of it, the speed and sureness of hand with which it touched open at least one petal of my locked-up heart; and the spiritual core of it was indistinguishable from John Coltrane's, the same search, the same discoveries, though instead of being bashed out in midnight basements of America it had been nurtured over centuries of material and spiritual culture to blossom with as little apparent struggle as a rose. Hearing it was a time-defying experience, an inextricable compound of rediscovery and revelation, and in the instant it felt like a life-altering event.

Weekday nights in the Front Room were spiritual improvisations that sometimes had a topic, with someone, according to temperament, nominally or actually in charge. When a specific subject wasn't addressed—meditation, study, *zikr*, the nature of work, Rumi, the Uwaysi—and even when one was, things drifted toward storytelling, reminiscence, the sifting of scripture and Sufi lore. People were fond of hearing about the adolescent Ibn 'Arabi's exchange with the philosopher Averroes, then at the height of his fame: the sage had heard about the prodigious young man and invited him to the house for a chat; the discussion was intense, and at the end of it the old man asked the fifteen-year-old, Are the conclusions reached by reason the same as those found by mystical experience? Ibn 'Arabi answered Yes, and the philosopher brightened, but then Ibn 'Arabi also said No, and added, famously, "Between the yes and the no, heads are severed from their bodies and spirits take flight." And the philosopher blanched.

At that point eyes flicked over, some of them nervously, to Jafar, who burned more intensely than the rest of us and seemed readiest to leap the lethal gap between that yes and no, or to Anton, who might already be living on the other side.

As would be true in a Sufi circle of any provenance, there was among us a strong emphasis on *fana*, the passing away or annihilation of the false, merely relative self, or *nafs*, in the face and constancy of the Real. Everything passes away save His face, went one admonition, and Die before death, ran another; and Reshad had quoted Bulent on the subject more than once—"Some say there are three deaths, others say there are five deaths, but I will tell you there are *many* deaths"—and he would delineate the various circumstances in which we might die to ourselves, in *zikr*, in the smallest of our doings, and if we only were aware of it, on every breath.

Since Beshara was predominantly a place of young men, it would have been remarkable if *fana* wasn't occasionally given the macho treatment. Perhaps especially when Reshad was around, one presumptive hero or another of *fana* would get an acknowledging nod and wink on the subject, and it began to seem like high school again, with its hierarchy of who'd gotten laid yet and who had not.

The talk ran subtler courses too. One evening the *nafs* was under discussion, its relation both linguistic and actual to the breath, the difficulty of getting rid of it despite its irreality, the inadvisability of substantiating it through thinking about it too much, and onward . . . Jafar's quiet voice filled a pause: "A man I met told me that the *nafs* wasn't so important, it was next to nothing, it was a 'knot tied with water.' At first I didn't understand what he meant, then I thought of the little whirlpools after the stroke of an oar . . ."

Machismo there was, but Beshara did not indulge, thank God, in the dramaturgy of necrophiliac destruction. A paperback copy of a recent "Sufi novel" passed casually from hand to hand but wasn't, I think, much read: *The Book of Strangers*, by Ian Dallas. I liked the title but not its first pages: the skies on fire, cities toppling, the world coming to an end, and two old women grinning as the black ashes fell, nodding and cackling to each other, *La ilaha ill'Allah*. Dallas was hooked up with a Naqshbandi shaikh from Morocco, one heard, had changed his name to something triple-barrelled in Arabic, and had recently "raided" Beshara's North London or perhaps Edinburgh centre with his Myrmidons, quizzed its innocents on points of Islamic doctrine, and had insisted that you couldn't be a Sufi if you weren't a Muslim first.

It was, after all, a fiery and vigorous tradition, and even if we weren't clinging to it, the lore was full of outrageous people who ranged beyond the normal definitions of humanity and any normal sense of Law or Order, and they were natural magnets to our youthful sense of rebellion and bravado. There was Khidr in the Quran, the Green man, although the Quran did not name or color him. Moses, the exemplar of the written Law, sought him out "in the place where the two seas meet"—the juncture, link, *barzakh* between the higher and lower worlds—and asked to travel with him. Khidr tells Moses that he won't be able to stand it, Moses pleads with him and Khidr finally allows Moses to come along, but only on the condition that he not question anything Khidr does. They set off, and in short order Khidr bashes in the hulls of the boats in a village of honest fisherman, kills a young boy they meet on the road and finally rebuilds a wall in a town whose inhabitants taunted Moses and Khidr as they passed through. Moses questions him all three times, and on the third strike he's out. Before they part ways Khidr explains his actions: the fishermen and their boats would have been recruited by a tyrant for an unjust war, a pious man's secret inheritance was protected by that wall, and the boy was bad, would have been the ruin of his good parents' lives, and they would be compensated with the birth of a good child.

Which didn't smooth the story over much: this was the rough incomprehensibility of life inarguable and compact in one man, who was either associated with or identical to Elijah, who had inititated Ibn 'Arabi and given him his cloak, and whose guidance, as apprentice Uwaysi, we were supposed to seek.

People tried, nervously, not to look at Anton.

Even in David Hornsby's occasional Rumi evenings, the swooning and melting responses to the poetry would part and the tale of Rumi's meeting with Shams-i-Tabriz take the stage: how in his thirties Rumi was "opened" by a man out of nowhere whose spiritual nature was so uncompromised that no one could stand to be in his presence. Shams threw Rumi's books down a well, implicitly along with the entirety of Rumi's prior life and self and, taking him into seclusion with him, blasted open Rumi's fullblown, universal nature. Later on Shams was murdered for his pains, and his body was stuffed down a well. Afterward Rumi not only dedicated his breakthrough verses to Shams but declared him their author.

Sometimes Jafar could be coaxed into telling us about his travels in the East: how when the war hit in Pakistan when he was with Sufi Barkat Ali, they'd thrown tarps across the domes of the mosques so that the beautiful turquoise tiles would not reflect the moonlight back and give the planes a target, and how when the planes did come over all the young dervishes stayed as close as possible to the Shaikh so that if the planes bombed them they could catch the corner of his robe and ride with him to Paradise; how in Afghanistan Jafar had visited the tomb of the patron saint of thieves—he had his reasons—and prayed fervently in front of it until one of the *incredibly* tough characters who lived in the niches tossed a contemptuous handful of coins at Jafar's feet as if to say, "If you came here to *beg* . . ." There was a Shaikh who lived on a hilltop in a tent lit inside with green fluorescent lights, who asked Jafar what he did, then handed him a rough handmade broom from the corner of the tent and told him to play his best flamenco for him and Jafar did it, every note of impassioned *cante jondo* played out across the straws, and then the Shaikh accepted him as a student; and there was his jailbird friend in Istanbul who flicked his ironball prayer beads and although typically swarthy insisted he looked like Steeva McQueen and would cut Jafar's heart out if he didn't give him that sweater . . .

At this point someone would ask Jafar if he would play the guitar, and sometimes Anton, whose departure had gone unnoticed, would walk into the room with the instrument in his hands.

On other evenings, especially on weekends, when visitors had come to pack the place, the handdrums would come out, and Latif would unwrap the shakuhachi he hadn't mastered but did make actual music on, and that would finish off the evening when talk outlasted inspiration.

One weeknight Lomand was finally allotted time to read Dr. Seuss to us—the copy of *Horton Hears a Who* I'd brought over. Although attendance was not required, almost everyone came—Lomand had hinted there'd be something special—and I shuddered inwardly for him as he launched his characteristic mixture of the drily sophisticated and the utterly cornball, chuckling to himself after every other line about all the Whos in Whoville on their Horton-guarded speck of dust, but it went over fine, and if he finished the evening by strumming his autoharp and singing gospel tunes in extremely ofay fashion, that went over too.

Letters from Reshad arrived from Turkey and were read out to us. Bulent was well, sent love. Significant experiences all over the place. Many tales to tell. Lovely weather. Sid sends *çok salaams*. We are about to embark upon a new phase of the Work. Expect a big shakeup when I return. Love to all.

AFTER TEN O'CLOCK I continued my late-night attempts upon the castle of the Turn, but the Big Experience didn't happen again, and I was left with the struggles of a normal learning process step by step: feet, heart, the swing of arms, trying to get some music into the motion.

At twice-daily meditations, and in solitary sessions after *wasifas* and before the Turn, I unstrung myself from known condition the best I could, offered up my smokes and soots as if they might pass for incense above, and labored to divest myself of every narrow meanness that parted me from the ocean of sheer Being, and it always seemed I was about to get there after one last surrendered wisp would give up its ghost but no. Hadn't I:

(1) suffered, and (2) loved enough?

What else could it possibly take? I had performed the interior pot-latch. How could there be this much self-evident love and mercy pouring down and still no final resolution? How could one be seated at such a banquet and still end up famished? All this partial, emotional spiritual experience was fine, but I wanted to be lifted up for good into that objective realm of pure cognition. Not just because it was exalted but because it was deeply normal. It corresponded to human nature, to the human need to know as so-called normal life never managed to. It was the meshing of form and function, lock and key.

As for all the local talk about the heart, the struggle with that organ was beyond my strength.

One night, asleep after my session in the Barn, I dreamed that I was heading to Turkey on a train—there had already been talk of everyone going in December, to Istanbul, the Virgin Mary's house in Ephesus, and the whirling dervish festival in Konya—and there were, vaguely, other Beshara people with me on the train, but as it pulled into Zagreb, with its station sign in big capital letters, I got off to do some quick, simple thing for a minute but got lost in the unexpected intricacy of the station and the train pulled out without me, and I woke up complexly hurt.

Zagreb was lightly encoded dreamspeak for Zabor, and I wondered if that's how it would be after all this illumination and slog: lost in the station of my own impediment, without issue into the Real.

A more usual, in fact recurrent dream, one I'm sure others had in their individual versions, found me naked in some public place—Beshara, Brooklyn, Grand Central Station—wondering how the hell I'd wound up like this, crouching clothesless under the microscope, wincing beneath the acuity and persistence of the lens.

THEN THERE WERE THE working days, the sting of nettles at the base of a wall, the repeated chocking of a shovel into rocky earth, the swing of a pick under the summer sun, the wipeaway of honest sweat and a grin shared with a fellow striver, or a pause to watch the clockwork figure of Hugh emerging from his office niche facing the car park, followed humbly by his black Labrador, Becca—heavy and old now, slow on stiffening legs, with sad, faithful eyes, her name had been Mecca until Bulent requested a change. Sometimes Hugh and Becca would escort an odd character named Mr. Green, who wore a blazer even on the hottest summer day, about the property to inspect the new drainage pipes here or the bit of digging there; sometimes Mr. Green carried a clipboard and made notes on its flip of sheets, but he seemed to be a crony of the place. For all Hugh's aristocratic distinction he seemed to do a lot of drudgework—papers, not the vigorous kind that was good for one's spiritual energies.

In the meantime I spoke no essential word to anyone. To whom would I speak it and what did I know how to say? In a place where spiritual courage was the byword what pronouncement could my weakness make?

I got along with the normal people, though my silence kept me from getting to know, for instance, the women I didn't cook with, and David Hyams, a tall beaky guy I liked instinctively: he was Beshara's third architect, and I didn't make him for Jewish even though he reminded me of my uncle Joe.

One day after lunch I was first in the scullery at the stainless steel sink and double tubs of wash and rinse, working the brushes, the water hot as I could stand it, and Anton pulled up alongside me, his warrior profile impassive in the steam, plates going in, plates coming out and onto the rack, and I felt upon me with greater fixity the suit of armor that locked me in place and shut my jaw, as if Anton, who said not a word as we sluiced and soaped and rinsed and dried, were the touchstone that told false from true. The ring of my coin upon the counter in his presence always came up leaden, and it was an ordeal working clamped in place beside him, a small terror of merciless exposure, and when we finished work and had laid the last tea towel aside to dry, Anton said in parting, his voice lightly fogged and unassertive, "Thank you for being so calm."

Right.

Another time I was part of a busier team at the sinks after dinner, scrub, dunk, rinse, dry, and Jafar was part of the workforce. "You know," he told someone over his shoulder in his variable accent, "I'll tell you something about service ... Most people ... it never occurs to most people ... the altruistic impulse hardly even arises in most people except in the cusp between ... just at the beginning of puberty, when the sexual impulse has arisen but hasn't really been expressed yet."

It rang a bell, and for a moment I was back there in my protracted adolescent melodrama, announcing to myself that Since I have no life of my own I will live it for others.

Where had Jafar come up with that one? It was not the kind of thing I expected to hear from him. And if I asked him would he come out with an It's got nothing to do with me?

One afternoon I was in and out of the workshop of the North Barn, getting a hammer out of its rack or putting one back, and Jafar, stalled in the middle of hauling some lengths of lumber, was telling someone about the time in his early adolescence when he was sniffing glue in an alley and suddenly heard an audible deep accelerating voice tell him, "In your mind's eye in your mind's eye in your mind's eye," and I wondered They sniff glue in Damascus or Cairo or wherever?

Another time we were carrying a length of lumber out into the field. Jafar was behind me, being improbably funny in his thick accent and I very nearly spun on him and said, Hey listen *Jack* ... but the penny never dropped.

One afternoon I happened to see Anton vanishing through the meditation room doorway and thought clearly, There goes my friend but I'm too fucked up to spend time with him now.

Anton and Jafar reminded me of those two seventh-century Chinese Buddhist cats I'd read about in one of Lomand's Zen books: Han Shan, author of the Cold Mountain Poems, a hero of the Beats, and the cook

Shieh-Teh, hanging out in the kitchen listening to Thelonious Monk records and laughing up their sleeves at the crowd of serious stiffbacked meditators who didn't get it, couldn't swing, and probably never would.

And I knew that laughter, was familiar with the syncopations. These guys were supposed to be my friends, and the exclusion—it was just another piece of my exile from the human world.

I WORKED AT THE SCHISM between my restricted spirituality and the rest of life in prayer and meditation, in *wasifas* and the Turn and while digging a shovel into the resistant earth; which at least was a struggle I could understand.

The 'Arabi sessions were more difficult, though, and I had begun to develop a suspicion, a creeping worry . . . Ibn 'Arabi so thoroughly dismantled the faith of the orthodox—the God created in the faiths was a false, subjective God; to assert His transcendence is to limit Him; no trace of association with existing things can touch Him and He is the very existence of the things—that I began to suspect that under the cover of a laboriously articulated concordance with Islamic diktat Ibn 'Arabi was delineating an essentially nontheistic if transcendent Order, and, if only because I'd had an accusing mother and a forgiving father—a pathetic basis at best—I had turned out, against all expectation, to be the sort of person who wanted God to Be There. Buddhism got along fine without a God, and seemed all the more sensible and realistic for the divestiture, but I couldn't live in such impersonal air. Neither could I sit still that long. Ibn 'Arabi was the man with the facts, but was he really some kind of crypto-Mahayana Buddhist one step ahead of the sword of Shariah? and if so, why did we, here, at Beshara, famously going straight up beyond formal restriction, have to do a fancy dance around it?

And what about the possibility that with all our lines of light and huffa-puffa we were only dialling up cartoons on our nervous systems?

So tell me, someone, tell it straight before I go completely nuts: what is the ultimate nature of Reality already?

8

AT LENGTH THERE CAME a certain day.

I must have demonstrated some kind of competence at simple physical tasks, because three weeks into Reshad's absence I was given a real job to do and the responsibility of directing someone else to help me do it. Which turned out to be a bit of a joke: Michael Frederick knew his way around tools and a ruler—or maybe *they* (meaning mostly Lomand von Rota, to whom my mechanical incompetence was archfamiliar) knew that, and gave me charge of Frederick and the job as a small, harmlessly deceptive boost. Michael Frederick was over from America three months early for Mr. Bennett's course at Sherborne House and was stopping off at Beshara for a week of the Sufi tasting menu before continuing his pre-course travel loop. Nice guy, could have been a year or three my senior, apparent straight-arrow American, neat black hair, regular features, didn't shamble and say uhh every second word, was intelligent and had proper manners besides. In any case that was all I clocked of him at the time.

The job was in Niagara Falls.

Niagara Falls was a room at the back of the house, up the stairs above the washroom to the left of the Quiet Room, where a wooden platform had been bolted together holding three large grey open plastic tubs, each a few bathtubsful in capacity, that held water for the ablution basins and toilets immediately below. The framework of the wooden platform had been extended to accommodate the needs of Beshara's planned shower block in the works beneath, and Frederick and I were to nail down slats we'd cut to measure. If I'd been given the job alone, or if Frederick hadn't known his stuff, the best one could have hoped for was a silent movie camera on the premises to record the ladder gags, whaps and pratfalls and finally the deluge.

The platform and its tubs were scaffolded eight or ten feet up beneath the slants of roof. There was a hanging lightbulb if we needed it, but for now sufficient light entered through a window at the back. It had rained on and off the past few days and again before dawn. The sky was overcast and a greyed light fell outside on saturated green. Having climbed the creaky staircase to the room and the ladder to the scaffold, Frederick and I eyeballed the newly built structural beams and supports, the pile of roughcut lumber, and went off to the North Barn workshop for our tools.

Out the front of the House the red clay walk was puddled here and there and it was rush hour in the shop, with someone bent rattling the boxes underneath the counter to find the, where's the, amid the smell of iron and oil and the gleam of the tablesaw's teeth. A work crew up to major work was sorting planks under the soiled plastic sheeting of the lumber rack down the open end, east: Big Hakim, Richard Waddington, Jafar, a kibitzer or two. Frederick and I took the things we needed and headed back to the Falls. When we set to work I fell in with his calm competence and followed his lead in measuring board against board, aligning them in parallel and cutting ends on a slant to fit the wall. The job going well relieved me of my habitual distress and I began to take pleasure in the surd solidity of the work . . . the beautiful necessary workness of life . . . the taskness of our being here . . . the fitness not just of things but abilities . . . so that it could not have been very long before I wanted to goof off for the length of a reflective smoke.

"Join me?" I asked my workmate.

"Don't smoke."

"Mind if I take a minute?"

"Go ahead."

The world was orderly and just, and the people in it pleasant.

I sat on the edge of the scaffold—we had added to it already—and rolled a ragged Golden Virginia or Old Holborn, scratched a match, lit up, then climbed down the ladder and ambled to the little window for a look at the piece of world outside. And—it probably took me a few seconds to confirm the view point by point, but the awe and chill and tremor had already started—and that was it, this was it, there I was, I was there, here it was, this can't be real it's real: I was looking at the Garden. Of Eden, of souls, of eternal individuation out of time and space, of the *a'yan-i-thabita*, infinity and grace: that bit of broken wall, that tree, that patch of ground, the brush-stroked stand of trees beyond—exact. I felt as if all my hair had leapt to its feet and stood on end—what what what what what what *what?*

My mind began to race, my mind outran the race, the race outran my mind: lying there in the fever sheets of my cold-sweat Oakland basement— paint me a picture, somebody!—I'd been not only outside time but ahead of it, my being here had preexisted my arrival—ordained! predestinate!— and in this sudden downpour of big news—Niagara Falls!—my doubts of worthiness, the sense that I was the beneficiary of a kind mistake, or of a grace so tenuously extended it might easily be broken by the normal tremors of my own incapacity, were swept away waving their arms across the floodplain and over the falls because, no, in reality it hadn't been like that at all. My being here had been established beyond time and ahead of it, and waitaminnit check it out, precognition did not require a lift beyond the world's dimensions, only sight, so the garden had also been the Garden . . . I think. Let's deal with that later. In any case I was certainly being given a show. The lid had been cranked up and I was looking down into the works and wheelies.

All of which in the racing moment seemed some small potatoes because, widening my eyes, it seemed to me that maybe this was it—I'm about to be lifted out of time and space to rejoin my essential self in the beauty of the Real, the two moments coinciding in eternal green, in the peace of completed mind, the all-including cadence, the manyness achieved as One, here it comes, I can feel it, my body suffused with higher energy, might as well call it Light and I am trembling, here it comes . . . and I stood there, full height, palms upraised to ease the pickup, it must be coming, this is it . . . I don't know how long I stood there waiting for the bus or the angel or for that matter what I did with the cigarette but the inconceivable music remained a suggestion only, amid rolled orchestral scores and laddered scales and the inscribed tones of final Light.

Aww come *on*!

The high tremulousness of the moment declined into a lower trough of merer pleasure and I was very slow to give the higher reaches up; but I was overjoyed anyway, it was a sign, my world shaken by the slam of major portent, every nerve and pore of me still atremble ready for the rest of it.

When the moment quieted and I climbed back up to the radiance of labor I must have been quite manic, and even if I half-suppressed it I must have laughed and jabbered irrelevancies at Michael Frederick and slapped his back, in the joy and tremble, then bent to bang big iron nails into the sturdy, bready wood, the world made of plied and layered code and the objects in it not things but meanings, each on the brink of speaking loud and clear its unforgettable, characteristic word. Yes, it's the real life at last, I could feel the wave of it rising behind the scrim of these last persisting things, the mass and force and majesty of all that it implied— Joel Joel Joel I told myself, and heard my name echo down the years through rooms and streets and schools and the calmed, medallion light beneath the leaves of trees to this living moment in which the Unific truth of it out of all-subsuming Mercy was about to shake off the fragments of its superficial show, light up its particulars with the blaze of their annihilation in pure meaning and finally stand revealed.

The lifting of the final Veil, now just all atremble.

The curtain going up, show about to start.

Real life at last, crude and dumbshow mummery at an end.

Mercy, mercy. Here comes the promised, foreseen moment . . .

So, *nu*, okay, where do I look?

And how long's this gonna take?

BY TEN-THIRTY I WAS GETTING pretty antsy, felt confined there banging nails into two-by-fours in Niagara Falls for all the smell of pine, and it occurred to me I could buy myself an intermission in the front hallway, where the morning mail had almost certainly been delivered. There might be something from Jake in Israel or a letter from my folks, my mother in block print for several paragraphs of We're well, business is slow and how are you, then below that something heartfelt and worried in my father's stricken ungrammatic scrawl, my parents still uneasy about the Thank Gods with which I'd begun to punctuate the aerogrammes I mailed them when I could. I wondered if my last explanation took: it's not what you think, it's certainly not religion, and if you knew what was happening your worries for me these last years would . . . It was hard to get across but maybe my last letter had put an atom of it over.

"You mind?" I asked Michael Frederick. "I'll just check. Want a drink of water? Cuppa tea?"

"Sure."

The mail was kept on a deep windowsill in the hallway, on the right as I saw it now, a heap of envelopes no one had sorted yet.

Went there and started shuffling through brochure, nothing, nothing, a lot of English nothing, wait, aha, here's, aha, an airmail envelope, edged in bands of red and blue, American stamp, for me? No, it's for *yyyyyyyyyyyyyyyyyyyyyyyyyyyywhaat?*

Waitaminnit waitaminnit this can't be happening it's for Jafar . . . from, it looks like, his mother in America, for Jafar *Shema*, and I stood there with my jaw dropped cliché open as a multipilicity of images kaleidoscoped and resolved in a hilarious jangle of changing names and faces, phantom accents, and it's ridiculous we didn't spot the setup.

I was banging out the front door laughing, supercharged from the window vision and now this new laughfest of coincidence, where the hell is he? and running on the rainslick clay I misstepped, my feet flew out from under me and I came down hard on my left hip in a puddle, leapt up again and continued limping on the run. I asked a passing someone if he knew where Jafar was and he said the North Barn workshop—where I'd seen him last, as if the picture were holding still. I ran up the slope streaked on one side with mud and antic how the coincidence was gonna blow Jafar's mind besides which he owed me a hundred and a half.

In other words I didn't see it coming.

Made the workshop, burst through the doorway, heard the planking of the planks off to the right and there they were, sorting through lumber in its long makeshift rack with the plastic sheet flung overtop, the building open on the end with grey day showing, and most conveniently Jafar Jack Shema stood just offside the action and I checked my pace to saunter up with what still must have been a major grin, for all my sense of realistic and in-character suppression. I got his attention in any case, and I pointed at him with the hammer, a stainless-steel one with a light blue rubber grip, noticing only then that I still had a hammer in my hand, conducting the moment's rhythm up and down with it, and asked him, "Hey, d'you know we already know each other from five or six years back, New York?"

"We do?" And the natural intentness in his face as he tried to unpuzzle it, redraw the features, subtract the years, a beard, find the moment: he shook his head no. For one thing I hadn't been so pale and cadaverous then. "When? Where?"

"I'll give you a hint. I gave you some money once."

"Whadjou do, bail me outa jail?" I hardly noticed his foreign accent gone.

The other human forms in his work crew had come away from the woodrack and now began to spectate. It was certainly not the time or place to mention abortions and besides, I wanted to stretch this out, see if he could find it on his own. "Think about it. New York City, say six years back, a hundred and fifty dollars. I'll give you till lunchtime, then I'll tell you. Meantime work on it."

And back down the hill grinning and feeling metaphysically stylish for once. See me? I was blind as a bat in a hat. No idea.

I must have hammered away in Niagara in some hilarity and if so would have unleashed on poor Michael Frederick such a cataract of narrative, not about Jafar but something funny about who knows what, that he might have felt he'd gone over the Falls in a barrel with the wrong unstoppably manic companion.

Came teatime I was sipping beverage in an armchair in the Quiet Room when Jafar rocketed in, pulled up a footstool and thrust his face at me. "Look, this is driving me crazy. Who the hell are you."

I'd wanted to hold it off till lunchtime but, okay, this'll do. "All right." I lowered my voice. "Once upon a time I lent you a hundred and fifty dollars," eyeballed the room, lowered my voice still further, "for an abortion."

And that's when this little day went a little zooey.

Even at his normal settings Jafar walked around with a head of steam beyond the boiler capacity or ten strong normal men, but now I watched his eyes bulge and his face thrust forward as he went right off the scale. *"You're the guy,"* he said.

"What guy? Which?"

Jafar's racing voice insisted, *"It all started with you."*

Say what? What all started with me? I was having trouble watching Jafar's face because it was as if some portion of his visionary capacity had been transferred to me, the room behind him struck by flares and strobes of aura-light, green to yellow, blue to purple, white to red as if on superimposed panes of painted glass, a combination of church window and arcade machine—which reminded me, how funny, of a scene in one of my favorite bbbbbbb—

"*What* started with me?" I asked him, trying to get a grip.

Across the room I saw Lomand sitting up straight with his teacup in an armchair and a psychedelic grin of anticipation setting up its tents and lights and Ferris wheels across his maned, bespectacled features, but quickly spun back to Jack Jafar Shema Yisroël Wake Up Already who was about to tell me—what was he about to tell me? I lacked the specifics but did have a highly ionized suspicion that the Garden and the garden, the Timeless and the timed were all about to shazam together full-force and bigtime.

"After the abortion," Jafar began, "after I took Gina to the doctor Sharon used in Jersey—"

"I know. I went there too the year after," I told him.

"You're kidding," Jafar said, with the Middle Eastern accent working again, rolling his *r*'s. "I hope you did better than us, because after Gina's abortion . . . We thought she was all right at first but then she started running a fever, and pains, then she started bleeding, and she didn't want me to take her to the hospital—"

"Jesus."

"I got her there. She was bleeding to death. They took her in and told me about the infection, the sepsis, and they didn't know if she was gonna make it . . . I sat in the hallway praying my ass off and when they told me I had to leave I ended up in Central Park in the middle of the night, went out there, fell on the ground and said Take me, and man, I offered my soul to God or the Devil, whoever would save Gina's life I'd sign it over . . . And that's how it started with me."

"You remember when that happened?" I asked him. Things were getting strange. "The date."

"The *date*? I don't remember what *date*."

"Because that summer when I was in London—how soon after I gave you the money did you have the abortion?—because when I was in London staying at this hotel off Russell Square, the sun had gone down and I was sitting in Russell Square and all this emotion was coming at me out of nowhere . . . I was going to fall down on the ground and surrender myself to the first person who came up the path because everyone was God and one was as good as another and I knew I had to give myself up . . . You think it could've been the same night? Would have been early July."

We furrowed our brows in the direction of the calendar but didn't find anything.

"Anyway Gina made it," Jafar said.

"I know. I saw her when I got back from Europe. I got the address from Sharon, went to her apartment kind of shamefaced, thinking I was supposed to ask for the money back even though I didn't really want it. She told me she didn't know where you were . . ."

"She was great, Gina. Look how she covered for me, man. I was living with her on the weekends and working in Jersey during the week, anatomical sculpture for the medical schools, doing all the musculature, veins and arteries, internal organs, and at the same time I was taking psychedelics and getting the same information on the esoteric level. I kept asking who I was. I entered the digestive system, the circulatory system, the breath, the nervous system nerve by nerve and out again, then out of the physical, and I was asking, always asking the Question and seeing that I wasn't this, I wasn't that . . . I was having all this esoteric experience and I told my friend Gregory about it and he said he needed a sign. We were around Times Square and I said Watch this. There was one esoteric bookstore in the neighborhood, it was late at night, everything was closed, we went to the bookshop and I turned the handle and—"

"You don't have to tell me this," I said. "I've seen it."

"—the door opened. We walked in and I told Gregory, Look, it's very important for us not to take anything, which wasn't automatic with Gregory and me. He wanted a second sign, so I said . . ."

We kept swapping narratives of what had happened after life had changed, Jafar going from a thief to visionary seeker . . .

"Sometimes," he told me, "I had so much love pouring through my heart I wasn't sure I was supposed to let it out, you know, like maybe it'd change the world in a way that wasn't supposed to happen. I was out there without a license, man, and this big hole blown through my heart. I was afraid that if I let the love out I might damage things . . . I was such a kid. What happened to you when you went to the abortionist?"

"She couldn't go through with it and we ended up in Japan."

Finally something that Jafar stalled and blinked at. *"Japan?"*

"Where'd you get the accent?" I asked him. "That was one of the reasons it never occurred to me that, you know . . ."

"All the years out there in Asia I was wide open. I picked up everything that came my way. . . . Hey man, you'll like this one. One time I went down to Birmingham Alabama and found an abandoned Baptist church in the black part of town and moved into it. The local people knew me but I had to keep an eye out for the cops. There was an old

Coke machine inside the church, I ran a wire from a streetlamp and kept my food inside. And down in the basement, believe it or not there was this big white egg, with an Alice in Wonderland door in it—"

"I've seen this," I told him.

"Can you imagine? I figured the preacher used to go down there to meditate. It was white outside and inside and just big enough to stand up in. I bought some paints and painted everything I was seeing, inside the egg, waves of the ocean, waves of energy from the organs of the body to the stars, and all the centers of what I called the Heat Body—I didn't know anything, I didn't have a terminology, I was a know-nothing kid in outer space. If I found that egg today I'd leave it just as it was, perfect, white . . ."

We banged stories back and forth, oblivious to everyone in the Quiet Room, and didn't notice the end of teatime and people leaving except— "Hah. Hah"—except for Lomand, laughing in his armchair, having a great time at the movies today.

"It all started for me after the abortion too," I told Jafar, "though it looks like I went a different route."

"Doesn't matter."

"I know." But still I was shaken by the chain of circumstance reaching back to some anchor buried in the seabed of years, and got some of this out to Jafar—the completely uncharacteristic move I'd made cutting in on Gene with Sharon, and before that, the second I'd recognized Sharon walking into that room. In any case neither of us knew what we were doing together . . . and then, the even stranger thing, when I'd offered Jafar the abortion money that night and heard as if aloud *You don't know why you're doing this.*

"You know," Jafar told me, "the idea was to get you stoned and hit you up for it."

"But you didn't have to."

"No."

And how years later in Berkeley, Lomand over there—

"Hah. Hah."

"—moves into the house I was living in and I was checking him out and thinking about that group of his, and then one night after he cut this guy Nick to pieces, friend of mine, you'll meet him, he's coming to Sherborne, cut Nick to bits and I thought it was kind of ugly, so the next day I told him, You know I've been thinking about your group but after what I heard you do to Nick, that's it, it's not for me . . . And there was the same sensation—I remembered it—outside my body about three feet up and left, and the next day I'm telling Lomand, hearing the same *You don't know why you're doing this* while I'm telling him I'd join his stupid fucking group."

"Hah. Hah."

"Oh shut up," I said, but I was punchdrunk, out on my feet: it was one thing to admit the experience and deal with the existence of a higher dimension or two as long as they were abstract and objective, but this was personal, this was design, this was plot and character, and in narrative terms this was *planted* back before abortion and catastrophe and collapse. And then the recognition scene luuudicrously deferred until right after I looked out the window and saw the Tree. This was a finger with personal intent coming down out of the higher blue . . . this was setup and instruction, this was grade school novel-writing with a credibility problem, and it . . . just can't be like this.

"It is," Jafar said.

It was such a stunning magic trick, a wonderful fluttering of the cards, a sudden turning inside-out of experience with all its details included to show a boggling revision of everything I'd known the world to be. It was too much to assimilate but there it was.

"God is . . ."

"We can't say what He is . . ."

"Jafar . . ."

"Brother."

Eventually we broke the set and staggered back to whatever our jobs were back on earth.

Banged and hammered in Niagara Falls between tea and lunchtime— laid those boards in parallel: parallel! It was part of the Logos, pure enunciation, every syllable.

You'd have thought that at some point I would have walked out into the view from Niagara's window and stood in the middle of its patch of grass, beneath its tree, or leaned an elbow on the wall of the stage-set, but I didn't feel the urge.

AT LUNCH I WAS STILL ATREMBLE, head on pivot and eyes awake, soul alert for the next blast of revelation—basically acting stoned because the day couldn't have finished all its business yet, the decisive cadence hadn't come.

I sat there so manic and alit that Lomand came over during the soup course and stopped me as I dunked a piece of homebaked bread. "Koren?"

"Uh-huh."

"How are you feeling?"

"Man oh man oh man . . . Look, let's get serious. Tell me what the hell's going on here. Who's working the switches and what for?"

"Hah. Hah. You've read The Twenty-Nine Pages and told me it was all pretty obvious."

"Lomand, this is me and you. Don't fuck around. This is really happening. How can this be happening? You got to tell me straight what's going on. And don't give me that Interesting and Amusing crap or tell me about the point of bewilderment. What is going on and how's it possible?"

"Koren, I think you could do with a massage."

"Yeah sure but tell me first."

"I think you need some looking after. . . Mea, would you come upstairs with Koren and me?"

"Whatabout lunch?" I asked. And Koren: what a stupid name. How'd I get into all this crap?

"They'll keep some for you. Mea? Would you come upstairs with us? I think he needs a little looking after."

I heard Mea's responding guffaw. Were other people watching? I'd lost track and didn't really care.

"I'm not going anywhere. I've been working and I want to eat my lunch. Lomand, get serious with me a minute. This can't be what spiritual life's about. This is too ridiculous. It can't be like this. How can it be like this?" I looked around the room. "You mean to tell me this is all they could come up with? God can't do any better than this?"

"Clearly one of the Names of God is 'He with the outrageous sense of humor,'" Lomand said. Then he fixed it with someone sitting near: they'd save us lunch: let's go.

Lunch. What a word. What a world. Lunch. What was lunch? I didn't have the full report. I'd grown up this serious intellectual and when they finally took the wraps off it was beyond ridiculous . . . "Lomand, you got to be kidding me. This is the real deal?" I gestured around the dining room. "Drop the act and clue me in. This is it?"

"Hah. Hah."

He didn't know how serious I was. I thought the last veil deserved to part or rise or rend, whatever it took, today. I wanted the body electric sung down to the ultimate spark of its final Zap.

As I climbed the stairs behind Lomand and Mea thinking how bizarre, one flight up and then the narrow staircase leading to their room, a buried memory returned to me intact.

Once upon a time . . . I couldn't have been more than four years old, and by then I'd heard Ruth and Gloria play guitars next door many times and liked the music well enough. Could I have been three?

Early one evening Gloria came into our apartment and asked me to come with her, there was someone she wanted me to meet. Did I ask my parents if it was all right? I toddled next door holding Gloria's hand, and just inside, seated on the small sofa in the foyer, was a man I'd never met before. Gloria introduced us and I obediently said hello: a man of Mediterranean complexion with thinning wavy black hair.

Gloria told me that he played the flute with an orchestra and asked if I would like to hear him play.

—Can I?

—Of course.

And the man—I wonder if he was someone Gloria was dating—picked up from beside him on the sofa an oblong case I hadn't noticed, placed it on his knees, unsnapped and opened it, and there in the case, laid out in three valved silver sections on blue plush, was an instrument I'd never seen before; and I watched fascinated and absorbed as he put it together and secured the fit, then raised it to an unexpected position, sideways, extended outward from himself so that his lips were atop a dou-bling of the silver, a kind of tablet with a hole in it, the silver valves and levers off to the side. He pursed his lips and blew into the flute-hole and the sound was so beautiful and unexpected that my knees went weak and I nearly fell down in front of him, the sound so pure and silver also inside myself somehow.

I'm willing to bet he played the flute theme from Debussy's *Prelude to the Afternoon of a Faun*—what else would he have played? It hung in the air and I listened to it without falling down or dying of its beauty but only just.

When he finished he smiled at me and asked me if I liked it and I said I did, and that was when I knew that a contract had been made between us. We wouldn't say a word, just as no one ever said a word about the real, the most essential things—everyone knew them but didn't speak them: that was the known arrangement of our being here—but I knew this time that the flute player and I would spend the next while speaking politely and he would let me touch the flute and work its silver buttons, but then, when he had taken it apart and put it back in the blue plush and shut the lid and snapped the snaps and it was time for him to go, he'd take my hand and lead me away from what I had always known were provisional parents and rooms and windows and life and name and take me to the real place, where the music was, the preparatory life over and the real one to begin.

I smiled to show him that I understood and he smiled back to say yes, that's right, and then I waited for it to happen.

When he got up, turned and left without me my heart fell through the music to the floor, although I didn't say a word about it to a soul. I was surprised, not even hurt or disappointed in the usual way, with the usual emotions. This was subtler, more inside. How to say it . . . couldn't.

And now, twenty-some years later as I ascended creaking wooden English stairs behind Lomand and Mea to their room, it was as if the moment had come again. When we got up there Lomand would stretch that smile of his wider still and spill the beans and the charade would end, everyone else would come in, and my parents, followed by all the multicolored Agrins and Zaborovskys, would emerge smiling from behind the wainscoting, shy and bent from their confinement but relieved at last of the arduous labor of such long pretense, the stage-set would be struck and the entire multiform troupe of mummers I had met in the course of my exhaustively particularized life would step from behind the curtain to take their bows, there'd be applause and congratulations all around as everything provisional packed its bags, and the wanderings I'd paced on earth and in myself would reveal themselves as the verticals, arabesques and diacritical points of God's own script, the text and meaning not only clear but all the way alive. Now we'd stop pretending. Everything would correspond in native intimacy and point for point with the Real and we'd all start living the true life at last.

This sounded crazy-silly to me even at the time—I can't assess the degree of Let's Pretend I was playing with—but it seemed that on this path of basic stupid human fuckup I'd been on, here at last was the real moment swinging open and a voice implying I could come inside for good.

We made it to their sunny upstairs room, went inside, Mea shut the door, and there was Lomand with that grin that told me Here it comes.

"So, Koren," he said. "You seem to be having an interesting day. Are you still with us?"

I probably wasn't at my most expository and concise but must have managed something about the Garden, the *a'yan*, Grace and predestination in case he'd missed the full enchainment of particulars in the Quiet Room with Jafar.

"Interesting," he might have said. I think he checked my shoulders and may have found a tightness, tension. Lomand had strong hands. "Yes, I think we need to loosen you up and give you a massage. Mea, will you help me? Koren, take your clothes off."

"Excuse me?"

"Take your clothes off and lie down on the bed so we can give you a massage." The old Hopi Indian Lion Massage: I'd learned it too, from Saaque, a powerful, more direct form of Japanese *shiatsu*: get those nerves and tromp them, bite the shoulder muscles where they join the neck.

"Uh, okay."

I stripped to my jockey shorts and socks and got on the bed.

"Take your socks off."

"I'd rather leave them on," I said. Oh no.

"Take them off. The feet are important," Lomand said.

No help for it. I took my socks off.

Mea gasped and Lomand said, "Oh Jesus."

"There was this shoestore," I began . . .

And this was it. This was the unveiling at the end of vision's day. Not the glory revelation of ever higher skies and light, not the ultimate re-union and the dumbshow over. Instead of a full translation to the transcendent sphere we were getting the denouement of "Gogol's Shoes."

"How long have your feet been like that?" Lomand wanted to know.

"Awhile." Pointless to go on about Gogol. Lomand wasn't into Russian literature or the Zaborovskian bizarre. I felt a truly Gogolian shame at my unlikelihood and unsuitability as a human actor.

"We'll have to get you to a doctor," Lomand said.

"In my family we don't go to the doctor until two weeks after we're dead already."

"You're going to see a doctor."

"You don't mean today do you?"

"No. We'll make an appointment for you with the local doctor we've been seeing."

I might have sighed or made some sign of consent to this conclusion of the tale and my day's run. It was true and I had to cop to it. It was so blatant even I should have seen the moral of the tale limping toward me in its rags and bracketed in its sandwich-board with the shopworn message on it: your heart may be set on heaven but you just can't go that far on fucked-up feet.

"How did this happen to your feet, Koren?"

I sighed. "There was this shoe store in Oakland," I began to tell him anyway.

I REMEMBER THE FESTIVAL and celebratory day Reshad came back, some of us bunched around him between the guillotine bell and Acacia Avenue. He had just alighted from the Shaikhmobile, his white new-model VW bus, not the old tin hippy-dippy breadbox of custom. I don't see Sid in the picture; she might have been hanging back, as she often did on state occasions, or stopped off at the Cottage.

The soundtrack is all "Hello hello hello, hello dahlings, *hell*o ducks, hello hello," and it was as if the ten or so of us were dancing around him, this wonderful central guy with his red beard and his face suntanned now, his heart like a hearth that warmed us all, and I was on the fringe acting polite but looking at him as if for the first time, since while he was away I'd had a taste of what the place was and what we were doing in it, and what was he?

"So much lovely light everywhere, oh look at all the light," Reshad said to the ring of glowing faces, and that's when he spotted me. His eyebrows shot up and his eyes increased their wattage, his mouth its grin. "Oh look at the light, look where the light is, look look, look everyone, there's even some of it breaking out over *there*," he said, laughing, pointing at me, pointing at my heart. "Look at all the lovely light all round and look look look, it's even there, now even *he's* got some."

I did a shucks and whut, and made as if to open the curtain o'er my heart and look down shrugging at it. Light?

"There, look there!" Reshad instructed everyone. "And may he never recover, hahaha!"

I felt like a schmuck with earlaps standing there stared at in this change of world, no idea what to do with my hands or with the involuntary grin that was determined to distort my features and lay them completely open and, what's worse, with the hapless heart of mine all those brighteyed faces were staring at or—who knows, anything's possible now—all the way into . . .

"Never recover! Ever recover! Ha-ha-ha!"

* * *

THIS ENDS the Tales of Wonder portion of our evening's entertainment for a while.

ACKNOWLEDGEMENTS

I must say a word in appreciation of the courage of the people who have permitted me to represent them freely in this book, as I remember them and as I chose, sometimes lightly covered by a pseudonym, more often not. The effort toward accuracy has been constant but of course impossible to satisfy completely, even after interviews and research. I appear to have an unusual memory for spoken dialogue, but even so, many of the book's conversations are approximations with verbatim nuggets distributed through them like plums in a pudding. Once or twice such approximations have been explicitly distinguished from exact quotations in the text.

Although I have tried to make the dialogue "work," I have resisted the temptation to juice a conversation with lines better, funnier, or more dramatic than those actually spoken, and as a rule of thumb, the more outrageous or improbable a line of dialogue (or an event) seems, the more likely it is to be an exact rendering—for example going up in that rocket, dinosaurs, or the matter of Gogol's Shoes.

Occasionally I have altered small matters of chronology in ways that are dramatically insignificant but tidy the narrative a bit. Otherwise I have kept to the facts, the unavoidable distortions of honest memory, and the questions I neglected to ask. Oh all right, I played around once or twice, but only in the margins.

Many people have helped the author clarify his teeming text: Brian Cullman (indispensably, as before: simply the best), Reshad Field, Salik Chalom, Aaron Cass, Lomand, Anthony Tierney, Peter Young, Angela Culme-Seymour, Layla

Shamash, Khalil Norland, Frances Emeleus, Richard and Cecilia Twinch (speaking of courage), Ewan McDonald, Lyndon Baker, Stephen Silver, Abdullah Gündoğdo, Daniel Furman, Arthur Sacks, Jerome Reese, Liz Ayre, Angela Jaffray, Michelle Mercer, David Breskin, Rebecca Saletan, Mary Cunnane, Jennifer McDonald, who was willing to try early . . . Poor list, you're leaving people out.

My agent, Kathleen Anderson, helped mightily to both expedite and refine the object, and my editor, Lorin Stein, has been skilled and sympathetic to an extraordinary degree. The faults of the book are my own, and would have been fewer if I had taken all his editorial advice but, like Popeye the Sailor Man, I yam, et cetera.

The peripatetic author has benefitted from relevant feats of hospitality across the globe: Mahmut Rauf, Sid repeatedly and beyond the call of duty, George and Maryam Steffen, Susan Kovner, Jack and Lydia DeJohnette, Philip and Alison Bradbury, Aziza Sterling, Sara Sterman, Chris Nation, Anthony Tierney, David Banon, Peter Giron, Nicole Pagliardini, Melinda Plant, Asım and Hüseyin Kaplan, Bob Towns and Jane Carroll, Chisholme House, Keith and Helen Farvis, Donna Tauscher, David Hyams, the old folks of Konya, Üsküdar, Hacıbektash . . .

I am also grateful to the Ucross Foundation: a room, three squares, brilliant prairie skies, and good company.

Special thanks to Richard Waddington for his fine rendering of Swyre Farm, and to Eduardo Garcia for the drum transcription, exact. Car repair credits will appear in a future volume.